Access Database Design and Programming

THIRD EDITION

Access Database Design and Programming

Steven Roman

O'REILLY®

Beijing · Cambridge · Farnham · Köln · Paris · Sebastopol · Taipei · Tokyo

Access Database Design and Programming, Third Edition
by Steven Roman

Copyright © 2002, 1999, 1997 Steven Roman. All rights reserved.
Printed in the United States of America.

Published by O'Reilly Media, Inc., 1005 Gravenstein Highway North,
Sebastopol, CA 95472.

O'Reilly & Associates books may be purchased for educational, business, or sales promotional use. On-line editions are also available for most titles (*safari.oreilly.com*). For more information contact our corporate/institutional sales department: (800) 998-9938 or *corporate@oreilly.com*.

Editor:	Ron Petrusha
Production Editor:	Jeffrey Holcomb
Cover Designer:	Edie Freedman
Interior Designer:	David Futato

Printing History:

June 1997:	First Edition.
July 1999:	Second Edition.
January 2002:	Third Edition.

 This book uses RepKover™, a durable and flexible lay-flat binding.

ISBN: 0-596-00273-4
[M]

Table of Contents

Preface xi

Part I.   Database Design

1.   Introduction **3**
    Database Design   3
    Database Programming   9

2.   The Entity-Relationship Model of a Database **11**
    What Is a Database?   11
    Entities and Their Attributes   11
    Keys and Superkeys   15
    Relationships Between Entities   16

3.   Implementing Entity-Relationship Models: Relational Databases **18**
    Implementing Entities   18
    A Short Glossary   21
    Implementing the Relationships in a Relational Database   22
    The LIBRARY Relational Database   27
    Index Files   31
    NULL Values   33

4.   Database Design Principles **35**
    Redundancy   35
    Normal Forms   37
    First Normal Form   38
    Functional Dependencies   39
    Second Normal Form   40

Third Normal Form   41
Boyce-Codd Normal Form   42
Normalization   43

Part II.   Database Queries

5. Query Languages and the Relational Algebra **51**
Query Languages   52
Relational Algebra and Relational Calculus   53
Details of the Relational Algebra   55

6. Access Structured Query Language (SQL) **81**
Introduction to Access SQL   81
Access Query Design   81
Access Query Types   83
Why Use SQL?   84
Access SQL   85
The DDL Component of Access SQL   86
The DML Component of Access SQL   90

Part III.   Database Architecture

7. Database System Architecture **115**
Why Program?   115
Database Systems   117
Database Management Systems   118
The Jet DBMS   119
Data Definition Languages   121
Data Manipulation Languages   122
Host Languages   123
The Client/Server Architecture   124

Part IV.   Visual Basic for Applications

8. The Visual Basic Editor, Part I **129**
The Project Window   129
The Properties Window   132
The Code Window   132

The Immediate Window 134
Arranging Windows 135

9. The Visual Basic Editor, Part II 137
Navigating the IDE 137
Getting Help 138
Creating a Procedure 138
Run Mode, Break Mode, and Design Mode 139
Errors 140
Debugging 143

10. Variables, Data Types, and Constants 146
Comments 146
Line Continuation 146
Constants 147
Variables and Data Types 149
VBA Operators 164

11. Functions and Subroutines 165
Calling Functions 165
Calling Subroutines 166
Parameters and Arguments 167
Exiting a Procedure 171
Public and Private Procedures 171
Fully Qualified Procedure Names 172

12. Built-in Functions and Statements 173
The MsgBox Function 174
The InputBox Function 176
VBA String Functions 177
Miscellaneous Functions and Statements 180
Handling Errors in Code 183

13. Control Statements 191
The If...Then Statement 191
The For Loop 192
The Exit For Statement 193
The For Each Loop 194
The Do Loop 194
The Select Case Statement 195
A Final Note on VBA 196

Part V. Data Access Objects

14. Programming DAO: Overview **201**
Objects   201
The DAO Object Model   207
The Microsoft Access Object Model   209
Referencing Objects   211
Collections Are Objects Too   215
The Properties Collection   220
Closing DAO Objects   225
A Look at the DAO Objects   226
The CurrentDb Function   234

15. Programming DAO: Data Definition Language **241**
Creating a Database   241
Opening a Database   243
Creating a Table and Its Fields   243
Creating an Index   246
Creating a Relation   248
Creating a QueryDef   250

16. Programming DAO: Data Manipulation Language **254**
Recordset Objects   254
Opening a Recordset   255
Moving Through a Recordset   257
Finding Records in a Recordset   260
Editing Data Using a Recordset   262

Part VI. ActiveX Data Objects

17. ADO and OLE DB **269**
What Is ADO?   269
Installing ADO   270
ADO and OLE DB   272
The ADO Object Model   274
Finding OLE DB Providers   304
A Closer Look at Connection Strings   309
An Example: Using ADO over the Web   322

18. **ADOX: Jet Data Definition in ADO** **326**

The ADOX Object Model   326

Part VII. Programming Problems

19. **Some Common Data Manipulation Problems** **337**

Running Sums   337

Overlapping Intervals I   340

Overlapping Intervals II   341

Making Assignments with Default   344

Time to Completion I   346

Time to Completion II   347

Time to Completion III—A MaxMin Problem   349

Vertical to Horizontal   352

A Matching Problem   354

Equality of Sets   355

Part VIII. Appendixes

A. **DAO 3.0/3.5 Collections, Properties, and Methods** **361**

B. **The Quotient: An Additional Operation of the Relational Algebra** **378**

C. **Open Database Connectivity (ODBC)** **381**

D. **Obtaining or Creating the Sample Database** **401**

E. **Suggestions for Further Reading** **411**

Index **413**

Preface

Preface to the Third Edition

As with the second edition, let me begin by thanking all of those readers who have helped to make this book so successful. In light of the recent release of Access 2003, I have taken a careful look to make certain that it is up to date with respect to this new release. As it happens, the new release has made no relevant impact on the topics covered in this book: database design, the VBA language, SQL, DAO, and ADO—so the changes for this printing have been minor (mostly fixing some errata).

The third edition of the book includes two new chapters; the first of which is Chapter 18, *ADOX: Jet Data Definition in ADO*. With the sad and, in my opinion, highly unfortunate demise of DAO at Microsoft's hands, it seemed necessary to bring the book up to speed on that aspect of ADO that gives the programmer most of the functionality of the Data Definition Language (DDL) portion of DAO.

ADOX is an acronym for *ADO Extensions for Data Definition and Security*. When making comparisons between ADO and DAO, proponents of DAO will point out that ADO does not include features for data definition—that is, features that can be used to create and alter databases and their components (tables, columns, indexes, etc.). This is precisely the purpose of ADOX. (Our concern here is with ADOX as it relates to Jet.)

Unfortunately, ADOX is not a complete substitute for DAO's data-definition features. For example, query creation in ADOX has a serious wrinkle. Namely, a query created using ADOX will not appear in the Access user interface! I elaborate on this in Chapter 18.

The other new chapter for the third edition is Chapter 19, *Some Common Data Manipulation Problems*. In this chapter, I present a number of problems that are commonly encountered when dealing with data, along with their solutions couched in terms of SQL. I hope that this chapter will provide some good food for thought, as well as useful examples for your own applications.

Preface to the Second Edition

Let me begin by thanking all of those readers who have helped to make the first edition of this book so very successful. Also, my sincere thanks go to the many readers who have written some very flattering reviews of the first edition on amazon.com and on O'Reilly's own web site. Keep them coming.

With the recent release of Office 2000, and in view of the many suggestions I have received concerning the first edition of the book, it seemed like an appropriate time to do a second edition. I hope that readers will find the second edition of the book to be even more useful than the first edition.

Actually, Access has undergone only relatively minor changes in its latest release, at least with respect to the subject matter of this book. Changes for the Second Edition are:

- A discussion (Chapters 8 and 9) of Access' new VBA Integrated Development Environment. At last Access shares the same IDE as Word, Excel, and Power-Point!

- In response to reader requests, I have significantly expanded the discussion of the VBA language itself, which now occupies Chapters 10, 11, 12, and 13.

- Chapter 17, which is new for this edition, provides a fairly complete discussion of ActiveX Data Objects (ADO). This is also accompanied by an appendix on Open Database Connectivity (ODBC), which is still intimately connected with ADO.

  As you may know, ADO is a successor to DAO (Data Access Objects) and is intended to eventually replace DAO, although I suspect that this will take considerable time. While the DAO model is the programming interface for the Jet database engine, ADO has a much more ambitious goal—it is a programming model for a *universal* data access interface called OLE DB. Simply put, OLE DB is a technology to connect to *any* type of data—traditional database data, spreadsheet data, web-based data, text data, email, and so on.

  Frankly, while the ADO object model is smaller than that of DAO, the documentation is much less complete. As a result, ADO seems far more confusing than DAO, especially when it comes to issues such as how to create the infamous *connection strings*. Accordingly, I have spent considerable time discussing this and other difficult issues, illustrating how to use ADO to connect to Jet databases, Excel spreadsheets, and text files.

I should also mention that while the Access object model has undergone significant changes, as you can see by looking at Figure 14-7, the DAO object model has changed only in one respect. In particular, DAO has been upgraded from Version 3.5 to Version 3.6. Here is what Microsoft itself says about this new release:

DAO 3.6 has been updated to use the Microsoft® Jet 4.0 database engine. This includes enabling all interfaces for Unicode. Data is now provided in unicode (internationally enabled) format rather than ANSI. No other new features were implemented.

Thus, DAO 3.6 does not include any new objects, properties, or methods.

This book appears to cover two separate topics—database design and database programming. It does. It would be misleading to claim that database design and database programming are intimately related. So why are they in the same book?

The answer is that while these two subjects are not related, in the sense that knowledge of one leads directly to knowledge of the other, they are definitely *linked*, by the simple fact that a power database user needs to know something about both of these subjects to effectively create, use, and maintain a database.

In fact, it might be said that creating and maintaining a database application in Microsoft Access is done in three broad steps—designing the database, creating the basic graphical interface (i.e., setting up the tables, queries, forms, and reports), and then getting the application to perform in the desired way.

The second of these three steps is fairly straightforward, for it is mostly a matter of becoming familiar with the relatively easy-to-use Access graphical interface. Help is available for this through Access' online help system, as well as through the dozens of overblown 1,000-plus-page tomes devoted to Microsoft Access. Unfortunately, none of the books that I have seen does any real justice to the other two steps. Hence this book.

To be a bit more specific, the book has two goals:

- To discuss the basic concepts of relational database theory and design
- To discuss how to extract the full power of Microsoft Access, through programming in the Access Structured Query Language (SQL) and the Data Access Object (DAO) component of the Microsoft Jet database engine

To accomplish the first goal, I describe the how and why of creating an efficient database system, explaining such concepts as:

- Entities and entity classes
- Keys, superkeys, and primary keys
- One-to-one, one-to-many, and many-to-many relationships
- Referential integrity
- Joins of various types (inner joins, outer joins, equi-joins, semi-joins, θ-joins, and so on)
- Operations of the relational algebra (selection, projection, join, union, intersection, and so on)
- Normal forms and their importance

Of course, once you have a basic understanding of how to create an effective relational database, you will want to take full advantage of that database, which can only be done through programming. In addition, many of the programming techniques I discuss in this book can be used to create and maintain a database from within other applications, such as Microsoft Visual Basic, Microsoft Excel, and Microsoft Word.

I should hasten to add that this book is not a traditional cookbook for learning Microsoft Access. For instance, I do not discuss forms and reports, nor do I discuss such issues as database security, database replication, and multiuser issues. This is why I've been able to keep the book to a (hopefully) readable few hundred pages.

This book is for Access users at all levels. Most of it applies equally well to Access 2.0, Access 7.0, Access 8.0, Access 9.0 (which is a component of Microsoft Office 2000), and Access 2002 (which is included with Office XP), and Access 2003. I will assume that you have a passing acquaintance with the Access development environment, however. For instance, I assume that you already know how to create a table or a query.

Throughout the book, I will use a specific modest-sized example to illustrate the concepts discussed. The example consists of a database called LIBRARY that is designed to hold data about the books in a certain library. Of course, the amount of data used will be kept artificially small—just enough to illustrate the concepts.

The Book's Audience

Most books on Microsoft Access focus primarily on the Access interface and its components, giving little attention to the more important issue of database design. After all, once the database application is complete, the interface components play only a small role, whereas the design continues to affect the usefulness of the application.

In attempting to restore the focus on database design, this book aspires to be a kind of "second course" in Microsoft Access—a book for Access users who have mastered the basics of the interface, are familiar with such things as creating tables and designing queries, and now want to move beyond the interface to create programmable Access applications. This book provides a firm foundation on which you can begin to build your database-application development skills.

At the same time that this book is intended primarily as an introduction to Access for aspiring database-application developers, it also is of interest to more experienced Access programmers. For the most part, such topics as normal forms or the details of the relational algebra are almost exclusively the preserve of the academic world. By introducing these topics to the mainstream Access audience, *Access Database Design and Programming* offers a concise, succinct, readable guide that experienced Access developers can turn to whenever some of the details of database design or SQL statements escape them.

The Sample Code

To follow along with the sample code, you will need to set a reference in the Visual Basic Editor to the DAO object model and the ADO and ADOX object models. Once in the VB Editor, go to the *Tools* menu, choose *References*, and select the references entitled:

- Microsoft DAO 3.XX Object Model
- Microsoft ActiveX Data Objects 2.X Library
- Microsoft ADO Ext. 2.5 for DLL and Security

Organization of This Book

Access Database Design and Programming consists of 19 chapters that are divided into six parts. In addition, there are five appendixes.

Part I, Database Design

The first part of the book focuses on designing a database—that is, on the process of decomposing data into multiple tables.

Chapter 1, *Introduction*, examines the problems involved in using a flat database—a single table that holds all of an application's data—and makes a case for using instead a relational-database design consisting of multiple tables. But because relational-database applications divide data into multiple tables, it is necessary to reconstitute that data in ways that are useful—that is, to piece data back together from their multiple tables. Hence, there is a need for query languages and programming, which are in many ways an integral part of designing a database.

Chapter 2, *The Entity-Relationship Model of a Database*, introduces some of the basic concepts of relational-database management, such as entities, entity classes, keys, superkeys, and one-to-many and many-to-many relationships.

Chapter 3, *Implementing Entity-Relationship Models: Relational Databases*, shows how these general concepts and principles are applied in designing a real-world database. In particular, the chapter shows how to decompose a sample flat database into a well-designed relational database.

Chapter 4, *Database Design Principles*, continues the discussion begun in Chapter 3 by focusing on the major problem of database design, that of eliminating data redundancy without losing the essential relationships between items of data. The chapter introduces the notion of functional dependencies and examines each of the major forms for database normalization.

Once a database is properly normalized or its data is broken up into discrete tables, it must, almost paradoxically, be pieced back together again to be of any value at all. The next part of the book focuses on the query languages that are responsible for doing this.

Part II, Database Queries

Chapter 5, *Query Languages and the Relational Algebra*, introduces procedural query languages based on the relational algebra and nonprocedural query languages based on the relational calculus, then focuses on the major operations—like unions, intersections, and inner and outer joins—that are available using the relational algebra.

Chapter 6, *Access Structured Query Language (SQL)*, shows how the relational algebra is implemented in Microsoft Access, both in the Access Query Design window and in Access SQL. Interestingly, the Access Query Design window is really a frontend that constructs Access SQL statements, which ordinarily are hidden from the user or developer. However, it does not offer a complete replacement for Access SQL—a number of operations can only be performed using SQL statements, and not through the Access graphical interface. This makes a basic knowledge of Access SQL important.

While SQL is a critical tool for getting at data in relational database management systems and returning recordsets that offer various views of their data, it is also an unfriendly tool. The Access Query Design window, for example, was developed primarily to hide the implementation of Access SQL from both the user and the programmer. But Access SQL, and the graphical query facilities that hide it, do not form an integrated environment on which the database programmer can rely to shield the user from the details of an application's implementation. Instead, creating this integrated application environment is the responsibility of a programming language (Visual Basic for Applications or VBA) and an interface between the programming language and the database engine (DAO). Parts IV and V examine these two tools for application development.

Part III, Database Architecture

Part III consists of a single chapter, Chapter 7, *Database System Architecture*, that describes the role of programming in database-application development and introduces the major tools and concepts needed to create an Access application.

Part IV, Visual Basic for Applications

When programming in Access VBA, you use the VBA integrated development environment (or IDE) to write Access VBA code. The former topic is covered in Chapter 8, *The Visual Basic Editor, Part I*, and Chapter 9, *The Visual Basic Editor, Part II*, while the following three chapters are devoted to the latter. In particular, separate chapters are devoted to VBA variables, data types, and constants (Chapter 10, *Variables, Data Types, and Constants*), to VBA functions and subroutines (Chapter 11, *Functions and Subroutines*), to VBA statements and intrinsic functions (Chapter 12, *Built-in Functions and Statements*), and to statements that alter the flow of program execution (Chapter 13, *Control Statements*).

Part V, Data Access Objects

Chapter 14, *Programming DAO: Overview*, introduces Data Access Objects, or DAO. DAO provides the interface between Visual Basic for Applications and the Jet database engine used by Access. The chapter provides an overview of working with objects in VBA before examining the DAO object model and the Microsoft Access object model.

Chapter 15, *Programming DAO: Data Definition Language*, focuses on the subset of DAO that is used to define basic database objects. The chapter discusses operations such as creating tables, indexes, and query definitions under program control.

Chapter 16, *Programming DAO: Data Manipulation Language*, focuses on working with recordset objects and on practical record-oriented operations. The chapter discusses such topics as recordset navigation, finding records, and editing data.

Part VI, ActiveX Data Objects

Chapter 17, *ADO and OLE DB*, explores ActiveX Data Objects, Microsoft's newest technology for data access, which offers the promise of a single programmatic interface to data in any format and in any location. The chapter examines when and why you might want to use ADO and shows you how to take advantage of it in your code.

Chapter 18, *ADOX: Jet Data Definition in ADO*, discusses the role of ADOX in various data-definition operations, such as creating a Jet database and creating and altering Jet database tables.

Part VII, Programming Problems

Chapter 19, *Some Common Data Manipulation Problems*, presents a number of problems commonly encountered when dealing with data, along with their solutions.

Part VIII, Appendixes

Appendix A, *DAO 3.0/3.5 Collections, Properties, and Methods*, is intended as a quick reference guide to DAO 3.0 (which is included with Access for Office 95) and DAO 3.5 (which is included with Access for Office 97).

Appendix B, *The Quotient: An Additional Operation of the Relational Algebra*, examines an additional, little-used query operation that was not discussed in Chapter 5.

Appendix C, *Open Database Connectivity (ODBC)*, examines how to use ODBC to connect to a data source.

Appendix D, *Obtaining or Creating the Sample Database*, contains instructions for either downloading a copy of the sample files from the book or creating them yourself.

Appendix E, *Suggestions for Further Reading*, lists some of the major works that provide in-depth discussion of the issues of relational database design and normalization.

Conventions in This Book

Throughout this book, we've used the following typographic conventions:

UPPERCASE
> Indicates a database name (e.g., LIBRARY) or the name of a table within a database (e.g., BOOKS). Keywords in SQL statements (e.g., SELECT) also appear in uppercase, as well as types of data (e.g., LONG), commands (e.g., CREATE VALUE), options (e.g., HAVING), etc.

`Constant width`
> Indicates a language construct such as a language statement, a constant, or an expression. Lines of code also appear in constant width, as do function and method prototypes in body text.

`Constant width italic`
> Indicates parameter and variable names in body text. In syntax statements or prototypes, constant width italic indicates replaceable parameters.

Italic
> Is used in normal text to introduce a new term, to represent menu options, and to indicate object names (e.g., *QueryDef*), collection names, the names of entity classes (e.g., the *Books* entity class), and VBA keywords.

Obtaining Updated Information

The sample tables in the LIBRARY database, as well as the sample programs presented in the book, are available online and can be freely downloaded. Alternately, if you don't have access to the Internet by either a web browser or a file transfer protocol (FTP) client, and if you don't use an email system that allows you to send and receive email from the Internet, you can create the database file and its tables yourself. For details, see Appendix D.

Updates to the material contained in the book, along with other Access-related developments, are available from the O'Reilly web site, *http://www.oreilly.com/catalog/accessdata3/*. Simply follow the links to the Windows section.

Request for Comments

Please address comments and questions concerning this book to the publisher:

O'Reilly & Associates, Inc.
1005 Gravenstein Highway North
Sebastopol, CA 95472
(800) 998-9938 (in the United States or Canada)
(707) 829-0515 (international/local)
(707) 829-0104 (fax)

There is a web page for this book, which lists errata, examples, or any additional information. You can access this page at:

http://www.oreilly.com/catalog/accessdata3/

To comment or ask technical questions about this book, send email to:

bookquestions@oreilly.com

For more information about books, conferences, Resource Centers, and the O'Reilly Network, see the O'Reilly web site at:

http://www.oreilly.com

Acknowledgments

My thanks to Ron Petrusha, editor at O'Reilly & Associates, for making many useful suggestions that improved this book.

Also thanks to the production staff at O'Reilly & Associates, including Jeffrey Holcomb, the production editor, Edie Freedman for the cover design, David Futato for interior design, Mihaela Maier for Tools support, Rob Romano and Jessamyn Read for the illustrations, Rachel Wheeler, Matt Hutchinson, and Claire Cloutier for quality and sanity control, and Brenda Miller for the index.

PART I

Database Design

CHAPTER 1

Introduction

Database Design

As mentioned in the Preface, one purpose of this book is to explain the basic concepts of modern relational-database theory and show how these concepts are realized in Microsoft Access. Allow me to amplify on this rather lofty goal.

To take a very simple view, which will do nicely for the purposes of this introductory discussion, a *database* is just a collection of related data. A *database management system*, or DBMS, is a system that is designed for two main purposes:

- To add, delete, and update the data in the database
- To provide various ways to *view* (on screen or in print) the data in the database

If the data is simple and there is not very much of it, then a database can consist of a single table. In fact, a simple database can easily be maintained even with a word processor!

To illustrate, suppose you want to set up a database for the books in a library. Purely for the sake of illustration, suppose the library contains 14 books. The same discussion would apply to a library of perhaps a few hundred books. Table 1-1 shows the LIBRARY_FLAT database in the form of a single table.

LIBRARY_FLAT (Table 1-1) was created using Microsoft Word. For such a simple database, Word has enough power to fulfill the two goals mentioned earlier. Certainly, adding, deleting, and editing the table presents no particular problems (provided we know how to manage tables in Word). In addition, if we want to sort the data by author, for example, we can just select the table and choose *Sort* from the *Table* menu in Microsoft Word. Extracting a portion of the data in the table (i.e., creating a view) can be done by making a copy of the table and then deleting appropriate rows and/or columns.

Table 1-1. The LIBRARY_FLAT sample database

ISBN	Title	AuID[a]	AuName	AuPhone	PubID[a]	PubName	PubPhone	Price
1-1111-1111-1	C++	4	Roman	444-444-4444	1	Big House	123-456-7890	$29.95
0-99-999999-9	Emma	1	Austen	111-111-1111	1	Big House	123-456-7890	$20.00
0-91-335678-7	Faerie Queene	7	Spenser	777-777-7777	1	Big House	123-456-7890	$15.00
0-91-045678-5	Hamlet	5	Shakespeare	555-555-5555	2	Alpha Press	999-999-9999	$20.00
0-103-45678-9	Iliad	3	Homer	333-333-3333	1	Big House	123-456-7890	$25.00
0-12-345678-9	Pride and Prujudice	1	Brontë	111-111-1111	3	Small House	714-000-0000	$49.00
0-99-777777-7	King Lear	5	Shakespeare	555-555-5555	2	Alpha Press	999-999-9999	$49.00
0-555-55555-9	Macbeth	5	Shakespeare	555-555-5555	2	Alpha Press	999-999-9999	$12.00
0-11-345678-9	Moby-Dick	2	Melville	222-222-2222	3	Small House	714-000-0000	$49.00
0-12-333433-3	On Liberty	8	Mill	888-888-8888	1	Big House	123-456-7890	$25.00
0-321-32132-1	Balloon	13	Sleepy	321-321-1111	3	Small House	714-000-0000	$34.00
0-321-32132-1	Balloon	11	Snoopy	321-321-2222	3	Small House	714-000-0000	$34.00
0-321-32132-1	Balloon	12	Grumpy	321-321-0000	3	Small House	714-000-0000	$34.00
0-55-123456-9	Main Street	10	Jones	123-333-3333	3	Small House	714-000-0000	$22.95
0-55-123456-9	Main Street	9	Smith	123-222-2222	3	Small House	714-000-0000	$22.95
0-123-45678-0	Ulysses	6	Joyce	666-666-6666	2	Alpha Press	999-999-9999	$34.00
1-22-233700-0	Visual Basic	4	Roman	444-444-4444	1	Big House	123-456-7890	$25.00

[a] Columns labeled *AuID* and *PubID* are included for identitification purposes, i.e., to identify an author or a publisher uniquely. In any case, their presence or absence will not affect the current discussion.

Why Use a Relational-Database Design?

Thus, maintaining a simple, so-called *flat database* consisting of a single table does not require much knowledge of database theory. On the other hand, most databases worth maintaining are quite a bit more complicated than that. Real-life databases often have hundreds of thousands or even millions of records, with data that is very intricately related. This is where using a full-fledged relational-database program becomes essential. Consider, for example, the Library of Congress, which has over 16 million books in its collection. For reasons that will become apparent soon, a single table simply will not do for this database!

Redundancy

Using a single table to maintain a database leads to problems of *unnecessary repetition* of data, that is, *redundancy*. Some repetition of data is always necessary, as we will see, but the idea is to remove as much *unnecessary* repetition as possible.

The redundancy in the LIBRARY_FLAT table (Table 1-1) is obvious. For instance, the name and phone number of Big House publishers is repeated six times in the table, and Shakespeare's phone number is repeated thrice.

In an effort to remove as much redundancy as possible from a database, a database designer must split the data into multiple tables. Here is one possibility for the LIBRARY_FLAT example, which splits the original database into four separate tables.

- A BOOKS table, shown in Table 1-2, in which each book has its own record
- An AUTHORS table, shown in Table 1-3, in which each author has his own record
- A PUBLISHERS table, shown in Table 1-4, in which each publisher has its own record
- BOOK/AUTHOR table, shown in Table 1-5, the purpose of which we will explain a bit later

Note that now the name and phone number of Big House appears only once in the database (in the PUBLISHERS table), as does Shakespeare's phone number (in the AUTHORS table).

Of course, there is still some duplicated data in the database. For instance, the PubID information appears in more than one place in these tables. As mentioned earlier, we cannot eliminate all duplicate data and still maintain the relationships between the data.

To get a feel for the reduction in duplicate data achieved by the four-table approach, imagine (as is reasonable) that the database also includes the address of each publisher. Then Table 1-1 would need a new column containing 14 addresses—many of which are duplicates. On the other hand, the four-table database needs only one new column in the PUBLISHERS table, adding a total of three *distinct* addresses.

Table 1-2. The BOOKS table from the LIBRARY_FLAT database

ISBN	Title	PubID	Price
0-555-55555-9	Macbeth	2	$12.00
0-91-335678-7	Faerie Queene	1	$15.00
0-99-999999-9	Emma	1	$20.00
0-91-045678-5	Hamlet	2	$20.00
0-55-123456-9	Main Street	3	$22.95
1-22-233700-0	Visual Basic	1	$25.00
0-12-333433-3	On Liberty	1	$25.00
0-103-45678-9	Iliad	1	$25.00
1-1111-1111-1	C++	1	$29.95
0-321-32132-1	Balloon	3	$34.00
0-123-45678-0	Ulysses	2	$34.00
0-99-777777-7	King Lear	2	$49.00
0-12-345678-9	Jane Eyre	3	$49.00
0-11-345678-9	Moby-Dick	3	$49.00

Table 1-3. The AUTHORS table from the LIBRARY_FLAT database

AuID	AuName	AuPhone
1	Austen	111-111-1111
12	Grumpy	321-321-0000
3	Homer	333-333-3333
10	Jones	123-333-3333
6	Joyce	666-666-6666
2	Melville	222-222-2222
8	Mill	888-888-8888
4	Roman	444-444-4444
5	Shakespeare	555-555-5555
13	Sleepy	321-321-1111
9	Smith	123-222-2222
11	Snoopy	321-321-2222
7	Spenser	777-777-7777

Table 1-4. The PUBLISHERS table from the LIBRARY_FLAT database

PubID	PubName	PubPhone
1	Big House	123-456-7890
2	Alpha Press	999-999-9999
3	Small House	714-000-0000

Table 1-5. The BOOK/AUTHOR table from the LIBRARY_FLAT database

ISBN	AuID
0-103-45678-9	3
0-11-345678-9	2
0-12-333433-3	8
0-12-345678-9	1
0-123-45678-0	6
0-321-32132-1	11
0-321-32132-1	12
0-321-32132-1	13
0-55-123456-9	9
0-55-123456-9	10
0-555-55555-9	5
0-91-045678-5	5
0-91-335678-7	7
0-99-777777-7	5
0-99-999999-9	1
1-1111-1111-1	4
1-22-233700-0	4

To drive the difference home, consider the 16-million-book database of the Library of Congress. Suppose the database contains books from 10,000 different publishers. A publisher's address column in a flat-database design would contain 16 million addresses, whereas a multitable approach would require only 10,000 addresses. Now, if the average address is 50 characters long, then the multitable approach would save:

$$(16,000,000 - 10,000) \times 50 = 799 \text{ million characters}$$

Assuming that each character takes 2 bytes (in the Unicode that is used internally by Microsoft Access), the single-table approach wastes about 1.6 gigabytes of space just for the address field!

Indeed, the issue of redundancy alone is quite enough to convince a database designer to avoid the flat-database approach. However, there are several other problems with flat databases, which we now discuss.

Multiple-value problems

It is clear that some books in our database are authored by multiple authors. This leaves us with three choices in a single-table flat database:

- We can accommodate multiple authors with multiple rows—one for each author, as in the LIBRARY_FLAT table (Table 1-1) for the books *Balloon* and *Main Street*.

- We can accommodate multiple authors with multiple columns in a single row—one for each author.
- We can include all authors' names in one column of the table.

The problem with the multiple-row choice is that *all* of the data about a book must be repeated as many times as there are authors of the book—an obvious case of redundancy. The multiple-column approach presents the problem of guessing how many Author columns we will *ever* need and creates a lot of wasted space (empty fields) for books with only one author. It also creates major programming headaches.

The third choice is to include all authors' names in one cell, which can lead to trouble of its own. For example, it becomes more difficult to search the database for a single author. Worse yet, how can we create an alphabetical list of the authors in the table?

Update anomalies

In order to update, say, a publisher's phone number in the LIBRARY_FLAT database (Table 1-1), it is necessary to make changes in every row containing that number. If we miss a row, we have produced a so-called *update anomaly*, resulting in an unreliable table.

Insertion anomalies

Difficulties will arise if we wish to insert a new publisher in the LIBRARY_FLAT database (Table 1-1), but we do not yet have information about any of that publisher's books. We could add a new row to the existing table and place NULL values in all but the three publisher-related columns, but this may lead to trouble. (A NULL is a value intended to indicate a missing or unknown value for a field.) For instance, adding several such publishers means that the ISBN column, which should contain unique data, will contain several NULL values. This general problem is referred to as an *insertion anomaly*.

Deletion anomalies

In contrast to the preceding problem, if we delete all book entries for a given publisher, for instance, then we will also lose all information about that publisher. This is a *deletion anomaly*.

Complications of Relational-Database Design

This list of potential problems should be enough to convince us that the idea of using a single-table database is generally not smart. Good database design dictates that the data be divided into several tables and that relationships be established between these tables. Because a table describes a "relation," such a database is called a *relational database*. On the other hand, relational databases do have their complications. Here are a few examples.

Avoiding data loss

One complication in designing a relational database is figuring out how to split the data into multiple tables so as not to lose any information. For instance, if we had left out the BOOK/AUTHOR table (Table 1-5) in our previous example, there would be no way to determine the author of each book. In fact, the sole purpose of the BOOK/AUTHOR table is so that we do not lose the book/author relationship!

Maintaining relational integrity

We must be careful to maintain the integrity of the various relationships between tables when changes are made. For instance, if we decide to remove a publisher from the database, it is not enough just to remove that publisher from the PUBLISHERS table, for this would leave *dangling references* to that publisher in the BOOKS table.

Creating views

When the data is spread throughout several tables, it becomes more difficult to create various *views* of the data. For instance, we might want to see a list of all publishers that publish books priced under $10.00. This requires gathering data from more than one table. The point is that, by breaking data into separate tables, we must *often* go to the trouble of piecing the data back together in order to get a comprehensive view of the data!

Summary

It is clear that to avoid redundancy problems and various unpleasant anomalies, a database needs to contain multiple tables with relationships defined between these tables. On the other hand, this raises some issues, such as how to design the tables in the database without losing any data, and how to piece together the data from multiple tables to create various views of that data. The main goal of the first part of this book is to explore these fundamental issues.

Database Programming

The motivation for learning database programming is quite simple—power. If you want to have as much control over your databases as possible, you will need to do some programming. In fact, even some simple things require programming. For instance, there is no way to retrieve the list of fields of a given table using the Access graphical interface—you can only get this list through programming. (You can *view* such a list in the table-design mode of the table, but you cannot get access to this list in order to, for example, present the end-user with the list and ask if she wishes to make any changes to it.)

In addition, programming may be the only way to access and manipulate a database from within another application. For instance, if you are working in Microsoft Excel, you can create and manipulate an Access database with as much power as with Access itself, but only through programming! The reason is that Excel does not have the capability to render graphical representations of database objects. Instead you can create the database within Access and then manipulate it programmatically from within Excel.

It is also worth mentioning that programming can give you a great sense of satisfaction. There is nothing more pleasing than watching a program that you have written step through the rows of a table and make certain changes that you have requested. It is often easier to write a program to perform an action such as this than to remember how to perform the same action using the graphical interface. In short, programming is not only empowering, but it also sometimes provides the simplest route to a particular end.

And let us not forget that programming can be just plain fun!

CHAPTER 2

The Entity-Relationship Model of a Database

Let us begin our discussion of database design by looking at an informal database model called the *entity-relationship model*. This model of a relational database provides a useful perspective, especially for the purposes of the initial database design.

I will illustrate the general principles of this model with the LIBRARY database example, which I will carry through the entire book. This example database is designed to hold data about the books in a certain library. The amount of data we will use will be kept artificially small—just enough to illustrate the concepts. (In fact, at this point, you may want to take a look at the example database. For details on downloading it from the Internet, or on using Microsoft Access to create it yourself, see Appendix D.) In the next chapter, we will actually implement the entity-relationship (E/R) model for our LIBRARY database.

What Is a Database?

A *database* may be defined as a collection of *persistent* data. The term persistent is somewhat vague, but is intended to imply that the data has a more-or-less independent existence or that it is *semipermanent*. For instance, data stored on paper in a filing cabinet, or stored magnetically on a hard disk, CD-ROM, or computer tape is persistent, whereas data stored in a computer's memory is generally not considered to be persistent. (The term *permanent* is a bit too strong, since very little in life is truly permanent.)

Of course, this is a very general concept. Most real-life databases consist of data that exist for a specific purpose and are thus persistent.

Entities and Their Attributes

The purpose of a database is to store information about certain types of objects. In database language, these objects are called *entities*. For example, the entities of the LIBRARY database include books, authors, and publishers.

It is very important at the outset to make a distinction between the entities that are contained in a database at a given time and the world of all possible entities that the database might contain. The reason this is important is that the contents of a database are constantly changing and we must make decisions based not just on what is contained in a database at a given time, but on what might be contained in the database in the future.

For example, at a given time, our LIBRARY database might contain 14 book entities. However, as time goes on, new books may be added to the database, and old books may be removed. Thus, the entities in the database are constantly changing. If, for example, based on the fact that the 14 books currently in the database have different titles, we decide to use the title to identify each book uniquely, we may be in for some trouble when, later on, a different book arrives at the library with the same title as a previous book.

The world of all possible entities of a specific type that a database might contain is referred to as an *entity class*. We will use italics to denote entity classes. Thus, for instance, the world of all possible books is the *Books* entity class, and the world of all possible authors is the *Authors* entity class.

We emphasize that an entity class is just an abstract description of something, whereas an entity is a concrete example of that description. The entity classes in our very modest LIBRARY example database are (at least so far):

- Books
- Authors
- Publishers

The set of entities of a given entity class that are in the database at a given time is called an *entity set*. To clarify the difference between entity set and entity class with an example, consider the BOOKS table in the LIBRARY database, which is shown in Table 2-1.

The entities are books, the entity class is the set of all possible books, and the entity set (at this moment) is the specific set of 14 books listed in the BOOKS table. As mentioned, the entity set will change as new books (book entities) are added to the table or old ones are removed. However, the entity class does not change.

Incidentally, if you are familiar with object-oriented programming concepts, you will recognize the concept of a *class*. In object-oriented circles, we would refer to an entity class simply as a class and an entity as an *object*.

The entities of an entity class possess certain properties, which are called *attributes*. We usually refer to these attributes as attributes of the entity class itself. It is up to the database designer to determine which attributes to include for each entity class. It is these attributes that will correspond to the fields in the tables of the database.

Table 2-1. The BOOKS table from the LIBRARY database

ISBN	Title	Price
0-12-333433-3	On Liberty	$25.00
0-103-45678-9	Iliad	$25.00
0-91-335678-7	Faerie Queene	$15.00
0-99-999999-9	Emma	$20.00
1-22-233700-0	Visual Basic	$25.00
1-1111-1111-1	C++	$29.95
0-91-045678-5	Hamlet	$20.00
0-555-55555-9	Macbeth	$12.00
0-99-777777-7	King Lear	$49.00
0-123-45678-0	Ulysses	$34.00
0-12-345678-9	Jane Eyre	$49.00
0-11-345678-9	Moby-Dick	$49.00
0-321-32132-1	Balloon	$34.00
0-55-123456-9	Main Street	$22.95

The attributes of an entity class serve three main purposes:

- Attributes are used to include *information* that we want in the database. For instance, we want the title of each book to be included in the database, so we include a Title attribute for the *Books* entity class.

- Attributes are used to help uniquely identify individual entities within an entity class. For instance, we may wish to include a publisher's ID-number attribute for the *Publishers* entity class, to uniquely identify each publisher. If combinations of other attributes (such as the publisher's name and publisher's address) will serve this purpose, the inclusion of an identifying attribute is not strictly necessary, but it can still be more efficient to include such an attribute, since often we can create a much shorter identifying attribute. For instance, a combination of title, author, publisher, and copyright date would make a very awkward and inefficient identifying attribute for the *Books* entity class—much more so than the ISBN attribute.

- Attributes are used to describe *relationships* between the entities in different entity classes. We will discuss this subject in more detail later.

For now, let us list the attributes for the LIBRARY database that we need to supply information about each entity and to identify each entity uniquely. I will deal with the issue of describing relationships later. Remember that this example is kept deliberately small—in real life we would no doubt include many other attributes.

The attributes of the entity classes in the LIBRARY database are:

Books attributes

> Title
> ISBN
> Price

Authors attributes

> AuName
> AuPhone
> AuID

Publishers attributes

> PubName
> PubPhone
> PubID

Let us make a few remarks about these attributes.

- From these attributes alone, there is no direct way to tell who is the author of a given book, since there is no author-related attribute in the *Books* entity class. A similar statement applies to determining the publisher of a book. Thus, we will need to add more attributes in order to describe these relationships.

- The ISBN (International Standard Book Number) of a book serves to identify the book uniquely, since no two books have the same ISBN (at least in theory). On the other hand, the Title alone does not uniquely identify the book, since many books have the same title. In fact, the sole purpose of ISBNs (here and in the real world) is to identify books uniquely. Put another way, the ISBN is a quintessential identifying attribute!

- We may reasonably assume that no two publishers in the world have the same name *and* the same phone number. Hence, these two attributes together uniquely identify the publisher. Nevertheless, we have included a publisher's ID attribute to make this identification more convenient.

Let us emphasize that an entity class is a description, not a set. For instance, the entity class *Books* is a description of the attributes of the entities that we identify as books. A *Books* entity is the "database version" of a book. It is not a physical book, but rather a book as defined by the values of its attributes. For instance, the following is a *Books* entity:

```
Title = Gone With the Wind
ISBN = 0-12-345678-9
Price = $24.00
```

Now, there is certainly more than one physical copy in existence of the book *Gone With the Wind*, with this ISBN and price, but that is not relevant to our discussion. As far as the database is concerned, there is only one *Books* entity defined by:

```
Title = Gone With the Wind
ISBN = 0-12-345678-9
Price = $24.00
```

If we need to model multiple copies of physical books in our database (as a real library would do), then we must add another attribute to the *Books* entity class, perhaps called CopyNumber. Even still, a book entity is just a set of attribute values.

These matters emphasize the point that it is up to the database designer to ensure that the set of attributes for an entity uniquely identify the entity from among all other entities that may appear in the database (now and forever, if possible!). For instance, if the *Books* entity class included only the Title and Price attributes, there would certainly be cause to worry that someday we might want to include two books with the same title and price. While this is allowed in some database-application programs, it can lead to great confusion and is definitely not recommended. Moreover, it is forbidden by definition in a true relational database. In other words, no two entities can agree on all of their attributes. (This *is* allowed in Microsoft Access, however.)

Keys and Superkeys

A set of attributes that uniquely identifies any entity from among all possible entities in the entity class that may appear in the database is called a *superkey* for the entity class. Thus, the set {ISBN} is a superkey for the *Books* entity class, and the sets {PubID} and {PubName, PubPhone} are both superkeys for the *Publishers* entity class.

Note that there is a bit of subjectivity in this definition of superkey, since it depends ultimately on our decision about which entities may ever appear in the database, and this is probably something of which we cannot be absolutely certain. Consider, for instance, the *Books* entity class. There is no law that says all books must have an ISBN (and many books do not). Also, there is no law that says that two books cannot have the same ISBN. (The ISBN is assigned, at least in part, by the publisher of the book.) Thus, the set {ISBN} is a superkey only if we are willing to accept the fact that all books that the library purchases have distinct ISBNs or that the librarian will assign a unique ersatz ISBN to any books that do not have a real ISBN.

It is important to emphasize that the concept of a superkey applies to entity classes, and not entity sets. Although we can define a superkey for an entity set, this is of limited use, since what may serve to identify the entities uniquely in a particular entity set may fail to do so if we add new entities to the set. To illustrate, the Title attribute does serve to identify each of the 14 books uniquely in the BOOKS table. Thus,

{Title} is a superkey for the entity set described by the BOOKS table. However, {Title} is not a superkey for the *Books* entity class, since there are many distinct books with the same title.

We have remarked that {ISBN} is a superkey for the *Books* entity class. Of course, so is {Title, ISBN}, but it is wasteful and inefficient to include the Title attribute purely for the sake of identification.

Indeed, one of the difficulties with superkeys is that they may contain more attributes than is absolutely necessary to indentify any entity uniquely. It is more desirable to work with superkeys that do not have this property. A superkey is called a key when it has the property that no proper subset of it is also a superkey. Thus, if we remove an attribute from a key, the resulting set is no longer a superkey. Put more succinctly, a key is a minimal superkey. Sometimes keys are called *candidate keys*, since it is usually the case that we want to select one particular key to use as an identifier. This particular choice is referred to as the *primary key*. The primary keys in the LIBRARY database are ISBN, AuID, and PubID.

I should remark that a key may contain more than one attribute, and different keys may have different numbers of attributes. For instance, it is reasonable to assume that both {SocialSecurityNumber} and {FullName, FullAddress, DateofBirth} are keys for a *US Citizens* entity class.

Relationships Between Entities

If we are going to model a database as a collection of entity sets (tables), then we also need to describe the *relationships* between these entity sets. For instance, an author relationship exists between a book and the authors who wrote that book. We might call this relationship *WrittenBy*. Thus, Hamlet is *WrittenBy* Shakespeare.

It is possible to draw a diagram, called an *entity-relationship diagram,* or *E/R diagram,* to illustrate the entity classes in a database model, along with their attributes and relationships. Figure 2-1 shows the LIBRARY E/R diagram, with an additional entity class called *Contributors* (a contributor may be someone who contributes to or writes only a very small portion of a book, and thus may not be accorded all of the rights of an author, such as a royalty).

Note that each entity class is denoted by a rectangle, and each attribute by an ellipse. The relations are denoted by diamonds. We have included the *Contributors* entity class in this model merely to illustrate a special type of relationship. In particular, since a contributor is considered an author, there is an *IsA* relationship between the two entity classes.

The model represented by an E/R diagram is sometimes referred to as a *semantic model* since it describes much of the meaning of the database.

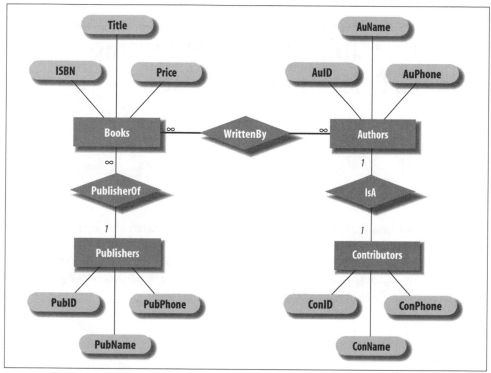

Figure 2-1. The LIBRARY entity-relationship diagram

Types of Relationships

Referring to Figure 2-1, the symbols 1 and ∞ represent the type of relationship between the corresponding entity classes. (The symbol ∞ is read "many.") Relationships can be classified into three types. For instance, the relationship between *Books* and *Authors* is *many-to-many*, meaning that a book may have many authors and an author may write many books. On the other hand, the relationship from *Publishers* to *Books* is *one-to-many*, meaning that one publisher may publish many books, but a book is published by at most one publisher (or so we will assume).

One-to-one relationships, where each entity on each side is related to at most one entity on the other side of the relationship, are fairly rare in database design. For instance, consider the *Contributors-Authors* relationship, which is one-to-one. We could replace the *Contributors* class by a contributor attribute of the *Authors* class, thus eliminating the need for a separate class and a separate relationship. On the other hand, if the *Contributors* class had several attributes that are not shared by the *Authors* class, then a separate class may be appropriate.

In Chapter 3 we will actually implement the full E/R model for our LIBRARY database.

CHAPTER 3

Implementing Entity-Relationship Models: Relational Databases

An E/R model of a database is an abstract model, visualized through an E/R diagram. For this to be useful, we must translate the abstract model into a concrete one. That is, we must describe each aspect of the model in the concrete terms that a database program can manipulate. In short, we must *implement* the E/R model. This requires implementing several things:

- The entities
- The entity classes
- The entity sets
- The relationships between the entity classes

The result of this implementation is a *relational database*.

As we will see, implementing the relationships usually involves some changes to the entity classes, perhaps by adding new attributes to existing entity classes or by adding new entity classes.

Implementing Entities

As discussed in the previous chapter, an entity is implemented (or described in concrete terms) simply by giving the values of its attributes. Thus, the following is an implementation of a *Books* entity:

```
Title = Gone With the Wind
ISBN = 0-12-345678-9
Price = $24.00
```

Implementing Entity Classes—Table Schemes

Since the entities in an entity class are implemented by giving their attribute values, it makes sense to implement an entity class by the set of attribute names. For instance, the *Books* entity class can be identified with the set:

```
{ISBN,Title,Price}
```

(We will add the PubID attribute name later, when we implement the relationships.)

Since attribute names are usually used as column headings for a table, a set of attribute names is called a *table scheme*. Thus, entity classes are implemented as table schemes. For convenience, we use notation such as:

```
Books(ISBN,Title,Price)
```

which shows not only the name of the entity class, but also the names of the attributes in the table scheme for this class. You can also think of a table scheme as the column headings row (the top row) of any table that is formed using that table scheme. (I will present an example of this shortly.)

We have defined the concepts of a superkey and a key for entity classes. These concepts apply equally well to table schemes, so we may say that the attributes {A,B} form a key for a table scheme, meaning that they form a key for the entity class implemented by that table scheme.

Implementing Entity Sets—Tables

In a relational database, each entity set is modeled by a *table*. For example, consider the BOOKS table shown in Table 3-1, and note the following:

- The first row of the table is the table scheme for the *Books* entity class.
- Each of the other rows of the table implements a *Books* entity.
- The set of all rows of the table, except the first row, implements the entity set itself.

Table 3-1. The BOOKS table from the LIBRARY database

ISBN	Title	Price
0-12-333433-3	On Liberty	$25.00
0-103-45678-9	Iliad	$25.00
0-91-335678-7	Faerie Queene	$15.00
0-99-999999-9	Emma	$20.00
1-22-233700-0	Visual Basic	$25.00
1-1111-1111-1	C++	$29.95
0-91-045678-5	Hamlet	$20.00
0-555-55555-9	Macbeth	$12.00
0-99-777777-7	King Lear	$49.00
0-123-45678-0	Ulysses	$34.00
0-12-345678-9	Jane Eyre	$49.00
0-11-345678-9	Moby-Dick	$49.00
0-321-32132-1	Balloon	$34.00
0-55-123456-9	Main Street	$22.95

More formally, a table T is a rectangular array of elements with the following properties:

- The top of each column is labeled with a distinct *attribute name* A_i. The label A_i is also called the *column heading*.

- The elements of the ith column of the table T come from a single set D_i, called the *domain* for the ith column. Thus, the domain is the set of all *possible* values for the attribute. For instance, for the BOOKS table in Table 3-1, the domain D_1 is the set of all possible ISBNs, and the domain D_2 is the set of all possible book titles.

- No two rows of the table are identical.

Let us make some remarks about the concept of a table:

- A table may (but is not required to) have a name, such as BOOKS, which is intended to convey the meaning of the table as a whole.

- The number of rows of the table is called the *size* of the table, and the number of columns is called the *degree* of the table. For example, the BOOKS table shown in Table 3-1 has size 14 and degree 3. The attribute names are ISBN, Title, and Price.

- As mentioned earlier, to emphasize the attributes of a table, it is common to denote a table by writing $T(A_1,...,A_n)$; for example, we denote the BOOKS table by:

      BOOKS(ISBN,Title,Price)

- The order of the rows of a table is not important, and so two tables that differ only in the order of their rows are thought of as being the same table. Similarly, the order of the columns of a table is not important as long as the headings are thought of as part of their respective columns. In other words, we may feel free to reorder the columns of a table, as long as we keep the headings with their respective columns.

- Finally, there is no requirement that the domains of different columns be different. (For example, it is possible for two columns in a single table to use the domain of integers.) However, there is a requirement that the attribute names of different columns be different. Think of the potential confusion that would otherwise ensue, in view of the fact that we may rearrange the columns of a table!

Now that we have defined the concept of a table, we can say that it is common to define a relational database as a finite collection of tables. However, this definition belies the fact that the tables also model the relationships between the entity classes, as we will see.

A Short Glossary

To help keep the various database terms clear, let us collect their definitions in one place:

Entity

An object about which the database is designed to store information. Example: a book; that is, an ISBN, a title, and a price, as in:

```
0-12-333433-3, On Liberty, $25.00
```

Attribute

A property that (partially or completely) describes an entity. Example: title.

Entity class

An abstract group of entities, with a common description. Example: the entity class *Books*, representing all books in the universe.

Entity set

The set of entities from a given entity class that are currently in the database. Example: the following set of 14 books:

```
0-12-333433-3, On Liberty, $25.00
0-103-45678-9, Iliad, $25.00
0-91-335678-7, Faerie Queene, $15.00
0-99-999999-9, Emma, $20.00
1-22-233700-0, Visual Basic, $25.00
1-1111-1111-1, C++, $29.95
0-91-045678-5, Hamlet, $20.00
0-555-55555-9, Macbeth, $12.00
0-99-777777-7, King Lear, $49.00
0-123-45678-0, Ulysses, $34.00
0-12-345678-9, Jane Eyre, $49.00
0-11-345678-9, Moby-Dick, $49.00
0-321-32132-1, Balloon, $34.00
0-55-123456-9, Main Street, $22.95
```

Superkey

A set of attributes for an entity class that serves to identify an entity uniquely from among all possible entities in that entity class. Example: the set {Title, ISBN} for the *Books* entity class.

Key

A minimal superkey; that is, a key with the property that, if we remove an attribute, the resulting set is no longer a superkey. Example: the set {ISBN} for the *Books* entity class.

Table

A rectangular array of attribute values whose columns hold the attribute values for a given attribute and whose rows hold the attribute values for a given entity. Tables are used to implement entity sets. Example: the BOOKS table shown earlier in Table 3-1.

Table scheme

The set of all attribute names for an entity class. Example:

{ISBN,Title,Price}

Since this is the table scheme for the entity class *Books*, we can use the notation *Books*(ISBN,Title,Price).

Relational database

A finite collection of tables that provides an implementation of an E/R database model.

Implementing the Relationships in a Relational Database

Now let us discuss how we might implement the relationships in an E/R database model. For convenience, we repeat the E/R diagram for the LIBRARY database in Figure 3-1.

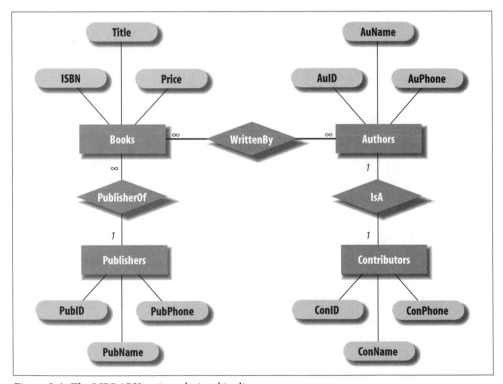

Figure 3-1. The LIBRARY entity-relationship diagram

Implementing a One-to-Many Relationship—Foreign Keys

Implementing a one-to-many relationship, such as the *PublisherOf* relationship, is fairly easy. To illustrate, since {PubID} is a key for the *Publishers* entity class, we simply add this attribute to the *Books* entity class. Thus, the *Books* entity class becomes:

```
Books(ISBN,Title,PubID,Price)
```

The *Books* table scheme is now:

```
{ISBN,Title,PubID,Price}
```

and the BOOKS table now appears as shown in Table 3-2 (sorted by PubID).

Table 3-2. The BOOKS table sorted by PubID

ISBN	Title	PubID	Price
0-12-333433-3	On Liberty	1	$25.00
0-103-45678-9	Iliad	1	$25.00
0-91-335678-7	Faerie Queene	1	$15.00
0-99-999999-9	Emma	1	$20.00
1-22-233700-0	Visual Basic	1	$25.00
1-1111-1111-1	C++	1	$29.95
0-91-045678-5	Hamlet	2	$20.00
0-555-55555-9	Macbeth	2	$12.00
0-99-777777-7	King Lear	2	$49.00
0-123-45678-0	Ulysses	2	$34.00
0-12-345678-9	Jane Eyre	3	$49.00
0-11-345678-9	Moby-Dick	3	$49.00
0-321-32132-1	Balloon	3	$34.00
0-55-123456-9	Main Street	3	$22.95

The PubID attribute in the Books entity class is referred to as a *foreign key,* because it is a key for a foreign entity class—that is, for the *Publishers* entity class.

Note that the value of the foreign key PubID in the BOOKS table provides a reference to the corresponding value in PUBLISHERS. Moreover, since {PubID} is a key for the *Publishers* entity class, there is at most one row of PUBLISHERS that contains a given value. Thus, for each book entity, we can look up the PubID value in the PUBLISHERS table to get the name of the publisher of that book. In this way, we have implemented the one-to-many *PublisherOf* relationship.

The idea just described is pictured in more general terms in Figure 3-2. Suppose that there is a one-to-many relationship between the entity classes (or, equivalently, table schemes) S and T. Figure 3-2 shows two tables S and T based on these table schemes. Suppose also that {A$_2$} is a key for table scheme S (the one side of the relationship). Then we add this attribute to the table scheme T (and hence to table T). In this way, for any row of the table T, we can identify the unique row in table S to which it is related.

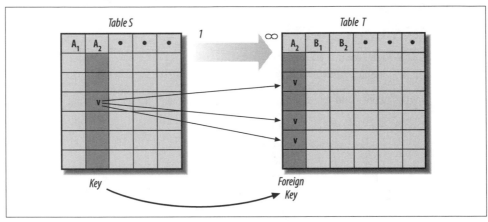

Figure 3-2. A one-to-many relationship shown in tables S and T

The attribute set {A$_2$} in table S is a key for the table scheme S. For this reason, the attribute set {A$_2$} is also called a foreign key for the table scheme T. More generally, a set of attributes of a table scheme T is a foreign key for T if it is a key for some other table scheme S. Note that a foreign key for T is not a key for T—it is a key for another table scheme. Thus, the attribute set {PubID} is a key for *Publishers*, but a foreign key for *Books*.

As with our example, a foreign key provides a reference to the entity class (table scheme) for which it is a key. The table scheme T is called the *referencing table scheme*, and the table scheme S is called the *referenced table scheme*. The key that is being referenced in the referenced table scheme is called the *referenced key*.

Note that adding a foreign key to a table scheme does create some duplicate values in the database, but we must expect to add some additional information to the database in order to describe the relationships.

Implementing a One-to-One Relationship

Of course, the procedure of introducing a foreign key into a table scheme works equally well for one-to-one relationships as for one-to-many relationships. For instance, we only need to rename the ConID attribute to AuID to make ConID into a foreign key that will implement the *Authors-Contributors IsA* relationship.

Implementing a Many-to-Many Relationship— New Entity Classes

The implementation of a many-to-many relationship is a bit more involved. For instance, consider the *WrittenBy* relationship between *Books* and *Authors*.

At first glance, we might think of just adding foreign keys to each table scheme, thinking of the relationship as two distinct one-to-many relationships. However, this approach is not good, since it requires duplicating table rows. For example, if we add the ISBN key to the *Authors* table scheme and the AuID key to the *Books* table scheme, then each book that is written by two authors must be represented by two rows in the BOOKS table, so we can have two AuIDs. To be specific, since the book *Main Street* is written by Smith and Jones, we would need two rows in the BOOKS table:

```
TITLE: Main Street, ISBN 0-55-123456-9, Price: $22.95 AuID: Smith
TITLE: Main Street, ISBN 0-55-123456-9, Price: $22.95 AuID: Jones
```

It is clear that this approach will bloat the database with redundant information.

The proper approach to implementing a many-to-many relationship is to add a new table scheme to the database in order to break the relationship into two one-to-many relationships. In our case, we add a *Book/Author* table scheme, whose attributes consist precisely of the foreign keys ISBN and AuID:

```
Book/Author(ISBN,AuID)
```

To get a pictorial view of this procedure, Figure 3-3 shows the corresponding E/R diagram. Note that it is not customary to include this as a portion of the original E/R diagram, since it belongs more to the implementation of the design than to the design itself.

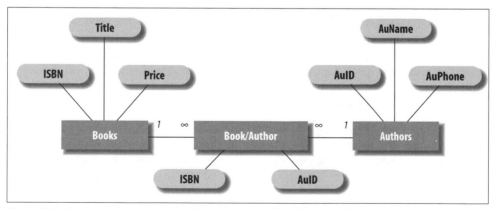

Figure 3-3. A many-to-many relationship in the BOOK/AUTHOR table

Referential Integrity

There are a few important considerations that we must discuss with regard to using foreign keys to implement relationships. First, of course, is the fact that each value of the foreign key must have a matching value in the referenced key. Otherwise, we would have a so-called *dangling reference*. For instance, if the PubID key in a BOOKS table did not match a value of the PubID key in the PUBLISHERS table, we would have a book whose publisher did not exist in the database—that is, a dangling reference to a nonexistent publisher.

The requirement that each value in the foreign key be a value in the referenced key is called the *referential constraint*, and the problem of ensuring that there are no dangling references is referred to as the problem of ensuring *referential integrity*.

There are several ways in which referential integrity might be compromised. First, we could add a value to the foreign key that is not in the referenced key. This would happen, for instance, if we added a new book entity to the BOOKS table, whose publisher is not listed in the PUBLISHERS table. Such an action will be rejected by a database application that has been instructed to protect referential integrity. More subtle ways to affect referential integrity are to change or delete a value in the *referenced* key—the one that is being referenced by the foreign key. This would happen, for instance, if we deleted a publisher from the PUBLISHERS table, but that publisher had at least one book listed in the BOOKS table.

Of course, the database program can simply disallow such a change or deletion, but there is sometimes a preferable alternative, as discussed next.

Cascading Updates and Cascading Deletions

Many database programs allow the option of performing *cascading updates*, which simply means that, if a value in the referenced key is changed, then all matching entries in the foreign key are automatically changed to match the new value. For instance, if cascading updates are enabled, then changing a publisher's PubID in a PUBLISHERS table, say from 100 to 101, would automatically cause all values of 100 in the PubID foreign key of the referencing table BOOKS to change to 101. In short, cascading updates keep everything "in sync."

Similarly, enabling *cascading deletions* means that if a value in the referenced table is deleted by deleting the corresponding row in the referenced table, then all rows in the referencing table that refer to that deleted key value will also be deleted. For instance, if we delete a publisher from a PUBLISHERS table, all book entries referring to that publisher (through its PubID) will be deleted from the BOOKS table automatically. Thus, cascading deletions also preserve referential integrity, at the cost of performing perhaps massive deletions in other tables. Thus, cascading deletions should be used with circumspection.

As you may know, Microsoft Access allows the user to enable or disable both cascading updates and cascading deletions. We will see just how to do this in Access later.

The LIBRARY Relational Database

We can now complete the implementation of the LIBRARY relational database (without the *Contributors* entity class) in Microsoft Access. If you open the LIBRARY database in Microsoft Access, you will see four tables:

- AUTHORS
- BOOK/AUTHOR
- BOOKS
- PUBLISHERS

(The LIBRARY_FLAT table is not used in the relational database.)

These four tables correspond to the following four entity classes (or table schemes):

- *Authors* (AuID, AuName, AuPhone)
- *Book/Author* (ISBN, AuID)
- *Books* (ISBN, Title, PubID, Price)
- *Publishers* (PubID, PubName, PubPhone)

The actual tables are shown in Tables 3-3 through 3-6.

Table 3-3. The AUTHORS table from the Access LIBRARY database

AuID	AuName	AuPhone
1	Austen	111-111-1111
10	Jones	123-333-3333
11	Snoopy	321-321-2222
12	Grumpy	321-321-0000
13	Sleepy	321-321-1111
2	Melville	222-222-2222
3	Homer	333-333-3333
4	Roman	444-444-4444
5	Shakespeare	555-555-5555
6	Joyce	666-666-6666
7	Spenser	777-777-7777
8	Mill	888-888-8888
9	Smith	123-222-2222

Table 3-4. The BOOK/AUTHOR table from the LIBRARY database

ISBN	AuID
0-103-45678-9	3
0-11-345678-9	2
0-12-333433-3	8
0-12-345678-9	1
0-123-45678-0	6
0-321-32132-1	11
0-321-32132-1	12
0-321-32132-1	13
0-55-123456-9	9
0-55-123456-9	10
0-555-55555-9	5
0-91-045678-5	5
0-91-335678-7	7
0-99-777777-7	5
0-99-999999-9	1
1-1111-1111-1	4
1-22-233700-0	4

Table 3-5. The BOOKS table from the LIBRARY database

ISBN	Title	PubID	Price
0-12-333433-3	On Liberty	1	$25.00
0-103-45678-9	Iliad	1	$25.00
0-91-335678-7	Faerie Queene	1	$15.00
0-99-999999-9	Emma	1	$20.00
1-22-233700-0	Visual Basic	1	$25.00
1-1111-1111-1	C++	1	$29.95
0-91-045678-5	Hamlet	2	$20.00
0-555-55555-9	Macbeth	2	$12.00
0-99-777777-7	King Lear	2	$49.00
0-123-45678-0	Ulysses	2	$34.00
0-12-345678-9	Jane Eyre	3	$49.00
0-11-345678-9	Moby-Dick	3	$49.00
0-321-32132-1	Balloon	3	$34.00
0-55-123456-9	Main Street	3	$22.95

Notice that we have included the necessary foreign key {PubID} in the BOOKS table in Table 3-5, to implement the *PublisherOf* relationship, which is one-to-many. Also, we have included the BOOK/AUTHOR table (Table 3-4) to implement the *WrittenBy* relationship, which is many-to-many.

Table 3-6. The PUBLISHERS Table from the LIBRARY Database

PubID	PubName	PubPhone
1	Big House	123-456-7890
2	Alpha Press	999-999-9999
3	Small House	714-000-0000

Even though all relationships are established through foreign keys, we must tell Access that these foreign keys are being used to implement the relationships. Here are the steps.

Setting Up the Relationships in Access

1. Just to illustrate a point, make the following small change in the BOOKS table: Open the table and change the PubID field for Hamlet to 4. Note that there is no publisher with PubID 4 and so we have created a dangling reference. Then close the BOOKS window.

2. Now choose *Relationships* from the *Tools* menu. You should get a window showing the table schemes in the database, similar to that in Figure 3-4. Relationships are denoted by lines between these table schemes. As you can see, there are as yet no relationships. Note that the primary key attributes appear in boldface.

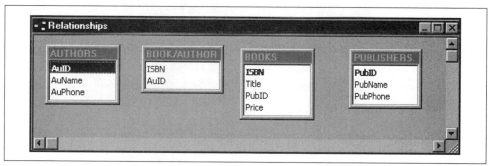

Figure 3-4. The Relationships view of the BOOKS table

3. To set the relationship between PUBLISHERS and BOOKS, place the mouse pointer over the PubID attribute name in the PUBLISHERS table scheme, hold down the left mouse button, and drag the name to the PubID attribute name in the BOOKS table scheme. You should get a window similar to Figure 3-5.

4. This window shows the relationship between PUBLISHERS and BOOKS, listing the key {PubID} in PUBLISHERS and the foreign key {PubID} in BOOKS. (We did not need to call the foreign key PubID, but it makes sense to do so, since it reminds us of the purpose of the attribute.)

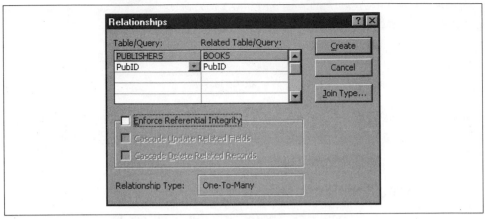

Figure 3-5. Relationship between the PUBLISHERS and BOOKS tables

5. Now check the *Enforce Referential Integrity* box, and click the *Create* button. You should get the message in Figure 3-6. The problem is, of course, the dangling reference that we created by changing the PubID field in the BOOKS table to refer to a nonexistent publisher.

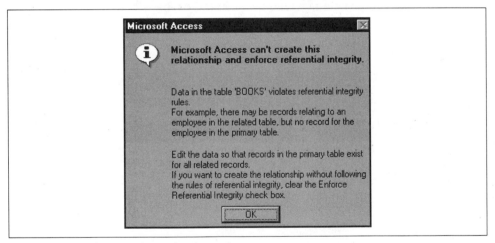

Figure 3-6. Error message due to dangling reference

6. Click the OK button, reopen the BOOKS table, and fix the offending entry (change the PubID field for *Hamlet* back to 2). Then close the BOOKS table, and re-establish the relationship between PUBLISHERS and BOOKS. This time, check the *Enforce Referential Integrity* checkbox, as well as the *Cascade Update Related Fields* checkbox. Do not check *Cascade Delete Related Fields*.

7. Next, drag the ISBN attribute name from the BOOKS table scheme to the ISBN attribute name in the BOOK/AUTHOR table scheme. Again check the *Enforce Referential Integrity* and *Cascade Update Related Fields* checkboxes.

8. Finally, drag the AuID attribute name from the AUTHORS table scheme to the AuID attribute name in the BOOK/AUTHOR table scheme. Check the *Enforce Referential Integrity* and *Cascade Update Related Fields* checkboxes. You should now see the lines indicating these relationships, as shown in Figure 3-7. Note the small 1s and ∞s, indicating the one side and many side of each relationship.

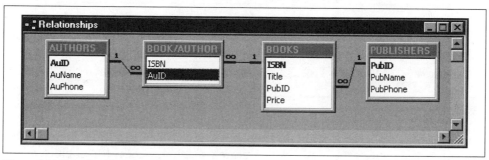

Figure 3-7. Relationships view showing various table relationships

9. To test the enforcement of referential integrity, try the following experiment: open the BOOKS and PUBLISHERS tables, and arrange them so that you can see both tables at the same time. Now change the value of PubID for Small House in the PUBLISHERS table from 3 to 4. As soon as you move the cursor out of the Small House row (which makes the change permanent), the corresponding PubID values in BOOKS should change automatically! When you are done, restore the PubID value in PUBLISHERS back to 3.

Index Files

When a table is stored on disk, it is often referred to as a *file*. In this case, each row of the table is referred to as a *record*, and each column is referred to as a *field*. (These terms are often used for any table.)

Since disk access is typically slow, an important goal is to reduce the amount of disk accesses necessary to retrieve the desired data from a file. Sequential searching of the data, record-by-record, to find the desired information may require a large number of disk accesses and is very inefficient.

The purpose of an *index file* is to provide direct (also called *random*) access to data in a database file.

Figure 3-8 illustrates the concept of an index file. For illustration purposes, we have changed the Publishers data, to include a city column. The file on the left is the index file and indexes the Publishers datafile by the City field, which is therefore called the indexed field. The city file is called an *index* for the PUBLISHERS table. (The index file is not a table in the same sense as the PUBLISHERS table is a table. That is to say, we cannot directly access the index file—instead we use it indirectly.) The index file contains the cities for each publisher, along with a pointer to the corresponding data record in the Publishers file.

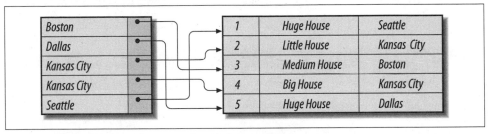

Figure 3-8. Index file between City and Publisher

An index file can be used in a variety of ways. For instance, to find all publishers located in Kansas City, Access can first search the alphabetical list of cities in the index file. Since the list is alphabetical, Access knows that the Kansas City entries are all together, and so once it reaches the first entry after Kansas City, it can stop the search. In other words, Access does not need to search the entire index file. (In addition, there are very efficient search algorithms for ordered tables.) Once the Kansas City entries are found in the index file, the pointers can be used to go directly to the Kansas City publishers in the indexed file.

Also, since the index provides a sorted view of the data in the original table, it can be used to efficiently retrieve a range of records. For instance, if the Books data were indexed on price, we could efficiently retrieve all books in the price range between $20.00 and $30.00.

A table can be indexed on more than one column; that is to say, a table can have more than one index file. Also, a table can be indexed on a combination of two or more columns. For instance, if the PUBLISHERS table also included a State column, we could index the table on a combination of City and State, as shown in Figure 3-9.

BostonMA		1	Huge House	Seattle	WA
DallasTX		2	Little House	Kansas City	MO
Kansas CityKS		3	Medium House	Boston	MA
Kansas CityMO		4	Big House	Kansas City	KS
SeattleWA		5	Huge House	Dallas	TX

Figure 3-9. Index file between City, State, and Publisher

An index on a primary key is referred to as a *primary index*. Note that Microsoft Access automatically creates an index on a primary key. An index on any other column or columns is called a *secondary index*. An index based on a key (not necessarily the primary key) is called a *unique index*, since the indexed column contains unique values.

Example

To view the indexes for a given table in Microsoft Access, open the table in design view, and then choose *Indexes* from the *View* menu. For the BOOKS table, you should see a window similar to Figure 3-10 (without the PubTitle entry).

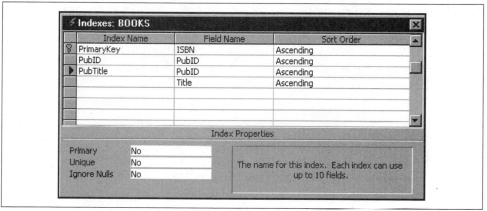

Figure 3-10. Index view of the BOOKS table

To add an index based on more than one attribute, you enter the multiple attributes on successive rows of the *Indexes* dialog box. We have done this in Figure 3-10, adding an index called PubTitle based on the PubID and the Title attributes. This index indexes the BOOKS entities first by PubID and then by Title (within each PubID).

NULL Values

The question of NULLs can be very confusing to the database user, so let us set down the basic principles. Generally speaking, a NULL is a special value that is used for two reasons:

- To indicate that a value is missing or unknown
- To indicate that a value is not applicable in the current context

For instance, consider an author's table:

    AUTHORS(AuID,AuName,AuPhone)

If a particular author's phone number is unknown, it is appropriate for that value to be NULL. This is not to say that the author does not have a phone number, but simply that we have no information about the number—it may or may not exist. If we knew that the person had no phone number, then the information would no longer be unknown. In this case, the appropriate value of the AuPhone attribute would be the empty string, or perhaps the string *no phone*, but not a NULL. Thus, the appropriateness of allowing NULL values for an attribute depends upon the context.

The issue of whether NULLs should appear in a key needs some discussion. The purpose of a key is to provide a means for uniquely identifying entities, and so it would seem that keys and NULLs are incompatible. However, it is impractical to never allow NULLs in any keys. For instance, for the *Publishers* entity, this would mean not allowing a PubPhone to be NULL, since {PubName,PubPhone} is a key. On the other hand, the so-called *entity integrity rule* says that NULLs are not allowed in a primary key.

As a final remark, the presence of a NULL as a foreign key value does not violate referential integrity. That is, referential integrity requires that every non-NULL value in a foreign key must have a match in the referenced key.

CHAPTER 4

Database Design Principles

In Chapter 1 I tried to present a convincing case for why most databases should be modeled as relational databases, rather than single-table flat databases. I tried to make it clear why I split the single LIBRARY_FLAT table into four separate tables: AUTHORS, BOOKS, PUBLISHERS, and BOOK/AUTHOR.

However, for large real-life databases, it is not always clear how to split the data into multiple tables. As I mentioned in Chapter 1, the goal is to minimize redundancy, without losing any information.

The problem of effective database design is a complex one. Most people consider it an art rather than a science. This means that intuition plays a major role in good design. Nonetheless, there is a considerable theory of database design, and it can be quite complicated. My goal in this chapter is to touch upon the general ideas, without becoming involved in the details. Hopefully, this discussion will provide a helpful guide to the intuition needed for database design.

Redundancy

As we saw in Chapter 1, redundant data tends to inflate the size of a database, which can be a very serious problem for medium to large databases. Moreover, redundancy can lead to several types of *anomalies*, as discussed earlier. To understand the problems that can arise from redundancy, we need to take a closer look at what redundancy means.

Let us begin by observing that the attributes of a table scheme can be classified into three groups:

- Attributes used strictly for identification purposes
- Attributes used strictly for informational purposes
- Attributes used for both identification and informational purposes

For example, consider the table scheme:

{PubID,PubName,PubPhone,YearFounded}

In this scheme, PubID is used strictly for identification purposes. It carries no informational content. On the other hand, YearFounded is strictly for informational purposes in this context. It gives the year that the publishing company was founded, but is not required for identification purposes.

Consider also the table scheme:

{Title,PubID,AuID,PageCount,CopyrightDate}

In this case, if we assume that there is only one book of a given title published by a given publisher and written by a given author, then {Title,PubID,AuID} is a key. Hence, each of these attributes is used (at least in part) for identification. However, Title is also an informational attribute.

I should hasten to add that these classifications are somewhat subjective and depend upon the assumptions made about the entity class. Nevertheless, this classification does provide a useful intuitive framework.

We can at least pin down the strictly informational attributes a bit more precisely by making the following observation. The sign that an attribute is being used (at least in part) for identification purposes is that it is part of some key. Thus, an attribute that is not part of any key is being used, in that table scheme, strictly for informational purposes. Let us call such an attribute a *strictly informational attribute*.

Now consider Table 4-1. In this case, both Title and PubName are strictly informational, since {ISBN} is the only key, and neither Title nor PubName is part of that key. However, the values of Title are not redundant (the fact that they are the same does not mean that they are not both required), whereas the values of PubName are redundant.

Table 4-1. A table with two informational attributes

ISBN	Title	PubID	PubName
1-1111-1111-1	C++	1	Big House
0-91-335678-7	Faerie Queene	1	Big House
1-011-22222-0	C++	2	ABC Press

The reason that Title is not redundant is that there is no way to eliminate any of these titles. Each book entity must have its title listed somewhere in the database—one title per ISBN. Thus, the two titles C++ must both appear somewhere in the database.

On the other hand, PubName is redundant, as can easily be seen from the fact that the same PubName is listed twice without adding any new information to the database. To look at this another way, consider the table with two cells blank in

Table 4-2. Can you fill in the title field for the last row? Not unless you call the publisher to get the title for that ISBN. In other words, some information is missing. On the other hand, you can fill in the blank PubName field.

Table 4-2. A table with blank cells to illustrate attribute dependency

ISBN	Title	PubID	PubName
1-1111-1111-1	Macbeth	1	Big House
2-2222-2222-2	Hamlet	1	
5-555-55555-5		2	ABC Press

The issue here is quite simple. The Title attribute depends only upon the ISBN attribute, and {ISBN} is a key. In other words, Title depends only upon a key. However, PubName depends completely upon PubID, which is not a key for this table scheme. (Of course, PubName also depends on the key {ISBN}, but that is not relevant.)

Thus, we have seen a case where redundancy results from the fact that one attribute depends upon another attribute that is not a key. Armed with this observation, we can move ahead.

Normal Forms

Those who make a study of database design have identified a number of special forms, properties, or constraints that a table scheme may possess, in order to achieve certain desired goals, such as minimizing redundancy. These forms are called *normal forms*. There are six commonly recognized normal forms, with the inspired names:

- First normal form (1NF)
- Second normal form (2NF)
- Third normal form (3NF)
- Boyce Codd normal form (BCNF)
- Fourth-normal form (4NF)
- Fifth normal form (5NF)

We will consider the first four of these normal forms, but only informally. Each of these normal forms is stronger than its predecessors. Thus, for instance, a table scheme that is in third normal form is also in second normal form. While it is generally desirable for the table schemes in a database to have a high degree of normalization, as we will see in this chapter, the situation is not as simple as it may seem.

For instance, requiring that all table schemes be in BCNF may cause some loss of information about the various relationships between the table schemes. In general, it is possible to manipulate the data to achieve third normal form for all table schemes, but this may turn out to be far more work than it is worth.

The plain fact is that forcing all table schemes to be in a particular normal form may require some compromises. Each individual situation (database) must be examined on its own merit. It is impossible to make general rules that apply in all situations.

The process of changing a database design to produce table schemes in normal form is called *normalization*.

First Normal Form

First normal form is very simple. A table scheme is said to be in first normal form if the attribute values are *indivisible*. To illustrate, we considered in Chapter 1 the question of including all the authors of a book in a single attribute, called Authors. Here is an example entity:

```
ISBN = 0-55-123456-9
Title = Main Street
Authors = Jones, H. and Smith, K.
Publisher = Small House
```

Since the table scheme in this case allows more than one author name for the Authors attribute, the scheme is not in first normal form. Indeed, one of the obvious problems with the Authors attribute is that it is impossible to sort the data by individual author name. It is also more difficult to, for instance, prepare a mailing label for each author, and so on.

Attributes that allow only indivisible values are said to be *scalar attributes* or *atomic attributes*. By contrast, an attribute whose values can be, for example, a list of items (such as a list of authors) is said to be a *structured attribute*. Thus, a table scheme is in first normal form if all of its attributes are atomic. Good database design almost always requires that all attributes be atomic, so that the table scheme is in first normal form.

In general, making the adjustments necessary to ensure first normal form is not hard, and it is a good general rule that table schemes should be put in first normal form. However, as with the other normal forms (and even more so the higher up we go) each situation must be considered on its own merits. For instance, a single field might be designed to hold a street address, such as "1333 Bessemer Street." Whether the house number and the street name should be separated into distinct attributes is a matter of context. Put another way, whether a street address is atomic depends upon the context. If there is reason to manipulate the street numbers apart from the street names, then they should certainly constitute their own attribute. Otherwise, perhaps not.

Functional Dependencies

Before we can discuss the other normal forms, we need to discuss the concept of *functional dependency*, which is used to define these normal forms. This concept is quite simple, and we have actually been using it for some time now. As an example, we have remarked that, for the Publishers table scheme, the PubName attribute depends completely on the PubID attribute. (More properly, we should say that the value of the PubName attribute depends completely on the value of the PubID attribute, but the earlier shorthand is convenient.) Thus, we can say that the functional dependency from PubID to PubName, written:

```
PubID → PubName
```

holds for the Publishers table scheme. This can be read "PubID determines Pub-Name" or "PubName depends on PubID."

More generally, suppose that $\{A_1,...,A_k\}$ are attributes of a table scheme and that $\{B_1,...,B_n\}$ are also attributes of the same table scheme. We do not require that the Bs be different from the As. Then the attributes $B_1,...,B_n$ depend on the attributes $A_1,...,A_k$, written:

```
{A₁,...,Aₖ} → {B₁,...,Bₙ}
```

if the values of $A_1,...,A_k$ completely determine the values of $B_1,...,B_n$. Our main interest is when there is only one attribute on the right:

```
{A₁,...,Aₖ} → {B}
```

For instance, it is probably safe to say that:

```
{PubName,PubPhone} → {PubID}
```

which is just another way of saying that there is only one publisher with a given name and phone number (including area code).

It is very important to understand that a functional dependency means that the attributes on the left completely determine the attributes on the right for now and for all time to come, no matter what additional data may be added to the database. Thus, just as the concept of a key relates to entity classes (table schemes) rather than individual entity sets (tables), so does functional dependency. Every table scheme has its set of associated functional dependencies, which are based on the meaning of the attributes.

Recall that a superkey is a set of attributes that uniquely determines an entity. Put another way, a superkey is a set of attributes upon which all other attributes of the table scheme are functionally dependent.

Some functional dependencies are obvious. For instance, an attribute functionally depends upon itself. Also, any set of attributes functionally determines any subset of these attributes, as in:

```
{A,B,C} → {A,B}
```

This just says that if we know the values of A, B, and C, then we know the value of A and B! Such functional dependencies are not at all interesting, and are called *trivial dependencies*. All other dependencies are called *nontrivial*.

Second Normal Form

Intuitively, a table scheme T is in second normal form if all of the strictly informational attributes (attributes that do not belong to any key) are attributes of the entities in the table scheme, and not of some other class of entities. In other words, the informational attributes provide information specifically about the entities in this entity class and not about some other entities.

Let us illustrate with an example. Consider a simplified table scheme designed to store house addresses. One possibility is:

    {City,Street,HouseNumber,HouseColor,CityPopulation}

The CityPopulation attribute is out of place here because it is an attribute of cities, not house addresses. More specifically, CityPopulation is strictly an informational attribute (not for identification of houses), but it gives information about cities, not house addresses. Thus, this table scheme is not in second normal form.

We can be a little bit more formal about the meaning of second normal form as follows. Referring to the previous example, we have the dependency:

    {City} → {CityPopulation}

where CityPopulation does not belong to any key, and where City is a proper subset of a key, namely, the key {City, Street, HouseNumber}. (By *proper* subset, we mean a subset that is not the whole set.)

A table scheme is in 2NF if it is not possible to have a dependency of the form:

    {A₁,...,Aₖ} → {B}

where B does not belong to any key (is strictly informational) and $\{A_1,...,A_k\}$ is a proper subset of some key, and thus does not identify the entities of this entity class, but rather identifies the entities of some other entity class.

Let us consider another example of a table scheme that is not in second normal form.

Consider the following table scheme, and assume for the purposes of illustration that, while there may be many books with the same title, no two of them have the same publisher and author:

    {Title,PubID,AuID,Price,AuAddress}

Thus, {Title, PubID, AuID} is the only key. Now, AuAddress does not belong to any key, but it depends upon {AuID}, which is a proper subset of the key, in symbols:

    {AuID} → {AuAddress}

Hence, this table scheme is not in second normal form. In fact, AuAddress is not a piece of information about the entities modeled in the table scheme (i.e., books), but rather about authors. Of course, we could remove the AuAddress attribute to bring the table scheme into second normal form. (If each publisher charged a single price for all of its books, then Price would also cause a violation of second normal form, but this is not the case, of course.)

Third Normal Form

Second normal form is good, but we can do better. We have seen that if a table scheme is in second normal form, then no strictly informational attribute depends on a proper subset of a key. However, there is another undesirable possibility. Let us illustrate with an example.

Consider the following table scheme and assume, for the purposes of illustration, that no two books with the same title have the same publisher:

> {Title,PubID,PageCount,Price}

The only key for this table scheme is {Title,PubID}. Both PageCount and Price are informational attributes only.

Now, let us assume that each publisher decides the price of its books based solely on the page count. First, we observe that this table is in second normal form. To see this, consider the proper subsets of the key. These are:

> {Title} and {PubID}

But none of the dependencies:

> {Title} → {PageCount}
> {Title} → {Price}
> {PubID} → {PageCount}
> {PubID} → {Price}

hold for this table scheme. After all, knowing the title does not determine the book, since there may be many books of the same title, published by different publishers. Hence, the table is in second normal form.

It is also not correct to say that:

> {PageCount} → {Price}

holds, because different publishers may use different price schemes based on page count. In other words, one publisher may price books over 1,000 pages at one price, whereas another may price books over 1,000 pages at a different price. However, it is true that:

> {PubID,PageCount} → {Price}

holds. In other words, here we have an informational attribute (Price) that depends not on a proper subset of a key, but on a proper subset of a key (PubID) together with another informational attribute (PageCount).

This is bad, since it may produce redundancy. For instance, consider Table 4-3. Note that the price attribute is redundant. After all, we could fill in the Price value for the third row if it were blank, because we know that PubID 2 charges $34.95 for 500-page books.

Table 4-3. Redundant data in a table

Title	PubID	PageCount	Price
Moby-Dick	1	500	29.95
Giant	2	500	34.95
Moby-Dick	2	500	34.95

We can summarize the problem with the dependency:

    {PubID,PageCount} → {Price}

by saying that the attribute Price depends upon a set of attributes:

    {PubID,PageCount}

that is not a key, not a superkey, and not a proper subset of a key. It is a mix containing one attribute from the key {Title,PubID} and one attribute that is not in any key.

With this example in mind, we can now define third normal form. A table scheme is in third normal form if it is not possible to have a dependency of the form:

    {A$_1$,...,A$_k$} → {B}

where B does not belong to any key (is strictly informational) and {A$_1$,...,A$_k$} is not a superkey. In other words, third normal form does not permit any strictly informational attribute to depend upon anything other than a superkey. Of course, superkeys determine all attributes, including strictly informational attributes, and so all attributes depend on any superkey. The point is that, with third normal form, strictly informational attributes depend only on superkeys.

Boyce-Codd Normal Form

It is possible to find table schemes that are in third normal form, but still have redundancy. Here is an example.

Consider the table scheme {City,StreetName,ZipCode}, with dependencies:

    {City,StreetName} → {ZipCode}

and:

    {ZipCode} → {City}

(Although in real life, a zip code may be shared by two different cities, we will assume otherwise for the purposes of illustration.) This table scheme is in third normal form. To see this, observe that the keys are {City,StreetName} and {Zip-Code,StreetName}. Hence, no attribute is strictly informational, and there is nothing to violate third normal form.

On the other hand, consider Table 4-4. We can fill in the blank city name because {ZipCode}→{City}.

Table 4-4. A table with dependencies

City	StreetName	ZipCode
Los Angeles	Hollywood Blvd	95000
	Vine St	95000

The problem here is with the dependency:

```
{ZipCode}→{City}
```

which does not violate third normal form because, as we have mentioned, {City} is not strictly informational.

The previous example gives us the idea to strengthen the condition in the definition of third normal form by dropping the requirement that B be strictly informational. Thus, we can define our last, and strongest, normal form. A table scheme is in Boyce-Codd normal form if it is not possible to have a dependency of the form:

$$\{A_1,\ldots,A_k\} \rightarrow \{B\}$$

where $\{A_1,\ldots,A_k\}$ is not a superkey. In other words, BCNF form does not permit any attribute to depend upon anything other than a superkey.

As mentioned earlier, all attributes must depend on any superkey by the very definition of superkey. Thus, BCNF is the strongest possible restriction of this type—it says that an attribute is not allowed to depend on anything other than a superkey.

Normalization

As mentioned earlier, the process of changing a database design to produce table schemes in normal form is called *normalization*.

As a very simple example, the table scheme:

```
{ISBN,Title,Authors}
```

is not even in first normal form, because the Authors attribute might contain more than one author and is therefore not atomic. By trading in this table scheme for the two schemes:

```
{ISBN,Title,AuID}
```

and:

    {AuID,AuName}

we have normalized the database into first normal form.

Here is another example involving the higher normal forms. Recall from an earlier example that the table scheme {City,StreetName,ZipCode}, with dependencies:

    {City,StreetName} → {ZipCode}

and:

    {ZipCode} → {City}

is in third normal form. However, Table 4-5 shows that there is still some redundancy in the table scheme. The table scheme is not in BCNF. In fact, this was the example we used to motivate our definition of BCNF. (The example violates BCNF.)

Table 4-5. A table with redundant data

City	StreetName	ZipCode
Los Angeles	Hollywood Blvd	95000
	Vine St	95000

However, we can split this table scheme into two schemes:

    {ZipCode,City}

and:

    {ZipCode,StreetName}

In this case, Table 4-5 gets split into two tables, Tables 4-6 and 4-7, and the redundancy is gone!

Table 4-6. First table derived from Table 4-5 to eliminate redundancy

ZipCode	City
95000	Los Angeles

Table 4-7. Second table derived from Table 4-5 to eliminate redundancy

ZipCode	StreetName
95000	Hollywood Blvd
95000	Vine St

Generally speaking, the design of a database may begin with an E/R diagram. This diagram can be implemented according to the principles discussed in Chapter 3. The result may very well be a perfectly satisfactory database design. However, if some of the table schemes have redundancies, it may be desirable to split them into smaller table schemes that satisfy a higher normal form, as in the previous example.

Decomposition

Although the decomposition of a table scheme into smaller (hopefully normalized) table schemes is desirable from an efficiency point of view (in order to reduce redundancy and avoid various anomalies), it does carry with it some risk, which primarily comes in two forms:

- The possible loss of information
- The possible loss of dependencies

The following example illustrates the first problem—loss of information. Consider the table scheme:

    {AuID,AuName,PubID}

The only dependency in this table scheme is:

    {AuID} → {AuName}

We could decompose this table scheme into the two schemes:

    {AuID,AuName}

and:

    {AuName,PubID}

Now consider Table 4-8, which has two different authors with the same name. The decomposition gives the two tables shown in Tables 4-9 and 4-10.

Table 4-8. A table with two identical author names

AuID	AuName	PubID
A1	John Smith	P1
A2	John Smith	P2

Table 4-9. Partial decomposition of Table 4-8

AuID	AuName
A1	John Smith
A2	John Smith

Table 4-10. Partial decomposition of Table 4-8

AuName	PubID
John Smith	P1
John Smith	P2

Unfortunately, if we were to ask Microsoft Access to show us the data for all authors named John Smith, we would get the table shown in Table 4-11, which is not the table we started with! Information has been lost, in the sense that we no longer know that both John Smiths together have published only two books, each author with a different publisher. (It may look as though we have more information, since the table is bigger, but in reality we have lost information.)

Table 4-11. An incorrect reconstruction of Table 4-8

AuID	AuName	PubID
A1	John Smith	P1
A1	John Smith	P2
A2	John Smith	P1
A2	John Smith	P2

The second problem I mentioned in connection with the decomposition of a table scheme is loss of dependencies. The issue is this: during the life of the database, we will be making changes (updates, insertions, and deletions) to the separate tables in the decomposition. Of course, we must be careful to preserve the functional dependencies that are inherited from the original table scheme. However, this does not necessarily guarantee that all of the original dependencies will be preserved!

Here is a simple example to illustrate the problem. Consider the table scheme:

    {ISBN,PageCount,Price}

with dependencies:

    {ISBN} → {PageCount}
    {PageCount} → {Price}

Consider the decomposition into the table schemes:

    {ISBN,PageCount}

and:

    {ISBN,Price}

Note that the key {ISBN} is in both schemes in the decomposition.

Unfortunately, the decomposition has caused us to lose the dependency {PageCount}→{Price}, in the sense that these two attributes are not in the same table scheme of the decomposition. To illustrate, consider Table 4-12, which has two different books with the same page count and price. The decomposition of this table into two tables is shown in Tables 4-13 and 4-14.

Table 4-12. Table example to show further decomposition

ISBN	PageCount	Price
0-111-11111-1	500	$39.95
0-111-22222-2	500	$39.95

Table 4-13. Partial decomposition of Table 4-12

ISBN	PageCount
0-111-11111-1	500
0-111-22222-2	500

Table 4-14. Partial decomposition of Table 4-12

ISBN	Price
0-111-11111-1	$39.95
0-111-22222-2	$39.95

Now here is the problem. Looking at the second table, we have no indication that the original scheme required that PageCount determine Price. Hence, we might change the price of the second book to $12.50, as we've done in Table 4-15.

Table 4-15. Decomposition example changing price

ISBN	Price
0-111-11111-1	$39.95
0-111-22222-2	$12.50

But putting the tables back together for a look at all of the data gives us Table 4-16, which reveals a violation of the requirement that PageCount determine Price. In fact, somebody at the publishing company is going to be very unhappy that the company is now selling a 500-page book below cost!

Table 4-16. Looking at data by combining Tables 4-12 through 4-15

ISBN	PageCount	Price
0-111-11111-1	500	$39.95
0-111-22222-2	500	$12.50

By contrast, consider the decomposition of the original table scheme into:

    {ISBN,PubPhone}

and:

    {PubPhone,PubName}

Here, no dependency is lost, so we can update each separate table without fear.

The previous two examples illustrate the pitfalls in decomposing a table scheme into smaller schemes. If a decomposition does not cause any information to be lost, it is called a *lossless decomposition*. A decomposition that does not cause any dependencies to be lost is called a *dependency-preserving decomposition*.

Now it is possible to show that any table scheme can be decomposed, in a lossless way, into a collection of smaller schemes that are in the very nice BCNF form. However, we cannot guarantee that the decomposition will preserve dependencies. On the other hand, any table scheme can be decomposed—in a lossless way that also preserves dependencies—into a collection of smaller schemes that are in the almost-as-nice third normal form.

However, before you get too excited, I must hasten to add that the algorithms given do not always produce desirable results. They can, in fact, create decompositions that are less intuitive than we might do just using our intuition. Nevertheless, they can be relied upon to produce the required decomposition, if we can't do it ourselves.

I should conclude by saying that there is no law that says that a database is always more useful or efficient if the tables have a high degree of normalization. These issues are more subjective than objective and must be dealt with, as a design issue, on an ad hoc basis. In fact, it appears that the best procedure for good database design is to mix eight parts intuition and experience with two parts theory. Hopefully, discussion of normalization has given you a general feel of the issues involved and will provide a good jumping-off place if you decide to study these somewhat complicated issues in greater depth. (See Appendix E for some books for further study.)

PART II

Database Queries

CHAPTER 5

Query Languages and the Relational Algebra

In the first part of this book, I have tried to make a convincing argument that good database design is important to the efficient use of a database. As you have seen, this generally involves breaking the data up into separate pieces (tables). Of course, this implies that we need methods for piecing the data back together again in various forms.

After all, one of the main functions of a database program is to allow the user to view the data in a variety of ways. When data is stored in multiple tables, it is necessary to piece the data back together to provide these various views. For instance, we might want to see a list of all publishers that publish books priced under $10.00. This requires gathering data from more than one table. The point is that, by breaking data into separate tables, we must often go to the trouble of piecing the data back together in order to get a comprehensive view of the data.

Thus, we can state the following important maxim:

> As a direct consequence of good database design, we often need to use methods for piecing data from several tables into a single coherent form.

Many database applications provide the user with relatively easy ways to create comprehensive views of data from many tables. For instance, Microsoft Access provides a graphical interface to create queries for that purpose. Our goal in this chapter is to understand how a database application such as Access goes about providing this service.

The short answer to this is the following:

1. The user of a database application, such as Access, asks the application to provide a specific view of the data by creating a *query*.

2. The database application then converts this query into a statement in its *query language*, which in the case of Microsoft Access is *Access Structured Query Language*, or Access SQL. (This is a special form of standard SQL.)

3. Finally, a special component of Access (known as the *Jet Query Engine*, which we will discuss again in Chapter 7) executes the SQL statement to produce the desired view of the data.

In view of this answer, it is time to turn away from a discussion of database-design issues and turn toward a discussion of issues that will lead us toward database programming and, in particular, programming in query languages such as Access SQL.

I will now outline my plan for this and the next chapter. In this chapter, I will discuss the underlying methods involved in piecing together data from separate tables. In short, I will discuss methods for making new tables from existing tables. This will give us a clear understanding as to the general tasks that must be provided by a query language.

In the next chapter, I will take a look at Access SQL itself. You will see that SQL is much more than just a simple query language, for not only is it capable of manipulating the components of an existing database (into various views), but it is also capable of creating those components in the first place.

Query Languages

A *query* can be thought of as a *request* of the database, the response to which is a new table, which I will refer to as a *result table*. For instance, referring to the LIBRARY database, we might request the titles and prices of all books published by Big House that cost over $20.00. The result table in this case is shown in Table 5-1.

Table 5-1. Books published by Big House costing over $20.00

Title	Price	PubName
On Liberty	$25.00	Big House
Iliad	$25.00	Big House
Visual Basic	$25.00	Big House
C++	$29.95	Big House

It is probably not necessary to emphasize the importance of queries, for what good is a database if we have no way to extract the data in meaningful forms?

Special languages that are are used to formulate queries—in other words, that are designed to create new tables from old ones—are known as *query languages*. (There does not seem to be agreement on the precise meaning of the term query language, so I have decided to use it in a manner that seems most consistent with the term query.)

There are two fundamental approaches to query languages: one is based on algebraic expressions, and the other is based on logical expressions. In both cases, an expression is formed that refers to existing tables, constants (i.e., values from the domains of tables), and operators of various types. How the expression is used to create the return table depends on the approach, as you will see.

Before proceeding, let us discuss a bit more terminology. A table whose data is actually stored in the database is called a *base table*. Base-table data is generally stored in a format that does not actually resemble a table—but the point is that the data is stored. A table that is not stored, such as the result table of a query, is called a *derived table*. It is generally possible to save (i.e., store) a result table, which then would become a base table of the database. In Microsoft Access, this is done by creating a so-called *make-table query*.

Finally, a *view* is a query expression that has been given a name and is stored in the database. For example, the expression:

all titles where (PubName = Big House) and (Price > $20.00)

is a view. Note that it is the expression that is the view, not the corresponding result table (as might be implied by the name view).

Whenever the expression (or view) is executed, it creates a result table. Therefore, a view is often referred to as a *virtual table*. Again, it is important not to confuse a view with the result table that is obtained by executing the expression. The virtue of a virtual table (or view) is that an expression generally takes up far less room in storage than the corresponding result table. Moreover, the data in a result table is redundant, since the data is already in the base tables, even though not in the same logical structure.

Relational Algebra and Relational Calculus

The most common algebraic query language is called the *relational algebra*. This language is *procedural*, in the sense that its expressions actually describe an explicit procedure for returning the results. Languages that use logic fall under the heading of the *relational calculus* (there is more than one such language in common use). These languages are *nonprocedural*, since their expressions represent statements that describe conditions that must be met for a row to be in the result table, without showing how to actually obtain those rows.

Let us illustrate these ideas with an example. Consider the following request, written in plain English:

Get the names and phone numbers for publishers who publish books costing under $20.00.

For reference, let us repeat the relevant tables for this request. The BOOKS table appears in Table 5-2, while the PUBLISHERS table is shown in Table 5-3.

Here is a procedure for executing this request. Don't worry if some of the terms do not make sense to you now; I will explain them later.

1. *Join* the BOOKS and PUBLISHERS tables, on the PubID attribute.
2. *Select* those rows (of the join) with Price attribute less than $20.00.
3. *Project* onto the columns PubName and PubPhone.

Table 5-2. The BOOKS table from the LIBRARY database

ISBN	Title	PubID	Price
0-555-55555-9	Macbeth	2	$12.00
0-91-335678-7	Faerie Queene	1	$15.00
0-99-999999-9	Emma	1	$20.00
0-91-045678-5	Hamlet	2	$20.00
0-55-123456-9	Main Street	3	$22.95
1-22-233700-0	Visual Basic	1	$25.00
0-12-333433-3	On Liberty	1	$25.00
0-103-45678-9	Iliad	1	$25.00
1-1111-1111-1	C++	1	$29.95
0-321-32132-1	Balloon	3	$34.00
0-123-45678-0	Ulysses	2	$34.00
0-99-777777-7	King Lear	2	$49.00
0-12-345678-9	Jane Eyre	3	$49.00
0-11-345678-9	Moby-Dick	3	$49.00

Table 5-3. The PUBLISHERS table from the LIBRARY database

PubID	PubName	PubPhone
1	Big House	123-456-7890
2	Alpha Press	999-999-9999
3	Small House	714-000-0000

In the relational algebra, this would be translated into the following expression:

$$proj_{PubName,PubPhone}(sel_{Price<20.00}(\text{BOOKS } join \text{ PUBLISHERS}))$$

The result table is shown in Table 5-4.

Table 5-4. Publishers with books under $20.00

PubName	PubPhone
Big House	123-456-7890
Alpha Press	999-999-9999

In a relational calculus, the corresponding expression might appear as:

$$\{(x,y) \mid \text{PUBLISHERS}(z,x,y) \text{ } and \text{ BOOKS}(a,b,z,c) \text{ } and \text{ } c < \$20.00\}$$

where the bar | is read "such that," and the entire expression is read:

The set of all pairs (x,y) such that (z,x,y) is a row in the PUBLISHERS table, (a,b,z,c) is a row in the BOOKS table, and c < $20.00.

Note that the variable z appears twice, and it must be the same for each appearance. This is precisely what provides the link between the BOOKS and PUBLISHERS tables. In other words, the row PUBLISHERS(z,x,y) in the PUBLISHERS table and the row BOOKS(a,b,z,c) in the BOOKS table have an attribute value in common (represented by the common letter z). This attribute, which is the first attribute in PUBLISHERS and the third attribute in BOOKS, is PubID.

As you can see from the previous example, the relational calculus is generally more complex (and perhaps less intuitive) than the relational algebra, and I will not discuss it further in this book, beyond making the following comments. First, it is important to at least be aware of the existence of the relational calculus, since there are commercially available applications, such as IBM's *Query-by-Example*, that use the relational calculus. Second, most relational calculus–based languages have exactly the same expressive power as the relational algebra. In other words, we get no more or less by using a relational calculus than we do by using the relational algebra.

Details of the Relational Algebra

We are now ready to discuss the details of the relational algebra. The operations that are part of the relational algebra are described in this section. You should find most of these operations intuitive.

Before beginning, however, I should say a word about how Microsoft Access implements the operations of the relational algebra. Most of these operations can be implemented in Microsoft Access by creating a query. This is most easily done in Access's Query Design mode, which provides the graphical environment shown in Figure 5-1.

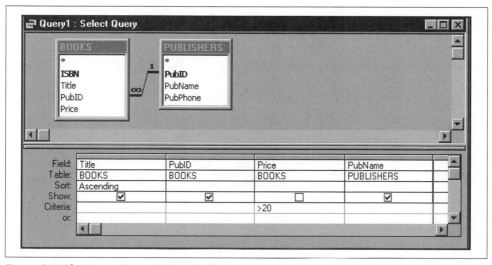

Figure 5-1. The Access Query Design window

The user can add table schemes from the database to the upper portion of the Query Design window. From there, various attributes can be moved to the design grid. Note that the second row of the grid shows the table from whence the attribute comes, just in case two tables have attributes of the same name (which happens often).

The grid has options for sorting and for determining whether to display a particular attribute in the result table. It also has room for criteria used to filter out data from the query.

Note also that we do not need to include the PubID field from both tables in the lower portion of the design window. Microsoft Access takes care of forming the appropriate join based on the information in the upper portion of the window.

Microsoft Access translates the final query design into a statement in the query language known as *structured query language,* or SQL. We will discuss the details of Access SQL (which differs somewhat from standard SQL) in Chapter 6, where the knowledge you gain here will prove very useful. I should also mention that Access SQL is more powerful than the Access Query Design interface, so some operations must be written directly in SQL. Fortunately, Access allows the user to write SQL statements.

Let us recall some notation used earlier in the book. In order to emphasize the attributes of a table (or table scheme), we use the notation $T(A_1,...,A_n)$. As an example, the BOOKS table can be written:

BOOKS(ISBN,Title,PubID,Price)

and the *Books* table scheme can be written:

Books(ISBN,Title,PubID,Price)

Renaming

Renaming refers simply to changing the name of an attribute of a table. If a table T has an attribute named A, we will denote the table resulting from the operation of renaming A to B by:

$ren_{A \rightarrow B}(T)$

For Table 5-5:

Table 5-5. The BOOKS table with original fields

ISBN	Title	Price	PubID
0-103-45678-9	The Firm	$24.95	1
0-11-345678-9	Moby-Dick	$49.00	2
0-12-333433-3	War and Peace	$25.00	1

the result of performing:

$ren_{ISBN}\rightarrow$BookID, Price$\rightarrow$Cost(BOOKS)

is shown in Table 5-6.

Table 5-6. The BOOKS table with renamed fields

BookID	Title	Cost	PubID
0-103-45678-9	The Firm	$24.95	1
0-11-345678-9	Moby-Dick	$49.00	2
0-12-333433-3	War and Peace	$25.00	1

Union

If S and T are tables with the same attributes, then we may form the *union* $S \cup T$, which is just the table obtained by including all of the rows from both S and T. Here is an example.

A_1	A_2
a	b
c	d
e	f

A_1	A_2
g	h
i	j

A_1	A_2
a	b
c	d
e	f
g	h
i	j

Note that if S and T do not have the same attributes, but do have the same *degree*—that is, the same number of columns—then we can first rename the attributes of one table to match the other and then take their union. Of course, this will not always make sense, since it may result in combining attribute values from different domains into one column.

Let us consider an example of how to take a union in Microsoft Access. Unions can be formed in one of two ways in Microsoft Access. The first is straightforward:

1. First, we need some expendable tables to use in this example. We can create these tables by copying the BOOKS table as follows. Highlight the BOOKS table in the Database Window, and choose *Copy* from the *Edit* menu. Then choose *Paste* from the *Edit* menu. You will get the dialog box in Figure 5-2.

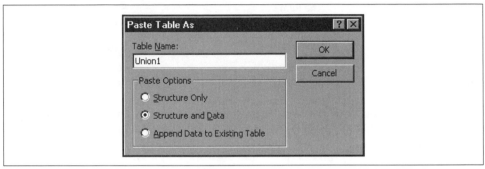

Figure 5-2. The Access Paste Table As dialog box

Type the table name Union1, and click *OK*. Choose *Paste* a second time to create a table named Union2. Open Union1, and delete the last seven rows from the table. (Just highlight the rows and hit the Delete key.) Open Union2, and delete the first seven rows of the table. Thus, Union1 will consist of the first half of the BOOKS, table and Union2 will consist of the second half of BOOKS.

2. The simplest way to take the union is to use the same *Copy...Paste* procedure that we used in Step 1. To illustrate, highlight Union2, and choose *Copy* from the *Edit* menu. Then choose *Paste*, and enter the table name Union1. Select the *Append Data to Existing Table* option. If you then click *OK*, the rows of the copied table (Union2) will be appended to the rows of the table Union1. In other words, Union1 will now contain the *union* of the original Union1 table and the Union2 table, which in this case is the complete contents of BOOKS. This is expressed in symbols as:

NewUnion1 = OriginalUnion1 ∪ Union2

Open Union1 to verify that it now has 14 rows. Then delete the last seven rows again to restore Union1 to its original condition.

Another way to create a union is to use an Append Query as follows:

1. From the *Query* tab in the Database window, choose the *New* button. Select *Design View*, and then add Union2 to the design window. Select *Append* from the *Query* menu to get the dialog box in Figure 5-3.

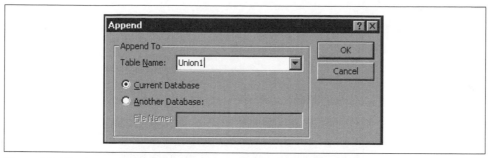

Figure 5-3. The Access Append dialog box

2. Click *OK* to get the window shown in Figure 5-4. Drag the asterisk (*) in the table scheme for Union2 to the first cell in the *Field* row of the design grid. This will fill in the first column of the design grid as shown in Figure 5-4. Run the query (choose *Run* from the *Query* menu). You will get a warning that you are about to append seven rows and that the process cannot be undone. Click *OK*, and then open the Union1 table to verify that it now has 14 rows.

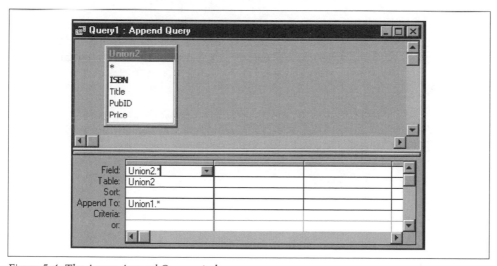

Figure 5-4. The Access Append Query window

Intersection

The *intersection* S ∩ T of two tables S and T with the same attributes is the table formed by keeping only those rows that appear in both tables. Here is an example:

A$_1$	A$_2$
a	b

A₁	A₂
c	d
e	f

A₁	A₂
c	d
i	j
e	f

A₁	A₂
c	d
e	f

We will see an example of how to form an intersection in Microsoft Access when we discuss differences, in the next section.

Difference

The *difference* S – T of two tables S and T with the same attributes is the table consisting of all rows of S that do not appear in T, as shown in the following tables:

A₁	A₂
a	b
c	d
e	f
g	h

A₁	A₂
c	d
i	j
e	f

A₁	A₂
a	b
g	h

Let us consider an example of how to take an intersection or difference in Microsoft Access.

1. First, we need some expendable tables. As in the first step of the example for creating a union, use the *Copy* and *Paste* features to create two tables named Diff1 and Diff2 that are exact copies of BOOKS. Open Diff1, and remove the last four

rows. Open Diff2, and remove the first four rows. Thus, Diff1 contains the first ten books from BOOKS, and Diff2 contains the last ten books from BOOKS.

2. Now switch to the Query tab, and start a new query. Add both Diff1 and Diff2 to the query. You may notice a connecting line between the two ISBN attributes. If there is no such line, drag one ISBN name to the other to create a line. Now right click on the line and choose *Join Properties* from the pop-up menu. This should produce the dialog box shown in Figure 5-5. Select option 2, which will include all records (rows) from Diff1 and all rows of Diff2 that have a matching ISBN in Diff1. This is a so-called *left outer join*. We will discuss this in more detail later in this section. Click *OK*.

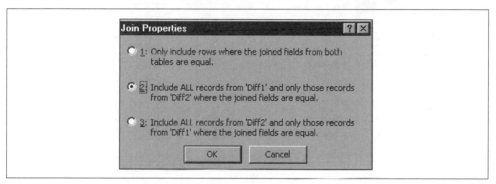

Figure 5-5. The Access Join Properties dialog box

3. Drag the asterisk (*) from Diff1 to the design grid, and then drag ISBN from Diff2 to the second column of the design grid. The design window should now appear as in Figure 5-6.

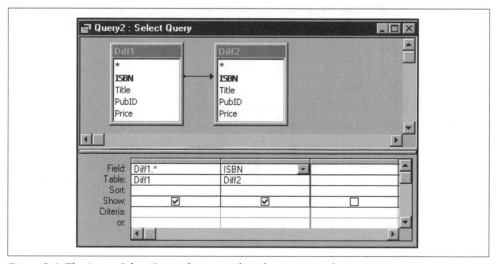

Figure 5-6. The Access Select Query design window showing a join between two properties

4. Now run the query. You should get a table as shown in Figure 5-7. This table contains the ten rows from Diff1, with an extra column that gives the matching ISBN from Diff2, if there is one. Otherwise, the column contains a NULL. We can see that the six rows that have a matching ISBN in column Diff2.ISBN form the intersection of the two tables. Also, the four rows that do not have a matching ISBN form the difference Diff1 − Diff2. Hence, we only need to add a simple criterion to the query to obtain either the intersection or the difference.

Diff1.ISBN	Title	PubID	Price	Diff2.ISBN
0-103-45678-9	Iliad	1	$25.00	
0-11-345678-9	Moby Dick	3	$49.00	
0-12-333433-3	On Liberty	1	$25.00	
0-12-345678-9	Jane Eyre	3	$49.00	
0-123-45678-0	Ulysses	2	$34.00	0-123-45678-0
0-321-32132-1	Balloon	3	$34.00	0-321-32132-1
0-55-123456-9	Main Street	3	$22.95	0-55-123456-9
0-555-55555-9	MacBeth	2	$12.00	0-555-55555-9
0-91-045678-5	Hamlet	2	$20.00	0-91-045678-5
0-91-335678-7	Faerie Queene	1	$15.00	0-91-335678-7

Figure 5-7. The Access Select Query window showing the intersection of two tables

5. To get the intersection Diff1 ∩ Diff2, return to the design view of the query, and add the words *Is Not Null* under the *Criteria* row in the Diff2.ISBN column. Run the query.

6. To get the difference Diff1 − Diff2, return to the design view of the query, and add the words *Is Null* under the *Criteria* row in the Diff2.ISBN column. Run the query.

Cartesian Product

To define the Cartesian product of tables, we need to adjust the way we write attribute names, just in case both tables have an attribute of the same name. If a table T has an attribute named A, the *fully qualified attribute name* (or just *qualified attribute name*) is T.A. Thus, we may write BOOKS.ISBN or AUTHORS.AuID.

If $S(A_1,...,A_n)$ and $T(B_1,...,B_m)$ are tables, then the *Cartesian product* $S \times T$ of S and T is the table whose attribute set contains the fully qualified attribute names of all attributes from S and T:

$$\{S.A_1,...,S.A_n,T.B_1,...,T.B_m\}$$

The rows of S × T are formed by combining each row s of S with each row t of T, to form a new row st. An example will help make this clear:

A₁	A₂
a	b
c	d
e	f

B₁	B₂	B₃
g	h	i
j	k	l

S.A₁	S.A₂	T.B₁	T.B₂	T.B₃
a	b	g	h	i
a	b	j	k	l
c	d	g	h	i
c	d	j	k	l
e	f	g	h	i
e	f	j	k	l

Notice that if S has *k* rows and T has *j* rows, then the Cartesian product has *kj* rows. Hence, the Cartesian product of two tables can be very large.

To form a Cartesian product of two tables in Microsoft Access, proceed as follows:

1. Create the two tables S and T in the previous example.
2. Create a new query, and add the tables S and T. Make certain that there are no lines joining the two table schemes. (If there are, right click on the lines, and choose *Delete* from the pop-up menu.)
3. Drag the asterisks from each table scheme to the design grid. You should now have a design window as shown in Figure 5-8. Run the query to get the Cartesian product.

Projection

Projection is a very simple concept. Intuitively, a projection of a table onto a subset of its attributes (columns) is the table formed by throwing away all other columns.

More formally, let $T(A_1,...A_n)$ be a table, where $A = \{A_1,...,A_n\}$ is the attribute set. If B is a subset of A, then the projection of T onto B is just the table obtained from T by keeping only those columns headed by the attribute names in B. We denote this table by $proj_B(T)$.

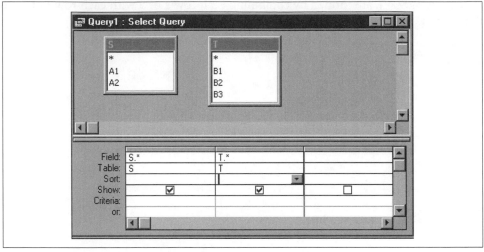

Figure 5-8. The Access Query window illustrating a Cartesian product of two tables

As an example, for the table:

ISBN	Title	Price	PubID
0-103-45678-9	The Firm	$24.95	1
0-11-345678-9	Moby-Dick	$49.00	2
0-12-333433-3	War and Peace	$25.00	1

the projection $proj_{ISBN,Price}$(BOOKS) is:

ISBN	Price
0-103-45678-9	$24.95
0-11-345678-9	$49.00
0-12-333433-3	$25.00

Note that, if the projection produces two identical rows, the duplicate rows must be removed, since a table is not allowed to have duplicate rows. (This rule of relational databases is not enforced by all commercial database products. In particular, it is not enforced by Microsoft Access. That is, some products allow identical rows in a table. By definition, these products are not true relational databases—but that is not necessarily a flaw.)

The Query Design window in Microsoft Access was tailor-made for creating projections. Just add the table to the design window, and drag the desired attribute names to the design grid. Run the query to get the projection. Figure 5-9 shows the Query Design window for computing the projection of *Books* onto the attributes ISBN and Price.

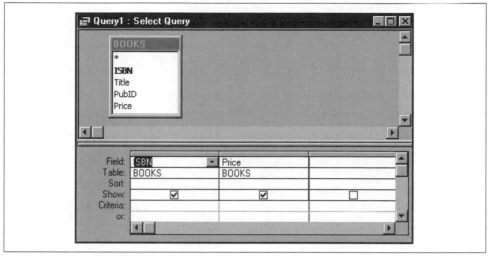

Figure 5-9. Creating a projection using the BOOKS table

Selection

Just as the operation of projection selects only a subset of the columns of a table, so the operation of *selection* selects a subset of the rows of a table. The first step in defining the operation of selection is to define a *selection condition* or *selection criterion* to be any legally formed expression that involves:

- Constants (i.e., members of any attribute domain)
- Attribute names
- Arithmetic comparison relations ($=, \neq, <, \leq, >, \geq$)
- Logical operators (*and*, *or*, *not*)

For example, the following are selection conditions:

- Price > $10.00
- Price ≤ $50.00 *and* AuName = "Bronte"
- (Price ≤ $50.00 *and* AuName = "Bronte") *or* (*not* AuName = "Austen")

If *condition* is a selection condition, then the result table obtained by applying the corresponding selection operation to a table T is denoted by:

$$sel_{condition}(T)$$

or sometimes by:

T where condition

and is the table obtained from T by keeping only those rows that satisfy the selection condition.

For example, see Table 5-7.

Table 5-7. The BOOKS table in the LIBRARY databse

ISBN	Title	PubID	Price
0-103-45678-9	Iliad	1	$25.00
0-11-345678-9	Moby-Dick	3	$49.00
0-12-333433-3	On Liberty	1	$25.00
0-12-345678-9	Jane Eyre	3	$49.00
0-123-45678-0	Ulysses	2	$34.00
0-321-32132-1	Balloon	3	$34.00
0-55-123456-9	Main Street	3	$22.95
0-555-55555-9	Macbeth	2	$12.00
0-91-045678-5	Hamlet	2	$20.00
0-91-335678-7	Faerie Queene	1	$15.00
0-99-777777-7	King Lear	2	$49.00
0-99-999999-9	Emma	1	$20.00
1-1111-1111-1	C++	1	$29.95
1-22-233700-0	Visual Basic	1	$25.00

The table $sel_{Price}>\$25.00$(BOOKS) is shown in Table 5-8:

Table 5-8. The resulting table

ISBN	Title	PubID	Price
0-12-345678-9	Jane Eyre	3	$49.00
0-11-345678-9	Moby-Dick	3	$49.00
0-99-777777-7	King Lear	2	$49.00
0-123-45678-0	Ulysses	2	$34.00
1-1111-1111-1	C++	1	$29.95
0-321-32132-1	Balloon	3	$34.00

Some authors refer to selection as *restriction*, which does seem to be a more appropriate term and has the advantage that it is not confused with the SQL SELECT statement, which is much more general than just selection. However, it is less common than the term selection, so we will use this term.

The Query Design window in Microsoft Access was also tailor-made for creating selections. We just use the *Criteria* rows to apply the desired restrictions. For example, Figure 5-10 shows the design window for the selection:

$sel_{Price}>\$25.00$(BOOKS)

from the previous example.

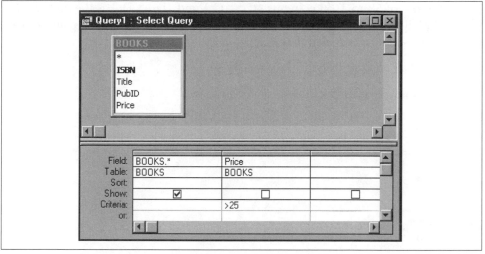

Figure 5-10. Creating a selection in the Query Design window

You will probably agree that the operations we have covered so far are pretty straightforward—union, intersection, difference, and Cartesian product are basic set-theoretic operations. Selecting rows and columns are clearly valuable table operations.

Actually, the six operations of renaming, union, difference, Cartesian product, projection, and selection are enough to form the complete relational algebra by combining these operations with constants and attribute names to create relational-algebra expressions.

However, it is very convenient to define some additional operations on tables, even though they can theoretically be expressed in terms of the six operations previously mentioned. So let us proceed.

Joins

The various types of joins are among the most important and useful of the relational-algebra operations. Loosely speaking, joining two tables involves combining the rows of two tables based on comparing the values in selected columns.

Equi-join

In an equi-join, rows are combined if there are equal attribute values in certain selected columns from each table.

To be specific, let S and T be tables, and suppose that $\{C_1,...,C_k\}$ are selected attributes of S and $\{D_1,...,D_k\}$ are selected attributes of T. Each table may have additional attributes as well. Note that we select the same number of attributes from each table.

The equi-join of S and T on columns $\{C_1,...,C_k\}$ and $\{D_1,...,D_k\}$ is the table formed by combining a row of S with a row of T, provided that corresponding columns have equal value—that is, provided that:

$$S.C_1 = T.D_1, S.C_2 = T.D_2, ..., S.C_k = T.D_k$$

As an example, consider the tables:

A₁	A₂
1	4
4	5
6	3

B₁	B₂	B₃
2	3	4
6	7	3
1	1	4

To form the equi-join:

$$S \; equi\text{-}join_{A_2 = B_3} T$$

we combine rows for which:

$$S.A_2 = T.B_3$$

This gives:

S.A₁	S.A₂	T.B₁	T.B₂	T.B₃
1	4	2	3	4
1	4	1	1	4
6	3	6	7	3

Notice that the equi-join can be expressed in terms of the Cartesian product and the selection operation as follows:

$$S \; equi\text{-}join_{C_1 = D_1, ..., C_k = D_k} T = sel_{C_1 = D_1, ..., C_k = D_k}(S \times T)$$

This simply says that, to form the equi-join, we take the Cartesian product $S \times T$ of S and T (i.e., the set of all combinations of rows from S and T) and then select only those rows for which:

$$S.C_1 = T.D_1, S.C_2 = T.D_2, ..., S.C_k = T.D_k$$

Natural join

The *natural join* (nat-join) is a variation on the equi-join, based on the equality of all common attributes in two tables.

To be specific, suppose that S and T are tables and that the set of all common attributes between these tables is $\{C_1,...,C_n\}$. Thus, each table may have additional attributes, but no further attributes in common. The natural join of S and T, which we denote by:

> S *nat-join* T

is formed in two steps:

1. Form the equi-join on the common attributes $\{C_1,...,C_n\}$.
2. Remove the second set of common columns from the table.

Consider these tables:

A₁	A₂	A₃	A₄
a	b	c	d
e	f	g	h
i	j	k	l
m	n	o	p

B₁	A₂	A₄	B₄
a	b	c	d
c	j	l	f
f	b	d	g
x	y	z	h
s	j	l	j

In this case, the set of common attributes is $\{A_2,A_4\}$. The corresponding columns are shaded for easier identification.

The equi-join on A_2 and A_4 is:

S.A₁	S.A₂	S.A₃	S.A₄	T.B₁	T.A₂	T.A₄	T.B₄
a	b	c	d	f	b	d	g
i	j	k	l	c	j	l	f
i	j	k	l	s	j	l	j

Deleting the second set of common columns (the columns that come from T, as shaded in the previous table) gives:

S.A$_1$	S.A$_2$	S.A$_3$	S.A$_4$	T.B$_1$	T.B$_4$
a	b	c	d	f	g
i	j	k	l	c	f
i	j	k	l	s	j

The importance of the natural join comes from the fact that, when there is a one-to-many relationship from S to T, we can arrange it—by renaming, if necessary—so that the only common attributes are the key of S and the foreign key in T. In this case, the natural join S *nat-join* T is simply the table obtained by matching rows that are related through the one-to-many relationship.

For example, consider the following BOOKS and PUBLISHERS tables in Tables 5-9 and 5-10, respectively.

Table 5-9. The BOOKS table

ISBN	Title	Price	PubID
0-103-45678-9	The Firm	$24.95	1
0-11-345678-9	Moby-Dick	$49.00	2
0-12-333433-3	War and Peace	$25.00	1
0-12-345678-9	Jane Eyre	$34.00	1
0-26-888888-8	Persuasion	$13.00	3
0-555-55555-9	Emma	$12.00	3
0-91-045678-5	The Chamber	$20.00	3
0-91-335678-7	Partners	$15.00	1
0-99-777777-7	Triple Play	$44.00	3
0-99-999999-9	Mansfield Park	$18.00	1

Table 5-10. The PUBLISHERS table

PubID	PubName	PubPhone
1	Big House	212-000-1212
2	Little House	213-111-1212
3	Medium House	614-222-1212

Then PUBLISHERS *nat-join* BOOKS is the table formed by taking each PUBLISHERS row and adjoining each BOOKS row with a matching PubID, as shown in Table 5-11.

Table 5-11. The PUBLISHERS nat-join BOOKS table

PubID	PubName	PubPhone	ISBN	Title	Price
1	Big House	212-000-1212	0-103-45678-9	The Firm	$24.95
1	Big House	212-000-1212	0-12-333433-3	War and Peace	$25.00
1	Big House	212-000-1212	0-12-345678-9	Jane Eyre	$34.00
1	Big House	212-000-1212	0-91-335678-7	Partners	$15.00
1	Big House	212-000-1212	0-99-999999-9	Mansfield Park	$18.00
2	Little House	213-111-1212	0-11-345678-9	Moby-Dick	$49.00
3	Medium House	614-222-1212	0-26-888888-8	Persuasion	$13.00
3	Medium House	614-222-1212	0-555-55555-9	Emma	$12.00
3	Medium House	614-222-1212	0-91-045678-5	The Chamber	$20.00
3	Medium House	614-222-1212	0-99-777777-7	Triple Play	$44.00

θ-Join

The θ-join (read *theta join*, since θ is the Greek letter *theta*) is similar to the equi-join and is used when we need to make a comparison other than equality between column values. In fact, the θ-join can use any of these arithmetic comparison relations:

$$=, \neq, <, \leq, >, \geq$$

Let S and T be tables, and suppose that $\{C_1,...,C_k\}$ are selected attributes of S and $\{D_1,...,D_k\}$ are selected attributes of T. Each table may have additional attributes as well. Note that we select the same number of attributes from each table. Let $\theta_1,...,\theta_k$ be comparison relations. Then the θ-join of tables S and T on columns $C_1,...,C_k$ and $D_1,...,D_k$ is:

$$S \text{ } \theta\text{-join}_{C_1\theta_1 D_1, ..., C_k\theta_k D_k} T = sel_{C_1\theta_1 D_1, ..., C_k\theta_k D_k}(S \times T)$$

Thus, to form the θ-join, we take the Cartesian product $S \times T$ of S and T and then select those rows for which the value in column C_1 stands in relation θ_1 to the value in column D_1 and similarly for each of the other columns.

As an example, consider these tables:

A₁	A₂
1	2
4	5
6	3

B₁	B₂	B₃
2	3	4
6	7	3

To form the θ-join:

$$S \ \theta\text{-}join_{A_2 \le B_3} T$$

we keep only those rows of the Cartesian product of the two tables for which the value in column A_2 is $\le$ the value in column B_3:

S.A$_1$	S.A$_2$	T.B$_1$	T.B$_2$	T.B$_3$
1	2	2	3	4
1	2	6	7	3
6	3	2	3	4
6	3	6	7	3

Notice that a θ-join, where all relations θ_i are equality (=), is precisely the equi-join.

Outer Joins

The natural join, equi-join, and θ-join are referred to as *inner joins*. Each inner join has a corresponding *left outer join* and *right outer join*, which are formed by first taking the corresponding inner join and then including some additional rows.

In particular, for the left outer join, if s is a row of S that was not used in the inner join, we include the row s, filled out to the proper size with NULL values. An example may help to clarify this concept.

In an earlier example, we saw that the natural join of the tables:

A$_1$	A$_2$	A$_3$	A$_4$
a	b	c	d
e	f	g	h
i	j	k	l
m	n	o	p

B$_1$	A$_2$	A$_4$	B$_4$
a	b	c	d
c	j	l	f
f	b	d	g
x	y	z	h
s	j	l	j

is:

A₁	A₂	A₃	A₄	B₁	B₄
a	b	c	d	f	g
i	j	k	l	c	f
i	j	k	l	s	j

The corresponding left outer join is the same as the nat-join, but with a few extra rows:

A₁	A₂	A₃	A₄	B₁	B₄
a	b	c	d	f	g
i	j	k	l	c	f
i	j	k	l	s	j
e	f	g	h	NULL	NULL
m	n	o	p	NULL	NULL

In particular, the left outer join also contains the two rows of S that were not involved in the natural join, with NULL values used to fill out the rows. The right outer join is defined similarly, where the rows of T are included, with NULL values in place of the S values.

One of the simplest uses for an outer join is to help see what is not part of an inner join! For instance, the previous table shows us instantly that the second and fourth rows:

e	f	g	h
m	n	o	p

of table S are not involved in the natural join S *nat-join* T. Put another way, the values:

$$A_2 = f, A_4 = h$$

and:

$$A_2 = n, A_4 = p$$

are not present in any rows of table T.

Implementing Joins in Microsoft Access

Now let us consider how to implement the various types of joins in Microsoft Access. The Access Query Design window makes it easy to create equi-joins. Of course, a natural join is easily created from an appropriate equi-join by using a projection. Let us illustrate this statement with an example.

Begin by creating the following two simple tables, S and T, shown in Tables 5-12 and 5-13.

Table 5-12. The S table

A_1	A_2
a	b
c	d
e	f

Table 5-13. The T table

B_1	B_2	B_3
g	h	i
j	k	l
c	d	x
c	d	y
c	y	z

Let us create the equi-join:

$$S \ equi\text{-}join_{A_1 = B_1, A_2 = B_2} T$$

Open the Query Design window (by asking for a new query), and add these two tables. To establish the associations:

$$S.A_1 = T.B_1 \ and \ S.A_2 = T.B_2$$

drag the attribute name A_1 to B_1, and drag the attribute name A_2 to B_2. This should create the lines shown in Figure 5-11. Drag the two asterisks down to the first two columns of the design grid, as in Figure 5-11. (Access provides the asterisk as a quick way to drag all of the fields to the design grid. It is the same as dragging each field separately with one exception—changes to the underlying table design are reflected in the asterisk. In other words, if new fields are added to the underlying table, they will be included automatically in the query.)

Now all we need to do is run the query. The result is shown in Table 5-14.

In other words, Microsoft Access uses the relationships defined graphically in the upper portion of the window to create an equi-join.

The Access Query Design window does not allow us to create a θ-join that does not use equality. However, we can easily create such a join from an equi-join by altering the corresponding SQL statement. We will discuss SQL in detail in Chapter 6. For now, let us modify the previous example to illustrate the technique.

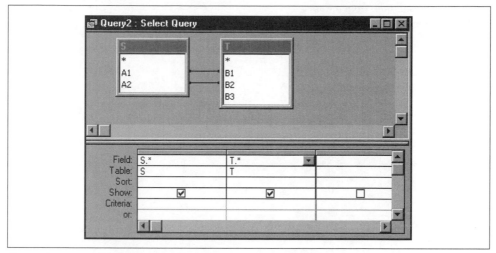

Figure 5-11. Establishing associations in the Access Query Design window

Table 5-14. An equi-join of tables S and T

A_1	A_2	B_1	B_2	B_3
c	d	c	d	y
c	d	c	d	x

From the design view for the query in the previous example, select *SQL* from the *View* menu. You should see the window shown in Figure 5-12.

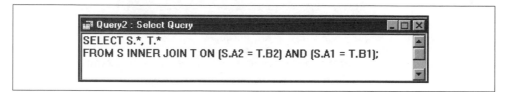

Figure 5-12. The SQL statement generated from Figure 5-11

This is the SQL statement that Access created from our query design for the previous example. Now, edit the two equal signs by changing each of them to <= (less than or equal to). Note that, for text, the less-than-or-equal-to sign refers to alphabetical order.

Now run the query. The result table should appear as shown in Table 5-15.

Notice that for each row of the table, A_1 precedes or equals B_1 in alphabetical order, and A_2 precedes or equals B_2.

Finally, observe that if we try to return to the design view of this query, Access issues the message in Figure 5-13, because the design view cannot create θ-joins that are not based strictly on equality.

Table 5-15. Result table from a θ-join

A₁	A₂	B₁	B₂	B₃
a	b	g	h	i
a	b	j	k	l
a	b	c	d	x
a	b	c	d	y
a	b	c	y	z
c	d	g	h	i
c	d	j	k	l
c	d	c	d	x
c	d	c	d	y
c	d	c	y	z
e	f	g	h	i
e	f	j	k	l

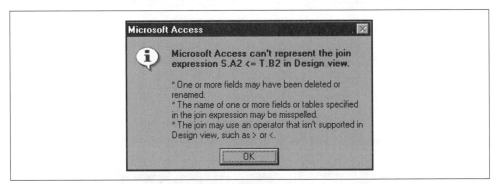

Figure 5-13. Access error for attempting to create unequal θ-joins

To create an outer join, return the SQL statement of the previous example back to its original form (with equal signs), and then return to design view. Click the right mouse button on one of the connecting lines between the table schemes, and choose *Join Properties* from the pop-up menu. This should produce the dialog box shown in Figure 5-14.

Select option 2, which will produce a left outer join. (Option 1 creates an inner join, option 2 creates a left outer join, and option 3 creates a right outer join.) Do the same for the other connecting line. Take a peek at the SQL statement, which should appear as in Figure 5-15.

Now you can run the query, which should produce the result table in Table 5-16, where the empty cells contain the NULL value.

Of course, a right outer join is created similarly, by choosing option 3 in Figure 5-14.

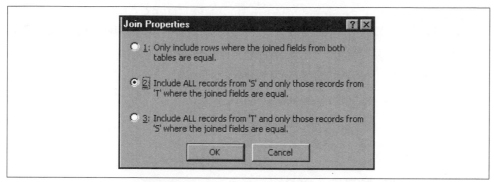

Figure 5-14. The Access dialog box for joining properties

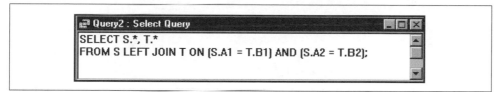

Figure 5-15. The SQL statement illustrating a left outer join

Table 5-16. A left outer join

A₁	A₂	B₁	B₂	B₃
a	b			
c	d	c	d	y
c	d	c	d	x
e	f			

Semi-Joins

A *semi-join* is formed from an inner join (or θ-join) by projecting onto one of the tables that participated in the join. In other words, we first form the join:

> S θ-joinT

and then just keep the columns that came from S or from T. Thus, the formula for the *left semi-join* is:

$$S\ \textit{left-semi-join}_{C_1\theta_1 D_1,\ ...,\ C_k\theta_k D_k} T = \textit{proj}_{\text{all columns of } S}(\text{sel}_{C_1\theta_1 D_1,\ ...,\ C_k\theta_k D_k}(S \times T))$$

Similarly, the formula for the *right semi-join* is:

$$S\ \textit{right-semi-join}_{C_1\theta_1 D_1,\ ...,\ C_k\theta_k D_k} T = \textit{proj}_{\text{all columns of } T}(\text{sel}_{C_1\theta_1 D_1,\ ...,\ C_k\theta_k D_k}(S \times T))$$

The concept of a semi-join occurs in relation to the DISTINCTROW keyword of the SELECT clause in Access SQL, which we will discuss in Chapter 6. For now, let us consider an example of the semi-join, which should indicate why semi-joins are useful.

Imagine that we add a new publisher to the PUBLISHERS table (Another Press in Table 5-17), but do not add any books for this publisher to the BOOKS table. Consider the inner join of the tables PUBLISHERS and BOOKS:

PUBLISHERS *join*_{PUBLISHERS.PubID = BOOKS.PubID} BOOKS

Table 5-17. The PUBLISHERS (new) table

PubID	PubName	PubPhone
1	Big House	123-456-7890
2	Alpha Press	999-999-9999
3	Small House	714-000-0000
4	Another Press	111-222-3333

For the LIBRARY database, the result table resulting from this join is shown in Table 5-18.

Table 5-18. Result table from an inner join

PUBLI- SHERS .PubID	Pub- Name	PubPhone	ISBN	Title	BOOKS. PubID	Price
3	Small House	714-000-0000	0-12-345678-9	Jane Eyre	3	$49.00
3	Small House	714-000-0000	0-11-345678-9	Moby-Dick	3	$49.00
3	Small House	714-000-0000	0-321-32132-1	Balloon	3	$34.00
3	Small House	714-000-0000	0-55-123456-9	Main Street	3	$22.95
1	Big House	123-456-7890	0-12-333433-3	On Liberty	1	$25.00
1	Big House	123-456-7890	0-103-45678-9	Iliad	1	$25.00
1	Big House	123-456-7890	0-91-335678-7	Faerie Queene	1	$15.00
1	Big House	123-456-7890	0-99-999999-9	Emma	1	$20.00
1	Big House	123-456-7890	1-22-233700-0	Visual Basic	1	$25.00
1	Big House	123-456-7890	1-1111-1111-1	C++	1	$29.95
2	Alpha Press	999-999-9999	0-91-045678-5	Hamlet	2	$20.00
2	Alpha Press	999-999-9999	0-555-55555-9	Macbeth	2	$12.00
2	Alpha Press	999-999-9999	0-99-777777-7	King Lear	2	$49.00
2	Alpha Press	999-999-9999	0-123-45678-0	Ulysses	2	$34.00

If we now project onto the PUBLISHERS table, we get the left semi-join:

PUBLISHERS *left-semi-join*$_{PUBLISHERS.PubID = BOOKS.PubID}$ BOOKS

for which the result table is shown in Table 5-19.

Table 5-19. Result table from a semi-join

PubID	PubName	PubPhone
3	Small House	714-000-0000
1	Big House	123-456-7890
2	Alpha Press	999-999-9999

This is the set of all publishers that have book entries in the BOOKS database.

Other Relational Algebra Operations

There is one more operation in relational algebra that occurs from time to time, called the *quotient*. However, since this operation is less common, and a bit involved, we will cover it in Appendix B. (You may turn to that appendix after finishing this chapter, if you are interested.)

Optimization

Let us conclude this discussion with a brief remark about *optimization*. As we have discussed, statements in the relational algebra are *procedural*; that is, they describe a procedure for carrying out the operations. However, this procedure is often not very efficient.

Let us illustrate with an extreme example. Consider the two table schemes:

{ISBN,Title,Price} and {ISBN,PageCount}

If S is a table based on the first scheme and T is a table based on the second scheme, then the natural join is:

$$S\ join\ T = proj_{S.ISBN,Title,Price,PageCount}(sel_{S.A_1 = T.A_1}(S \times T))$$

According to this formula, the join is carried out in the following steps:

1. Form the Cartesian product.
2. Take the appropriate selection.
3. Take the appropriate projection.

Now imagine two tables S and T, where S has 10,000 rows and T has 10,000 rows. Assume also that the tables have only one common attribute, for which no values are the same in both tables. In this case, according to the definition of natural join, the join is actually the empty table.

However, according to the procedure described, the first step in computing this join is to compute the product $S \times T$, which has $10,000 \times 10,000 = 100,000,000$ rows—that is, one hundred million rows! Obviously, this is not the best procedure for computing the join!

Fortunately, database programs that use a procedural language have *optimization routines* to avoid problems such as this. Such a routine looks at the task it is requested to perform and tries to find an alternative procedure that will produce the same output with less computation. Thus, from a practical standpoint, procedural languages sometimes behave similarly to nonprocedural ones.

CHAPTER 6

Access Structured Query Language (SQL)

Introduction to Access SQL

As we have said, Microsoft Access uses a form of query language referred to as *Structured Query Language*, or SQL. (I prefer to pronounce SQL by saying each letter separately, rather than saying "sequel." Accordingly, I will write "an SQL statement" rather than "a SQL statement.")

SQL is the most common database query language in use today. It is actually more than just a query language, as I have defined the term in the previous chapter. It is a complete *database management system* (DBMS) language, in that it has the capability not only to manipulate the components of a database, but also to create them in the first place. In particular, SQL has the following components:

1. A *data definition language* (DDL) component, to allow the definition (creation) of database components, such as tables.
2. A *data manipulation language* (DML) component, to allow manipulation of database components.
3. A *data control language* (DCL) component, to provide internal security for a database.

We will discuss the first two components of SQL in some detail in this chapter.

SQL (also known as SEQUEL) was developed by IBM in San Jose, California. The current version of SQL is called SQL-92. However, Microsoft Access, like all other commercial products that support SQL, does not implement the complete SQL-92 standard and in fact adds some additional features of its own to the language. Since this book uses Microsoft Access, we will discuss the Access version of SQL.

Access Query Design

In Microsoft Access, queries can be defined in several different ways, but they all come down to an SQL statement in the end. The *Query Wizard* helps create a query by asking the user to respond to a series of questions. This approach is the most user friendly, but also the least powerful. Access also provides a *Query Design window* with two different views. The *Design View* is shown in Figure 6-1.

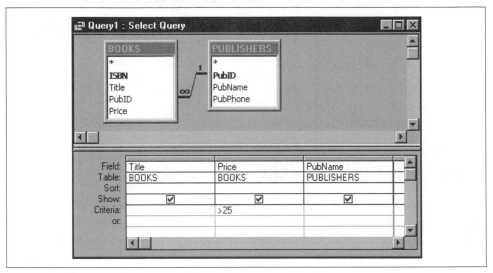

Figure 6-1. The Access Query Design View

Query Design View displays table schemes, along with their relationships, and allows the user to select columns to return (*projection*) and specify criteria for the returned data (*selection*). Figure 6-1 shows a query definition that joins the BOOKS and PUB-LISHERS table and returns the Title, Publisher, and Price of all books whose price is over $25.00.

The Query Design window also has an *SQL View*. Switching to this view shows the SQL statement that corresponds to the Design View query. Figure 6-2 shows the corresponding SQL statement for the query in Figure 6-1.

Figure 6-2. The Access SQL View of Figure 6-1

In addition to using the Design View, users can enter SQL statements directly into the SQL View window. In fact, some constructions, such as directly creating the union of two tables in a third table, cannot be accomplished using Design View and therefore must be entered in SQL View. However, such constructs are rare, and it is often possible to complete a project without the need to enter SQL statements directly.

Access Query Types

Access supports a variety of query types. Here is a list, along with a brief description of each:

Select query

> These queries return data from one or more tables and display the results in a result table. The table is (usually) *updatable*, which means that we can change the data in the table, and the changes will be reflected in the underlying tables. Select queries can also be used to group rows and calculate sums, counts, averages, and other types of totals for these groups.

Action queries

> These are queries that take some form of action. The action queries are:

> *Make-table query*
>> A query that is designed to create a new table with data from existing tables.

> *Delete query*
>> A query that is used to delete rows from a given table or tables.

> *Append query*
>> A query that is used to append additional rows to the bottom of an existing table.

> *Update query*
>> A query that is used to make changes to one or more rows in a table.

SQL queries

> These are queries that must be entered in SQL View. The SQL queries are:

> *Union query*
>> A query that creates the union of two or more tables.

> *Pass-through query*
>> A query that passes the *uninterpreted* SQL statement through to an external database server. (We will not discuss these queries in this book.)

> *Data-definition query*
>> Queries that use the DDL component of SQL, such as CREATE TABLE or CREATE INDEX.

Crosstab query

> This is a special type of select query that displays values in a spreadsheet format, with both row and column headings. For instance, we might wish to know how many books are published by each publisher at each price. This is most conveniently pictured as a crosstab query, as shown in Table 6-1.

Parameter query

> For select or crosstab queries, we may choose to let the user supply certain data at runtime by filling in a dialog box. This can be done in both Design View and SQL View. When the query asks for information from the user, it is referred to as a *parameterized query*, or *parameter query*.

Table 6-1. A CROSSTAB Query

Price	Total	Big House	Medium House	Small House
$12.00	1		1	
$13.00	3	2	1	
$15.00	1	1		
$18.00	1	1		
$20.00	6		1	5
$25.00	2	2		
$34.00	5	1	4	
$44.00	1		1	
$49.00	6	1	4	1
$99.00	1		1	

Finally, I mention that Access allows a select or action query to contain another select query. This is done by nesting SQL SELECT statements, as we will see. The internal query is called a *subquery* of the external query. Access allows multiple levels of subqueries.

Why Use SQL?

As you look through the syntax of the SQL statements in this chapter, you may be struck by the fact that SQL is not a particularly pleasant language. Moreover, as I have said, many features of SQL can be accessed through the Access Query Design Window. So why program in SQL at all?

Here are some reasons:

- There are some important features of SQL that cannot be reached through the Query Design Window. For instance, there is no way to create a union query, a subquery, or an SQL pass-through query (which is a query that passes through Access to an external database server, such as Microsoft SQL Server) using the Query Design Window.

- You cannot use the DDL component of SQL from within the Query Design Window. To use this component, you must write SQL statements directly.

- SQL can be used from within other applications, such as Microsoft Excel, Word, and Visual Basic, to run the Access SQL engine.

- SQL is an industry-standard language for querying databases, and as such it is useful outside of the Microsoft Access environment.

Despite these important reasons, we suggest that, on first reading, you go lightly over the SQL commands to get a flavor for how they work. Then you can use this chapter as a reference whenever you actually need to write SQL statements yourself. Fortunately, SQL has relatively few actual commands, which makes it easy to get an over-all picture of the language. (For instance, SQL is single-statement oriented. It does not have control structures such as *For...Next...* loops, nor conditional statements such as *If...Then...* statements.)

We should also mention that using the Query Design Window itself is a good way to learn SQL, for you can create a query in the Design Window and then switch to SQL View to see the corresponding SQL statement, obligingly created by Microsoft Access.

Access SQL

SQL is a nonprocedural language, meaning, as we have seen, that expressions in SQL state *what* needs to be done, but not *how* it should be done. This frees the programmer to concentrate on the logic of the SQL program. The Access Query Engine takes care of optimization.

One way to experiment with SQL is to enter a query using Design View and then switch to SQL View to see how Access resolves the query into SQL. It is also worth mentioning that the Help system has complete details on the syntax and options of each SQL statement.

Incidentally, reading the definition of SQL statements can be tiresome. You may wish to just skim over the syntax of each statement and go directly to the examples. The main goal here is to get a reasonable feel for SQL statements and what they can do. You can then look up the correct syntax for the relevant statement when needed (as I do).

Syntax Conventions

In looking at the SQL commands, we need to establish a consistent syntax. I will employ the following conventions:

- Uppercase words are SQL keywords and should be typed in as written.
- Words in constant width italic are intended to be replaced with something else. For instance, in the statement:

      CREATE TABLE *TableName*

  we must replace *TableName* with the name of a table.
- An item in square brackets [ ] is optional.
- Braces ({}) are used to (hopefully) clarify the syntax. They are *never* to be included in the statement proper.
- Parentheses should be typed as shown.

- The symbol ::= means "defined as" and the symbol | means "or." For instance, the line:

    ```
    TableElement ::= ColumnDefinition | TableConstraint
    ```

  means that a table element is *defined as* either a column definition *or* a table constraint.

- The syntax item, ... means that you can repeat item as often as desired, separated by commas. For instance, in the line:

    ```
    CREATE TABLE TableName (TableElement, ...)
    ```

  you may repeat the TableElement as many times as desired but at least once, since it is not enclosed in square brackets, so it is not optional. (The parentheses must be included.) If a group of items may be repeated, then we use curly braces to enclose those items (for easier reading). For instance, the following expression means that you may repeat the clause *ColName* [ASC|DESC]:

    ```
    {ColName [ASC|DESC]}, ...
    ```

Notes

- You may break the lines in an SQL statement at any point, which is useful for improving readability.

- Each SQL statement should end with a semicolon (although Access SQL does not require this).

- If a table name (or other name) contains a character that SQL regards as illegal, then the name must be enclosed in square brackets. For instance, the forward slash character is illegal in SQL and so the table name BOOK/AUTHOR is also illegal. Thus, it must be enclosed in square brackets: [BOOK/AUTHOR]. This should not be confused with the use of square brackets to denote optional items in SQL syntax descriptions.

The DDL Component of Access SQL

We begin by looking at the data definition commands in Access SQL. These commands do not have a counterpart in Query Design View (although, of course, you can perform these functions through the Access graphical environment). Access SQL supports these four DDL commands:

- CREATE TABLE
- ALTER TABLE
- DROP TABLE
- CREATE INDEX

I should mention now that there is some duplication of features in the DDL commands. For instance, you can add an index to a table using either the ALTER TABLE command or the CREATE INDEX command.

The CREATE TABLE Statement

The CREATE TABLE command has the following syntax:

```
CREATE TABLE TableName
  (ColumnDefinition,...
  [,Multi-ColumnConstraint,...] );
```

In words, the parameters to the CREATE TABLE statement are a table name, followed by one or more column definitions, followed by one or more (optional) multi-column constraints. Note that the parentheses are also part of the syntax.

Column definition

A column definition is defined as follows:

```
ColumnDefinition ::= ColumnName
                     DataType[(Size)]
                        [Single-ColumnConstraint]
```

In words, a ColumnDefinition is a ColumnName, followed by a DataType (with size if appropriate), followed by a Single-ColumnConstraint.

There are several data types available in Access SQL. For comparison, the list in Table 6-2 includes the corresponding selection in the Access Table Design window. (We have not included all synonyms for the data types.) Note that the SQL type INTEGER corresponds with the Access data type *Long*. Note also that the *Size* option affects only TEXT columns, indicating the length of the field. (If it is omitted, the text length defaults to 255.)

Table 6-2. Access SQL data types

SQL data type	Table Design field type
BOOLEAN, LOGICAL, or YES/NO	Yes/No
BYTE or INTEGER1	Number, Field Size = Byte
COUNTER or AUTOINCREMENT	AutoNumber, Field Size = Long Integer
CURRENCY or MONEY	Currency
DATETIME, DATE, or TIME	Date/Time
SHORT, INTEGER2, or SMALLINT	Number, Field Size = Integer
LONG, INT, INTEGER, or INTEGER4	Number, Field Size = Long
SINGLE, FLOAT4, or REAL	Number, Field Size = Single
DOUBLE, FLOAT, FLOAT8, NUMBER, or NUMERIC	Number, Field Size = Double
TEXT, ALPHANUMERIC, CHAR, CHARACTER, or STRING	Text
LONGTEXT, LONGCHAR, MEMO, or NOTE	Memo
LONGBINARY, GENERAL, or OLEOBJECT	(OLE) Object
GUID	AutoNumber, Field Size = Replication ID

Constraints

Constraint clauses can be used to:

- Designate a primary key
- Designate a foreign key, thus establishing a relationship between two tables
- Force a column to contain only unique values

(In SQL-92, these clauses have two other uses: to disallow NULLs and to restrict allowable values to a specified range.)

There are two types of constraint clauses in a CREATE TABLE command. The single-column constraint is used (as indicated in the syntax) within a column definition. Its syntax is:

```
Single-ColumnConstraint ::=
CONSTRAINT
IndexName
[PRIMARY KEY |
UNIQUE |
    REFERENCES ReferencedTable [(ReferencedColumn,...)] ]
```

The first option designates the column as a primary key and creates an index file of the name *IndexName* on that column. The second option designates the column as a (candidate) key and creates a unique index file on that key, by the name *IndexName*. The third option designates the column as a foreign key that references the *ReferencedColumn,...* column(s) of the *ReferencedTable*. The *ReferencedColumn,...* clause is optional if the referenced table has a primary key, since that key will be the referenced key.

For multicolumn constraints, the CONSTRAINT clause must appear after all column definitions and has the syntax:

```
Multi-ColumnConstraint ::=
CONSTRAINT
IndexName
[PRIMARY KEY (ColumnName,...) |
UNIQUE (ColumnName,...) |
FOREIGN KEY (ReferencingColumn,...)
    REFERENCES ReferencedTable [(ReferencedColumn,...)] ]
```

Here are some examples.

Create the *Publishers* table scheme:

```
CREATE TABLE PUBLISHERS
(PubID TEXT(10) CONSTRAINT PrimaryKeyName PRIMARY KEY,
PubName TEXT(100),
PubPhone TEXT(20));
```

Create the *Books* table scheme, and link to *Publishers* using PubID as foreign key:

```
CREATE TABLE BOOKS
(ISBN TEXT(13) CONSTRAINT PrimaryKeyName PRIMARY KEY,
TITLE TEXT(100),
PRICE MONEY,
PubID TEXT(10), CONSTRAINT Test FOREIGN KEY (PubID) REFERENCES
    Publishers
(PubID) );
```

Notes

- The CREATE TABLE statement does not provide a way to create an index with nonunique values. This can be done using the CREATE INDEX statement, however.

- In specifying a foreign key, the CREATE TABLE statement does enable referential integrity rules, but does not allow the option of enabling cascading updates or deletes. (This is one place where Access SQL is weaker than SQL-92, which has a FOREIGN KEY clause that allows the programmer to specify ON UPDATE CASCADE and/or ON DELETE CASCADE.)

The ALTER TABLE Statement

The ALTER TABLE command is used to:

- Add a new column to a table
- Delete a column from a table
- Add or delete single- or multiple-column index

The syntax for the ALTER TABLE command is:

```
ALTER TABLE
  TableName
  ADD COLUMN ColName ColType[(size)] [Single-ColumnConstraint] |
  DROP COLUMN ColName |
  ADD CONSTRAINT Multi-ColumnConstraint |
  DROP CONSTRAINT MultiColumnIndexName;
```

As you can see, the Single- and Multi-Column Constraint clauses (as defined earlier) can be used here to add or delete (DROP) an index.

Notes

- New columns are added at the beginning of the table, immediately following any primary key columns.

- You cannot delete a column that is part of an index. The index must first be removed using a DROP CONSTRAINT statement (or DROP INDEX).

The CREATE INDEX Statement

The CREATE INDEX command has the following syntax:

```
CREATE [ UNIQUE ] INDEX IndexName
ON TableName ({ColName [ASC|DESC]},...])
[WITH {PRIMARY | DISALLOW NULL | IGNORE NULL}]
```

where ASC stands for *ascending* and DESC for *descending*. Note that:

- The UNIQUE keyword prevents duplicate values in the index.
- WITH PRIMARY designates the primary key and creates a primary index file. In this case, the UNIQUE keyword is redundant.
- WITH DISALLOW NULL disallows NULL values in the key.
- WITH IGNORE NULL allows NULL values in the key, but does not include them in the index file. (Hence, they will be skipped in any searches that use the index.)

Note

The CREATE INDEX command is specific to Access SQL and is not part of the SQL-92 standard.

The DROP Statement

The syntax for the DROP statement, which is used for deleting tables and indexes, is:

```
DROP TABLE TableName | DROP INDEX IndexName ON TableName
```

Note

A table must be closed before it can be deleted or an index can be removed from it.

The DML Component of Access SQL

We now turn to the DML component of SQL. The commands we will consider are:

- SELECT
- UNION
- UPDATE
- DELETE
- INSERT INTO
- SELECT INTO
- TRANSFORM
- PARAMETER

Before getting to these statements, however, we must discuss a few relevant points.

Updatable Queries

In many situations, a query is *updatable*, meaning that we may edit the values in the result table, and the changes are automatically reflected in the underlying tables. The details of when this is permitted are fairly involved, but they are completely detailed in the Access Help facility. (This information is not easy to find, however. You can locate it by entering "updatable query" in the Access Answer Wizard and choosing *Determine when I can update data from a query*.)

Joins

Let's begin with a brief discussion of how Access SQL denotes joins. Note that a join clause is not an SQL statement by itself, but must be placed within an SQL statement.

Inner joins

The INNER JOIN clause in Access SQL actually denotes a θ-join on one or more columns. (See the discussion of joins in Chapter 5.) In particular, the syntax is:

```
Table1 INNER JOIN Table2
 ON Table1.Column1 θ1 Table2.Column1
 [{AND|OR ON Table1.Column2 θ2 Table2.Column2},...]
```

where each θ is one of =, <, >, <=, >=, <> (not equal to).

Outer joins

The syntax for an outer join clause is:

```
Table1 {LEFT [OUTER]} | {RIGHT [OUTER]} JOIN Table2
 ON Table1.Column1 θ1 Table2.Column1
 [{AND|OR ON Table1.Column2 θ2 Table2.Column2},...]
```

where θ is one of =, <, >, <=, >=, or <>. Note that the word OUTER is optional.

Nested joins

JOIN statements can be nested. Here is an example that joins the BOOKS, AUTHORS, PUBLISHERS, and BOOK/AUTHOR tables and then selects the Title, AuName, and PubName columns. I have indented some lines in the hope of increasing readability. (I will describe the SELECT statement soon.)

```
SELECT Title, AuName, PubName
FROM
AUTHORS INNER JOIN
 (PUBLISHERS INNER JOIN
 (BOOKS INNER JOIN [BOOK/AUTHOR]
 ON BOOKS.ISBN=[BOOK/AUTHOR].ISBN)
 ON PUBLISHERS.PubID = BOOKS.PubID)
ON AUTHORS.AuID = [BOOK/AUTHOR].AuID;
```

To see how this was constructed, it helps to look at the relationships between the tables involved. Figure 6-3 shows a portion of the relationships window in Access.

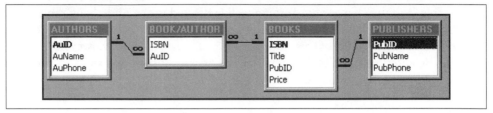

Figure 6-3. A portion of the Relationships window in Access

One way to create the previous join statement is to work from the inside out. We first join BOOKS and BOOK/AUTHOR by the statement:

```
(BOOKS INNER JOIN [BOOK/AUTHOR]
    ON BOOKS.ISBN=[BOOK/AUTHOR].ISBN)
```

We then join this to PUBLISHERS on the PubID column:

```
(PUBLISHERS INNER JOIN
 (BOOKS INNER JOIN [BOOK/AUTHOR]
 ON BOOKS.ISBN=[BOOK/AUTHOR].ISBN)
 ON PUBLISHERS.PubID = BOOKS.PubID)
```

and finally we join this to AUTHORS on the AuID column.

Self-joins

A table can be joined to itself, resulting in a *self-join*. In order to do this, SQL requires the use of the AS *AliasName* syntax. For instance, we can write:

```
BOOKS INNER JOIN BOOKS AS BOOKS2 ON ...
```

The least confusing way to think of this statement is as though Access creates a second copy of the BOOKS table and calls it BOOKS2. We can now refer to the columns of BOOKS as BOOKS.*ColumnName* or BOOKS2.*ColumnName*.

Notes

- An outer join may be nested inside an inner join, but an inner join may not be nested inside an outer join.

- We may use Access expressions, which involve functions (such as *Left$*, *Len*, *Trim$*, and *Instr*) in SQL statements (even though the "official" syntax does not describe this).

- In Access, we can define relationships between tables. However, these relationships have no effect on SQL statements. Thus, an INNER JOIN statement does not require that a relationship already exist between the participating tables.

Relationships are used in Design View, however, and translate into INNER JOIN statements. For example, if we add BOOKS and PUBLISHERS to the Query Design View window, move Title and PubName to the Design grid, and then view the SQL equivalent, we will see an INNER JOIN clause in the SQL statement.

The SELECT Statement

The SELECT statement is the workhorse of SQL commands (as you can tell by the length of our discussion on this statement). The statement returns a table and can perform both of the relational algebra operations *selection* and *projection*. The syntax of the SELECT statement is:

```
SELECT [predicate] ReturnColumnDescription,...
FROM TableExpression
[WHERE RowCondition]
[GROUP BY GroupByCriteria]
[HAVING GroupCriteria]
[ORDER BY OrderByCriteria]
```

Let us describe the various components of this statement. We note immediately that the keyword SELECT is in some ways unfortunate, since it denotes the relational algebra operation of projection, not selection. It is the WHERE clause that performs selection.

Predicate

The *predicate* is used to describe how to handle duplicate return rows. It can have one of the following values: ALL, DISTINCT, DISTINCTROW, or TOP.

The default option ALL returns all qualifying rows, including duplicates. If there is more than one qualifying row with the same values in all of the columns that are requested in the ReturnColumnDescription, then the option DISTINCT returns only the first such row. The:

```
TOP number
```

or:

```
TOP percent PERCENT
```

option returns the top *number* (or percent) of rows in the sort order determined by the ORDER BY clause.

The DISTINCTROW option can be a bit confusing, so let us see if we can straighten it out. The Access Help system says that the DISTINCTROW option "Omits data based on entire duplicate records, not just duplicate fields." It doesn't say *how* this is done. Microsoft Technet is a bit less vague:

> In contrast, DISTINCTROW is unique to Microsoft Access. It causes a query to return unique records, not unique values. For example, if 10 customers are named Jones, a query based on the SQL statement "SELECT DISTINCTROW Name FROM

Customers" returns all 10 records with Jones in the Name field. The major reason for adding the DISTINCTROW reserved word to Microsoft Access SQL is to support updatable semi-joins, such as one-to-many joins in which the output fields all come from the table on the "one" side. DISTINCTROW is specified by default in Microsoft Access queries and is ignored in queries in which it has no effect. You should not delete the DISTINCTROW reserved word from the SQL dialog box.

The intended purpose of DISTINCTROW is simple. DISTINCTROW applies only when the FROM clause involves more than one table. Consider this statement:

```
SELECT ALL PubName
FROM PUBLISHERS INNER JOIN BOOKS
ON PUBLISHERS.PubID = BOOKS.PubID;
```

Since there are many books published by the same publisher, the result table tblALL shown in Table 6-3 has many duplicate publisher names.

Table 6-3. The tblALL table

PubName
Small House
Small House
Small House
Small House
Big House
Big House
Big House
Big House
Big House
Big House
Alpha Press
Alpha Press
Alpha Press
Alpha Press

To remove duplicate publisher names, we can include the DISTINCT keyword. Thus, the statement

```
SELECT DISTINCT PubName
FROM PUBLISHERS INNER JOIN BOOKS
ON PUBLISHERS.PubID = BOOKS.PubID;
```

produces the table tblDISTINCT that is shown in Table 6-4.

Now consider what happens if the PUBLISHERS table is changed by adding a new publisher with the same name as an existing publisher (but a different PubID and phone), as we have done in Table 6-5. The previous DISTINCT statement will give the same result table as before, thus leaving out the new publisher.

Table 6-4. The tblDISTINCT table

PubName
Alpha Press
Big House
Small House

Table 6-5. The PUBLISHERS (altered) table

PubID	PubName	PubPhone
1	Big House	123-456-7890
2	Alpha Press	999-999-9999
3	Small House	714-000-0000
4	Small House	555-123-1111

What is called for is a selection criterion that will return both publisher names simply because they come from different rows of the PUBLISHERS table. This is the purpose of DISTINCTROW. Thus, the statement:

```
SELECT DISTINCTROW PubName
FROM PUBLISHERS INNER JOIN BOOKS
ON PUBLISHERS.PubID = BOOKS.PubID;
```

produces the result table tblDISTINCTROW shown in Table 6-6 (note that we also had to add a book to the BOOKS table, with PubID 4).

Table 6-6. The tblDISTINCTROW table

PubName
Small House
Big House
Alpha Press
Small House

We can now describe how DISTINCTROW works. Consider the following SQL skeleton:

```
SELECT DISTINCTROW ColumnsRequested
FROM TablesClause
```

Here *ColumnsRequested* is a list of columns requested by the statement, and *TablesClause* is a join of tables. Let us refer to a table mentioned in *TablesClause* as a *return table* if at least one of its columns is mentioned in *ColumnsRequested*. Thus, in the statement:

```
SELECT DISTINCTROW PubName
FROM PUBLISHERS INNER JOIN BOOKS
ON PUBLISHERS.PubID = BOOKS.PubID;
```

PUBLISHERS is a return table, but BOOKS is not. Here is how DISTINCTROW works:

1. Form the join(s) described in *TablesClause*.

2. Project the resulting table onto all of the columns from all return tables (not just the columns requested). Put another way, remove all columns that are not part of a return table.

3. Remove all duplicate rows, where two rows are considered duplicates if they are composed of the same rows from each result table. It is not the values that are compared, but the actual rows. It is necessary to add this because two different rows may have identical values in an Access table.

Let us illustrate with a simple example.

Consider the following tables, named Temp1, Temp2, and Temp3, respectively:

A_1	A_2
a1	x
a2	link
a3	link

B_1	B_2	B_3
b1	y	z
b2	link	link2

C_1	C_2	C_3
c1	t	link2
c2	v	link2
c3	a	x

The statement:

```
SELECT *
FROM
(Temp1 INNER JOIN Temp2 ON Temp1.A2 = Temp2.B2)
INNER JOIN Temp3 ON Temp2.B3 = Temp3.C3;
```

gives the result table tblALL:

A_1	A_2	B_1	B_2	B_3	C_1	C_2	C_3
a3	link	b2	link	link2	c2	v	link2
a3	link	b2	link	link2	c1	t	link2
a2	link	b2	link	link2	c2	v	link2
a2	link	b2	link	link2	c1	t	link2

Now let us add the DISTINCTROW keyword and select a single column from just tblA:

```
SELECT DISTINCTROW A1
FROM
(Temp1 INNER JOIN Temp2 ON Temp1.A2 = Temp2.B2)
INNER JOIN Temp3 ON Temp2.B3 = Temp3.C3;
```

Now we consider the projection onto the rows of the only return table (tblA):

A_1	A_2
a3	link
a3	link
a2	link
a2	link

It is clear that the first two rows of this table are the same row of tblA, so they produce only one row in the final result table. The same holds for the last two rows. Hence, the result table is:

A_1
a2
a3

Let us now change this by requesting a column from tblC, thus making it a return table as well:

```
SELECT DISTINCTROW A1,C1
FROM
(Temp1 INNER JOIN Temp2 ON Temp1.A2 = Temp2.B2)
INNER JOIN Temp3 ON Temp2.B3 = Temp3.C3;
```

The projection onto return table rows is now:

A_1	A_2	C_1	C_2	C_3
a3	link	c2	v	link2
a3	link	c1	t	link2
a2	link	c2	v	link2
a2	link	c1	t	link2

These row "pairs" are all distinct. In fact:

- Row 1 comes from row 3 of tblA and row 2 of tblC.
- Row 2 comes from row 3 of tblA and row 1 of tblC.
- Row 3 comes from row 2 of tblA and row 2 of tblC.
- Row 4 comes from row 2 of tblA and row 1 of tblC.

It follows that the return table includes all rows:

A₁	C₁
a2	c1
a2	c2
a3	c1
a3	c2

Finally, consider what happens if we change the third row of tblA to:

A₁	A₂
a1	x
a2	link
a2	link

Running the first DISTINCTROW statement:

```
SELECT DISTINCTROW A1
FROM
(Temp1 INNER JOIN Temp2 ON Temp1.A2 = Temp2.B2)
INNER JOIN Temp3 ON Temp2.B3 = Temp3.C3;
```

gives:

A₁
a2
a2

Comparing this to the previous result table DISTINCTROW, A1 emphasizes the fact that, even though the second and third rows of tblNewA are identical in values, they are different rows, so they both contribute to the final result table. If we were to replace the DISTINCTROW keyword with the word DISTINCT, then the result table would have only one row, since then it is the values in each row that form the basis for comparison.

Of course, this would not be an issue if all tables had a key, since then the values in a row would determine the row. You may now see why I recommended against having two different rows with the same column values, even though Access permits this possibility (but true relational databases do not).

Notice what happens if all tables mentioned in the *TablesClause* are return tables. This would happen, for instance, if there is only one table in *TablesClause*. In this case, the projection does nothing; since each row of the *TablesClause* result table must come from a distinct combination of rows of the result tables, we deduce that DISTINCTROW has exactly the same effect as ALL. To put it another way, DISTINCTROW is ignored.

It is useful to compare DISTINCTROW and DISTINCT. We can see that the only difference is that a DISTINCT statement will return distinct values, rather than values from distinct rows. However, these will be the same if the requested columns from each return table uniquely identify their rows.

Let us illustrate with the PUBLISHERS example. Suppose we return a key (PubID) for PUBLISHERS, as in the statement:

```
SELECT DISTINCTROW PUBLISHERS.PubID, PUBLISHERS.PubName
FROM PUBLISHERS INNER JOIN BOOKS
ON PUBLISHERS.PubID = BOOKS.PubID;
```

Then the result table will return all PUBLISHERS rows that have at least one book in the BOOKS table, as Table 6-7 shows.

Table 6-7. Publishers with at least one book in BOOKS

PubID	PubName
3	Small House
1	Big House
2	Alpha Press
4	Small House

This is, in fact, the *semi-join:*

$$PUBLISHERS \; semi\text{-}join_{PUBLISHERS.PubID=BOOKS.PubID} \; BOOKS$$

Recall that the semi-join is the projection of the join onto one of the tables (in this case, the PUBLISHERS table). Thus, as Microsoft itself says, the purpose of the DISTINCTROW option is to return an *updatable semi-join.*

Of course, the same statement with DISTINCT in place of DISTINCTROW will return the same result table. However, there is one big difference. Since DISTINCT statements can completely hide the origin of the returned values, it would be a disaster if Access allowed such a result table to be updatable—and indeed it does not. For instance, recall the table tblDISTINCT discussed earlier and shown in Table 6-8.

Table 6-8. The tblDISTINCT table

PubName
Alpha Press
Big House
Small House

Changing the name of Small House in this result table would be disastrous, since we would not know which Small House was being affected!

On the other hand, the result table of the DISTINCTROW statement has a "representative" from each row of the PUBLISHERS table, as Table 6-9 shows. Hence, while it still may not be a good idea to change this particular table, since we cannot tell which Small House is which, it would be reasonable to make a change to both names, for instance.

Table 6-9. The tblDISTINCTROW table

PubName
Small House
Big House
Alpha Press
Small House

More generally, Access does not permit updating of the result table of a DISTINCT statement, but it does permit updating of the result table for a DISTINCTROW statement.

Finally, we mention that Microsoft Access includes the DISTINCTROW keyword by default when you create a query using the Access Query Design Window.

ReturnColumnDescription

The *ReturnColumnDescription* describes the columns, or combination of columns, to return. It can be any of the following:

- * (indicating all columns)
- The name of a column
- An expression involving column names, enclosed in brackets, along with strings and string operators; for example, `[PubID] & "-" & [Title]`

(Note that, according to the syntax of the SELECT statement, *ReturnColumnDescription* can be repeated as many times as desired.)

When two returned columns (from different tables) have the same name, it is necessary to *qualify* the column names using the table names. For instance, to qualify the PubID column name, we write BOOKS.PubID and PUBLISHERS.PubID. We can also write BOOKS.* to indicate all columns of the BOOKS table.

Finally, each *ReturnColumnDescription* can end with:

```
[AS AliasName]
```

to give the return column a (new) name. For example, the following statement:

```
SELECT DISTINCTROW
[ISBN] & " from " & [PubName] AS [ISBN from PubName]
FROM PUBLISHERS INNER JOIN BOOKS ON PUBLISHERS.PubID = BOOKS.PubID;
```

returns a single-column result table ISBN-PUB, as shown in Table 6-10.

Table 6-10. The ISBN-PUB table

ISBN from PubName
0-12-345678-9 from Small House
0-11-345678-9 from Small House
0-321-32132-1 from Small House
0-55-123456-9 from Small House
0-12-333433-3 from Big House
0-103-45678-9 from Big House
0-91-335678-7 from Big House
0-99-999999-9 from Big House
1-22-233700-0 from Big House
1-1111-1111-1 from Big House
0-91-045678-5 from Alpha Press
0-555-55555-9 from Alpha Press
0-99-777777-7 from Alpha Press
0-123-45678-0 from Alpha Press

Not only does the AS *AliasName* option allow us to name a *compound column*, it also allows us to rename duplicate column names without having to qualify the names.

FROM TableExpression

The FROM clause specifies the tables (or queries) from which the SELECT statement is to take its rows. The expression *TableExpression* can be a single table name, several table names separated by commas, or a join clause. The *TableExpression* may also include the AS *AliasName* syntax for table-name aliases.

When tables are separated by commas in the FROM clause, a Cartesian product is formed. For example, the statement:

```
SELECT *
FROM AUTHORS, PUBLISHERS;
```

will produce the Cartesian product of the two tables.

WHERE RowCondition

The *RowCondition* is any Access expression that specifies which rows are included in the result table. Expressions can involve column names, constants, arithmetic (=, <, >, <=, >=, <>, BETWEEN) and logical (AND, OR, XOR, NOT, IMP) relations, as well as functions. Here are some examples:

- WHERE Title LIKE "F*"
- WHERE Len(Trim(Title)) > 10
- WHERE Instr(Title, "Wind") > 0 AND Len(Trim(Title)) > 10
- WHERE DateSold = #5/21/96#

Note that dates are enclosed in number signs (#) and the strings are enclosed in quotation marks (" ").

GROUP BY GroupByCriteria

The GROUP BY option allows records to be grouped together for the purpose of computing the value of an *aggregate function* (*Avg*, *Count*, *Min*, *Max*, *Sum*, *First*, *Last*, *StDev*, *StDevP*, *Var*, and *VarP*). It is equivalent to creating a so-called *totals query*. The *GroupByCriteria* can contain the names of up to 10 columns. The order of the column names determines the grouping levels, from highest to lowest.

For example, the following statement lists each publisher by name, along with the minimum price of each publisher's books in the BOOKS table:

```
SELECT PUBLISHERS.PubName, MIN(Price) AS [Minimum Price]
FROM PUBLISHERS INNER JOIN BOOKS
ON PUBLISHERS.PubID = BOOKS.PubID
GROUP BY PUBLISHERS.PubName;
```

The result table appears in Table 6-11.

Table 6-11. Each publisher's least expensive book

PubName	Minimum Price
Alpha Press	$12.00
Big House	$15.00
Small House	$22.95

HAVING GroupCriteria

The HAVING option is used in conjunction with the GROUP BY option and allows us to specify a criterion, in terms of aggregate functions, for deciding which data to display.

For example, the following command is the same as the previous one, with the additional HAVING option that restricts the return table to those publishers whose minimum price is less than $20.00:

```
SELECT PUBLISHERS.PubName, MIN(Price) AS [Minimum Price]
FROM PUBLISHERS INNER JOIN BOOKS
ON PUBLISHERS.PubID = BOOKS.PubID
GROUP BY PUBLISHERS.PubName
HAVING MIN(Price)<20.00;
```

The result table is shown in Table 6-12.

Table 6-12. Each publisher's cheapest book under $20.00

PubName	Minimum Price
Alpha Press	$12.00
Big House	$15.00

Note that the WHERE clause restricts which rows participate in the grouping and hence contribute to the value of the aggregate functions, whereas the HAVING clause affects only which values are displayed.

ORDER BY OrderByCriteria

The ORDER BY option describes the order in which to return the rows in the return table. The *OrderByCriteria* has the form:

```
OrderByCriteria ::= {ColumnName [ASC | DESC ]},...
```

In other words, it is just a list of columns to use in the ordering. Rows are sorted first by the first column listed, then rows with identical values in the first column are sorted by the values in the second column, and so on.

The UNION Statement

The UNION statement is used to create the union of two or more tables. The syntax is:

```
[TABLE] Query
{UNION [ALL] [TABLE] Query},...
```

where *Query* is either a SELECT statement, the name of a stored query, or the name of a stored table preceded by the TABLE keyword. The ALL option forces Access to include all records. Without this option, Access does not include duplicate rows. The use of ALL increases performance as well and is thus recommended even when there are no duplicate rows.

Example

The following statement takes the union of all rows of BOOKS and those rows of NEWBOOKS that have Price > $25.00, sorting the result table by Title:

```
TABLE BOOKS
UNION ALL
SELECT * FROM NEWBOOKS WHERE Price > 25.00
ORDER BY Title;
```

Notes

- All queries in a UNION operation must return the same number of fields. However, the fields do not need to have the same size or data type.
- Columns are combined in the union by their order in the query clauses, not by their names.
- Aliases may be used in the first SELECT statement (if there is one) to change the names of returned columns.
- An ORDER BY clause can be used at the end of the last *Query* to order the returned data. Use the column names from the first *Query*.

- GROUP BY and/or HAVING clauses can be used in each query argument to group the returned data.
- The result table of a UNION is not updatable.
- UNION is not part of SQL-92.

The UPDATE Statement

The UPDATE statement is equivalent to an Update query and is used for updating data in a table or tables. The syntax is:

```
UPDATE TableName | QueryName
SET NewValueExpression,...
WHERE Criteria;
```

The WHERE clause is used to restrict updating to qualifying rows.

Example

The following example updates the Price column in the BOOKS table with new prices from a table called NEWPRICES that has an ISBN and a Price column:

```
UPDATE
BOOKS INNER JOIN NEWPRICES ON BOOKS.ISBN = NEWPRICES.ISBN
SET BOOKS.Price = NEWPRICES.Price
WHERE BOOKS.Price <> NEWPRICES.Price;
```

Note that UPDATE does not produce a result table. To determine which rows will be updated, first run a corresponding SELECT query, as in:

```
SELECT * FROM
BOOKS INNER JOIN NEWPRICES ON BOOKS.ISBN = NEWPRICES.ISBN
WHERE BOOKS.Price <> NEWPRICES.Price
```

The DELETE Statement

The DELETE statement is equivalent to a Delete query and is used to delete rows from a table. Here is the syntax:

```
DELETE
FROM TableName
WHERE Criteria
```

Criteria is used to determine which rows to delete.

This command can be used to delete all data from a table, but it will not delete the structure of the table. Use DROP for that purpose.

You can use DELETE to remove records from tables that have a one-to-many relationship. If cascading delete is enabled when you delete a row from the one side of the relationship, all matching rows are deleted from the many side. The action of the

DELETE statement is not reversable. Always make backups before deleting! You can run a SELECT operation before DELETE to see which rows will be affected by the DELETE operation.

The INSERT INTO Statement

The INSERT INTO statement is designed to insert new rows into a table. This can be done by specifying the values of a new row using this syntax:

```
INSERT INTO Target [(FieldName,...)]
VALUES (Value1,...)
```

If you do not specify the *FieldName*(s), then you must include values for each field in the table.

Let's look at several examples of the INSERT INTO statement. The following statement inserts a new row into the BOOKS table:

```
INSERT INTO BOOKS
VALUES ("1-000-00000-0", "SQL is Fun",1,25.00);
```

The following statement inserts a new row into the BOOKS table. The Price and PubID columns have NULL values.

```
INSERT INTO BOOKS (ISBN,Title)
VALUES ("1-1111-1111-1","Gone Fishing");
```

To insert multiple rows, use this syntax:

```
INSERT INTO Target [(FieldName,...)]
SELECT FieldName,...
FROM TableExpression
```

In both syntaxes, *Target* is the name of the table or query into which rows are to be inserted. In the case of a query, that query must be updatable and all updates will be reflected in the underlying tables. *TableExpression* is the name of the table from which records are inserted, the name of a saved query, or a SELECT statement.

Assume that NEWBOOKS is a table with three fields: ISBN, PubID, and Price. The following statement inserts rows from BOOKS into NEWBOOKS. It inserts only those books with Price > $20.00.

```
INSERT INTO NEWBOOKS
SELECT ISBN, PubID, Price
FROM BOOKS
WHERE Price>20;
```

Note

Text field values must be enclosed in quotation marks.

The SELECT...INTO Statement

The SELECT...INTO statement is equivalent to a MakeTable query. It makes a new table and inserts data from other tables. The syntax is:

```
SELECT FieldName,...
INTO NewTableName
FROM Source
WHERE RowCondition
ORDER BY OrderCondition
```

FieldName is the name of the field to be copied into the new table. *Source* is the name of the table from which data is taken. This can also be the name of a query or a join statement.

For example, the following statement creates a new table called EXPENSIVEBOOKS and includes books from the BOOKS table that cost more than $45.00:

```
SELECT Title, ISBN
INTO EXPENSIVEBOOKS
FROM BOOKS
WHERE Price>45
ORDER BY Title;
```

Notes

- This statement is unique to Access SQL.
- This statement does not create indexes in the new table.

TRANSFORM

The TRANSFORM statement (which is not part of SQL-92) is designed to create crosstab queries. The basic syntax is:

```
TRANSFORM AggregateFunction
SelectStatement
PIVOT ColumnHeadingsColumn [IN (Value,...)]
```

The *AggregateFunction* is one of Access' aggregate functions (*Avg*, *Count*, *Min*, *Max*, *Sum*, *First*, *Last*, *StDev*, *StDevP*, *Var*, and *VarP*). The *ColumnHeadingsColumn* is the column that is pivoted to give the column headings in the crosstab result table. The *Values* in the IN clause option specify fixed column headings.

The *SelectStatement* is a SELECT statement that uses the GROUP BY clause, with some modifications. In particular, the select statement must have at least two GROUP BY columns and no HAVING clause.

As an example, suppose we wish to display the total number of books from each publisher by price. The SELECT statement:

```
SELECT PubName, Price, COUNT(Title) AS Total
FROM PUBLISHERS INNER JOIN BOOKS
 ON PUBLISHERS.PubID=BOOKS.PubID
GROUP BY PubName, Price;
```

whose result table is shown in Table 6-13, doesn't really give the information in the desired form. For instance, it is difficult to tell how many books cost $20.00. (Remember, this small table is just for illustration.)

Table 6-13. Book prices by publisher

PubName	Price	Total
Big House	$15.00	1
Big House	$20.00	1
Big House	$25.00	2
Big House	$49.00	1
Medium House	$12.00	2
Medium House	$20.00	1
Medium House	$34.00	1
Medium House	$49.00	1
Small House	$49.00	1

We can transform this into a crosstab query in two steps:

1. Add a TRANSFORM clause at the top, and move the aggregate function whose value is to be computed to that clause.

2. Add a PIVOT line at the bottom, and move the column whose values will form the column headings to that clause. Also, delete the reference to this column in the SELECT clause.

This gives:

```
TRANSFORM COUNT(Title)
SELECT Price
FROM PUBLISHERS INNER JOIN BOOKS
 ON PUBLISHERS.PubID=BOOKS.PubID
GROUP BY Price
PIVOT PubName;
```

with the result table shown in Table 6-14.

Table 6-14. A cross-tabulation of book prices by publisher

Price	Big House	Medium House	Small House
$12.00		2	
$15.00	1		
$20.00	1	1	
$25.00	2		
$34.00		1	
$49.00	1	1	1

We can group the rows by the values in more than one column. For example, suppose that the BOOKS table also had a DISCOUNT column that gave the discount from the regular price of the book (as a percentage). Then by including the DISCOUNT column in the SELECT and GROUP BY clauses, we get:

```
TRANSFORM COUNT(Title)
SELECT Price, Discount
FROM PUBLISHERS INNER JOIN BOOKS
 ON PUBLISHERS.PubID=BOOKS.PubID
GROUP BY Price, Discount
PIVOT PubName;
```

for which the result table is shown in Table 6-15.

Table 6-15. Book prices and discount by publisher

Price	Discount	Big House	Medium House	Small House
$12.00	30%		2	
$15.00	20%	1		
$20.00	20%		1	
$20.00	30%	1		
$25.00	10%	1		
$25.00	20%	1		
$34.00	10%		1	
$49.00	10%	1		
$49.00	30%		1	1

In this case, each row represents a unique price/discount pair.

A crosstab can also include additional row aggregates by adding additional aggregate functions to the SELECT clause, as follows:

```
TRANSFORM COUNT(Title)
SELECT Price, COUNT(Price) AS Count, SUM(Price) AS Sum
FROM PUBLISHERS INNER JOIN BOOKS
 ON PUBLISHERS.PubID=BOOKS.PubID
GROUP BY Price
PIVOT PubName;
```

which gives the result table shown in Table 6-16.

Finally, by including fixed column names, we can reorder or omit columns from the crosstab result table. For instance, the next statement is just like the previous one except for the PIVOT clause:

```
TRANSFORM COUNT(Title)
SELECT Price, COUNT(Price) AS Count, SUM(Price) AS Sum
FROM PUBLISHERS INNER JOIN BOOKS
 ON PUBLISHERS.PubID=BOOKS.PubID
GROUP BY Price
PIVOT PubName IN ("Small House", "Medium House");
```

Table 6-16. Aggregating results in a crosstab table

Price	Count	Sum	Big House	Medium House	Small House
$12.00	2	$24.00		2	
$15.00	1	$15.00	1		
$20.00	2	$40.00	1	1	
$25.00	2	$50.00	2		
$34.00	1	$34.00		1	
$49.00	3	$147.00	1	1	1

The result table is shown in Table 6-17. Note that the order of the columns has changed and Big House is not shown.

Table 6-17. Omitting columns from a crosstab table

Price	Count	Sum	Small House	Medium House
$12.00	2	$24.00		2
$15.00	1	$15.00		
$20.00	2	$40.00		1
$25.00	2	$50.00		
$34.00	1	$34.00		1
$49.00	3	$147.00	1	1

Subqueries

SQL permits the use of SELECT statements within the following:

- Other SELECT statements
- SELECT…INTO statements
- INSERT…INTO statements
- DELETE statements
- UPDATE statements

The internal SELECT statement is referred to as a *subquery* and is generally used in the WHERE clause of the main query.

The syntax of a subquery takes three possible forms, described as follows.

Syntax 1

```
Comparison [ANY | SOME | ALL] (SQLStatement)
```

where *Comparison* is an expression followed by a comparison relation that compares the expression with the return value(s) of the subquery. This syntax is used to compare a value against the values obtained from another query.

For example, the following statement returns all titles and prices of books from the BOOKS table, whose prices are greater than the maximum price of all books in the table BOOKS2:

```
SELECT Title, Price
FROM BOOKS
WHERE Price > (SELECT Max(Price) FROM BOOKS2);
```

Note that since the subquery returns only one value, we do not need to use any of the keywords ANY, SOME, or ALL.

The following statement selects all BOOKS titles and prices for books that are more expensive than ALL of the books published by Big House:

```
SELECT Title, Price
FROM BOOKS
WHERE Price > ALL
    (SELECT Price
    FROM PUBLISHERS INNER JOIN BOOKS ON PUBLISHERS.PubID =
    BOOKS.PubID
    WHERE PubName = "Big House");
```

Note that ANY and SOME have the same meaning and return all choices that make the comparison true for at least one value returned by the subquery. For example, if we were to replace ALL by SOME in the previous example, the return table would consist of all book titles and prices for books that are more expensive than the cheapest book published by Big House.

Syntax 2

```
Expression [NOT] IN (SQLStatement)
```

This syntax is used to look up a column value in the result table of another query.

For example, the following statement returns all book titles from BOOKS that do not appear in the table BOOKS2:

```
SELECT Title
FROM BOOKS
WHERE Title NOT IN (SELECT Title FROM BOOKS2);
```

Syntax 3

```
[NOT] EXISTS (SQLStatement)
```

This syntax is used to check whether an item exists (is returned) in the subquery.

For example, the following statement selects all publishers that do not have books in the BOOKS table:

```
SELECT PubName
FROM PUBLISHERS
WHERE NOT EXISTS
  (SELECT * FROM BOOKS WHERE BOOKS.PubID =
  PUBLISHERS.PubID);
```

Notice that the PUBLISHERS table is referenced in the subquery. This causes Access to evaluate the subquery once for each value of PUBLISHERS.PubID in the PUBLISHERS table.

Notes

- When using Syntax 1 or 2, the subquery must return a single column, or an error will occur.
- The SELECT statement that constitutes the subquery follows the same format and rules as any other SELECT statement. However, it must be enclosed in parentheses.

Parameters

Access SQL allows the use of *parameters* to obtain information from the user when the query is run. The PARAMETERS line must be the first line in the statement and has the syntax:

```
PARAMETERS Name DataType, ...
```

An example will illustrate the technique.

The following statement will prompt the user for a portion of the title of a book and return all books from BOOKS with that string in the title. Note the semicolon at the end of the PARAMETERS line.

```
PARAMETERS [Enter portion of title] TEXT;
SELECT *
FROM BOOKS
WHERE Instr(Title, [Enter portion of title]) > 0;
```

The function Instr(Text1, Text2) returns the first location of the text string *Text2* within the text string *Text1*. Note that *Name* is repeated in the WHERE clause and will be filled in by the value that the user enters as a result of *Name* appearing in the PARAMETERS clause.

Database Architecture

CHAPTER 7

Database System Architecture

Why Program?

There is no doubt that SQL is a powerful language—as far as it goes. However, it is a somewhat unfriendly language, and it lacks the sophisticated control structures of a more traditional language, such as *For...Next...* loops and *If...Then...* statements.

This is not really a problem, since SQL is designed for a very specific purpose related to database-component creation and manipulation. SQL is not designed to provide an overall programming environment for Microsoft Access itself. This role is played by *Visual Basic for Applications* (VBA).

VBA is the macro or scripting language for all of the major Microsoft Office products: Microsoft Access, Excel, PowerPoint, and Word (starting with Word 97). It is a very powerful programming language that gives the programmer access to the full features of these applications, as well as the means to make the applications work together.

One of the major components of VBA is its support for *Data Access Objects* model, (DAO). DAO is the programming-language interface for the Jet database management system (DBMS) that underlies Microsoft Access. It provides a more-or-less object-oriented data definition language (DDL) and data manipulation language (DML), thereby allowing the VBA programmer to define the structure of a database and manipulate its data.

Of course, it is natural to wonder why you would want to use DAO, and VBA in general, rather than using the built-in graphical interface of Microsoft Access. The answer is simple. While the graphical interface is very easy to use and is quite adequate for many purposes, it is simply not as powerful as the programming languages. The database creator gains more power and flexibility over the database by directly manipulating the basic objects of the database (such as the tables, queries, relationships, indexes, and so on) through programming.

As a simple example, there is no way to get a list of the fields of a given table (i.e, the table's *table scheme*) using the Access graphical interface. However, this is a simple matter using programming techniques. The following short program:

```
Sub Example( )
    Dim db As DATABASE
    Dim tdf As TableDef
    Dim fld As Field

    Set db = CurrentDb
    Set tdf = db.TableDefs("BOOKS")
    For Each fld In tdf.Fields
        Debug.Print fld.Name
    Next
End Sub
```

displays the following list of fields for the BOOKS table in the Debug window:

```
ISBN
Title
PubID
Price
```

This is a good place to discuss the relationship between DAO and SQL. The fact is that DAO both uses SQL and overlaps SQL. That is, there are many commands in DAO that can accept an SQL statement as an argument. For instance, the following VBA code opens a recordset (discussed later in the book) using an SQL statement to define the records in the recordset:

```
' Get current database
Set dbs = CurrentDb( )

' Write SQL statement
strSelect = "Select * FROM Books WHERE Price=10"

' Open recordset using SQL statement
Set rsCheap = dbs.OpenRecordset(strSelect)
```

On the other hand, DAO overlaps SQL in the sense that many actions can be performed using either language. For instance, a table can be created using either the SQL statement CREATE TABLE or the DAO method *CreateTable*. The choice is up to the programmer.

Our main goal in the remaining portion of this book is to discuss the DAO model. Before doing so, however, we need to set the stage by discussing the overall architecture of a database management system, and of the Jet DBMS in particular, so we can put DAO in its proper context. We will do so in this chapter and also take a quick peek at DAO programming. In Part IV, *Visual Basic for Applications*, I will present a brief introduction to programming in VBA. Then I will turn to DAO itself in the following chapters of the book. Finally, I'll conclude by examining *ActiveX Data Objects* (ADO), Microsoft's recent technology for universal data access.

Database Systems

A *database system* is often pictured as a three-level structure, as shown in Figure 7-1.

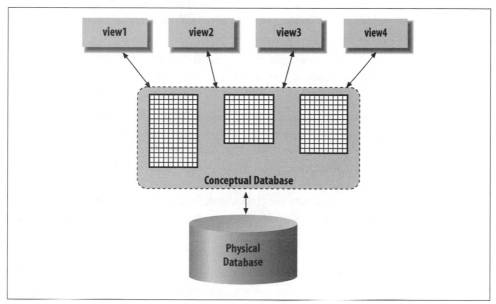

Figure 7-1. The three-level structure of a database system

At the lowest level of the structure is the *physical database*, which consists of the raw data existing on a physical object, such as a hard disk. At this level, the data has no logical meaning, as related to the database. However, the data does have a very definite physical structure to allow efficient access. In other words, the data is more than just a string of bits.

In fact, there are a variety of structures in which the data might be stored, including hash tables, balanced trees, linked lists, nested records, and so on, and the choice of data structure is not a simple one. However, I will not pursue a discussion of the physical database in this book. Suffice it to say that, at the physical level, the data is viewed as a *structured* collection of bits, and the sole purpose of the structure is to provide efficient access to the data. The physical level of a database is often referred to as the *internal level*.

The *conceptual database* is a conceptual view of the database as a whole. It gives the data a *logical structure*. For instance, in a relational database system, the data is viewed as a collection of tables, with column headings describing the attributes of the corresponding entity class. Moreover, tables are related to one another through certain columns.

The conceptual model is intended to model the entire database. However, individual users may be interested in views of only specific portions of the data. For instance, in the LIBRARY database, a student using the library's online database catalog is probably not interested in the price of the book, but is interested in where it is located on the shelves. Thus, a single database, such as LIBRARY, may need different views for the student than for the librarian.

The highest level in the three-tier structure consists of the individual *views* of the data that may be held by users of the database. Views are also referred to as *subschemes*, and this level of the tier is also referred to as the *external level*.

As another example, we can think of the Microsoft Visual Basic programming language as providing an external view of the Jet database management system that is geared toward database programmers. We can think of Microsoft Access as providing an external view that is geared, not just to programmers, but also to high-level users of varying degrees of sophistication. After all, a user does not need to know anything about database programming to create a database in Microsoft Access, although he does need to have a familiarity with the *conceptual level* of a relational database.

Thinking of a database system as a three-tier structure has distinct advantages. One advantage is that it allows for a certain level of independence that permits the individual tiers to be changed or replaced without affecting the other tiers. For instance, if the database is moved to a new computer system that stores the data in hash tables rather than balanced trees, this should not affect the conceptual model of the data, nor the views of users of the database. Also, if we switch from the Visual Basic view of the database to the Access view, we can still use the same conceptual database model. Put more bluntly, a database table in Visual Basic is still a database table in Microsoft Access.

Database Management Systems

A DBMS is a software system that is responsible for managing all aspects of a database, at all levels. In particular, a DBMS should provide the following features, and perhaps more:

- A mechanism for defining the structure of a database, in the form of a *data definition language*, or DDL.
- A mechanism for data manipulation, including data access, sorting, searching, and filtering. This takes the form of a *data manipulation language*, or DML.
- Interaction with a high-level *host language* or *host application*, allowing programmers to write database applications designed for specific purposes. The host language can be a standard programming language, such as C or Visual Basic, or a database application language, such as Microsoft Access.

- Efficient and correct *multiuser access* to the data.
- Effective *data security*.
- *Robustness*—that is, the ability to recover from system failures without data loss.
- A *data dictionary*, or *data catalog*. This is a database (in its own right) that provides a list of the *definitions* of all objects in the main database. For instance, it should include information on all entities in the database, along with their attributes and indexes. This "data about data" is sometimes referred to as *metadata*. The data dictionary should be accessible to the user of the database, so that she can obtain this metadata.

The Jet DBMS

As the title of the book suggests, our primary interest is in the DBMS that underlies Microsoft Access (and also Visual Basic). Accordingly, we will take our examples from this DBMS, called the *Jet DBMS* or the *Jet Database Engine*. The relationship between the Jet DBMS and other database-related programs, including Microsoft Access and Visual Basic, can be pictured as in Figure 7-2.

Microsoft's application-level products Visual Basic, Access, and Excel play host to VBA, which is the underlying programming language (also called *scripting* or *macro* language) for these applications. (Microsoft Word Version 7 does not use VBA—it uses a similar language called *Word Basic*. However, as of Microsoft Word 97, Word does use VBA.) As expected, each of these applications integrates VBA into its environment in a specific way, since each application has a different purpose.

In turn, Visual Basic for Applications is the host language for the Jet DBMS. The Jet DBMS contains the DAO component, which is the programming-language interface for the Jet DBMS. The DAO provides a more-or-less object-oriented DDL and DML, thereby allowing the VBA programmer to define the structure of a database and manipulate its data.

The Jet Database Engine is a collection of components, generally in the form of dynamic link libraries (DLLs), designed to provide specific functions within the Jet DBMS. (A DLL is essentially a collection of functions for performing various tasks.) The *Jet Query Engine* handles the translation of database queries into Access SQL, and the subsequent compilation, optimization, and execution of these queries. In short, it handles queries. The *Internal ISAM component* is responsible for storing and retrieving data from the physical database file. ISAM stands for *Indexed Sequential Access Method* and is the method by which data is stored in a Jet database file. The *Replication Engine* allows exact duplicates of a database to coexist on multiple systems, with periodic synchronization.

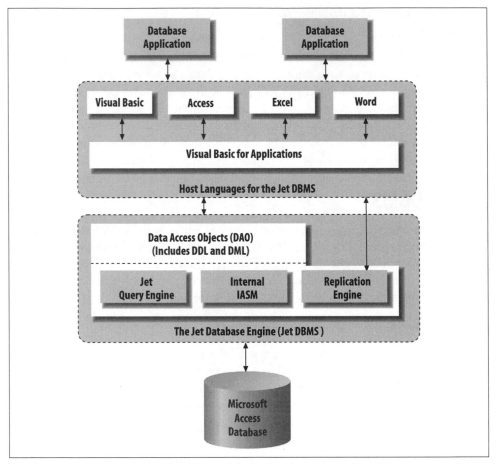

Figure 7-2. The relationships and structure of the Jet Database Engine (DBMS)

The host languages for the Jet DBMS, such as Visual Basic and Access, are used by database programmers to create database applications for specific purposes. For instance, we might create a *Library* database application, which a library can use to maintain information about its books, or an *Order Entry* database application for a small business.

Incidentally, the Jet DBMS is also capable of interfacing with non-Access-formatted databases, such as those with format Xbase (dBase), Paradox, Btrieve, Excel, and delimited text formats. It can also interface with *open database connectivity* (ODBC is discussed in Appendix C) to access server database applications across networks.

Let us take a closer look at the components of the Jet DBMS. We will study these components in much greater detail in separate chapters of the book.

Data Definition Languages

We have already mentioned that a DBMS needs to provide a method for defining new databases. This is done by providing a *data definition language* (DDL) to the programmer. A DDL is not a *procedural language;* that is, its instructions do not actually perform operations. Rather, a DDL is a *definitional language.*

The Jet Data Definition Language

Example 7-1 illustrates the use of the Jet data definition language. The code will run in Visual Basic or in an Access code module, so feel free to key it in and try it yourself. (Use a new database in Access, since some of this code will conflict with the LIBRARY database that we have been working with in earlier chapters.) The purpose is to create a new database called LIBRARY, along with a table called BOOKS, containing two fields, ISBN and TITLE, and one index. (Don't worry if some portions of this code don't make sense to you at this point.) Note that Access uses a space followed by an underscore character (_) to indicate that the next line is a continuation of the current line.

Example 7-1. Use of the Jet data definition language

```
' Data Definition Language example

' Declare variables of the required types
Dim ws As Workspace
Dim dbLibrary As Database
Dim tblBooks As TableDef
Dim fldBooks As Field
Dim idxBooks As Index

' Use the default workspace, called Workspaces(0)
Set ws = DBEngine.Workspaces(0)

' Create a new database named LIBRARY
' in the default Workspace
Set dbLibrary = _
ws.CreateDatabase("d:\dao\library.mdb", _
dbLangGeneral)

' Create a new table called BOOKS
Set tblBooks = dbLibrary.CreateTableDef("BOOKS")

' Define ISBN field and append to the
' table's Fields collection
Set fldBooks = tblBooks.CreateField("ISBN", dbText)
fldBooks.Size = 13
tblBooks.Fields.Append fldBooks

' Define Title field and append to the
' table's Fields collection
Set fldBooks = tblBooks.CreateField("Title", dbText)
```

Example 7-1. Use of the Jet data definition language (continued)

```
fldBooks.Size = 100
tblBooks.Fields.Append fldBooks

' Add the table to the db's Tables collection
dbLibrary.TableDefs.Append tblBooks

' Create an index
Set idxBooks = tblBooks.CreateIndex("ISBNIdx")
idxBooks.Unique = False

' Indices need their own fields
Set fldBooks = idxBooks.CreateField("ISBN")

' Append to the proper collections
idxBooks.Fields.Append fldBooks
tblBooks.Indexes.Append idxBooks
```

As you can see, the clue that we are dealing with a DDL are the commands Create-Database, CreateTableDef, CreateField, and CreateIndex (in boldface for easier identification). You can also see from this code that the Jet DBMS uses the *collections* to hold the properties of an object. For instance, the fields that we create for a table must be appended to the *Fields* collection for that table. This has the advantage that we don't need to keep a separate reference to each field—the collection does that for us. This approach is typical of object-oriented programming.

Data Manipulation Languages

A DBMS must also provide a language designed to manipulate the data in a database. This language is called a *database manipulation language*, or DML. To the database programmer, however, the distinction between a DDL and a DML may be just a logical one, defined more by the purpose of the language than the syntax.

The Jet Data Manipulation Language

Example 7-2 is Jet DML code to add two records to the BOOKS table, set the index, and display the records.

Example 7-2. Jet DML code altering the BOOKS table

```
' Data Manipulation Language example

Dim rsBooks As Recordset

' Open the database
Set dbLibrary = DBEngine.OpenDatabase("d:\dao\library.mdb")

' Create a recordset for the BOOKS table
Set rsBooks = dbLibrary.OpenRecordset("BOOKS")
```

Example 7-2. Jet DML code altering the BOOKS table (continued)

```
' Add two records
rsBooks.AddNew
rsBooks!ISBN = "0-99-345678-0"
rsBooks!Title = "DB Programming is Fun"
rsBooks.Update
rsBooks.AddNew
rsBooks!ISBN = "0-78-654321-0"
rsBooks!Title = "DB Programming isn't Fun"
rsBooks.Update

' Set index
rsBooks.Index = "ISBNIdx"

' Show the records
rsBooks.MoveFirst
MsgBox "ISBN: " & rsBooks!ISBN & "  TI: " & rsBooks!Title
rsBooks.MoveNext
MsgBox "ISBN: " & rsBooks!ISBN & "  TI: " & rsBooks!Title
```

As you can see even from this small example, the DML is designed to perform a variety of actions, such as:

- Moving through the data in the database
- Adding data to the database
- Editing or updating data in the database
- Deleting data from the database
- Querying the data and returning those portions of the data that satisfy the query

Host Languages

Data is seldom manipulated without some intended purpose. For instance, consider a LIBRARY database consisting of information about the books in a library. If a student wishes to access this data, it is probably with the intention of finding a certain book, for which the student has some information, such as the title. On the other hand, if a librarian wishes to access the information, it may be for other purposes, such as determining when the book was added to the library or how much it cost. These issues probably don't interest the student.

The point here is that a DBMS should supply an interface with a high-level language with which programmers can program the database to provide specific services—that is, with which programmers can create database applications. Thus, when a student logs onto a library's computer to search for a book, he may be accessing a different database application than the librarian might access. The language that is used for *database application programming* is the host language for the DBMS. As mentioned earlier, a host language may be a traditional programming language, such as C or COBOL, or it may be an application-level language, such as Microsoft Access or Visual Basic, as it is for the Jet DBMS.

In fact, the Jet DBMS is so tightly integrated into both of these applications that it is hard to tell where one leaves off and the other begins. Put another way, it sometimes seems as though Microsoft Access *is* the Jet DBMS, whereas it is more accurate to say that Access and Visual Basic are *front ends*, or *host applications*, for the Jet DBMS.

The Client/Server Architecture

The client/server model of a database system is really very simple, but its meaning has evolved somewhat through popular usage. The client/server model is shown in Figure 7-3.

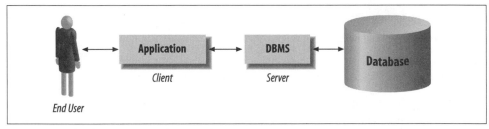

Figure 7-3. The client/server mode example

The server in a client/server model is simply the DBMS, whereas the client is the database application serviced by the DBMS. (We could also think of Visual Basic and Access as clients of the Jet DBMS server.)

The basic client/server model says nothing about the location of the various components. However, since the components are distinct, it is common to find them on different computers. The two most common configurations are illustrated in Figures 7-4 and 7-5. The *distributed client/server model* (Figure 7-4), wherein the client is on one computer and the server and database are on another, is so popular that it is usually simply referred to as the *client/server model*. The *remote database* model (Figure 7-5) refers to the case in which the client and server are on the same computer, but the database is on a remote computer.

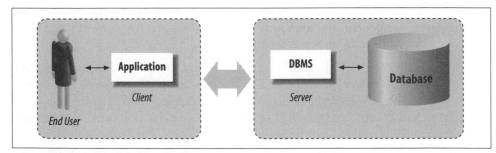

Figure 7-4. The distributed client/server model example

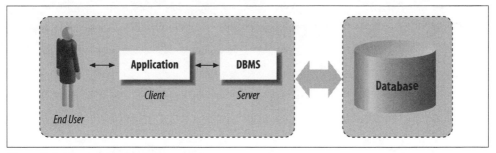

Figure 7-5. The remote database example

PART IV

Visual Basic for Applications

CHAPTER 8

The Visual Basic Editor, Part I

The first step in becoming an Access VBA/DAO programmer is to become familiar with the environment in which Access programming is done. Each of the main Office applications has a programming environment referred to as its *Integrated Development Environment* or IDE. Microsoft also refers to this programming environment as the *Visual Basic Editor*.

My plan in this chapter and the next is to describe the major components of the Access IDE. I realize that you are probably anxious to get to some actual programming, but it is necessary to gain some familiarity with the IDE before you can use it. Nevertheless, you may want to read quickly through this chapter and the next and then refer back to them as needed.

Until the release of Office 2000, not all of the Office Suite applications used the same IDE. In Office 97, Word, Excel, and PowerPoint use the full VBA IDE, whereas Access 97 uses a simple code module environment. However, with the appearance of Access 9 for Office 2000, all four of the Office applications use the same IDE, as show in Figure 8-1. To start the Access IDE, simply choose *Visual Basic Editor* from the *Macros* submenu of the *Tools* menu, or hit Alt+F11.

Let us take a look at some of the components of this IDE.

The Project Window

The window in the upper-left corner of the client area (below the toolbar) is called the *Project Explorer*. Figure 8-2 shows a close-up of this window.

Note that the Project Explorer has a tree-like structure, similar to the Windows Explorer's folders pane (the left-hand pane). Each entry in the Project Explorer is called a *node*. The top nodes, of which there are two in Figure 8-2, represent the currently open Access VBA *projects* (hence the name Project Explorer). The view of each project can be expanded or contracted by clicking on the small boxes (just as with Windows Explorer).

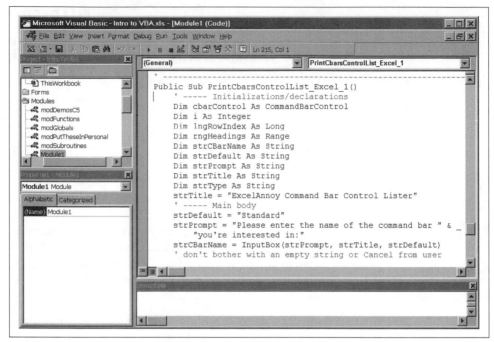

Figure 8-1. The Access VBA IDE

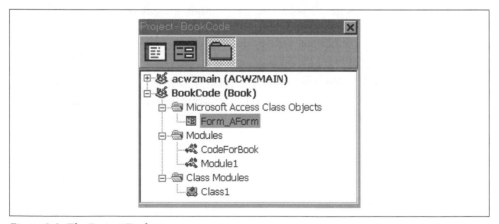

Figure 8-2. The Project Explorer

As you know, Access is a *single document interface* (SDI) program, meaning that you can only open one database for each session of Access. Each Access session has its own IDE as well. Hence, the project window for a given instance of the IDE will contain only one *user* project. However, as you can see in Figure 8-2, Access may add another project to the project window. The ACWZMAIN project in Figure 8-2 was added when I invoked the Access wizard to create a table, for instance. If you try to access any of the code in the ACWZMAIN project, you will be rewarded with a "Project Unviewable" error message.

Project Names

Each project has a name, which the programmer can choose. The default name for a project is the name of the database. The top node for each project is labeled:

    ProjectName (DatabaseName)

where *ProjectName* is the name of the project and *DatabaseName* is the name of the Access database. The name of the project can be changed using the Properties window, which I will discuss a bit later.

Project Contents

At the level immediately below the top (project) level, as Figure 8-2 shows, there are nodes named:

> Microsoft Access Class Objects
> Modules
> Class Modules

Under the Microsoft Access Class Objects node, there is a node for each Access form in the database that contains some code (just creating a form does not add a node to the Projects window). The form nodes provide access to the code module "behind" the form, where we can write code to implement events, such as clicking on a command button.

In fact, Access forms have two components—a user-interface component (the form's background and any controls on the form) and a code component. By right-clicking on a form node, we can choose to view the object itself or the code component for that object. I will not discuss creating Access forms in this book, however.

Standard modules

Under the Modules node, there is a node for each *standard module* in the project. By double-clicking on the node for a standard module, Access will display the code window for that module. A standard module is a code module that contains general procedures. VBA allows two kinds of procedures: functions and subroutines. The only difference between a function and a subroutine is that a function returns a value, whereas a subroutine does not. I will discuss functions and subroutines in Chapter 11.

These procedures may be intended to be run by the user (in response to a button click, for instance), or they may be support programs that are intended to be run by code from within other procedures (in the same or other modules).

Class modules

Under the Classes node, there is a node for each *class module* in the project. By double-clicking on a class module node, Access will display the code window for the corresponding class module.

Class modules are code modules that contain code related to custom objects. The Access object model contains built-in objects representing such objects as forms and reports. It is also possible to create custom objects and endow them with various properties. To do so, we would place the appropriate code within a class module.

However, since creating custom objects is beyond the scope of this book, we will not be using class modules. (For an introduction to object-oriented programming using VB, allow me to suggest my book, *Concepts of Object-Oriented Programming with Visual Basic*, published by Springer-Verlag, New York.)

The Properties Window

The Properties window (see Figure 8-1) displays the properties of an object and allows us to change them.

When a standard module is selected in the Project window, the only property that appears in the Properties window is the module's name. However, when a form is selected in the Projects window, many of the object's properties appear in the Properties window, as shown in Figure 8-3.

The Properties window can be used to change some of the properties of the object while no code is running, that is, at *design time*. (Note that while most properties can be changed either at design time or *runtime*, some properties can only be changed at design time and some can only be changed at runtime. Runtime properties generally do not appear in the Properties window.)

The Code Window

The Code window displays the code that is associated with the selected item in the Projects window. To view this code, select the item in the Projects window, and either choose *Code* from the *View* menu or hit the F7 function key. For objects with only a code component (that is, standard or class modules), you can just double-click on the item in the Projects window.

Procedure and Full-Module Views

Generally, a code module contains more than one procedure. The IDE offers the choice between viewing one procedure at a time (called *procedure view*) or all procedures at one time (called *full-module view*), with a horizontal line separating the procedures. Each view has its advantages and disadvantages, and you will probably want to use both views at different times. Unfortunately, Microsoft has not supplied a menu choice for selecting the view. (I've complained about this in my other books as well, but Microsoft does not seem to be listening to me. Strange.) To change views, click on the small buttons in the lower-left corner of the Code window. (The default view can be set using the *Editor* tab of the *Options* dialog box.)

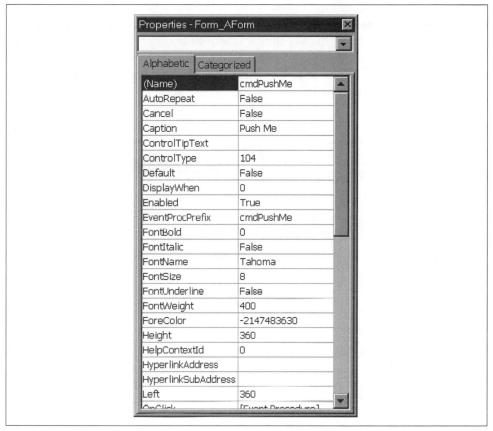

Figure 8-3. The Properties window

Incidentally, the default font for the module window is Courier, which has a rather thin looking appearance and may be somewhat difficult to read. You may want to change the font to FixedSys (on the *Editor Format* tab of the *Options* dialog box, under the *Tools* menu), which is much more readable.

The Object and Procedure Listboxes

At the top of the Code window there are two drop-down listboxes (see Figure 8-1). The Object box contains a list of the objects that are associated with the current project, and the Procedure box contains a list of all of the procedures associated with the object selected in the Object box. The precise contents of these boxes vary depending on the type of object selected in the Project Explorer.

When a standard module is selected in the Project window, the Object box contains only the entry (*General*), because there are no objects in a standard module with which to associate code (or any objects at all). In this case, the Procedure listbox contains a list of the current procedures in that module.

When a form is selected, the Objects listbox contains a list of each control on the form, as well as entries for page and form headers and footers, the detail section of the form, and so on. As Figure 8-4 shows, when we select an object, such as a command button, in the Objects listbox, the Procedures listbox contains a list of procedures for that object. When selecting a procedure, Access will automatically place the cursor in the appropriate location in the code window, so we can start entering code.

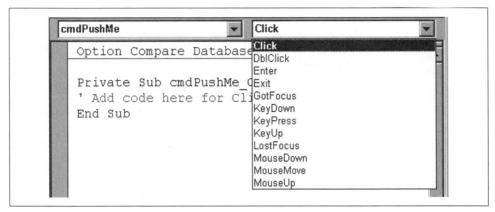

Figure 8-4. The events for a Workbook object

For example, if we choose the *Click* event in the Procedures box, Access will create the following code shell for this event, and place the cursor within this procedure:

```
Private Sub cmdPushMe_Click( )

End Sub
```

The Immediate Window

The Immediate window (see Figure 8-1) has two main functions. First, we can send output to this window using the command Debug.Print. For instance, the code shown in Figure 8-5 produces the result shown in the Immediate window (there were four records in the recordset when I executed this code). (We will see how to execute the code in a procedure shortly.) This provides a nice way to experiment with different code snippets.

The other main function of the Immediate window is to execute commands. We can enter a line of code directly in the Immediate window. Hitting the Enter key at the end of the line asks Access to execute that line of code. Note that this only works for single physical lines of code, but you can place more than one logical line of code on the same physical line by separating the logical lines with colons, as in:

```
For i = 1 To 10: Debug.Print i: Next i
```

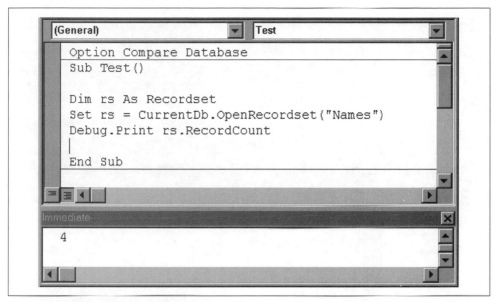

Figure 8-5. The Immediate window

The Immediate window is an extremely valuable tool for debugging a program, and you will probably use it often (as I do).

Arranging Windows

If you need more space for writing code, you can close the Properties window, the Project window, and the Immediate window. On the other hand, if you are fortunate enough to have a large monitor, then you can split your screen as shown in Figure 8-6 in order to see the Access VBA IDE and the corresponding Access database at the same time. In some cases (but not all), you can trace through each line of your code and watch the results in the database! (You can toggle between Access and the IDE using the Alt+F11 function key combination.)

Docking

Many of the windows in the IDE (including the Project, Properties, and Immediate windows) can be in one of two states: docked or floating. This state can be set using the Docking tab on the Options dialog box, which is shown in Figure 8-7.

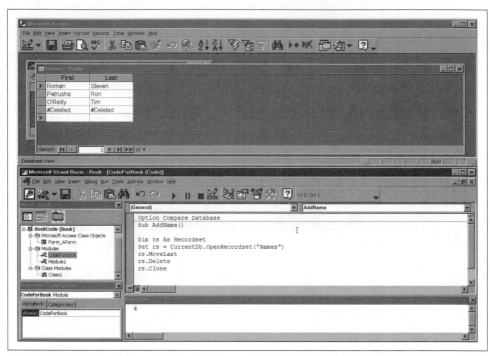

Figure 8-6. A split-screen approach

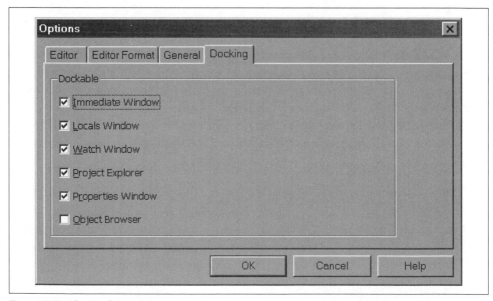

Figure 8-7. The Docking options

A *docked* window is attached, or anchored, to an edge of another window or an edge of the main VBA window's client area. When a dockable window is moved, it snaps to an anchored position. A floating window can be placed anywhere on the screen.

CHAPTER 9

The Visual Basic Editor, Part II

In this chapter, we conclude our discussion of the Visual Basic Editor. Again, I remind the reader that she may want to read quickly through this chapter and refer to it later as needed.

Navigating the IDE

If you prefer the keyboard to the mouse (as I do), then you may want to use keyboard shortcuts. Here are some tips.

General Navigation

The following keyboard shortcuts are used for navigating the IDE:

F7	Go to the Code window.
F4	Go to the Properties window.
Ctrl-R	Go to the Project window.
Ctrl-G	Go to the Immediate window.
Alt+F11	Toggle between Access and VB IDE.

Navigating the code window at design time

Within the code window, the following keystrokes are very useful:

F1	Help on the item under the cursor.
Shift+F2	Go to the definition of the item under the cursor. (If the cursor is over a call to a function or subroutine, hitting Shift+F2 sends you to the definition of that procedure.)
Control+ Shift+F2	Return to the last position where editing took place.

Tracing code

The following keystrokes are useful when tracing through code (discussed later):

F8	Step into
Shift+F8	Step over
Ctrl+Shift+F8	Step out
Ctrl+F8	Run to cursor
F5	Run
Ctrl+Break	Break
Shift+F9	Quick watch
F9	Toggle breakpoint
Ctrl+Shift+F9	Clear all breakpoints

Bookmarks

It is also possible to insert *bookmarks* within code. A bookmark marks a location to which we can return easily. To insert a bookmark, or to move to the next or previous bookmark, use the *Bookmarks* submenu of the *Edit* menu. The presence of a bookmark is indicated by a small blue square in the left margin of the code.

Getting Help

The simplest way to get help on any particular item is to place the cursor on that item and hit the F1 key. This works not only for VBA language keywords but also for portions of the VBA IDE.

Note that Microsoft provides multiple help files for Access, the VBA language, and the Access object model. While this is quite reasonable, occasionally the help system gets a bit confused and refuses to display the correct help file when I strike the F1 key.

Note also that a standard installation of Microsoft Office does not install the VBA help files for the various applications. Thus, you may need to run the Office setup program and install Access VBA help by selecting that option in the appropriate setup dialog box. (Do not confuse Access help with Access VBA help.)

Creating a Procedure

There are two ways to create a new procedure (that is, a subroutine or a function) within a code module. First, after selecting the correct project in the Project Explorer, we can select the *Procedure* option from the *Insert* menu. This will produce the dialog box shown in Figure 9-1. Just type in the name of the procedure, and select *Sub* or *Function* (the *Property* choice is used with custom objects in a class module). We will discuss the issue of Public versus Private procedures and static variables later in this chapter.

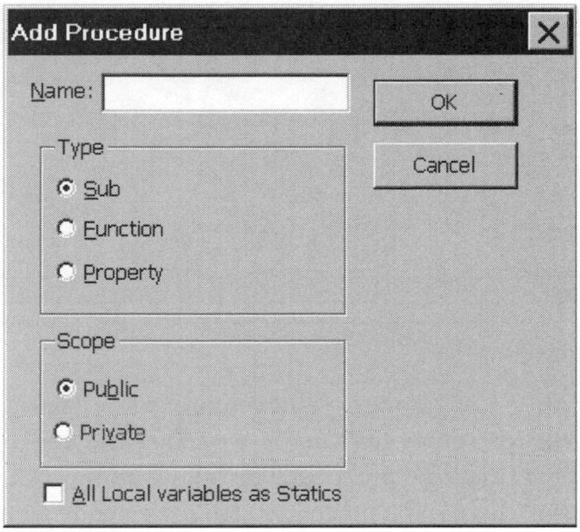

Figure 9-1. The Add Procedure dialog box

A simpler alternative is to begin typing:

```
Sub SubName
```

or:

```
Function FunctionName
```

in any code window (following the current End Sub or End Function statement, or in the general declarations section). As soon as the Enter key is struck, Access will move the line of code to a new location and thereby create a new subroutine. (It will even add the appropriate ending—End Sub or End Function.)

Run Mode, Break Mode, and Design Mode

The VBA IDE can be in any one of three modes: *run mode*, *break mode*, or *design mode*. When the IDE is in design mode, we can write code.

Run mode occurs when a procedure is running. To run (or execute) a procedure, just place the cursor anywhere within the procedure code, and hit the F5 key (or select *Run* from the *Run* menu). If for some reason a running procedure seems to be hanging, we can usually stop the procedure by hitting Ctrl+Break (hold down the Control key and hit the Break key).

Break mode is entered when a running procedure stops because of either an error in the code or a deliberate act on our part (described a bit later). In particular, if an error occurs, Access will stop execution and display an error dialog box, an example of which is shown in Figure 9-2.

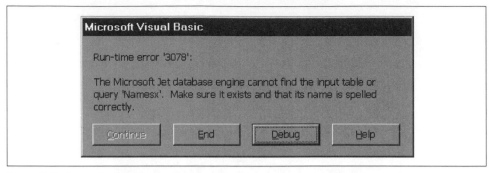

Figure 9-2. An error message

Error dialog boxes offer a few options: end the procedure, get help (such as it may be) with the problem, or enter break mode to debug the code. In the latter case, Access will stop execution of the procedure at the offending code and highlight that code in yellow. We will discuss the process of debugging code a bit later.

Aside from encountering an error, there are several ways we can deliberately enter break mode for debugging purposes:

- Hit the Ctrl+Break keys, and choose *Debug* from the resulting dialog box.

- Include a Stop statement in the code, which causes Access to enter break mode.

- Insert a *breakpoint* on an existing line of executable code. This is done by placing the cursor on that line and hitting the F9 function key (or using the *Toggle Breakpoint* option on the *Debug* menu). Access will place a red dot in the left margin in front of that line and stop execution when it reaches the line. You may enter more than one breakpoint in a procedure. This is generally preferred over using the Stop statement, because breakpoints are automatically removed when we close down the Visual Basic Editor; therefore, we don't need to remember to remove them, as we do with Stop statements.

- Set a watch statement that causes Access to enter break mode if a certain condition becomes true. We will discuss watch expressions a bit later.

To exit from break mode, choose *Reset* from the *Run* menu.

Note that the caption in the title bar of the VBA IDE indicates which mode is currently active. The caption contains the word "[running]" when in run mode and "[break]" when in break mode.

Errors

In computer jargon, an error is referred to as a *bug*. In case you are interested in the origin of this word, the story goes that when operating the first large-scale digital computer, called the Mark I, an error was traced to a moth that had found its way into the hardware. Incidentally, the Mark I (circa 1944) had 750,000 parts, was

51 feet long, and weighed over 5 tons. How about putting that on your desktop? It also executed about one instruction every 6 seconds, as compared to over 200 million instructions per second for a Pentium!

Errors can be grouped into three types based on when they occur—*design time*, *compile time*, or *runtime*.

Design-Time and Compile-Time Errors

As the name implies, a *design-time error* occurs during the writing of code. Perhaps the nicest feature of the Visual Basic Editor is that it can be instructed to watch as we type code and stop us when we make a syntax error. This automatic syntax checking can be enabled or disabled in the Options dialog box shown in Figure 9-3, but I strongly suggest that you keep it enabled.

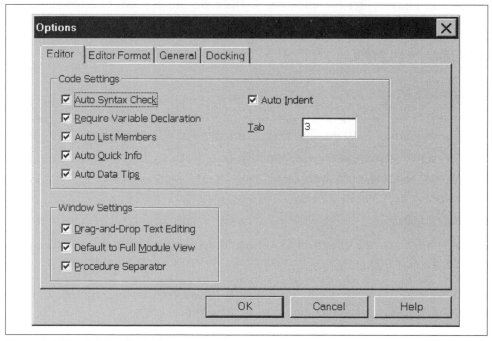

Figure 9-3. The Options dialog box

Notice also that there are other settings related to the design-time environment, such as how far to indent code in response to the Tab key. We will discuss some of these other settings a bit later.

Illustrating automatic syntax checking, Figure 9-4 shows what happens when we deliberately enter the syntactically incorrect statement x == 5 and then attempt to move to another line. Note that Microsoft refers to this type of error as a *compile error* in the dialog box, and perhaps we should as well. However, it seems more descriptive to call it a design-time error or just a syntax error.

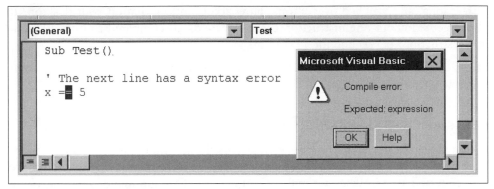

Figure 9-4. A syntax error message

Before a program can be executed, it must be *compiled*—or translated into a language that the computer can understand. The compilation process occurs automatically when we request that a program be executed. We can also specifically request compilation by choosing the *Compile Project* item under the *Debug* menu. If Access encounters an error while compiling code, it displays a compile-error message.

Runtime Errors

An error that occurs while a program is running is called a *runtime error*. Figure 9-2 illustrates a runtime error message that occurred in response to the line:

```
Set rs = CurrentDb.OpenRecordset("Namesx")
```

because no table named *Namesx* exists.

Logical Errors

There is one more type of error that we should discuss, since it is the most insidious type of all. A *logical error* can be defined as the production of an unexpected and incorrect result. As far as Access is concerned, there is no error, because Access has no way of knowing what we intend. (Thus, a logical error is *not* a runtime error in the traditional sense, even though it does occur at runtime.)

To illustrate, the following code purports to compute the average of some numbers:

```
Dim x(3) As Integer
Dim Ave As Single
x(0) = 1
x(1) = 3
x(2) = 8
x(3) = 5
Ave = (x(0) + x(1) + x(2) + x(3)) / 3
MsgBox "Average is: " & Ave
```

The result is the message box shown in Figure 9-5. Unfortunately, it is incorrect. The penultimate line in the preceding program should be:

```
Ave = (x(0) + x(1) + x(2) + x(3)) / 4
```

Note the 4 in the denominator, since there are 4 numbers to average. The correct average is 4.25. Of course, Access will not complain because it has no way of knowing whether we really want to divide by 3.

Figure 9-5. The result of a logical error

Precisely because Access cannot warn us about logical errors, they are the most dangerous, because we *think* that everything is correct.

Debugging

Invariably, you will encounter errors in your code. Design-time and compile-time errors are relatively easy to deal with because Access helps us out with error messages and by indicating the offending code. Logical errors are much more difficult to detect and fix. This is where debugging plays a major role. The Access IDE provides some very powerful ways to find bugs.

Debugging can be quite involved, and we could include a whole chapter on the subject. There are even special software applications designed to assist in complex debugging tasks. However, for most purposes, a few simple techniques are sufficient. In particular, Access makes it easy to *trace* through a program, executing one line at a time, watching the effect of each line as it is executed.

Let us discuss some of the tools that Access provides for debugging code.

Tracing

The process of executing code one line at a time is referred to as *tracing* or *code stepping*. Access provides three options related to tracing: stepping into, stepping over, and stepping out of. The difference between these methods refers to handling calls to other procedures.

To illustrate the difference, consider the code shown in Example 9-1. In ProcedureA, the first line of code adds a new record to a recordset denoted by rs. The second line calls ProcedureB, and the third line updates the recordset. ProcedureB sets the value of the LastName and FirstName fields for the current record. Don't worry about the exact syntax of this code. The important thing to notice is that the second line of ProcedureA calls ProcedureB.

Example 9-1. Sample code for tracing methods

```
Sub ProcedureA( )
    rs.AddNew              ' Add a new record
    Call ProcedureB
    rs.Update              ' Update recordset
End Sub

Sub ProcedureB( )
    rs!LastName = "Smith"
    rs!FirstName = "John"
End Sub
```

Step Into (F8 or choose Step Into from the Debug menu)

Step Into executes code one statement (or instruction) at a time. If the statement being executed calls another procedure, stepping into that statement simply transfers control to the first line in the called procedure. For instance, with reference to the previous code, stepping into the line:

```
Call ProcedureB
```

in ProcedureA transfers control to the first line of ProcedureB:

```
rs!LastName = "Smith"
```

Further tracing proceeds in ProcedureB. Once all of the lines of ProcedureB have been traced, control returns to ProcedureA at the line immediately following the call to ProcedureB, that is, at the line:

```
rs.Update
```

Step Into has another important use. If we choose Step Into while still in design mode—that is, before any code is running—execution begins, but break mode is entered *before* the first line of code is actually executed. This is the proper way to begin tracing a program.

Step Over (Shift+F8 or choose Step Over from the Debug menu)

Step Over is similar to Step Into, except that if the current statement being traced is a call to another procedure, the entire called procedure is executed without stopping (rather than tracing through the called procedure). Thus, for instance, stepping over the line:

```
Call ProcedureB
```

in the previous procedure executes `ProcedureB` and stops at the next line:

```
rs.Update
```

in `ProcedureA`. This is useful if we are certain that `ProcedureB` is not the cause of the problem and we don't want to trace through that procedure line by line.

Step Out (Ctrl+Shift+F8 or choose Step Out from the Debug menu)

Step Out is intended to be used within a called procedure (such as `ProcedureB`). Step Out executes the remaining lines of the called procedure and returns to the calling procedure (such as `ProcedureA`). This is useful if we are in the middle of a called procedure, and we decide that we don't need to trace any more of that procedure but want to return to the calling procedure. (If you trace into a called procedure by mistake, just do a Step Out to return to the calling procedure.)

Run to Cursor (Ctrl+F8 or choose Run To Cursor from the Debug menu)

If the Visual Basic Editor is in break mode, we may want to execute several lines of code at one time. This can be done using the *Run To Cursor* feature. Simply place the cursor on the statement immediately following the last line you want to execute and then execute.

Set Next Statement (Ctrl+F9 or choose Set Next Statement from the Debug menu)

We can also change the flow of execution while in break mode by placing the cursor on the next statement that we want to execute and selecting *Set Next Statement* from the *Debug* menu. This will set the selected statement as the next statement to execute, but not execute it until we continue tracing.

Breaking out of Debug mode

When we no longer need to trace our code, we have two choices. To return to design mode, we can choose *Reset* from the *Run* menu (there is no hotkey for this). To have Access finish executing the current program, we can hit F5 or choose Run from the *Run* menu.

CHAPTER 10

Variables, Data Types, and Constants

In the next few chapters, we will discuss the basics of the VBA programming language, which underlies all of the Microsoft Office programming environments. During our discussion, we will consider many short coding examples. I hope that you will take the time to key in some of these examples and experiment with them.

Comments

We have already discussed the fact that comments are important. Any text that follows an apostrophe is considered a comment and is ignored by Access. For example, the first line in the following code is a comment, as is everything following the apostrophe on the third line:

```
' Declare a recordset variable
Dim rs As Recordset
Set rs = CurrentDb.OpenRecordset("Names")    ' Get recordset for Names
```

When debugging code, it is often useful to comment out lines of code temporarily so they will not execute. The lines can subsequently be uncommented to restore them to active duty. The CommentBlock and UncommentBlock buttons, which can be found on the Edit toolbar, will place or remove comment marks from each currently selected line of code and are very useful for commenting out several lines of code in one step. (Unfortunately, there are no keyboard shortcuts for these commands, but they can be added to a menu and given menu accelerator keys.)

Line Continuation

The very nature of Access VBA syntax often leads to long lines of code, which can be difficult to read, especially if we need to scroll horizontally to see the entire line. For this reason, Microsoft recently introduced a line-continuation character into VBA. This character is the underscore, which *must* be preceded by a space and cannot be followed by any other characters (including comments). For example, the following code:

```
Set rs = CurrentDb.OpenRecordset("Names", _
    dbOpenForwardOnly)
```

is treated as one line by Access.

It is important to note that a line-continuation character cannot be inserted in the middle of a literal string constant, which is enclosed in quotation marks.

Constants

The VBA language has two types of constants. A *literal constant* (also called a *constant* or *literal*) is a specific value, such as a number, date, or text string, that does not change and is used exactly as written. Note that string constants are enclosed in double quotation marks, as in "Donna Smith", and date constants are enclosed between number signs, as in #1/1/96#.

For instance, the following code stores a date in the variable called *dt*:

```
Dim dt As Date
dt = #1/2/97#
```

A *symbolic constant* (also sometimes referred to simply as a *constant*) is a name for a literal constant. To define or declare a symbolic constant in a program, we use the Const keyword, as in:

```
Const InvoicePath = "d:\Invoices\"
```

In this case, Access will replace every instance of InvoicePath in our code with the string "d:\Invoices\". Thus, InvoicePath is a constant, since it never changes value, but it is not a literal constant, since it is not used as written.

The virtue of using symbolic constants is that, if we decide later to change "d:\Invoices\" to "d:\OldInvoices\", we only need to change the definition of InvoicePath to:

```
Const InvoicePath = "d:\OldInvoices\"
```

rather than searching through the entire program for every occurrence of the phrase "d:\Invoices\".

Note that it is generally good programming practice to declare any symbolic constants at the beginning of the procedure in which they are used (or in the Declarations section of a code module). This improves readability and makes housekeeping simpler.

In addition to the symbolic constants that you can define using the Const statement, VBA has a large number of built-in symbolic constants (about 700), whose names begin with the lowercase letters *vb*. Access VBA adds several hundred additional symbolic constants that begin with the letters *ac*.

Among the most commonly used VBA constants are `vbCrLf`, which is equivalent to a carriage return followed by a line feed, and `vbTab`, which is equivalent to the tab character.

Enums

Microsoft has introduced a structure into VBA to categorize the plethora of symbolic constants. This structure is called an *enum*, which is short for *enumeration*. For instance, the built-in enum for the constant values that can be returned when the user dismisses a message box (by clicking on a button) is:

```
Enum VbMsgBoxResult
    vbOK = 1
    vbCancel = 2
    vbAbort = 3
    vbRetry = 4
    vbIgnore = 5
    vbYes = 6
    vbNo = 7
End Enum
```

When the user hits the OK button on a dialog box (assuming it has one), VBA returns the value `vbOK`. Certainly, it is a lot easier to remember that VBA will return the symbolic constant `vbOK` than to remember that it will return the constant 1. (We will discuss how to get and use this return value later.)

VBA also defines some symbolic constants that are used to set the types of buttons that will appear on a message box. These are contained in the following enum (which includes some additional constants not shown):

```
Enum VbMsgBoxStyle
    vbOKOnly = 0
    vbOKCancel = 1
    vbAbortRetryIgnore = 2
    vbYesNoCancel = 3
    vbYesNo = 4
    vbRetryCancel = 5
End Enum
```

To illustrate, consider the following code:

```
If MsgBox("Proceed?", vbOKCancel) = vbOK Then
    ' place code to execute when user hits OK button
Else
    ' place code to execute when user hits any other button
End If
```

In the first line, the code `MsgBox("Proceed?", vbOKCancel)` causes Access to display a message box with an OK button and a Cancel button and the message "Proceed?", as shown in Figure 10-1.

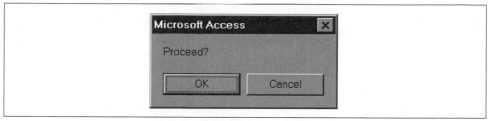

Figure 10-1. Example message box

If the user clicks the OK button, Access returns the constant value vbOK; otherwise, it returns the value vbCancel. Thus, the If statement in the first line distinguishs between the two responses. (We will discuss the If statement in detail in Chapter 13. Here we are interested in the role of symbolic constants.)

In case you are not yet convinced of the value of symbolic constants, consider the following enum for color constants:

```
Enum ColorConstants
    vbBlack = 0
    vbBlue = 16711680
    vbMagenta = 16711935
    vbCyan = 16776960
    vbWhite = 16777215
    vbRed = 255
    vbGreen = 65280
    vbYellow = 65535
End Enum
```

Which would you rather type:

```
ATextBox.ForeColor = vbBlue
```

or:

```
ATextBox.ForeColor = 16711680
```

Need I say more?

Variables and Data Types

A *variable* can be thought of as a memory location that can hold values of a specific type. The value in a variable may change during the life of the program—hence the name variable.

In VBA, each variable has a specific *data type*, which indicates which type of data it may hold. For instance, a variable that holds text strings has a String data type and is called a string variable. A variable that holds integers (whole numbers) has an Integer data type and is called an integer variable. For reference, Table 10-1 shows the complete set of VBA data types, along with the amount of memory that they consume and their range of values. We will discuss a few of the more commonly used data types in a moment.

Table 10-1. VBA data types

Type	Size in memory	Range of values
Byte	1 byte	0 to 255
Boolean	2 bytes	True or False
Integer	2 bytes	−32,768 to 32,767
Long (long integer)	4 bytes	−2,147,483,648 to 2,147,483,647
Single (single-precision real)	4 bytes	Approximately −3.4E38 to 3.4E38
Double (double-precision real)	8 bytes	Approximately −1.8E308 to 4.9E324
Currency (scaled integer)	8 bytes	Approximately −922,337,203,685,477.5808 to 922,337,203,685,477.5807
Date	8 bytes	1/1/100 to 12/31/9999
Object	4 bytes	Any Object reference
String	Variable length: 10 bytes + string length; Fixed length: string length	Variable length: <= about 2 billion (65,400 for Win 3.1) Fixed length: up to 65,400
Variant	16 bytes for numbers	Number: same as Double
	22 bytes + string length	String: same as String
User-defined	Varies	

Variable Declaration

To *declare* a variable means to define its data type. Variables are declared with the Dim keyword (or with the keywords Private and Public, which we will discuss later in this chapter). Here are some examples:

```
Dim Name As String
Dim Holiday As Date
Dim Age As Integer
Dim Height As Single
Dim Money As Currency
Dim db as Database
Dim rs as Recordset
```

The general syntax of a variable declaration is:

```
Dim VariableName As DataType
```

If a particular variable is used without first being declared, or if it is declared without a data type mentioned, as in Dim Age, then VBA will treat the variable as having type Variant. As we can see from Table 10-1, this is generally a waste of memory, since variants require more memory than most other types of variables.

For instance, an integer variable requires 2 bytes, whereas a variant that holds the same integer requires 16 bytes, which is a waste of 14 bytes. It is common to have hundreds or even thousands of variables in a complex program, and so the memory waste could be significant. For this reason, it is a good idea to declare all variables.

Perhaps more importantly, much more overhead is involved in maintaining a Variant than its corresponding String or Integer, for example. This in turn means that using Variants typically results in worse performance than using an equivalent set of explicit data types.

We can place more than one declaration on a line to save space. For instance, the line:

```
Dim Age As Integer, Name As String, Money As Currency
```

declares three variables. Note, however, that a declaration such as:

```
Dim Age, Height, Weight As Integer
```

is legal, but Age and Height are declared as Variants, not Integers. In other words, we must specify the type for each variable explicitly.

It is also possible to tell VBA the type of the variable by appending a special character to the variable name. In particular, VBA allows the type-declaration suffixes shown in Table 10-2. (I personally dislike these suffixes, but they do save space.)

Table 10-2. Type-declaration suffixes

Suffix	Type
%	integer
&	long
!	single
#	double
@	currency
$	string

For instance, the line:

```
Dim Name$
```

declares a variable called Name$ of type String. We can then write:

```
Name$ = "Donna"
```

Finally, let us note that although Access allows variable and constant declarations to be placed anywhere within a procedure (before the item is used, that is), it is generally good programming practice to place all such declarations at the *beginning* of the procedure. This improves code readability and makes housekeeping much simpler.

The Importance of Explicit Variable Declaration

I have said that using the Variant data type generally wastes memory and often results in poorer performance, and that all variables are assumed to be variants unless you specify otherwise. There is an additional, even more important reason to declare all variables explicitly. This has to do with making typing errors, which we all do from time to time. In particular, if we accidentally misspell a variable name, VBA will think we mean to create a new variable!

Option Explicit

To avoid this problem, we need a way to make Access refuse to run a program if it contains any variables that we have not explicitly declared. This is done simply by placing the line:

```
Option Explicit
```

in the Declarations section of each code module. Since it is easy to forget to do this, VBA provides an option called *Require Variable Declaration* in its *Options* dialog box. When this option is selected, VBA automatically inserts the `Option Explicit` line for us. Therefore, I strongly recommend that you enable this option.

Now let us briefly discuss some of the data types in Table 10-1.

Numeric Data Types

The numeric data types include Integer, Long, Single, Double, and Currency. A long is also sometimes referred to as a *long integer*.

Boolean Data Type

A Boolean variable is a variable that takes on one of two values: `True` or `False`. This is a very useful data type that was only recently introduced into VBA. Prior to its introduction, VBA recognized 0 as `False` and any nonzero value as `True`, and you may still see this usage in older code.

String Data Type

A string is a sequence of characters. (An empty string has no characters, however.) A string may contain ordinary text characters (letters, digits, and punctuation), as well as special control characters such as `vbCrLf` (carriage return/line feed characters) or `vbTab` (tab character). As we have seen, a string constant is enclosed within quotation marks. An empty string is denoted by a pair of adjacent quotation marks, as in:

```
EmptyString = ""
```

There are two types of string variables in VBA: fixed-length and variable-length. A fixed-length string variable is declared as follows:

```
Dim FixedStringVarName As String * StringLen
```

where `StringLen` specifies the number of characters reserved for the string. For instance, the following statement declares a fixed-length string of length 10 characters:

```
Dim sName As String * 10
```

Observe that the following code, which concatenates two strings:

```
Dim s As String * 10
s = "test"
Debug.Print s & "/"
```

produces the output:

```
test      /
```

This shows that the content of a fixed-length string is padded with spaces in order to reach the correct length.

A variable-length string variable is a variable that can hold strings of varying lengths (at different times, of course). Variable-length string variables are declared simply as:

```
Dim VariableStringVarName as String
```

As an example, the code:

```
Dim s As String
s = "test"
Debug.Print s & "/"
s = "another test"
Debug.Print s & "/"
```

produces the output:

```
test/
another test/
```

Variable-length string variables are used much more often than fixed-length strings, although the latter have some very specific and important uses (which I will not go into in this book).

Date Data Type

Variables of the Date data type require 8 bytes of storage and are actually stored as decimal (floating-point) numbers that represent dates ranging from January 1, 100 to December 31, 9999 (no year 2000 problem here) and times from 0:00:00 to 23:59:59.

As discussed earlier, literal dates are enclosed within number signs, but when assigning a date to a date variable, we can also use valid dates in string format. For example, the following are all valid date/time assignments:

```
Dim dt As Date
dt = #1/2/98#
dt = "January 12, 2001"
dt = #1/1/95#
dt = #12:50:00 PM#
dt = #1/13/76 12:50:00 PM#
```

VBA has a large number of functions that can manipulate dates and times. If you need to manipulate dates or times in your programs, you should probably spend some time with the Access VBA help file. (Start by looking under "Date Data Type.")

Variant Data Type

The Variant data type provides a catch-all data type that is capable of holding data of any other type except fixed-length string data and user-defined types. I have already noted the virtues and vices of the Variant data type and discussed why variants should generally be avoided.

Access Object Data Types

Access VBA/DAO has a number of additional data types that fall under the general category of Object data type. Here is a sampling:

Some Access objects
    Form
    Module
    Report
    Control
    Section

Some DAO objects
    Workspace
    Database
    Recordset
    Field
    Error
    User

Thus, we can declare variables such as:

```
Dim fm As Form
Dim ws As Workspace
Dim db As Database
Dim rs As Recordset
Dim fld As Field
```

I devote much of this book to studying the objects in the DAO object model, for it is through these objects that we can manipulate Access databases programmatically. (I will briefly describe the Access object model as well, but not go into its details, for its primary use is to manipulate Access forms and reports, not actual data. In fact, the Access object model does not even have a Table object!)

The generic As Object declaration

It is also possible to declare any Access object using the generic-object data type Object, as in the following example:

```
Dim rs As Object
```

While you may see this declaration from time to time, it is much less efficient than a specific object declaration, such as:

```
Dim rs As Recordset
```

This is because Access cannot tell what type of object the variable rs refers to until the program is running, so it must use some execution time to make this determination. This is referred to as *late binding* and can make programs run significantly more slowly.

The Set statement

Declaring object variables is done in the same way as declaring nonobject variables. For instance, here are two variable declarations:

```
Dim int As Integer     ' nonobject (standard) variable declaration
Dim db As Database     ' object variable declaration
```

On the other hand, when it comes to assigning a value to variables, the syntax differs for object and nonobject variables. In particular, we must use the Set keyword when assigning a value to an object variable. For example, the following line assigns the current Access database to the variable db:

```
Set db = CurrentDb
```

Arrays

An *array variable* is a collection of variables that use the same name, but are distinguished by an index value. For instance, to store 10 fields objects in variables, we could declare an array variable as follows:

```
Dim MyFields(1 To 10) As Field
```

The array variable is MyFields. It has size 10. The lower bound of the array is 1, and the upper bound is 10. Each of the variables:

```
MyFields(1), MyFields(2),..., MyFields(10)
```

are Field variables. Note that if we omit the first index in the declaration, as in:

```
Dim MyFields(10) As Field
```

then VBA will automatically set the first index to 0, so the size of the array will be 11.

The virtue of declaring array variables is clear, since it would be very unpleasant to have to declare 10 separate variables. In addition, as we will see, there are ways to work collectively with all of the elements in an array, using a few simple programming constructs. For instance, the following code sets all 10 Field types to Integer:

```
For i = 1 To 10
    MyFields(i).Type = dbInteger
Next i
```

The dimension of an array

The MyFields array defined in the previous example has *dimension* one. We can also define arrays of more than one dimension. For instance, the array:

```
Dim Stats(1 To 10, 1 To 100) As Integer
```

is a two-dimensional array whose first index ranges from 1 to 10 and whose second index ranges from 1 to 100. Thus, the array has size $10 \times 100 = 1000$.

Dynamic arrays

When an array is declared, as in:

```
Dim FileName(1 To 10) As String
```

the upper and lower bounds are both specified, and so the size of the array is fixed. However, there are many situations in which we do not know at declaration time how large an array we may need. For this reason, VBA provides dynamic arrays and the ReDim statement.

A dynamic array is declared with empty parentheses, as in:

```
Dim FileName( ) as String
```

Dynamic arrays can be sized (or resized) using the ReDim statement, as in:

```
ReDim FileName(1 to 10)
```

This same array can later be resized again, as in:

```
ReDim FileName(1 to 100)
```

Note that resizing an array will destroy its contents unless we use the Preserve keyword, as in:

```
ReDim Preserve FileName(1 to 200)
```

However, when Preserve is used, we can only change the upper bound of the array (and only the last dimension in a multidimensional array).

The UBound function

The *UBound* function is used to return the current upper bound of an array. This is very useful in determining when an array needs redimensioning. To illustrate, suppose we want to collect an unknown number of filenames in an array named

FileName. If the next file number is iNextFile, the following code checks to see if the upper bound is less than iNextFile and if so, it increases the upper bound of the array by 10, preserving its current contents, to make room for the next filename:

```
If UBound(FileName) < iNextFile Then
    ReDim Preserve FileName(UBound(FileName) + 10)
End If
```

Note that redimensioning takes time, so it is wise to add some "working room" at the top to cut down on the number of times the array must be redimensioned. This is why we added 10 to the upper bound in this example, rather than just 1. (There is a tradeoff here between the extra time it takes to redimension and the extra space that may be wasted if we do not use the entire redimensioned array.)

Variable Naming Conventions

VBA programs can get very complicated, and we can use all the help we can get in trying to make them as readable as possible. In addition, as time goes on, the ideas behind the program begin to fade, and we must rely on the code itself to refresh our memory. This is why adding copious comments to a program is so important.

Another way to make programs more readable is to use a consistent *naming convention* for constants, variables, procedure names, and other items. In general, a name should have two properties. First, it should remind the reader of the purpose or function of the item. For instance, suppose we want to assign Field variables to some fields in an Access table. The code:

```
Dim fld1 As Field, fld2 as Field
Set fld1 = Fields("Sales")
Set fld2 = Fields("Transactions")
```

is perfectly legal, but 1,000 lines of code and 6 months later, will we remember which field is fld1 and which is fld2? Since we went to the trouble of naming the fields in a descriptive manner, we should do the same with the fld variables, as in:

```
Dim fldSales As Field, fldTrans as Field
Set fldSales = Fields("Sales")
Set fldTrans = Fields("Transactions")
```

Of course, there are exceptions to all rules, but in general, it is better to choose descriptive names for variables (as well as other items that require naming, such as constants, procedures, controls, forms, and code modules).

Second, a variable name should reflect something about the properties of the variable, such as its data type. Many programmers use a convention in which the first few characters of a variable's name indicate the data type of the variable. This is sometimes referred to as a Hungarian naming convention, after the Hungarian programmer Charles Simonyi, who is credited with its invention.

Tables 10-3 and 10-4 describe the naming convention that we will generally use for nonobject and object variables, respectively. Of course, you are free to make changes for your own personal use, but you should at least try to be reasonably consistent. These prefixes are intended to remind us of the data type, but it is not easy to do this perfectly using only a couple of characters, and the longer the prefix, the less likely it is that we will use it! (Note the c prefix for integers or longs. This is a commonly used prefix when the variable is intended to *count* something.)

Table 10-3. Naming convention for nonobject variables

Variable	Prefix
Boolean	bool, b, or f
Byte	b, byt, or bt
Currency	cur
Date	d or dte
Double	d or dbl
Integer	i, c, or int
Long	l, c, or lng
Single	s or sng
String	s or str
User-defined type	typ, u, or ut
Variant	v or var

Table 10-4. Naming convention for some object variables

Variable	Prefix
Database	db
Workspace	ws
Recordset	rs
TableDef	tdef
Field	fld
Index	idx
QueryDef	qdef

In addition to a data type, every variable has a *scope* and a *lifetime*. Some programmers advocate including a hint as to the scope of a variable in the prefix, using g for global and m for module level. For example, the variable giSize is a global variable of type Integer. I will discuss the scope and lifetime of a variable next (but I will not generally include scope prefixes in variable names).

Variable Scope

Variables and constants have a *scope*, which indicates where in the program the variable or constant is recognized (or visible to the code). The scope of a variable or constant can be either procedure-level (also called local), module-level private, or module-level public. The rules may seem a bit involved at first, but they do make sense.

Procedure-level (local) variables

A *local* or *procedure-level* variable or constant is a variable or constant that is declared within a procedure, as is the case with the variable LocalVar and the constant LocalConstant in Figure 10-2. A local variable or constant is not visible outside of the procedure. Thus, for instance, if we try to run *ProcedureB* in Figure 10-2, we will get the error message, "Variable not defined," and the name LocalVar will be highlighted.

One of the advantages of local variables is that we can use the same name in different procedures without conflict, since each variable is visible only in its own procedure.

Module-level variables

A *module-level* variable (or constant) is one that is declared in the declarations section of a code module. Module-level variables and constants come in two flavors: private and public.

Simply put, a module-level *public* variable (or constant) is available to all procedures in all of the modules in the project, not just the module in which it is declared, whereas a module-level *private* variable (or constant) is available only to the procedures in the module in which it was declared.

Public variables and constants are declared using the Public keyword, as in:

```
Public APubInt As Integer
Public Const APubConst = 7
```

Private variables and constants are declared using the Private keyword, as in:

```
Private APrivateInt As Integer
Private Const APrivateConst = 7
```

The Dim keyword, when used at the module level, has the same scope as Private, but is not as clear, so it should be avoided.

Public variables are also referred to as *global variables*, but this descriptive term is not *de rigueur*.

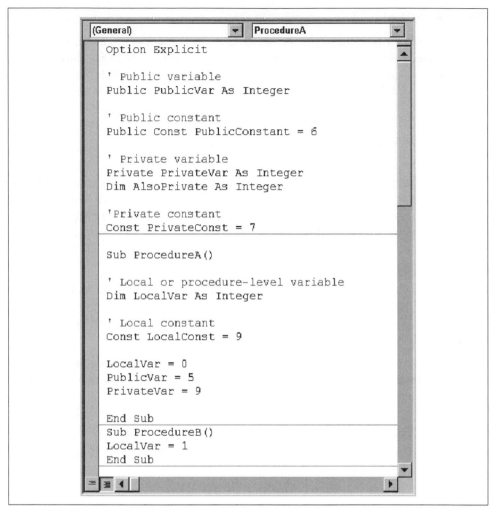

```
(General)                    ▼    ProcedureA              ▼
    Option Explicit

    ' Public variable
    Public PublicVar As Integer

    ' Public constant
    Public Const PublicConstant = 6

    ' Private variable
    Private PrivateVar As Integer
    Dim AlsoPrivate As Integer

    'Private constant
    Const PrivateConst = 7

    Sub ProcedureA()

    ' Local or procedure-level variable
    Dim LocalVar As Integer

    ' Local constant
    Const LocalConst = 9

    LocalVar = 0
    PublicVar = 5
    PrivateVar = 9

    End Sub
    Sub ProcedureB()
    LocalVar = 1
    End Sub
```

Figure 10-2. Examples of variable scope

Variable Lifetime

Variables also have a lifetime. The difference between lifetime and scope is quite simple: *lifetime* refers to how long (or when) the variable is valid (that is, retains a value), whereas *scope* refers to where the variable is accessible or visible.

To illustrate the difference, consider the following procedure:

```
Sub ProcedureA( )
    Dim LocalVar As Integer
    LocalVar = 0
    Call ProcedureB
    LocalVar = 1
End Sub
```

Note that LocalVar is a local variable. When the line:

```
Call ProcedureB
```

is executed, execution switches to *ProcedureB*. While the lines of *ProcedureB* are being executed, the variable LocalVar is out of scope, since it is local to *ProcedureA*. But it is still valid. In other words, the variable still exists and has a value, but it is simply not accessible to the code in *ProcedureB*. In fact, *ProcedureB* could also have a local variable named LocalVar, which would have nothing to do with the variable of the same name in *ProcedureA*.

Once *ProcedureB* has completed, execution continues in *ProcedureA* with the line:

```
LocalVar = 1
```

which is a valid instruction, since the variable LocalVar is back in scope.

Thus, the lifetime of the local variable LocalVar extends from the moment that *ProcedureA* is entered to the moment that it is terminated. This includes the period during which *ProcedureB* is executed as a result of the call to this procedure, even though during that period, LocalVar is out of scope.

Incidentally, you may notice that the Microsoft help files occasionally get the notions of scope and visibility mixed up a bit. The creators of the files seem to understand the difference, but they don't always use the terms correctly.

Static variables

To repeat, a variable may go in and out of scope and yet remain valid during that time—that is, retain a value during that time. However, once the lifetime of a variable expires, the variable is destroyed, and its value is lost. It is the lifetime that determines the *existence* of a variable; its scope determines its visibility.

Thus, consider the following procedures:

```
Sub ProcedureA( )
    Call ProcedureB
    Call ProcedureB
    Call ProcedureB
    Call ProcedureB
    Call ProcedureB
End Sub
Sub ProcedureB( )
    Dim x As Integer
    x = 5
    . . .
End Sub
```

When *ProcedureA* is executed, it simply calls *ProcedureB* five times. Each time *ProcedureB* is called, the local variable x is created anew and destroyed at the end of that call. Thus, x is created and destroyed five times.

Normally, this is just want we want. However, there are times when we would like the lifetime of a local variable to persist longer than the lifetime of the procedure in which it is declared. As an example, we may want a procedure to do something special the first time it is called, but not subsequent times.

A *static variable* is a local variable whose lifetime is the lifetime of the entire module, not just the procedure in which it was declared. In fact, a static variable retains its value as long as the document or template containing the code module is active (even if no code is running). Thus, a static variable has the scope of a local variable, but the lifetime of a module-level variable. *C'est tout dire!*

For instance, the procedure in Example 10-1 uses a static variable to execute some code only the first time the procedure is called, other code only after the first time, and still other code every time the procedure is run.

Example 10-1. Using a static variable

```
Sub StaticExample( )

' Declare static Boolean variable
Static NotFirstTime As Boolean

' If first time, then run special code
If NotFirstTime = False Then

    ' Code here that runs only the first time procedure is called

    ' No longer the first time
    NotFirstTime = True

Else

    ' Not the first time
    ' Code here will run if not first time

End If

    ' Code here will always run (unless procedure is exited beforehand)

End Sub
```

The If statement checks to see if the value of NotFirstTime is False, as it will be the first time the procedure is called. During this first call, the line:

```
    NotFirstTime = True
```

will execute, so that in subsequent calls to this procedure, the If condition:

```
    If NotFirstTime = False
```

will be False, and the alternate code will execute.

Static variables are not used very often, but they can be quite useful at times.

It may have occurred to you that we could accomplish the same effect by using a module-level private variable to keep a record of whether the procedure has been called, instead of a static local variable. However, it is considered better programming style to use the most restrictive scope possible, which, in this case, is a local variable with an "extended" lifetime. This helps prevent accidental alteration of the variable in other portions of the code. (Remember that this code may be part of a much larger code module, with a lot of things going on. It is better to hide the NotFirstTime variable from this other code.)

Variable Initialization

When a procedure begins execution, all of its local variables are automatically *initialized*, that is, given initial values. In general, however, it is not good programming practice to rely on this initialization, since it makes the program less readable and somewhat more prone to logical errors. Thus, it is a good idea to initialize all local variables explicitly, as in the following example:

```
Sub Example( )

Dim x As Integer
Dim s As String

x = 0        ' Initialize x to 0
s = ""       ' Initialize s to empty string

' more code here . . .

End Sub
```

Note, however, that static variables cannot be initialized, since that defeats their purpose! Thus, it is important to know the following rules that VBA uses for variable initialization (note also that they are intuitive):

- Numeric variables (Integer, Long, Single, Double, and Currency) are initialized to zero.
- A variable-length string is initialized to a zero-length (empty) string.
- A fixed-length string is filled with the character represented by the ASCII character code 0, or *Chr* (0).
- Variant variables are initialized to Empty.
- Object variables are initialized to Nothing.

The Nothing keyword actually has several related uses in Access VBA. It is used to release an object variable, as in:

```
Set rs = Nothing
```

and to determine if an object variable references a valid object, as in:

```
If rs Is Nothing
```

It is also sometimes used as a return value for some functions, generally to indicate that some operation has failed. Finally, it is used to initialize object variables.

VBA Operators

VBA uses a handful of simple operators and relations, the most common of which are shown in Table 10-5.

Table 10-5. VBA operators and relations

Type	Name	Symbol
Arithmetic operators	Addition	+
	Subtraction	-
	Multiplication	*
	Division	/
	Division with Integer result	\
	Exponentiation	^
	Modulo	Mod
String operator	Concatenation	&
Logical operators	AND	AND
	OR	OR
	NOT	NOT
Comparison relations	Equal	=
	Less than	<
	Greater than	>
	Less than or equal to	<=
	Greater than or equal to	>=
	Not equal to	<>

The Mod operator returns the remainder after division. For example:

```
8 Mod 3
```

returns 2, since the remainder after dividing 8 by 3 is 2.

To illustrate string concatenation, the expression:

```
"To be or " & "not to be"
```

is equivalent to:

```
"To be or not to be"
```

CHAPTER 11

Functions and Subroutines

VBA allows two kinds of procedures: functions and subroutines. The only difference between a function and a subroutine is that a function returns a value, whereas a subroutine does not.

Calling Functions

A function declaration has the form:

```
[Public or Private] Function FunctionName(Param1 As DataType1, _
        Param2 As DataType2,...) As ReturnType
```

Note that we must declare the data types not only of each parameter to the function, but also of the return type. Otherwise, VBA declares these items as variants.

I will discuss the optional keywords `Public` and `Private` later in this chapter, but you can probably guess that they are used here to indicate the scope of the function, just as they are used in variable declarations. For example, the `AddOne` function in Example 11-1 adds 1 to the original value.

Example 11-1. The AddOne function

```
Public Function AddOne(Value As Integer) As Integer
    AddOne = Value + 1
End Function
```

To use the return value of a function, we just place the call to the function within the expression, in the location where we want the value. For instance, the code:

```
MsgBox "Adding 1 to 5 gives: " & AddOne(5)
```

produces the message box in Figure 11-1, where the expression `AddOne(5)` is replaced by the return value of `AddOne`, which in this case is 6.

Note that, in general, any parameters to a function must be enclosed in parentheses within the function call.

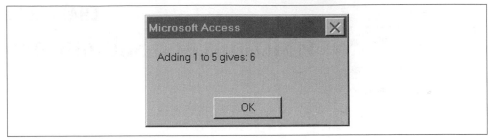

Figure 11-1. The message dialog box displayed by Example 11-1

In order to return a value from a function, we must assign the function's name to the return value somewhere within the body of the function. Example 11-2 shows a slightly more complicated example of a function.

Example 11-2. Assigning a function's return value

```
Function ReturnCount() As Variant

' Return count of records in recordset

If rs Is Nothing Then
    ReturnCount = "No recordset"
Else
    ReturnCount = rs.RecordCount
End If

End Function
```

This function returns a count of the number of records in the recordset referenced by the variable *rs*. However, if *rs* does not currently reference a recordset, then the function returns the words "No recordset".

Note that since the return value may be a number or a string, we declare the return type as Variant. Note also that *ReturnCount* is assigned twice within the body of the function. Its value, and hence the value of the function, is set differently depending upon the value returned by the If statement.

Calling Subroutines

A subroutine declaration has the form:

```
[Public or Private] Sub SubroutineName(Param1 As DataType1, _
        Param2 As DataType2,...)
```

This is similar to the function declaration, with the notable absence of the As ReturnType portion. (Note also the word Sub in place of Function.)

Since subroutines do not return a value, they cannot be used within an expression. To call a subroutine named *SubroutineA*, we can write either:

```
Call SubroutineA(parameters, . . .)
```

or simply:

```
SubroutineA parameters, . . .
```

Note that any parameters must be enclosed in parentheses when using the `Call` keyword, but not otherwise.

Parameters and Arguments

Consider the following very simple subroutine, which does nothing more than display a message box declaring a person's name:

```
Sub DisplayName(sName As String)
    MsgBox "My name is " & sName
End Sub
```

To call this subroutine, we would write, for example:

```
DisplayName "Wolfgang"
```

or:

```
Call DisplayName("Wolfgang")
```

The variable *sName* in the procedure declaration:

```
Sub DisplayName(sName As String)
```

is called a *parameter* of the procedure. The call to the procedure should contain a string variable or a literal string that is represented by the variable *sName* in this procedure (but see the discussion of optional arguments in the next section). The value used in place of the parameter when we make the procedure call is called an *argument*. Thus, in the previous example, the argument is the string "Wolfgang."

Note that many programmers fail to make a distinction between parameters and arguments, using the names interchangeably. However, since a parameter is like a variable and an argument is like a *value* of that variable, failing to make this distinction is like failing to distinguish between a variable and its value!

Optional Arguments

In VBA, the arguments to a procedure may be specified as optional, using the `Optional` keyword. (It makes no sense to say that a parameter is optional; it is the *value* that is optional.)

For instance, the definition of the OpenRecordset method is:

```
Set recordset = object.OpenRecordset(source, type, options, lockedits)
```

where *type*, *options*, and *lockedits* are optional. Thus, for instance, each of the following lines of code are legal:

```
Dim rs As Recordset
Set rs = CurrentDb.OpenRecordset("Names")
Set rs = CurrentDb.OpenRecordset("Names", dbOpenForwardOnly)
Set rs = CurrentDb.OpenRecordset("Names", dbOpenForwardOnly, dbReadOnly)
Set rs = CurrentDb.OpenRecordset("Names", dbOpenForwardOnly, _
    dbReadOnly, dbOptimistic)
```

To define a function with optional arguments, we just include the keyword `Optional` in the parameter declaration, as in Example 11-3.

Example 11-3. Using an optional argument

```
Sub ChangeFieldType(sFieldName As String, _
                    Optional NewSize As Variant)

' Change type to integer
rs!Fields(sFieldName).Type = dbInteger

' If size supplied, use it. Else use 25.
If Not IsMissing(NewSize) Then
   rs!Fields(sFieldName).Size = CInt(NewSize)
Else
   rs!Fields(sFieldName).Size = 25
End If

End Sub
```

The second parameter is declared with the `Optional` keyword. Because of this, we may call the procedure with or without an argument for this parameter, as in:

```
ChangeFieldType("Age", 10)
```

and:

```
ChangeFieldType("Age")
```

Note that the `IsMissing` function is used in the body of the procedure to test whether the argument is present. If the argument is present, then the font size is changed. Note also that we declared the *NewSize* parameter as type Variant because `IsMissing` works only with parameters of type Variant. (Other types of variables are given default values, which precludes the possibility of them going missing.) Thus, we converted the Variant to type Integer using the `CInt` function.

Note that a procedure may have any number of optional arguments, but they must all come at the end of the parameter list.

Named Arguments

Normally, the arguments to a function are matched to the parameters by their *position* in the function call. For instance, in the function call:

```
Set rs = CurrentDb.OpenRecordset("Objects", dbOpenForwardOnly)
```

Access can tell that the argument `dbOpenForwardOnly` is the value for the second parameter (*Type*) of the function. Such arguments are called *positional arguments*.

Many built-in VBA/DAO functions also allow *named arguments*. For example, the OpenRecordset function can be called as follows:

```
Set rs = CurrentDb.OpenRecordset(Name:="Objects", _
    Type:=dbOpenForwardOnly)
```

Here, each argument has the form:

```
ParameterName:=Argument
```

There are three main advantages to named arguments:

- Named arguments can improve readability and clarity.
- Blank spaces (separated by commas) are required for missing optional arguments when using a positional declaration, but not when using named arguments.
- The order in which named arguments are listed is immaterial, which, of course, is not the case for positional arguments. For instance, the previous function call could be written:

```
Set rs = CurrentDb.OpenRecordset(Type:=dbOpenForwardOnly, _
    Name:="Objects")
```

Named arguments can improve readability quite a bit, and they are highly recommended. However, they can require considerably more space, so for the short examples in this book, I usually will not use them.

ByRef Versus ByVal Parameters

Parameters come in two flavors: `ByRef` and `ByVal`. Many programmers do not have a clear understanding of these concepts, but they are very important and not that difficult to understand.

To explain the difference, I present the two procedures in Example 11-4. *ProcedureA* simply sets the value of the module-level variable *x* to 5, displays that value, calls the procedure AddOne with the argument *x*, and then displays the value of *x* again.

Example 11-4. Testing the ByVal and ByRef keywords

```
Sub ProcedureA( )
    x = 5               ' Set x to 5
    MsgBox x            ' Display x
    Call AddOne(x)      ' Call AddOne
    MsgBox x            ' Display x again
End Sub

Sub AddOne(ByRef i As Integer)
    i = i + 1
End Sub
```

Note the presence of the ByRef keyword in the AddOne procedure declaration. This keyword tells VBA to pass a reference to the variable *x* to the AddOne procedure. Therefore, the AddOne procedure, in effect, replaces its parameter *i* by the variable *x*. As a result, the line:

```
i = i + 1
```

effectively becomes:

```
x = x + 1
```

So, after AddOne is called, the variable *x* has the value 6.

On the other hand, suppose we change the AddOne procedure, replacing the keyword ByRef with the keyword ByVal:

```
Sub AddOne(ByVal i As Integer)
    i = i + 1
End Sub
```

In this case, VBA does not pass a reference to the variable *x*, but rather it passes its value. Hence, the variable *i* in AddOne simply takes on the value 5. Adding 1 to that value gives 6. Thus, *i* equals 6, but the value of the argument *x* is not affected! Hence, both message boxes will display the value 5 for *x*.

ByRef and ByVal both have their uses. When we want to change the value of a variable, we must declare the corresponding parameter as ByRef so that the called procedure has access to the actual variable itself. This is the case in the previous example. Otherwise, the AddOne procedure does absolutely nothing, since the local variable *i* is incremented, but it is destroyed immediately afterwards, when the procedure ends.

On the other hand, when we pass an argument for informational purposes only, and we do not want the argument to be altered, it should be passed by value, using the ByVal keyword. In this way, the called procedure gets only the *value* of the argument.

There is one downside to passing arguments by value: it can take a lot of memory (and time). When passing a string variable that contains a large string by value, the entire string must be duplicated.

Thus, we can summarize by saying that if we want the procedure to modify an argument, the argument must be passed by reference. If not, the argument should be passed by value unless this will produce an unacceptable decrease in performance, or unless we are very sure that it will not get changed by accident.

It is important to note that VBA defaults to ByRef if we do not specify otherwise. This means that the values of arguments are subject to change by the called procedure, unless we explicitly include the keyword ByVal. *Caveat scriptor!*

Exiting a Procedure

VBA provides the `Exit Sub` and `Exit Function` statements, should we wish to exit from a procedure before the procedure would terminate naturally. For instance, if the value of a parameter is not suitable, we may want to issue a warning to the user and exit, as Example 11-5 shows.

Example 11-5. Using the Exit Sub statement
```
Sub DisplayName(sName As String)
   If sName = "" then
      Msgbox "Please enter a name."
      Exit Sub
   End If
   MsgBox "Name entered is " & sName
End Sub
```

While we are on the subject of exiting, we should comment on the use of the `End` statement, which will terminate a procedure. Simply put, you should *almost never* use the `End` statement in VBA programming, since it produces a rather abrupt termination of a program. (I never like to say never.) Here is a partial list of what happens when the `End` statement is executed:

- Code execution stops abruptly, without invoking the Unload, QueryUnload, or Terminate event of any forms in the application, which means that forms are not given the opportunity to prevent the program from terminating or from performing any necessary cleanup.
- All module-level variables and all static local variables are reset. (Nonstatic local variables go out of scope, as expected.) Objects created from class modules are destroyed.
- Files opened using the `Open` statement are closed.

While there may be some rather specialized situations in which this behavior is desirable, you will no doubt recognize such a situation if and when it arises. In the meantime, it is probably best to simply avoid using the `End` statement.

Public and Private Procedures

Just as variables and constants have a scope, so do procedures. We can declare a procedure using the `Public` or `Private` keyword, as in:

```
Public Function AddOne(i As Integer) As Integer
```

or:

```
Private Function AddOne(i As Integer) As Integer
```

The difference is simple: a `Private` procedure can only be called from within the module in which it is defined, whereas a `Public` procedure can be called from within any module in the project.

Note that if the `Public` or `Private` keyword is omitted from a procedure declaration, then the procedure is considered to be `Public`.

Fully Qualified Procedure Names

When we call a public procedure that lies in another code module, there is a potential problem with ambiguity, for there may be more than one public procedure with the same name in another module. VBA will execute the first one it finds, and this may not be the one we had in mind!

The solution is to use a *qualified procedure name*, which has the form:

```
ModuleName.ProcedureName
```

For instance, if a public procedure named `AddOne` lies in a module named Utilities, then we can call this procedure using the syntax:

```
Utilities.AddOne
```

CHAPTER 12

Built-in Functions and Statements

VBA has a large number of built-in functions and statements. For possible reference, Table 12-1 shows the VBA functions, and Table 12-2 shows the statements. We will take a look at a few of the more commonly used functions and statements in this chapter and the next.

Table 12-1. VBA functions

Abs	CreateObject	Error	InputB	Len	PPmt	StrComp
Array	CSng	Exp	InputBox	LenB	PV	StrConv
Asc	CStr	FileAttr	InStr	LoadPicture	QBColor	String
AscB	CurDir	FileDateTime	InStrB	Loc	Rate	Switch
AscW	Cvar	FileLen	Int	LOF	RGB	SYD
Atn	CVDate	Fix	Ipmt	Log	Right	Tab
CBool	CVErr	Format	IRR	Ltrim	RightB	Tan
CByte	Date	FreeFile	IsArray	Mid	Rnd	Time
CCur	DateAdd	FV	IsDate	MidB	RTrim	Timer
CDate	DateDiff	GetAllSettings	IsEmpty	Minute	Second	TimeSerial
CDbl	DatePart	GetAttr	IsError	MIRR	Seek	TimeValue
CDec	DateSerial	GetAutoServerSettings	IsMissing	Month	Sgn	Trim
Choose	DateValue	GetObject	IsNull	MsgBox	Shell	TypeName
Chr	Day	GetSetting	IsNumeric	Now	Sin	UBound
ChrB	DDB	Hex	IsObject	Nper	SLN	UCase
ChrW	Dir	Hour	Lbound	NPV	Space	Val
CInt	DoEvents	Iif	Lcase	Oct	Spc	VarType
CLng	Environ	IMEStatus	Left	Partition	Sqr	Weekday
Command	EOF	Input	LeftB	Pmt	Str	Year
Cos						

Table 12-2. VBA statements

AppActivate	DefDec	Error	Kill	Open	Randomize	Set
Beep	DefInt	Event	Let	Option Base	ReDim	SetAttr
Call	DefLng	Exit	Line Input #	Option Compare	Rem	Static
ChDir	DefObj	FileCopy	Load	Option Explicit	Reset	Stop
ChDrive	DefSng	For Each...Next	Lock	Option Private	Resume	Sub
Close	DefStr	For...Next	LSet	Print #	Return	Time
Const	DefVar	Function	Mid	Private	RmDir	Type
Date	DeleteSetting	Get	MidB	Property Get	RSet	Unload
Declare	Dim	GoSub...Return	MkDir	Property Let	SavePicture	Unlock
DefBool	Do...Loop	GoTo	Name	Property Set	SaveSetting	While...Wend
DefByte	End	If...Then...Else	On Error	Public	Seek	Width #
DefCur	Enum	Implements	On...GoSub	Put	Select Case	With
DefDate	Erase	Input #	On...GoTo	RaiseEvent	SendKeys	Write #
DefDbl						

To help simplify the exposition, we will follow Microsoft's lead and use square brackets to indicate optional parameters. Thus, for instance, the second parameter in the following procedure is optional:

```
Sub ChangeFieldType(sFieldName, [NewSize])
```

Note that we have also omitted the data type declarations, which will be discussed separately.

The MsgBox Function

We have been using the `MsgBox` function unofficially for some time now. Let us introduce it officially. The `MsgBox` function is used to display a message and wait for the user to respond by pushing a button. The most commonly used syntax is:

```
MsgBox(prompt [, buttons] [, title])
```

(This is not the function's complete syntax. There are some additional optional parameters related to help contexts that you can look up in the help documentation.)

prompt is a String parameter containing the message to be displayed in the dialog box. Note that a multiline message can be created by interspersing the `vbCrLf` constant within the message.

buttons is a Long parameter giving the sum of values that specify various properties of the message box. These properties are the number and type of buttons to display, the icon style to use, the identity of the default button, and the modality of the message box. (A *system modal* dialog box remains on top of all currently open windows and captures the input focus systemwide, whereas an *application modal* dialog box remains on top of the application's windows only and captures the application's focus.) The various values of *buttons* that we can sum are shown in Table 12-3. (They are officially defined in the VbMsgBoxStyle enum.)

Table 12-3. The MsgBox buttons argument values

Purpose	Constant	Value	Description
Button types	vbOKOnly	0	Display OK button only
	vbOKCancel	1	Display OK and Cancel buttons
	vbAbortRetryIgnore	2	Display Abort, Retry, and Ignore buttons
	vbYesNoCancel	3	Display Yes, No, and Cancel buttons
	vbYesNo	4	Display Yes and No buttons
	vbRetryCancel	5	Display Retry and Cancel buttons
Icon types	vbCritical	16	Display Critical Message icon
	vbQuestion	32	Display Warning Query icon
	vbExclamation	48	Display Warning Message icon
	vbInformation	64	Display Information Message icon
Default button	vbDefaultButton1	0	First button is default
	vbDefaultButton2	256	Second button is default
	vbDefaultButton3	512	Third button is default
	vbDefaultButton4	768	Fourth button is default
Modality	vbApplicationModal	0	Application modal message box
	vbSystemModal	4096	System modal message box

For instance, the code:

```
MsgBox "Proceed?", vbQuestion + vbYesNo
```

displays the message box shown in Figure 12-1, which includes a question-mark icon and two command buttons, labeled *Yes* and *No*.

Figure 12-1. A MsgBox dialog box

The *title* parameter is a string expression that is displayed in the title bar of the dialog box. If we omit this argument, then *Microsoft Access* will be displayed, as in Figure 12-1.

The `MsgBox` function returns a number indicating which button was selected. These return values are given in Table 12-4. (They are officially defined in the `VbMsgBoxResult` enum.)

Table 12-4. MsgBox return values

Constant	Value	Description
vbOK	1	OK button pressed
vbCancel	2	Cancel button pressed
vbAbort	3	Abort button pressed
vbRetry	4	Retry button pressed
vbIgnore	5	Ignore button pressed
vbYes	6	Yes button pressed
vbNo	7	No button pressed

The InputBox Function

The `InputBox` function is designed to get input from the user. The most commonly used (but not complete) syntax is:

```
InputBox(prompt [, title] [, default])
```

where `prompt` is the message in the input box, `title` is the title for the input box, and `default` is the default value that is displayed in the text box. For instance, the code:

```
sName = InputBox("Enter your name.", "Name", "Albert")
```

produces the dialog box in Figure 12-2.

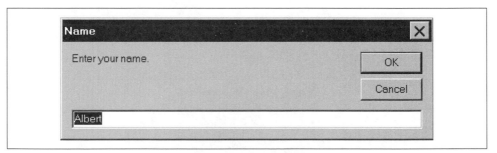

Figure 12-2. An InputBox dialog box

The `InputBox` function returns the string that the user enters into the text box. Thus, in our example, the string variable *sName* will contain this string.

Note that if we want a number from the user, we can still use the `InputBox` function and simply convert the returned string (such as `"12.55"`) to a number (12.55) using the `Val` function, discussed later in the chapter.

VBA String Functions

Here are a handful of useful functions that apply to strings (both constants and variables):

The Len function

The Len function returns the length of a string, that is, the number of characters in the string. Thus, the code:

```
Len("January Invoice")
```

returns the number 15.

The UCase and LCase functions

These functions return an all-uppercase or all-lowercase version of the string argument. The syntax is:

```
UCase(string)
LCase(string)
```

For instance:

```
MsgBox UCase("Donna")
```

will display the string DONNA.

The Left, Right, and Mid functions

These functions return a portion of a string. In particular:

```
Left(string, number)
```

returns the leftmost *number* characters in *string*, and:

```
Right(string, number)
```

returns the rightmost *number* characters in *string*. For instance:

```
MsgBox Right("Donna Smith", 5)
```

displays the string Smith.

The syntax for Mid is:

```
Mid(string, start, length)
```

This function returns the first *length* number of characters of *string*, starting at character number *start*. For instance:

```
Mid("Library.xls",9,3)
```

returns the string xls. If the *length* parameter is missing, as in:

```
Mid("Library.xls",9)
```

the function will return the rest of the string, starting at *start*.

The InStr function

The syntax for this very useful function is:

```
InStr(Start, StringToSearch, StringToFind)
```

The return value is the position, starting at *Start*, of the first occurrence of *StringToFind* within *StringToSearch*. If *Start* is missing, then the function starts searching at the beginning of *StringToSearch*. For instance:

```
MsgBox InStr(1, "Donna Smith", "Smith")
```

displays the number 7, because "Smith" begins at the seventh position in the string "Donna Smith".

The Str and Val functions

The Str function converts a number to a string. For instance:

```
Str(123)
```

returns the string 123. Conversely, the Val function converts a string that represents a number into a number (so that we can do arithmetic with it, for instance). For example:

```
Val("4.5")
```

returns the number 4.5 and:

```
Val("1234 Main Street")
```

returns the number 1234. Note, however, that Val does not recognize dollar signs or commas. Thus:

```
Val($12.00)
```

returns 0, not 12.00.

The type-conversion functions

The Str and Val functions have been replaced by the more modern type-conversion functions: CBool, CByte, CCur, CDate, CDbl, CDec, CInt, CLng, CSng, CVar, and CStr. For instance, the function CStr converts its argument to a string, as in:

```
CStr(123)
```

One advantage of the newer type-conversion functions over the older Str and Val functions is that the new functions are international-aware. For instance, the *CCur* function converts an expression to currency format, taking into account the particular decimal separators, thousands separators, and other currency options that are determined by the locale setting of the computer upon which the function is being used.

The Trim, LTrim, and RTrim functions

The LTrim function removes leading spaces from a string. Similarly, RTrim removes trailing spaces, and Trim removes both leading and trailing spaces. Thus:

```
Trim("  extra   ")
```

returns the string extra.

The String and Space functions

The String function provides a way to create a string quickly that consists of a single character repeated a number of times. For instance:

```
sText = String(25, "B")
```

sets *sText* to a string consisting of 25 Bs. Also, the Space function returns a string consisting of a given number of spaces. For instance:

```
sText = Space(25)
```

sets *sText* to a string consisting of 25 spaces.

The Like *operator and* StrCmp *function*

The Like operator is very useful for comparing two strings. Of course, we can use the equal sign:

```
string1 = string2
```

which is true when the two strings are identical. However, Like will also make a case-insensitive comparison or allow the use of pattern matching.

The expression:

```
string Like pattern
```

returns True if *string* fits *pattern* and returns False otherwise. (Actually, the expression can also return Null.) We will describe *pattern* in a moment.

The type of string comparison that the Like operator uses depends upon the setting of the Option Compare statement. There are two possibilities:

```
Option Compare Binary
Option Compare Text
```

one of which should be placed in the Declarations section of a module (in the same place as Option Explicit). Note that the default is Option Compare Binary.

Under Option Compare Binary, string comparison is in the order given by the ANSI character code, as shown here:

```
A < B < . . . < Z < a < b < . . . < z < À < . . . < Ø < à < . . . < ø
```

Under Option Compare Text, string comparison is based on a case-insensitive sort order (determined by your PC's locale setting). This gives a sort order as shown here:

```
A = a < À = à < B = b < . . . < Z = z < Ø = ø
```

By the way, the last item in the Text sort order is the left bracket ([) character, with ANSI value 91. This is useful to know if you want to place an item last in alphabetical order—just surround it by square brackets.

The pattern-matching features of the Like operator allow the use of wildcard characters, character lists, or character ranges. For example:

?

Matches any single character

*

Matches zero or more characters

#

Matches any single digit (0–9)

[charlist]

Matches any single character in *charlist*

[!charlist]

Matches any single character not in *charlist*

For more details, check the VBA help file.

The StrComp function also compares two strings. Its syntax is:

```
StrComp(string1, string2 [, compare])
```

and it returns a value indicating whether *string1* is equal to, greater than, or less than *string2*. For more details, check the VBA help file.

Miscellaneous Functions and Statements

We'll conclude our discussion of Access VBA functions and statements by examining a hodgepodge of language constructs that perform such tasks as evaluating objects or variables, evaluating an expression, and altering program flow based on an expression's values.

The Is Functions

VBA has several Is functions that return Boolean values indicating whether a certain condition holds. We have already discussed the IsMissing function in connection with optional arguments. Here are some additional Is functions.

The IsDate function

This function indicates whether an expression can be converted to a date. For instance, the code:

```
Dim x As String
x = "1/1/45"
Debug.Print IsDate(x)
```

will print True to the Immediate window.

The IsEmpty function

This function indicates whether a variable has been initialized. For example, the code:

```
Dim x As Variant
If IsEmpty(x) Then . . .
```

tests whether the variable *x* is empty.

The IsNull function

This function is used to test whether a variable or field is Null (that is, contains no data). Note that code such as:

```
If var = Null Then
```

will always return False because most expressions that involve Null automatically return Null. The proper way to determine if the variable *var* is Null is to write:

```
If IsNull(var) Then
```

Here is a typical scenario:

```
Dim rs As Recordset
Dim s As String
Set rs = CurrentDb.OpenRecordset("Names")
rs.MoveFirst
If Not IsNull(rs!LastName) Then
    s = rs!LastName
    . . .
End If
```

The IsNumeric function

This function indicates whether an expression can be evaluated as a number. For instance, consider the code:

```
Dim s As String
s = "123"
If IsNumeric(s) Then Debug.Print "Number"
```

This will print the word "Number." However, if we change the second line to:

```
s = "123 Main St"
```

then the Debug.Print statement will not execute.

The Immediate If Function

The Immediate If function has the syntax:

```
IIf(Expression, TruePart, FalsePart)
```

If *Expression* is True, then the function returns *TruePart*. If *Expression* is False, the function returns *FalsePart*. For instance, consider the following code:

```
Dim rs As Recordset
Dim s As String

Set rs = CurrentDb.OpenRecordset("Names")
rs.MoveFirst

If Not IsNull(rs!LastName) Then
    s = rs!LastName)
End If
```

This code fills a string variable with a field value. We must make a distinction between a Null and non-Null field value because the code:

```
s = rs!Lastname
```

will produce the error "Invalid use of Null" if we try to assign a Null value to a string variable.

It is very important to note that the Immediate If function always evaluates both *TruePart* and *FalsePart*, even though it returns only one of them. Hence, we must be careful about undesirable side effects. For example, the following code will produce a "Division by Zero" error because even though the IIf function returns 1/x only when x is not equal to 0, the expression 1/x is evaluated in all cases, including when x = 0:

```
x = 0
y = IIf(x = 0, x ^ 2, 1 / x)
```

The Switch Function

The syntax of the Switch function is:

```
Switch(expr1, value1, expr2, value2, ... , exprn, valuen)
```

where *exprn* and *valuen* are expressions. Note that there need only be one expression-value pair, but the function is more meaningful if there are at least two such pairs.

The Switch function evaluates each expression *exprn*. When it encounters the first True expression, it returns the corresponding value. As with the IIf function, Switch always evaluates all of the expressions. If none of the expressions is True, the function returns Null. This can be tested with the IsNull function.

The procedure in Example 12-1 displays the type of file based on its extension: Access database, text, or dbase database.

Example 12-1. The Switch function

```
Sub ShowFileType(FileExt As String)

Dim FileType As Variant

FileType = Switch(FileExt = "mdb", "Database", _
                  FileExt = "txt", "Text", _
                  FileExt = "dbf", "dBase")

' Display result
If Not IsNull(FileType) Then
   MsgBox FileType
Else
   MsgBox "Unrecognized type"
End If

End Sub
```

There is one subtlety in this code. Since the Switch function can return a Null value, we cannot assign the return value to a String variable, as we might first try to do:

```
Dim FileType As String

FileType = Switch(FileExt = "mdb", "Database", _
                  FileExt = "txt", "Text", _
                  FileExt = "dbf", "dBase")
```

This will produce an error if *FileExt* is *not* "mdb", "txt", or "dbf", in which case we will get the very annoying error message, "Invalid use of Null." The solution is to declare *FileType* as a Variant, which can hold any data type, including *no* data type, which is indicated by the Null keyword. (This issue can be avoided by using a Select Case statement, discussed in Chapter 13.)

The Beep Statement

This simple statement, whose syntax is:

```
Beep
```

sounds a single tone through the computer's speakers. It can be useful (when used with restraint) if we want to get the user's attention. However, there is a caveat: the results are dependent upon the computer's hardware, and so the statement may not produce a sound at all! Thus, if you use this statement in your code, be sure to warn the user.

Handling Errors in Code

I discussed the various types of errors in Chapter 9, but I have scrupulously avoided the question of how to handle runtime errors in code. Indeed, VBA provides several tools for handling errors (On Error, Resume, the *Err* object, and so on), and we could include an entire chapter on the subject in this book.

Proper error handling is *extremely* important. Indeed, if you are, or intend to become, a professional application developer, then you should familiarize yourself with error-handling procedures.

On the other hand, if your intention is to produce Access VBA code for your own personal use, then the reasons for adding error-handling routines are somewhat mitigated. When an error occurs within one of your own programs, VBA will stop execution, display an error message, and highlight the offending code. This should enable you to debug the application and fix the problem. (It would be unreasonable to expect another user of your program to debug your code, however.)

Let us undertake a brief discussion of the highlights of error handling. (For more details, may I suggest my book *Concepts of Object-Oriented Programming in Visual Basic*, published by Springer-Verlag. It has a detailed chapter on error handling.)

The On Error Goto Label Statement

The On Error statement tells VBA what to do when a runtime error occurs. The most common form of the statement is:

```
On Error GoTo label
```

where *label* is a label. For instance, consider the following code:

```
Sub RecordCt()

On Error GoTo ERR_EXAMPLE

Dim rs As Recordset
Set rs = CurrentDb.OpenRecordset("Name")

MsgBox rs.RecordCount

Exit Sub

ERR_EXAMPLE:
  MsgBox "Error " & Err.Number & " - " & Err.Description, vbCritical
  Exit Sub

End Sub
```

The purpose of this procedure is simply to display the number of rows in a table. However, the database does not happen to have a table called Name. Hence, when VBA encounters the line:

```
Set rs = CurrentDb.OpenRecordset("Name")
```

a runtime error will occur.

To deal with this possibility in a friendly manner, we add some error checking. The line:

```
On Error GoTo ERR_EXAMPLE
```

tells VBA to move execution to the label ERR_EXAMPLE if an error does occur. The code following this label is called the *error-handling code*. If an error should occur, the next line executed is the MsgBox line, in which case the dialog box in Figure 12-3 will be displayed. This message gives a description of the error, obtained from the error object, which we discuss in the next section.

Figure 12-3. An error dialog box

It is important to note the:

```
Exit Sub
```

line just before the ERR_EXAMPLE label. Without this statement, the error-handling code will always be executed, even when there is no error! Omitting this line is a common mistake. Note also that labels always end with a colon.

The process of adding error-handling code to a procedure is sometimes referred to as *error-trapping*.

Handling Errors in the Calling Procedure

Consider the following version of the RecordCt function:

```
Function RecordCt(TableName As String) As Integer

On Error GoTo ERR_EXAMPLE

Dim rs As Recordset

Set rs = CurrentDb.OpenRecordset(TableName)
RecordCt = rs.RecordCount
rs.Close

Exit Function

ERR_EXAMPLE:
  RecordCt = -1  ' Indicates error
  rs.Close

Exit Function

End Function
```

In this case, if there is an error, the function will simply return the value -1, rather than displaying a message box. This behavior is better than that of the previous version, because in this case the calling procedure can decide what to do.

Here is a procedure that calls RecordCt:

```
Sub Main()

On Error GoTo Err_Main

Dim rc As Long
rc = RecordCt("Object")

If rc = -1 Then
   ' code here to handle error
Else
   ' code here for no error
End If
Exit Sub

Err_Main:
  MsgBox "Error " & Err.Number & " - " & Err.Description, vbCritical
  Exit Sub

End Sub
```

Note that a return value of -1 is not perceived by VBA as an error at all, so we need to handle the error using code such as:

```
If rc = -1 Then
```

The Calls Stack

What happens if we do not trap errors in a procedure?

If the procedure was *not* called by another procedure, but rather was called directly by the user, or if the procedure is an *event* procedure—that is, code that executes in response to a user manipulating a control on a form (for instance, clicking on a command button)—then VBA just displays an error message and halts the program.

However, if the procedure in which the error occurred was called by another procedure, then VBA passes the error to the calling procedure, just as though the calling procedure had caused the error.

To illustrate this, consider the following procedures:

```
Function RecordCt2(TableName As String) As Integer
Dim rs As Recordset
Set rs = CurrentDb.OpenRecordset(TableName)
RecordCt2 = rs.RecordCount
rs.Close
End Function

' -----

Sub Main2()

On Error GoTo Err_Main

Dim rc As Long
rc = RecordCt2("Objects")

' More code here

Exit Sub

Err_Main:
  MsgBox "Error " & Err.Number & " - " & Err.Description, vbCritical
  Exit Sub

End Sub
```

The RecordCt2 function has no error-trapping code. If Main2 calls RecordCt2 with a bad table name, the error in RecordCt2 will be passed to Main2, whose error-trapping code will execute. Thus, we will get an error message from Main2. (This may be just fine.)

More generally, if *ProcedureA* calls *ProcedureB*, which calls *ProcedureC*, and so on, then an error in any one procedure will be passed up the *call stack* (list of procedures in reverse order of execution) until a procedure with error-handling code is encountered. If none is encountered, then VBA will issue its own error message and terminate the program.

Incidentally, you can view the call stack while in break mode by choosing *Call Stack* from the *View* menu.

The Error Object

The *error object*, denoted by `Err`, belongs to the VBA object model. The most important properties of this object are:

Number
> The VBA error number

Source
> The name of the current VBA project

Description
> A description of the error

Thus, for instance, the line:

```
MsgBox "Error " & Err.Number & " - " & Err.Description, vbCritical
```

displays the error number and its description.

The *Err* object has a *Clear* method:

```
Err.Clear
```

that will clear all of the properties of the `Err` object, setting its `Number` property to `0` (which indicates the absence of an error).

The On Error GoTo 0 Statement

The statement:

```
On Error GoTo 0
```

turns off any previous `On Error GoTo label` statements. Any error occurring subsequently will be handled by VBA in its own inimitable way.

The On Error Resume Next Statement

The syntax:

```
On Error Resume Next
```

tells VBA to continue executing the code immediately following the line that caused the error. There are two important uses for this form of On Error. The first is to cause VBA to ignore an error. For instance, the code:

```
Sub example( )

On Error Resume Next
MsgBox rs.RecordCount

End Sub
```

will report the record count when rs is a valid recordset and do nothing otherwise.

Another important use for the On Error Resume Next syntax is for *in-line error checking*, where we check for errors immediately following the line that may have caused an error. For instance, another way to handle errors in the RecordCount property is as follows:

```
Sub example( )

On Error Resume Next

MsgBox rs.RecordCount

If Err.Number <> 0 Then
  ' code to handle error here
End If
End Sub
```

The Resume Statement

It is also possible to include the Resume statement in the error-handling portion of the code. This will cause VBA to resume execution at the line that follows the one that caused the error. Thus, the previous code is equivalent to the following:

```
Sub example( )

On Error GoTo ERR_EXAMPLE
MsgBox rs.RecordCount

' An error will cause execution to resume here after
' displaying an error message

Exit Sub
ERR_EXAMPLE:
  MsgBox Err.Description, vbCritical
  Resume Next

End Sub
```

There are three variations on the Resume statement:

- Resume
- Resume Next
- Resume *ALabel*

The first version will cause VBA to resume with the line that caused the error. This is useful if your error-handling code actually repairs the error condition and you want the line that caused the original error to be executed again.

To illustrate, if the procedure in Example 12-2 encounters an error, it branches to an error handler. This handler checks for error number 3078, which is the "Can't find table" error. If this is the error, then the procedure displays a dialog box asking for a new table name. If the user enters a new name, the Resume statement is executed, and so the line:

```
Set rs = CurrentDb.OpenRecordset(TableName)
```

is repeated. Note that it is vital to give the user a way out, however. This is done by letting the user leave the dialog box blank. (Incidentally, I got the correct error number 3078 by simulating the error and reading the resulting error-message dialog box.)

Example 12-2. Error handling with the Resume statement

```
Function RecordCt3(TableName As String) As Integer

On Error GoTo ERR_EXAMPLE

Dim rs As Recordset

Set rs = CurrentDb.OpenRecordset(TableName)

RecordCt = rs.RecordCount

rs.Close
Exit Function

ERR_EXAMPLE:
    If Err.Number = 3078 Then
        ' Can't find table
        sTable = InputBox("Can't find table " & sTable & _
                ". Please enter table name again or leave blank to end.")
        If sTable = "" Then
            rs.Close
            TableName = sTable
            Exit Function
        Else
            Resume
        End If
```

Example 12-2. Error handling with the Resume statement (continued)

```
Else
    ' Unknown error
    MsgBox "Error " & Err.Number & " - " & Err.Description, vbCritical
    rs.Close
    Exit Function
End If
```

```
End Function
```

The third variation:

```
Resume ALabel
```

causes VBA to resume execution at the line labeled ALabel.

CHAPTER 13

Control Statements

I conclude our discussion of the VBA language with the main VBA *control statements*, which are statements that affect the flow of control (or flow of execution) in a program.

The If . . . Then Statement

The If...Then statement is used for conditional control. The syntax is:

```
If Condition Then
    ' statements go here . . .
ElseIf AnotherCondition Then
    ' more statements go here . . .
Else
    ' more statements go here . . .
End If
```

Note that we may include more than one ElseIf part, and that both the ElseIf part(s) and the Else part are optional. We can also squeeze all parts of this statement onto a single line, which is generally only a good idea when the ElseIf and Else parts are not required.

To illustrate, the following code checks to see if the FirstName field is null. If so, it replaces the Null value with a question mark. If not, it capitalizes the first name.

```
rs.Edit

If IsNull(rs!FirstName) Then
    rs!FirstName = "?"
Else
    rs!FirstName = UCase(rs!FirstName)
End If

rs.Update
```

The For Loop

The `For...Next` statement provides a method for repeatedly looping through a block of code (that is, one or more lines of code). This loop is naturally referred to as a `For` loop. The basic syntax is:

```
For counter = start To end

    ' block of code goes here . . .

Next counter
```

The first time that the block of code is executed, the variable *counter* (called the loop variable for the `For` loop) is given the value *start*. Each subsequent time that the block of code is executed, the loop variable `counter` is incremented by 1. When `counter` exceeds the value end, the block of code is no longer executed. Thus, the code block is executed a total of end - start + 1 times, each time with a different value of `counter`.

Note that we can omit the word *counter* in the last line of a `For` loop (replacing `Next counter` with just `Next`). This may cause the `For` loop to execute a bit more quickly, but it also detracts a bit from readability.

To illustrate, the following code prints the names of the fields in the Objects table:

```
Sub PrintFields()

Dim i As Integer
Dim rs As Recordset
Set rs = CurrentDb.OpenRecordset("Objects")

For i = 0 To rs.Fields.Count - 1
    Debug.Print rs.Fields(i).Name
Next

rs.Close

End Sub
```

Note that the limits of the `For` statement are 0 to `rs.Fields.Count - 1` because the fields are indexed starting at 0 (rather than 1). We will discuss this issue in more detail when we talk about DAO programming.

`For` loops are often used to initialize an array. For instance, the code:

```
For i = 0 To 10
    iArray(i) = 0
Next i
```

assigns a value of 0 to each of the 11 variables `iArray(0)` through `iArray(10)`.

Note that the loop variable counter will usually appear within the block of code, as it does in this array-initialization example, but this is not a requirement. However, if it does appear, we need to be very careful not to change its value, since that will certainly mess up the For loop. (VBA automatically increments the loop variable each time through the loop, so we should leave it alone.)

The Exit For Statement

VBA provides the Exit For statement to exit a For loop prematurely. For instance, the code in Example 13-1 finds the first field whose type is Integer.

Example 13-1. Finding the First Integer field

```
Sub FindFirstIntegerField( )

Dim i As Integer
Dim rs As Recordset
Set rs = CurrentDb.OpenRecordset("Objects")

For i = 0 To rs.Fields.Count - 1
   If rs.Fields(i).Type = dbInteger Then Exit For
Next

If i < rs.Fields.Count Then
   ' First Integer field found
Else
   ' No such field exists
End If

rs.Close

End Sub
```

We can also control the step size and direction for the counter in a For loop using the Step keyword. For instance, in the following code, the counter *i* is incremented by 2 each time the block of code is executed:

```
For i = 1 to 10 Step 2
   ' code block goes here
Next i
```

The following loop counts down from 10 to 1 in increments of –1. This can be useful when we want to examine a collection (such as the cells in a row or column) from the bottom up.

```
For i = 10 to 1 Step -1
   ' code block goes here
Next i
```

The For Each Loop

The For Each loop is a variation on the For loop that was designed to iterate through a collection of objects (as well as through elements in an array) and is generally much more efficient than using the traditional For loop. The general syntax is:

```
For Each ObjectVar In CollectionName

    ' block of code goes here . . .

Next ObjectVar
```

where ObjectVar is a variable of the same object type as the objects within the collection. The code block will execute once for each object in the collection.

The following version of *PrintFields* uses a For Each loop. It is more elegant than the previous version (and more efficient as well):

```
Sub PrintFields2()

Dim fld As Field
Dim rs As Recordset
Set rs = CurrentDb.OpenRecordset("Objects")

For Each fld In rs.Fields
    Debug.Print fld.Name
Next

rs.Close

End Sub
```

Thus, when iterating through a collection of objects, we have two choices:

```
For Each object in Collection
    ' code block here
Next object
```

or:

```
For i = 1 to Collection.Count
    ' code block here
Next i
```

It is important to keep in mind that the For Each loop can be much faster than the For loop when dealing with collections of objects.

The Do Loop

The Do loop has several variations. To describe these variations, we use the notation:

```
{While | Until}
```

to represent either the word While or the word Until, but not both. With this in mind, here are the possible syntaxes for the Do loop:

```
Do {While | Until} condition

    ' code block here

Loop
```
or:
```
Do

    ' code block here

Loop {While | Until} condition
```
Actually, there is a fifth possibility, because we can dispense with `condition` completely and write:
```
Do

    ' code block here

Loop
```
The Do loop is used quite often in DAO programming to iterate through a recordset. Here is a typical example that prints all values of a particular field in a recordset:
```
Sub DoExample( )

Dim rs As Recordset
Set rs = CurrentDb.OpenRecordset("Objects")

rs.MoveFirst

Do While Not rs.EOF
    Debug.Print rs!Name
    rs.MoveNext
Loop

rs.Close

End Sub
```
We will discuss the EOF property, as well as the MoveFirst and MoveNext methods, when we discuss Recordset objects later in the book.

Just as the For loop has an Exit For statement for terminating the loop, a Do loop has an Exit Do statement for exiting the Do loop.

The Select Case Statement

As we have seen, the If...Then... construct is used to perform different tasks based on different possibilities. An alternative construct that is often more readable is the Select Case statement, whose syntax is:

```
Select Case testexpression
   Case value1
      ' statements to execute if testexpression = value1
   Case value2
      ' statements to execute if testexpression = value2


   . . .


   Case Else
      ' statements to execute otherwise
End Select
```

Note that the Case Else part is optional. To illustrate, the following code is the
Select Case version of Example 12-1 in Chapter 12 (see the discussion of the "The
Switch Function") that displays the type of a file based on its extension. I think you
will agree that this is a bit more readable than the previous version:

```
Sub ShowFileType(FileExt As String)

Dim FileType As Variant

Select Case FileExt
  Case "mdb"
    FileType = "Database"
  Case "txt"
    FileType = "text"
  Case "dbf"
    FileType = "dBase"
  Case Else
    FileType = "unknown"
End Select

' Display result
MsgBox FileType

End Sub
```

Note that VBA allows us to place more than one condition in the same Case statement (separated by commas). This is useful when more than one case produces the
same result.

A Final Note on VBA

There is a lot more to the VBA language than we have covered here. In fact, the
Microsoft VBA reference manual is about 300 pages long. However, we have covered the main points needed to begin Access VBA/DAO programming. (For a reference on the VBA language, you might want to check out the book *VB & VBA in a
Nutshell*, by Paul Lomax, also published by O'Reilly.)

Actually, many Access VBA programming tasks require only a small portion of VBA's features, and you will probably find yourself wrestling much more with DAO's object model than with the VBA language itself.

I conclude our discussion of the VBA language *per se* with a brief outline of topics for further study, which you can do using the VBA help files.

File-Related Functions

VBA has a large number of functions related to file and directory housekeeping. Table 13-1 contains a selection of them.

Table 13-1. Some VBA file and directory functions

Function	Description
Dir	Find a file with a certain name.
FileLen	Get the length of a file.
FileTimeDate	Get the date stamp of a file.
FileCopy	Copy a file.
Kill	Delete a file.
Name	Rename a file or directory.
RmDir	Delete a directory.
MkDir	Make a new directory.

In addition to the file-related functions in Table 13-1, there may be times when it is useful to create new text files to store data. VBA provides a number of functions for this purpose, headed by the Open statement, whose (simplified) syntax is:

```
Open pathname For mode As [#]filenumber
```

Once a file has been opened, we can read or write to it.

Date- and Time-Related Functions

VBA has a large number of functions related to manipulating dates and times. Table 13-2 contains a selection.

Table 13-2. Some date- and time-related functions

Function	Description
Date, Now, Time	Get the current date or time.
DateAdd, DateDiff, DatePart	Perform date calculations.
DateSerial, DateValue	Return a date.
TimeSerial, TimeValue	Return a time.
Date, Time	Set the date or time.
Timer	Time a process.

The Format Function

The Format function is used to format strings, numbers, and dates. Table 13-3 gives a few examples.

Table 13-3. Format function examples

Expression	Return value[a]
Format(Date, "Long Date")	Thursday, April 30, 1998
Format(Time, "Long Time")	5:03:47 PM
Format(Date, "mm/dd/yy hh:mm:ss AMPM")	04/30/98 12:00:00 AM
Format(1234.5, "$##,##0.00")	$1,234.50
Format("HELLO", "<")	"hello"

[a] The exact format of the return value is governed by certain system settings.

PART V

Data Access Objects

CHAPTER 14

Programming DAO: Overview

We have seen that Access SQL provides a way to create and manipulate database objects, such as tables and queries, through its DDL and DML components. In addition, users can enter SQL statements directly into the Access *SQL View* window.

On the other hand, Microsoft Access allows us to program the Jet database engine directly, through its programming interface, which is known as *Data Access Objects*, or DAO. This gives the user far more control over a database.

DAO is a complicated structure, and I won't discuss all of its aspects. Our focus in this book will be on gaining a general understanding of the following concepts and components:

- The organization of DAO, which is at least partly object-oriented
- The DDL component of DAO
- The DML component of DAO

I will certainly not cover all aspects of the DDL and DML components. My main goal is to prepare you so that you can get whatever additional information you need from Microsoft Access' extensive online help for the DAO model or from similar hardcopy reference manuals.

Objects

Before discussing the various components of the DAO model, we must discuss the concept of an *object*. In the parlance of object-orientation, an object is something that is identified by its *properties* and its *methods* (or *actions*).

As we will see (and as the name implies) DAO is full of objects. For example, each saved table in an Access database is an object, called a *TableDef* object. (Actually, it is the *definition* of the table, rather than its data, that is an object of type *TableDef*.) Some of the properties of *TableDef* objects are *Name, RecordCount, DateCreated,* and *LastUpdated*.

An object's methods can be thought of as procedures or functions that act on the object. For instance, one of the methods of a *TableDef* object is CreateField, which, as the name implies, is used to create a new field for the *TableDef* object. Another method is OpenRecordset, which creates a *Recordset* object that can be used to manipulate the data in the table. (A more object-oriented view of methods is that they are messages sent to the object, saying, in effect, perform the following action.)

Object Variables

In order to access the properties or invoke the methods of an object, we need to first define an *object variable* to reference that object.

VBA and DAO offer a wide variety of *object data types*. There is a slight difference in syntax when declaring and setting an object variable, as opposed to a standard variable. For instance, here is an example using the *Database* object type. Note that the full pathname of the LIBRARY database on my PC is *d:\dbase\library.mdb*:

```
Dim dbLibrary as Database
Set dbLibrary = "d:\dbase\library.mdb"
```

In general, the syntax is:

```
Dim objectVariable as ObjectDataType
Set objectVariable = ObjectName
```

Note that the only difference between setting object variables and setting standard variables is the keyword *Set*. However, this minor syntactic difference belies a much more significant difference between standard variables and object variables.

In particular, a standard variable can be thought of as a name for a location in the computer's memory that holds the data. For instance, in the code:

```
Dim intVar As Integer
intVar = 123
```

the variable *intVar* is a 4-byte memory location that holds the integer value 123. Figure 14-1 illustrates the variable *intVar*. (Actually, the 4-byte memory location holds the value 123 in *binary* format, but that is not relevant to our discussion.)

Figure 14-1. An example of the intVar variable

Of course, if we were to write:

```
Dim intVar As Integer
Dim intVar2 As Integer
intvar = 123
intVar2 = intVar
intVar2 = 567
```

we would not expect the last line of code to have any effect upon the value of the variable *intVar*, which should still be 123.

On the other hand, an object variable is not the name of a memory location that holds the object's "value," whatever that means. Rather, an object variable holds the *address* of the area of memory that holds the object. Put another way, the object variable holds a reference to, or points to, the object. It is therefore called a *pointer variable*. The idea is pictured in Figure 14-2, where *rsBooks* and *rsBooks2* are object variables, both pointing to an object of type *Recordset*.

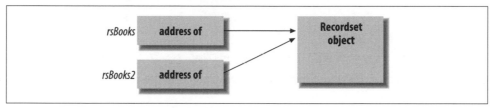

Figure 14-2. An example of a pointer variable

To illustrate this further, consider the code in Example 14-1.

Example 14-1. An object variable example

```
Sub exaObjectVar( )

'Declare some object variables
Dim dbLib As DATABASE
Dim rsBooks As Recordset
Dim rsBooks2 As Recordset

'Set dbLib to the current database (i.e. LIBRARY)
Set dbLib = CurrentDb

'Open a recordset object for the BOOKS table
Set rsBooks = dbLib.OpenRecordset("BOOKS")

'Two object variables will refer to the same object
Set rsBooks2 = rsBooks

'Use a property of this object
MsgBox "BOOKS record count: " & rsBooks.RecordCount

'Destroy the object using rsBooks2 reference
rsBooks2.Close

'Now rsBooks has nothing to refer to, so we get error
MsgBox "BOOKS record count: " & rsBooks.RecordCount

End Sub
```

First, we declare two object variables of type *Recordset* (we will discuss this type in detail later). The line:

```
Set rsBooks = dbLib.OpenRecordset("BOOKS")
```

sets *rsBooks* to point to (or refer to) a *Recordset* object created from the BOOKS table. Note again that, unlike standard variables, setting an object variable requires the use of the keyword *Set*. The line:

```
Set rsBooks2 = rsBooks
```

sets *rsBooks2* to point to the same *Recordset* object as *rsBooks*, as shown in Figure 14-2.

Next, the line:

```
MsgBox "BOOKS record count: " & rsBooks.RecordCount
```

displays the message box in Figure 14-3, showing that there are 14 books in the recordset.

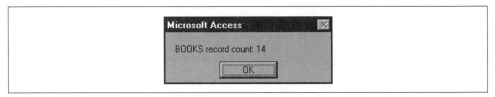

Figure 14-3. The message box from the exaObjectVar() example

To illustrate the fact that both variables point to the same object, the line:

```
rsBooks2.Close
```

uses the pointer *rsBooks2* to destroy (or close) the *Recordset* object. Then, when the line:

```
MsgBox "BOOKS record count: " & rsBooks.RecordCount
```

is executed, the *Recordset* object that both variables referred to is gone, and so the expression rsBooks.RecordCount causes an "Object invalid or no longer set" error, as shown in Figure 14-4.

Figure 14-4. Error message from the exaObjectvar() example

The moral of this example is that it is important to remember that object variables refer to objects and that more than one variable can refer to the same object. Despite this, it is customary to use the misleading statement "the *objVar* object" when we really should be saying "the object referred to by *objVar*."

Object-Variable Naming Conventions

Tables 14-1 and 14-2 describe the naming convention for both standard and object variables that we will (try to) use in this book. (Table 14-1 is a repeat of Table 10-3.) We will explain the various object types as we proceed through this chapter.

Table 14-1. Standard-variable naming for VBA

Variable	Prefix
Boolean	bool, b, or f
Byte	b, byt, or bt
Currency	cur
Date	dt or dte
Double	d or dbl
Integer	i, c, or int
Long	l, c, or lng
Single	s or sng
String	str
User-defined type	typ, u, or ut
Variant	v or var

Table 14-2. Object-variable naming for VBA

Variable	Prefix
Container	con
Database	db
Document	doc
Dynaset	dyn
Error	err
Field	fld
Form	frm
Index	idx
Object	obj
Parameter	prm
Property	prp

Table 14-2. Object-variable naming for VBA (continued)

Variable	Prefix
QueryDef	qdf
Recordset	rs
Relation	rel
Report	rpt
Snapshot	snp
Table	tbl
TableDef	tdf or tbl
User	usr
Workspace	ws

Referencing the Properties and Methods of an Object

The general syntax for referring to an object's properties and methods is very simple. Suppose that *objVar* is a variable that refers to an object. If AProperty is a property of this object, then we can access this property using the syntax:

```
objVar.AProperty
```

If AMethod is a method for this object, then we can invoke that method with the syntax:

```
objVar.AMethod(any required parameters)
```

To illustrate, consider the code in Example 14-2.

Example 14-2. A property and method example

```
Sub exaPropertyMethod( )

Dim dbLib As DATABASE
Dim qdfExpensive As QueryDef

' Get current database (LIBRARY)
Set dbLib = CurrentDb

' Show Name property
MsgBox dbLib.Name

' Invoke the CreateQueryDef method to create a query
Set qdfExpensive = dbLib.CreateQueryDef("Expensive",_
"SELECT * FROM BOOKS WHERE Price > 20")

End Sub
```

The line:

```
Set dbLib = CurrentDb
```

sets the object variable of type Database to point to the current database, that is, the LIBRARY database. The line:

```
MsgBox dbLib.Name
```

displays the value of the Name property of *dbLib*. The line:

```
Set qdfExpensive = dbLib.CreateQueryDef("Expensive",_
"SELECT * FROM BOOKS WHERE Price > 20")
```

invokes the CreateQueryDef method to create a new query named Expensive and defined by the SQL statement:

```
SELECT * FROM BOOKS WHERE Price > 20
```

Note that the code:

```
dbLib.CreateQueryDef("Expensive","SELECT * FROM BOOKS WHERE Price > 20")
```

invokes the method, which returns the *QueryDef* object, which is then pointed to by the object variable *qdfExpensive*. If you run this program, you will notice a new entry in the *Query* tab of the *Database* window. (If the query Expensive is already in the database, delete it before running this program. Also, you may need to switch away from and then return to the *Query* tab to refresh the list.)

The DAO Object Model

As the name Data Access Objects suggests, the DAO is, at least in part, an object-oriented environment. In particular, the DAO is implemented as a hierarchy of collections of objects. Figure 14-5 shows the DAO Object Model, describing the collections and their objects.

Each of the shaded boxes represents a collection of objects. (Thus *DBEngine* is the only noncollection.) The name of the objects contained within a given collection is just the singular of the collection name. For instance, the *TableDefs* collection holds *TableDef* objects, and the *Documents* collection holds *Document* objects. *DBEngine* is the only standalone object—not contained in any collection.

There is a potential point of confusion about the DAO object hierarchy in Figure 14-5 that we should address. Consider, for example, the relationship between the *Databases* and *Workspaces* collections. It would be incorrect to say, as one might infer from the diagram, that the *Databases* collection is contained in the *Workspaces* collection. Indeed, the line from *Workspaces* to *Databases* means that each Workspace object has (or as Microsoft would say, "contains") a *Databases* collection.

Perhaps the best way to view the situation is to say that each object in the DAO hierarchy has three things associated with it: *collections*, *methods*, and *properties*. For instance, a *Workspace* object has the following items associated with it:

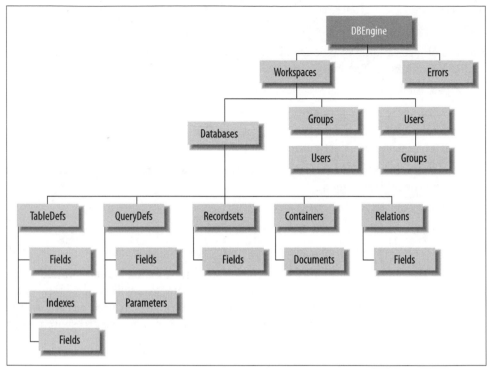

Figure 14-5. The DAO object model

Collections
    Databases
    Groups
    Users
    Properties (not shown in Figure 14-5)

Methods
    BeginTrans
    Close
    CommitTrans
    CreateDatabase
    CreateGroup
    CreateUser
    OpenDatabase
    Rollback

Properties
    IsolateODBCTrans
    Name
    UserName

Let us pause for a brief aside. In an object-oriented environment such as C++, or even Visual Basic, a collection is also considered an object. Moreover, the value of one object's property can be another object (these are so-called *object properties*). Hence, in such an object-oriented environment, we would probably think of the collections associated with an object as just additional properties of that object. However, Microsoft chose not to express this explicitly in the DAO.

Figure 14-6 shows a more detailed example of the object-collection relationship. The *Containers* collection in this case contains three *Container* objects, each of which has (the same) properties and methods. Each object also "contains" a *Documents* collection, which contains some *Document* objects.

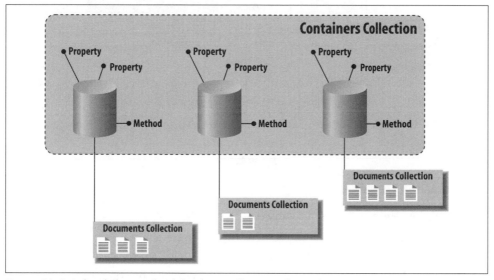

Figure 14-6. A detailed example of the object-collection relationship

Thus, according to this model, there may be more than one *Documents* collection. Indeed, there is one *Documents* collection for every *Container* object. Similarly, there is one *Databases* collection for each *Workspace* object and one *TableDefs* collection for each *Database* object.

The Microsoft Access Object Model

You may have noticed that there are no collections in the DAO object model corresponding to Access forms or reports. The fact is that DAO is not the whole object story. Microsoft Access defines its own collections of objects, as shown in Figure 14-7.

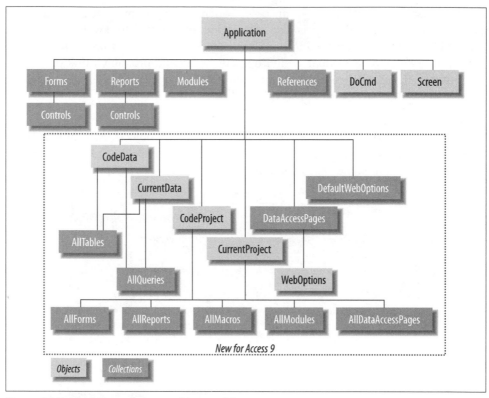

Figure 14-7. The Microsoft Access object model

Access defines the Forms collection to hold all currently open forms. (Note the words "currently open.") Similarly, the Reports collection holds all currently open reports. The *Application*, *DoCmd*, and *Screen* objects are not contained in a collection. The *Modules* collection holds all open code modules.

The *References* collection holds all *Reference* objects. A *Reference* object is a reference to another application's type library, which is a file containing information on the objects that the application exposes through Automation. It is through Automation objects that an application can share some of its features with other applications. However, we will not go further into this subject in this book. (Allow me to recommend my book *Concepts of Object-Oriented Programming with Visual Basic*, published by Springer-Verlag, for more information on OLE Automation geared toward the Visual Basic programmer.)

As you can see in Figure 14-7, Microsoft has added several new objects to the object model for Access 9 for Office 2000. (In fact, there are a few more objects not shown in the figure.) Several of these objects relate to the Internet. The *CodeData* and *CurrentData* objects have child collections containing all tables and all queries (whether open or not). The *CodeProject* and *CurrentProject* objects have child collections containing all forms, reports, modules, macros, and *DataAccessPages* (whether open or not).

We will not discuss the Access object model in general in this book, since it belongs more to issues related to the Access user interface (forms and reports) than to database manipulation.

On the other hand, we will discuss some aspects of the Access object model. For instance, the line:

```
Set db = CurrentDb
```

sets the variable *db* to point to the currently open database. The function `CurrentDb`, which we will discuss in more detail later, is not a DAO function—you will not find it in the DAO reference manual. It is a part of the Access object model: it is a method of the Application object, to be precise. Thus, the Access object model and DAO both provide supporting objects and instructions for database management.

Referencing Objects

The first step in understanding the objects in the DAO and Microsoft Access object hierarchies is to understand how to refer to an object in the hierarchy. In particular, we can refer to an object by the name of *ObjectName* that belongs to a collection named *CollectionName*, by any of the following syntaxes:

- `CollectionName!ObjectName`, or `CollectionName![ObjectName]` when `ObjectName` has illegal characters, such as spaces.
- `CollectionName("ObjectName")`.
- `CollectionName(StringVar)`, where `StringVar` holds the string `ObjectName`.
- `CollectionName(Index)`, where `Index` is the index number of the object in the collection. Indexes start with 0 and go up to one less than the number of objects in the collection. (As we will see, the number of elements in a collection is denoted by `CollectionName.Count`.)

For instance, the *TableDef* object named BOOKS in the *TableDefs* collection is denoted by:

```
TableDefs!BOOKS
```

or:

```
TableDefs("BOOKS")
```

or:

```
Dim strBooks as String
strBooks = "BOOKS"
TableDefs(strBooks)
```

or, if BOOKS happens to be the first *TableDef* object in the *TableDefs* collection:

```
TableDefs(0)
```

The exclamation point (!) used in the first syntax is called the *bang operator*.

Fully Qualified Object Names

There is a problem with these names. For instance, to which object does *Fields(0)* refer? There are several *Fields* collections in the DAO hierarchy, as can be seen from Figure 14-5. Let us refer to the names described in the previous syntax as *semiqualified names*. To avoid the problem that a semiqualified name may not be unique, we must use the *fully qualified object name*, which is formed by tracing the *entire* hierarchy from the top (*DBEngine*) to the desired object. For instance, the fully qualified name for BOOKS is:

```
DBEngine.Workspaces(0).Databases![d:\dbase\library.mdb].TableDefs!BOOKS
```

Let us examine this name. It is composed of four separate semiqualified object names, separated by periods. These periods are referred to as *dot operators*:

```
DBEngine.
Workspaces(0).
Databases![d:\dbase\library.mdb].
TableDefs!BOOKS
```

Perhaps the easiest way to make sense of this name is to start from the bottom. The semiqualified name of the object we are interested in is:

```
TableDefs!BOOKS
```

This object is contained in the *TableDefs* collection for the *Database* object named:

```
Databases![d:\dbase\library.mdb]
```

This object is, in turn, contained in the *Databases* collection of the default *Workspace* object (more on this later), which is:

```
Workspaces(0)
```

which, in turn, is contained in the *DBEngine* object. Separating each of these object names by the dot operator gives the fully qualified object name.

In general, the syntax for a semiqualified object name is:

```
Collection!Object
```

and for a fully qualified object name, it is:

```
DBEngine.Collection1!Object1. · · · .CollectionN!ObjectN
```

There seems to be much confusion over when to use the bang operator (!) and when to use the dot operator (.). Perhaps the following will help:

- The bang operator is used to separate an object's name from the name of the collection of which it is a member. In other words, bang signifies a member of a collection. It therefore appears in semiqualified object names.
- The dot operator is used to separate each semiqualified object name in a fully qualified object name. In other words, it signifies the next step in the hierarchy.
- The dot operator is also used to denote a property or method of an object.

This naming convention is really not as confusing as it may look at first, if you remember the previous three maxims. However, if you want confusing, stay tuned for default collections.

Using Object Variables to Your Advantage

As you can see, a fully qualified object name can be quite lengthy. This problem is compounded by the fact that it may be necessary to refer to the same object many times in a program. There are two common ways to deal with this issue.

One way is to use object variables. Consider the code in Example 14-3 to display the RecordCount property of the BOOKS table.

Example 14-3. An object variable example

```
Sub exaObjVar( )

Dim ws As Workspace
Dim dbLib As DATABASE
Dim tdfBooks As TableDef

Set ws = DBEngine.Workspaces(0)
Set dbLib = ws.Databases![d:\dbase\library.mdb]
Set tdfBooks = dbLib.TableDefs!BOOKS

MsgBox tdfBooks.RecordCount

End Sub
```

By defining three object variables, *ws*, *dbLib*, and *tdfBooks*, we were able to avoid writing the fully qualified name of BOOKS (on a single line, that is). Also, the line:

```
    MsgBox tdfBooks.RecordCount
```

is much easier to read. (It reads: "Message me the record count of TableDef tdf-Books.")

The use of object variables in this way has several advantages and is highly recommended. First, it tends to make the lines of code shorter and more readable. Second, we can refer to the object variable *tdfBooks* many times without having to write the fully qualified object name each time. As a result, the program will run somewhat faster, since VBA does not have to resolve the object name by climbing down the object hierarchy more than once.

Default Collections

There is another method that can be used for shortening fully qualified object names. In particular, each object has a *default collection*, which can be used as follows. Consider a portion of a fully qualified name:

```
    Collection1!Object1.Collection2!Object2
```

If *Collection2* is the default collection of *Object1*, then this name may be shortened to:

```
Collection1!Object1!Object2
```

where we have omitted the default collection name *Collection2*, as well as the preceding dot.

For instance, the default collection of *DBEngine* is *Workspaces*. Hence:

```
DBEngine.Workspaces!MyWorkspace
```

can be shortened to:

```
DBEngine!MyWorkspace
```

and the phrase:

```
DBEngine.Workspaces(0)
```

can be shortened to:

```
DBEngine(0)
```

Also, since the default collection for a *Workspace* object is *Databases*, the phrase:

```
DBEngine.Workspaces(0).Databases(0)
```

can be shortened to:

```
DBEngine(0)(0)
```

Table 14-3 shows the default collections in the DAO and Access object model.

Table 14-3. DAO and Access object default collections

Object	Default collection
DBEngine	Workspaces
Workspace	Databases
Database	TableDefs
TableDef	Fields
Recordset	Fields
QueryDef	Parameters
Index	Fields
Relation	Fields
Container	Documents
User	Groups
Group	Users
Forms	Controls
Reports	Controls

The use of default collections can save space. However, it does very little for readability (to say the least) and is probably best left to programmers with so much experience that they hardly read the names anyway! To emphasize the point, each of the lines in Example 14-4 displays the RecordCount property of the BOOKS table. Note that the full name of the database library file on my computer is *d:\dbase\library.mdb*.

Example 14-4. A default collections example

```
Sub exaDefaultCollections()

MsgBox DBEngine.Workspaces(0).Databases![d:\dbase\library.mdb]. _
TableDefs!BOOKS.RecordCount

MsgBox _
DBEngine(0).Databases![d:\dbase\library.mdb].TableDefs!BOOKS.RecordCount

MsgBox DBEngine(0)![d:\dbase\library.mdb].TableDefs!BOOKS.RecordCount

MsgBox DBEngine(0)![d:\dbase\library.mdb]!BOOKS.RecordCount

MsgBox DBEngine(0)(0)!BOOKS.RecordCount

End Sub
```

Collections Are Objects Too

In a true object-centric environment, *everything* is an object. While Access, VBA, and DAO may not go this far, it is true that collections are objects, and so they have their own properties and methods.

In the Access environment, collections can be divided into three types:

Microsoft Access collections
> Which are part of the Access object hierarchy

DAO collections
> Which are part of the DAO hierarchy

User-defined collections
> Which are VBA objects of type *Collection*

Note that only user-defined collections are of type *Collection*, which is a VBA data type, not a DAO data type. The properties and methods of collections are not very complicated, so let us list them here.

Properties and Methods of Access Collections

The Access collections *Forms, Reports,* and *Controls* have no methods and only one property, *Count*, which reports the number of objects in the collection. Thus, the line:

```
Forms.Count
```

reports the number of opened forms in the current database. (When we discuss *Container* objects, we'll see that there is a way to get the number of saved forms as well.)

Properties and Methods of DAO Collections

DAO collections fall into two categories with respect to their properties and methods. All DAO collections have a single property: Count. All DAO collections also have the Refresh method, which we will discuss a bit later. In addition, some of the collections have the Append and corresponding Delete methods, while others do not.

Collections that have Append and Delete methods:
> Workspaces
> TableDefs
> QueryDefs
> Groups
> Users
> Relations
> Fields
> Indexes
> Properties (explained later)

Collections that do not have Append and Delete methods:
> Databases
> Errors
> Recordsets
> Containers
> Documents
> Parameters

Evidently, some collections do not have Append or Delete methods because DAO does not want the user to append or delete objects from these collections. This is reasonable because DAO takes care of collection housekeeping automatically for these collections. For example, DAO automatically appends new databases to the *Databases* collection whenever they are created using the CreateDatabase method. However, it does not do so for new *TableDef* or *QueryDef* objects, for instance.

Note that Microsoft Access will do the housekeeping chores for you when objects are created and saved using the Access interface.

Properties and Methods of User-Defined Collections

User-defined *Collection* objects have one property: Count. They have three methods: Add, Remove, and Item. Add and Remove perform as advertised by their names, and we will see an example shortly. The Item method is used to identify the items in the collection, since they may or may not have names.

A single user-defined collection can contain objects of various types, including other collections. Here is an example to illustrate the Add method.

In Example 14-5, we create two collections: *colParent* and *colChild*. We then place *colChild* inside *colParent*, along with the BOOKS *TableDef* object. Thus, the *colParent* collection contains two objects of very different types—one *Collection* object and one *TableDef* object. (While this example is not of much practical value, it does illustrate the point.)

Example 14-5. A collections example

```
Sub exaCollections()

' Declare two variables of type collection
Dim colParent As New Collection
Dim colChild As New Collection

Dim tdfBooks As TableDef
Dim objVar As Object

Set tdfBooks = DBEngine(0)(0).TableDefs!Books

' Use Add method of collection object
' to add objects to colParent collection
colParent.Add colChild
colParent.Add tdfBooks

' Display size of collection
MsgBox "Size of Parent collection " & colParent.Count

' Iterate through collection. Note use of
' TypeOf statement
For Each objVar In colParent
    If TypeOf objVar Is Collection Then
        MsgBox "Collection"
    ElseIf TypeOf objVar Is TableDef Then
        MsgBox objVar.Name
    End If
Next

End Sub
```

In Example 14-5, we used the Add method of the *Collection* object to add items to the collection and the Count property of the *Collection* object, which returns the size of the collection. Note also the use of the TypeOf statement to determine the type of each object in the collection.

Now let us consider the Item method, which returns a specific object from a collection. The general syntax is:

```
Collection.Item(index)
```

where *index* is an index into the collection. Note that DAO collections begin with index 0 and go to index Collection.Count - 1.

To illustrate the Item method, in place of the code:

```
For Each tbl In db.TableDefs
    strTbls = strTbls & vbCrLf & tbl.Name
Next tbl
```

we could have written:

```
For i = 0 To db.TableDefs.Count - 1

  strTbls = strTbls & vbCrLf & _
db.TableDefs.Item(i).Name

  Next i
```

We should remark that an object's ordinal position in a collection is never guaranteed and can sometimes change without warning. Thus, for example, it is unwise to rely on the fact that the object that is *Item(0)* at some time will always be *Item(0)*.

Incidentally, one of the drawbacks of collections that contain different types of objects, as in the previous example, is that we can seldom do the same thing to all of the objects in the collection. For this reason, creating collections containing different types of objects is generally not very useful.

Say It Again

It is worth re-emphasizing that the collections in the DAO hierarchy are *not* contained in their parent collections (as is the case for the user-defined collections in the previous example). For example, the *TableDefs* collection contains only *TableDef* objects (table definitions). It does not contain the *Fields* collection. Rather, each *TableDef* object contains a *Fields* collection. We can confirm this with the code in Example 14-6, which displays the size of the *TableDefs* collection for the LIBRARY database as 14 and then displays the names of each of its 14 objects, showing that there is nothing but *TableDef* objects in the *TableDefs* collection.

Example 14-6. A TableDef example

```
Sub exaCheckTableDefs( )

Dim db As DATABASE
Dim tbl As TableDef
Dim strTbls As String

Set db = CurrentDb

strTbls = ""
MsgBox db.TableDefs.Count
For Each tbl In db.TableDefs
    strTbls = strTbls & vbCrLf & tbl.Name & " - " & TypeName(tbl)
Next

MsgBox strTbls

End Sub
```

Running the code in Example 14-6 produces two message boxes; the second is shown in Figure 14-8, which also shows that most of the *TableDefs* in the database are system-table definitions, created by Microsoft Access for its own use. (Just in case some additional tables get added to the LIBRARY database after this book goes to print, you may find a different list of tables when you run this example.) Figure 14-8 also illustrates the use of the function TypeName.

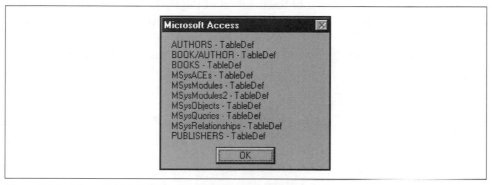

Figure 14-8. A list of TableDefs generated by exaCheckTableDefs()

Refreshing Certain Collections

There are times when the Microsoft Jet engine does not have the latest information on the contents of a collection. For example, this can happen in a multiuser environment, when one user makes a change to a collection. It can also happen when a host environment, such as Microsoft Access, makes a change to the environment. To see this, try the following simple experiment.

Enter the following code:

```
Sub temp( )

Dim db As DATABASE
Set db = DBEngine(0)(0)

' db.TableDefs.Refresh
MsgBox "Table count: " & db.TableDefs.Count

End Sub
```

Run the procedure. You should get a message that there are 13 tables in the *TableDefs* collection. Now use Microsoft Access to create a new table, and save the table. Then rerun the previous code. It will still report that there are 13 tables! Now remove the comment mark on the line:

```
' db.TableDefs.Refresh
```

and rerun the code. You should now get an accurate table count.

The point here is that the Jet engine does not keep track of the machinations of its host application—Microsoft Access. Hence, to be certain that a collection is up to date, you may need to use the Refresh method.

The Properties Collection

One item that has been left out of the diagram of the DAO object model shown earlier in Figure 14-5 (and is done so in most DAO diagrams) is the *Properties* collection. This is because every DAO object has a *Properties* collection, so it would clutter up the diagram considerably without adding much information. Figure 14-9 shows a *Properties* collection.

Figure 14-9. An Access properties collection diagram

The purpose of the *Properties* collections is simple. Properties are objects too, and so they are contained in collections, just like all other objects of the DAO (except *DBEngine*). Thus, the *Properties* collection of an object contains the *Property* objects (better known simply as properties) for the object.

The fact that the properties of an object are themselves objects and thus reside in a collection, implies that we may access these properties in several different ways. For example, the RecordCount property of the BOOKS *TableDef* object can be referred to in any of the following ways (among others):

```
TableDefs!BOOKS.Properties!RecordCount
TableDefs("BOOKS").Properties("RecordCount")
```

or just:

```
TableDefs!BOOKS.RecordCount
```

Of course, the latter form is the simplest and most commonly used. Note that the *Properties* collection is never the default collection for any object. Hence, for example, the syntax:

```
TableDefs!BOOKS!RecordCount
```

(which differs from the previous only by a bang) will cause VBA to look for the *RecordCount* object in the default *Fields* collection for the BOOKS *TableDef* object. Of course, it will not find such an object and so the error message "Item not found in this collection" will result.

The Virtues of Properties Collections

There are several virtues to the existence of *Properties* collections. One is that it is possible to iterate through all of the properties of an object, using the For Each syntax discussed earlier, for instance, without even knowing the names of the properties.

For example, the following simple code:

```
Dim db As DATABASE
Dim prp As Property
Set db = CurrentDb

For Each prp In db.TableDefs!BOOKS.Properties
    Debug.Print prp.Name
Next prp
```

produces the following list of all properties of the BOOKS object:

```
Name
Updatable
DateCreated
LastUpdated
Connect
Attributes
SourceTableName
RecordCount
ValidationRule
ValidationText
ConflictTable
OrderByOn
OrderBy
```

Another virtue of *Properties* collections is that they allow for the creation (and storage) of new properties. We discuss this next.

Types of Properties

In general, the properties of an object can be classified into three groups, depending upon their origin:

- Built-in properties
- Application-defined properties
- User-defined properties

The Jet database engine defines *built-in properties* for its objects. For instance, a *TableDef* object has a built-in Name property. In addition, Microsoft Access (and other applications that may be using the Jet engine) can create *application-defined properties*. For example, if you create a table in Microsoft Access and fill in the *Description* field in the *View...Properties* dialog box, Access creates a *Description* property for the table and appends it to the *Properties* collection for that *TableDef* object. Finally, as we will see later, the user can create his own properties.

It is important to note that an application-defined property is created *only* if the user assigns a value to that property. For example, if you do not specifically type a description in the *Description* field, as discussed earlier, then Access will not create a *Description* property. In other words, Access does not create a blank *Description* property. If you then use this property in your code, an error will result. Thus, when you write programs that refer to either application-defined or user-defined properties, it is important to check for errors, in case the referenced property does not exist.

Of course, each *Property* object, being an object, has its own properties, but you will be glad to hear that these properties do not have *Property* objects. (Where would this end?)

We should also mention that properties can be classified as *read/write, read-only,* or *write-only*. A read/write property can be both read and written to (i.e., changed), whereas a read-only property can be read but not changed, and a write-only property can be changed but not read. When an object is first created, its read/write properties can be set. However, in many cases, once the object is appended to a collection, some of these properties may become read-only and can therefore no longer be changed.

The properties of a *Property* object are described as follows. A *Property* object has no methods.

Property: Inherited

For the built-in *Property* objects, this value is always 0 (False). For user-defined properties, this value is true if the property exists because it was inherited from another object. For instance, any *Recordset* object that is created from a *QueryDef* object inherits the *QueryDef*'s properties.

Property: Name

The usual Name property, which in this case is the name of the property represented by this *Property* object.

Property: Type

This value gives the data type of the object. Note that the Type property is read/write until the *Property* object is appended to a *Properties* collection, after which it becomes read-only. The value of the *Type* property is an integer. VBA provides built-in constants so that we do not need to remember integer values. Table 14-4 gives these values, along with their numerical values, which are returned in code such as `MsgBox Property.Type`.

Table 14-4. Constants for the Type property in VBA

Data type	Constant	Numerical value
Boolean	dbBoolean	1
Byte	dbByte	2
Integer	dbInteger	3
Long	dbLong	4
Currency	dbCurrency	5
Single	dbSingle	6
Double	dbDouble	7
Date/Time	dbDate	8
Text	dbText	10
Long Binary (OLE Object)	dbLongBinary	11
Memo	dbMemo	12
GUID	dbGUID	15

Property: Value

Finally, we get to the main property of a *Property* object—its value, which can be any value commensurate with the assigned *Type* property of the *Property* object.

Let us consider another example of how to use the *Properties* collection. The code in Example 14-7 will display the entire contents of the *Properties* collection for the BOOKS *TableDef* object in the LIBRARY database.

Example 14-7. A Properties collection example

```
Sub exaProperties()

Dim db As DATABASE
Dim tbl As TableDef
Dim prp As Property
Dim str As String

Set db = CurrentDb
Set tbl = db!BOOKS

str = ""
For Each prp In tbl.Properties

    str = str & prp.Name
    str = str & " = " & prp.Value
    str = str & " (" & prp.Type & ") "
    str = str & prp.Inherited & vbCrLf

Next prp
```

Example 14-7. A Properties collection example (continued)

```
MsgBox "BOOKS has " & tbl.Properties.Count _
& " properties: " & vbCrLf & str

End Sub
```

Running this procedure gives the window shown in Figure 14-10, where each line has the form `Name = Value (Type) Inherited`.

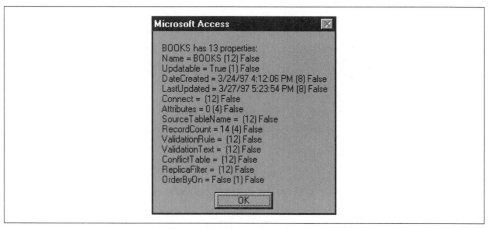

Figure 14-10. Window generated from executing exaProperties

User-Defined Properties

We mentioned that a user can add user-defined properties to an object. Let us consider an example of adding a new property to the BOOKS *TableDef* object.

The code in Example 14-8 adds the user-defined property named `UserProperty` to the BOOKS table. It uses the `CreateProperty` method of the *TableDef* object.

Example 14-8. A user-defined properties example

```
Sub exaUserDefinedProperty()

' Add user-defined property to BOOKS TableDef object

Dim db As DATABASE
Dim tbl As TableDef
Dim prp As Property

Dim str As String

Set db = CurrentDb
Set tbl = db!BOOKS

' Create new property using CreateProperty method
Set prp = tbl.CreateProperty("UserProperty", dbText,"Programming DAO is fun.")
```

Example 14-8. A user-defined properties example (continued)

```
' Append it to Properties collection
tbl.Properties.Append prp

' List all properties
str = ""
For Each prp In tbl.Properties
    str = str & prp.Name
    str = str & " = " & prp.Value
    str = str & " (" & prp.Type & ") "
    str = str & prp.Inherited & vbCrLf
Next prp

MsgBox "BOOKS has " & tbl.Properties.Count & " properties: " & vbCrLf & str
```

End Sub

This procedure produces the window shown in Figure 14-11. Note the last property on the list.

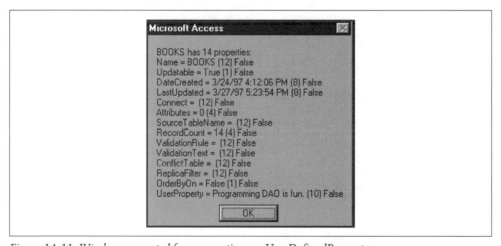

Figure 14-11. Window generated from executing exaUserDefinedProperty

Closing DAO Objects

We should make a few remarks about closing DAO objects that have been opened programmatically. The *Database*, *Recordset*, and *Workspace* objects each have a Close method. This method will remove these objects from their respective collections. This is appropriate for the three object types mentioned previously for the following reasons:

- The *Databases* collection is defined to be the collection of all open database objects.

- The *Recordset* objects are temporary objects, to be used only for data-manipulation purposes.

- Attempts to close the default *Workspace* object are ignored, but you can close other *Workspace* objects.

Note that objects of types other than the three mentioned are intended to be persistent members of their collections, stored on disk in the Access *mdb* file. However, they can be removed from their respective collections by using the Delete method.

Here are some caveats to keep in mind with respect to closing objects:

- As we will see in Chapter 16, you should update (i.e., complete) all pending edits before closing an open *Recordset* object.

- When a procedure that declares a *Recordset* or *Database* object is exited, the recordset or database is closed, and any unsaved changes or pending edits are lost.

- If you close a *Database* object while any *Recordset* objects are still open, or if you close a *Workspace* object while any of its *Database* objects are open, those *Recordset* objects will be automatically closed, and any pending updates or edits will be lost.

A Look at the DAO Objects

Now we can look briefly at each of the collections (and their objects) in the DAO Object Model. I will discuss each object and mention a few of the more commonly used properties and methods. A complete list of all collections, methods, and properties of each object is given in Appendix A.

DBEngine Object

The *DBEngine* object, of which there is only one, represents the Jet database engine. This is the only object in the DAO that is not contained in a collection. We have seen several examples of its use, along with the fact that the default collection for the *DBEngine* object is *Workspaces*, and so:

```
DBEngine.Workspaces(0)
```

is equivalent to:

```
DBEngine(0)
```

We have also seen that:

```
DBEngine(0)(0)
```

denotes the first database in the first (default) workspace.

The *DBEngine* object has methods to create a new workspace (CreateWorkspace), to compact a database (CompactDatabase), and to repair a database (RepairDatabase), among others.

Errors

From time to time, an operation may cause one or more errors to occur (or so I am told). When this happens, the *Errors* collection is first emptied and then filled with one *Error* object for each error that the operation caused. (Some operations may cause more than one error.) Note that if no errors occur, the *Errors* collection remains as it was before the operation.

Example 14-9, which deliberately produces an error, illustrates the use of the *Errors* collection. It also demonstrates the use of three *Error* object properties: Number (the VBA error number), Description (a description in words of the error), and Source (the object or application that generated the error).

Example 14-9. An Errors collection example

```
Sub exaErrorsCollection( )

' Note declaration of object variable of type Error
Dim dbsTest As DATABASE
Dim txtError As String
Dim errObj As Error

On Error GoTo ehTest

' A statement that produces an error
Set dbsTest = _
DBEngine.Workspaces(0).OpenDatabase("NoSuchDatabase")

Exit Sub

ehTest:

txtError = ""
' Loop through the Errors collection,
' to get the Number, Description and Source
' for each error object
For Each errObj In DBEngine.Errors
    txtError = txtError & Format$(errObj.Number)
    txtError = txtError & ": " & errObj.Description
    txtError = txtError & " (" & errObj.Source & ")"
    txtError = txtError & vbCrLf
Next

MsgBox txtError

Exit Sub

End Sub
```

Running this code produces the window in Figure 14-12.

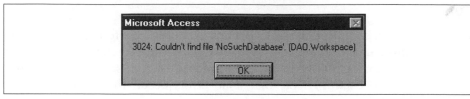

Figure 14-12. Error message from executing exaErrorsCollection

Workspaces

There is one *Workspace* object for each Access user session. In a single-user environment, there is generally only one session running. When a user starts Access with no security options enabled, Access automatically creates a *Workspace* called:

```
DBEngine.Workspaces(0)
```

Since we are not concerned in this book with multiple users or with database-security issues, we will not be creating multiple workspaces.

The values of the Name and UserName properties of the default *Workspace* object are easily determined by running the following code:

```
Sub Test( )

MsgBox "Count: " & DBEngine.Workspaces.Count
MsgBox "Name: " & DBEngine.Workspaces(0).Name
MsgBox "UserName: " & DBEngine.Workspaces(0).UserName

End Sub
```

This code should produce three message boxes, indicating that there is only one open workspace, with name *#Default Workspace#* and username *admin*.

Among the methods of a *Workspace* object are CreateDatabase (for creating a new database) and OpenDatabase (for opening an existing database). Another interesting group of methods is BeginTrans, CommitTrans, and Rollback, which allow the programmer to group several operations into one transaction. At the end of the transaction, the programmer can commit the operations—or rollback the database to its state prior to any of the operations in the transaction. One use for this is in updating related tables (as in transferring money from one table to another). If the entire group of operations is not completed successfully, then a rollback is probably desirable.

Workspace objects also have a Close method for closing opened workspaces. However, the method is ignored when applied to the default *Workspace* under Microsoft Access.

Users

The Jet engine provides security by assigning *access permissions* to users of the engine. A *User* object represents a user of the Jet engine. The *Users* collection contains all *User* objects. (Of course, female users are never to be considered objects.)

Groups

A *Group* object represents a set of *User* objects (users) that have a common set of access permissions. By using *Group* objects, a new user can be given a set of access permissions simply by adding the corresponding *User* object to the appropriate *Group* object. The *Groups* collection holds all *Group* objects.

Databases

A *Database* object represents a currently open database. In Microsoft Jet, you can have multiple databases open at one time (using the `OpenDatabase` function, discussed in Chapter 15). However, the Microsoft Access environment can display a graphical interface for only one database. In the Microsoft Access environment, when a database is opened, it is assigned to `DBEngine.Workspaces(0).Databases(0)`.

Database objects have a variety of methods for creating new objects: `CreateProperty`, `CreateQueryDef`, `CreateTableDef`, and `OpenRecordset`. There is also an `Execute` method for running action queries or executing SQL statements on the database. As mentioned earlier, *Database* objects also have a `Close` method.

TableDefs

A *TableDef* object represents a table definition for a saved table in the database. A *TableDef* object is more than a table scheme, in that it also has a *RecordCount* property that gives the number of rows in the table (and thus, in some sense, reflects the data in the table). However, it is less than a table, in that it does not describe the actual data in the table. The *TableDefs* collection contains all *TableDef* objects for a given database. *TableDef* objects have methods for creating fields (`CreateField`), indexes (`CreateIndex`), and opening recordsets (`OpenRecordset`).

QueryDefs

A *QueryDef* object represents a saved query in the database. The *QueryDefs* collection contains all *QueryDef* objects for a given database. One of the most interesting properties of a *QueryDef* object is *SQL*, which can be used to set or read the SQL definition of the *QueryDef* object.

Recordsets

A *Recordset* object represents data from one or more tables or queries, and is used to manipulate that data. Note that a *Recordset* object is temporary, in that it is not saved with the application. In fact, recordsets are created in code using the OpenRecordset function. The *Recordsets* collection contains all open *Recordset* objects in the current database.

Recordset objects are the workhorses of the DAO object model, with about 15 different methods and about 20 different properties. There are actually three types of *Recordset* objects—*Table-type, Dynaset,* and *Snapshot*—used for different purposes. We will discuss recordsets in Chapter 15.

Relations

A *Relation* object represents a relationship between certain fields in tables or queries. The *Relation* object can be used to view or create relationships. The *Relations* collection contains all *Relation* objects for a given database. We will discuss how to create a relation in Chapter 15.

Containers

The Microsoft Jet engine provides the *Containers* collection as a location where a host application, such as Microsoft Access, can store its own objects. This is done through the use of *Container* objects, as shown in Figure 14-13.

The Jet engine itself creates three *Container* objects:

- A *Databases* container object, containing information about the database
- A *Tables* container object, containing information about each saved table and query
- A *Relations* container object, containing information about each saved relationship

It is important not to confuse these *Container* objects (which are *not* collections, despite their names) with the *Databases*, *TableDefs,* and *Relations* collections. Indeed, these objects are at entirely different locations in the DAO object hierarchy and serve different purposes, as we will see.

In addition to the *Container* objects created by the Jet engine, Microsoft Access stores its forms, reports, macros, and modules in the *Containers* collection. Hence, the *Containers* collection also contains:

- A *Forms* container object, containing information about all saved forms
- A *Reports* container object, containing information about all saved reports
- A *Macros* container object, containing information about all saved macros
- A *Modules* container object, containing information about all saved modules

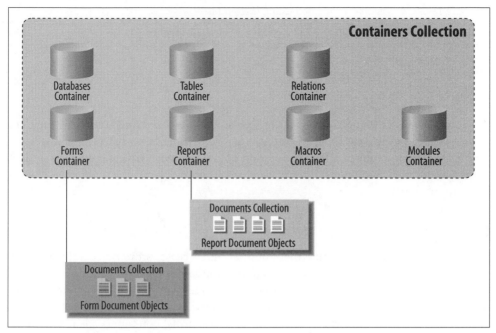

Figure 14-13. Container objects diagram of the MS Jet engine

The *Forms* and *Reports Container* objects should not be confused with the Microsoft Access collections of the same name (in the Access object model). In particular, the former contains information about all saved objects, whereas the latter contains information about all open objects.

To illustrate the aforementioned difference, create and save two forms in an Access session, and make sure that only one form is open. Then run the code in Example 14-10, which should report that the open form count is 1 but the saved form count is 2.

Example 14-10. A Containers collection example

```
Sub exaFormsContainer( )

Dim db As DATABASE
Dim frm As Form
Dim doc As Document      '

Set db = CurrentDb

Debug.Print "Opened form count: " & Forms.Count
For Each frm In Forms
    Debug.Print frm.Name
Next
Debug.Print
```

Example 14-10. A Containers collection example (continued)

```
Debug.Print "Saved form count: " & db.Containers!Forms.Documents.Count
For Each doc In db.Containers!Forms.Documents
    Debug.Print doc.Name
Next

End Sub
```

Note that a user cannot create new or delete existing *Container* objects—they are controlled by the Jet engine only. Put another way, there is no such thing as a user-defined *Container* object. The properties of a *Container* object generally reflect security-related issues, such as permission and user/group names. *Container* objects have no methods.

Documents

We have seen that applications (including Jet and Access) store objects through the use of *Container* objects. However, the *Forms Container* object, for example, is not of any real interest per se. The *Form* objects that reside within the *Forms* container are of interest. Actually, these *Form* objects are referred to as *Document* objects and are contained in the *Documents* collection of the *Forms* container, also shown in Figure 14-6. (If you are getting a bit confused, Figure 14-6 should help—it always helps me.)

Thus, it is the *Document* objects (in a *Documents* collection) that are the raison d'être for the *Container* objects. Example 14-11 illustrates a few of the properties of a *Document* object: Container, DateCreated, LastUpdated, Name, and Owner. It displays the value of various properties of the *Document* objects in the *Documents* collection of the *Tables Container* object.

Example 14-11. Properties of the Document object

```
Sub exaTablesDocuments( )
Dim db As DATABASE
Set db = CurrentDb
Dim docs As Documents
Dim doc As Document

Set docs = db.Containers!Tables.Documents
Debug.Print "Count: " & docs.Count

For Each doc In docs

    Debug.Print "Container: " & doc.Container
    Debug.Print "DateCreated: " & doc.DateCreated
    Debug.Print "LastUpdated: " & doc.LastUpdated
    Debug.Print "Name: " & doc.Name
    Debug.Print "Owner: " & doc.Owner
    Debug.Print
```

Example 14-11. Properties of the Document object (continued)

Next doc

End Sub

Here is a portion of the output from executing Example 14-11:

```
Count: 16
Container: Tables
DateCreated: 10/22/96 3:16:44 PM
LastUpdated: 10/24/96 1:36:16 PM
Name: AUTHORS
Owner: admin

Container: Tables
DateCreated: 10/22/96 3:19:47 PM
LastUpdated: 10/24/96 1:36:16 PM
Name: BOOK/AUTHOR
Owner: admin

Container: Tables
DateCreated: 5/15/96 6:16:29 PM
LastUpdated: 5/15/96 6:16:29 PM
Name: MSysACEs
Owner: Engine

Container: Tables
DateCreated: 5/15/96 6:16:31 PM
LastUpdated: 5/15/96 6:16:31 PM
Name: MSysIMEXColumns
Owner: admin
```

Fields

The *Fields* collection contains *Field* objects, which describe the various fields in a *TableDef*, *QueryDef*, *Index*, *Relation,* or *Recordset* object.

Parameters

The parameters of a parameter query are represented by *Parameter* objects, contained in the *Parameters* collection for that *QueryDef* object. Note that *Parameter* objects cannot be added to or deleted from the *Parameters* collection—*Parameter* objects represent existing parameters. Let us consider an example.

The code in Example 14-12 creates a parameter query named ParameterQuery and demonstrates some of the properties of a *Parameter* object—namely, Name, Type, and Value.

Example 14-12. A parameter query example

```
Sub exaParameters()
Dim db As DATABASE
Dim qdf As QueryDef
Dim strSQL As String

Set db = CurrentDb

' Create an SQL statement with parameters
strSQL = "SELECT * FROM BOOKS WHERE _
Price > [Enter minimum price]"

' Create a new QueryDef object
Set qdf = db.CreateQueryDef("ParameterQuery", strSQL)

' Supply value for parameter
qdf.PARAMETERS![Enter minimum price] = 15

' Now query query
Debug.Print qdf.PARAMETERS![Enter minimum price].Name
Debug.Print qdf.PARAMETERS![Enter minimum price].Type
Debug.Print qdf.PARAMETERS![Enter minimum _
price].Value

End Sub
```

Indexes

An *Indexes* collection contains all of the saved *Index* objects (i.e., indexes) for a *TableDef* object. We will discuss how to create an index in Chapter 15.

The CurrentDb Function

We have seen that DAO refers to the current database as:

> DBEngine.Workspaces(0).Databases(0)

or, through default collections, as:

> DBEngine(0)(0)

However, within Microsoft Access, there is a preferred way to refer to this database, since, unlike DBEngine(0)(0), it is always current with respect to changes made using the Access graphical interface. This preferred way is to use the Access function CurrentDb. Unfortunately, there is some confusion as to precisely what this function does.

Here is part of what the Access help system says about this function:

> The CurrentDb function returns an object variable of type *Database* that represents the database currently open in the Microsoft Access window.

The CurrentDb function provides a way to access the current database from Visual Basic code without having to know the name of the database. Once you have a variable that points to the current database, you can also access and manipulate other objects and collections in the data access object hierarchy.

You can use the CurrentDb function to create multiple object variables that refer to the current database. In the following example, the variables *dbsA* and *dbsB* both refer to the current database:

```
Dim dbsA As Database, dbsB As Database
Set dbsA = CurrentDb
Set dbsB = CurrentDb
```

This certainly makes it appear as though the object variables *dbsA* and *dbsB* point to a single *Database* object, namely, the currently open database. In other words, executing the instruction:

```
Set db = CurrentDb
```

implies that db points to the *Database* object known to DAO as DBEngine(0)(0). However, the Help system goes on to say:

> Note: In previous versions of Microsoft Access, you may have used the syntax *DBEngine.Workspaces(0).Databases(0),* or *DBEngine(0)(0)* to return a pointer to the current database. In Microsoft Access for Windows 95, you should use the *CurrentDb* function instead. The *CurrentDb* function creates another instance of the current database, while the *DBEngine(0)(0)* syntax refers to the open copy of the current database. Using the *CurrentDb* function enables you to create more than one variable of type *Database* that refers to the current database. Microsoft Access still supports the *DBEngine(0)(0)* syntax, but you should consider making this modification to your code in order to avoid possible conflicts in a multiuser database.

This seems to contradict the previous statements, by indicating that each time *CurrentDb* is executed, it creates a new *Database* object. Actually, if the current database is considered an object, then the statement "...creates another instance of the current database..." makes no sense, since you cannot create an instance of an *object*. (In object-oriented terms, you can create an instance of a *class*, and such an instance is called an *object*.)

In any case, each call to CurrentDb does seem to create a new object, as we can see from the experiment in Example 14-13, which checks the Count property of the *Databases* collection both before and after calling CurrentDb, showing that the count goes up.

Example 14-13. A CurrentDb function example

```
Sub exaCurrentDB( )

Dim db, dbExtra, dbOriginal As DATABASE
Dim str As String
Dim i As Integer

Set dbOriginal = DBEngine(0)(0)
```

Example 14-13. A CurrentDb function example (continued)

```
' Check the database count
MsgBox "Initial db count: " & _
DBEngine.Workspaces(0).Databases.Count

' Invoke CurrentDB
Set dbExtra = CurrentDb()

' Check the database count again
MsgBox "Count after CurrentDb run: " & _
DBEngine.Workspaces(0).Databases.Count

' Display the two database names
str = ""
For Each db In DBEngine.Workspaces(0).Databases
    str = str & vbCrLf & db.Name
Next db
MsgBox "Db Names: " & vbCrLf & str

dbExtra.Close

End Sub
```

If each call to CurrentDb produces a pointer to a new object, then it is natural to wonder what happens if we change the object pointed to by one of these pointers. Does it affect the other objects? What about DBEngine(0)(0)? Consider the code in Example 14-14, which does the following:

- Creates two *Database* object variables *dbOne* and *dbTwo* and sets both equal to CurrentDb
- Adds a new field *NewField1* to the BOOKS table using *dbOne*
- Adds a new field *NewField2* to the BOOKS table using *dbTwo*
- Displays the list of fields for BOOKS using *dbOne*
- Displays the list of fields for BOOKS using *dbTwo*
- Closes *dbOne* and *dbTwo*; that is, it removes their objects from the *Databases* collection

Example 14-14. The dbOne and dbTwo variable example

```
Sub exaCurrentDb2()

Dim dbOne As Database, dbTwo As DATABASE
Dim fldNew As Field
Dim str As String

Set dbOne = CurrentDb
Set dbTwo = CurrentDb

' Get field list in BOOKS
str = "Fields before: " & vbCrLf
```

Example 14-14. The dbOne and dbTwo variable example (continued)

```
''MsgBox dbOne.TableDefs!Books.Fields.Count
For Each fldNew In dbOne.TableDefs!Books.Fields
    str = str & fldNew.Name & vbCrLf
Next

' Use dbOne to add a new field to BOOKS
Set fldNew = dbOne.TableDefs!Books.CreateField("NewField1", dbInteger)
dbOne.TableDefs!Books.Fields.Append fldNew

' Use dbTwo to add a new field to BOOKS
Set fldNew = dbTwo.TableDefs!Books.CreateField("NewField2", dbInteger)
dbTwo.TableDefs!Books.Fields.Append fldNew

''Stop - (see the explanation in the text)

' Refresh Fields collection using dbOne!!!
dbOne.TableDefs!BOOKS.Fields.Refresh

' Get field list now using dbOne
str = str & vbCrLf & "Fields after using dbOne: " & vbCrLf
For Each fldNew In dbOne.TableDefs!Books.Fields
    str = str & fldNew.Name & vbCrLf
Next

' Get field list now using dbTwo
str = str & vbCrLf & "Fields after using dbTwo: " & vbCrLf
For Each fldNew In dbTwo.TableDefs!Books.Fields
    str = str & fldNew.Name & vbCrLf
Next

MsgBox str

dbOne.Close
dbTwo.Close

End Sub
```

Running this code produces the window shown in Figure 14-14.

Thus, it appears that changing the *Database* object pointed to by *dbTwo* does in fact also change the *Database* object pointed to by *dbOne*. However, if we do not refresh the *Fields* collection using the variable *dbOne*, or if we refresh using the variable *dbTwo* instead, we get the message box shown in Figure 14-15. Note that *NewField2* is missing from the second group.

Note also that even before the two objects *dbOne* and *dbTwo* have been closed, the Access graphical interface has been updated to reflect the two new fields. In fact, if you uncomment the Stop line in Example 14-14 and check the design of the BOOKS table though Access, you will find that both new fields appear, even before the Refresh method is called.

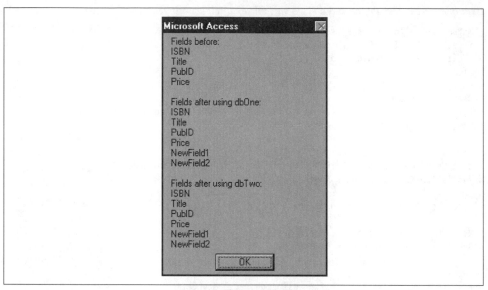

Figure 14-14. Message box from executing exaCurrentDb2

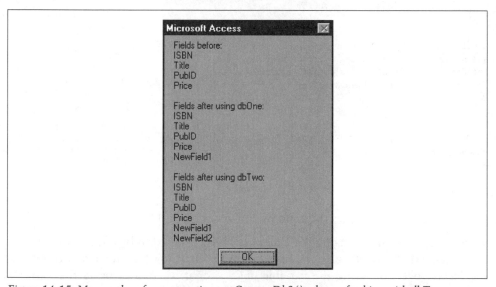

Figure 14-15. Message box from executing exaCurrentDb2() when refreshing with dbTwo

All of this experimenting leaves us with a feeling that there are some mysteries associated with CurrentDb that Microsoft is not revealing (at least not readily). We can summarize as follows:

- Invoking CurrentDb creates another member of the *Databases* collection.

- On the other hand, each variable set through CurrentDb seems to affect the same database.

Running exaCurrentDb2

To examine the behavior of the procedure shown in Example 14-14, do the following:

1. Run the program as is. Access displays the dialog in Figure 14-14.
2. Delete *NewField1* and *NewField2* from the BOOKS table. You can do this by opening the table in *Design* view, selecting each field separately, and choosing the *Delete Row* option from the *Edit* menu.
3. Comment out (using either the Rem statement or the ' character) the call to the Refresh method, then run the procedure. Access displays the dialog box in Figure 14-15.
4. Once again, delete *NewField1* and *NewField2* from the BOOKS table.
5. Remove the comment from the call to the Refresh method, and change it to read dbTwo.TableDefs!Books.Fields.Refresh. When you run the procedure, Access once again displays the dialog box shown in Figure 14-15.
6. Once again, delete *NewField1* and *NewField2* from the BOOKS table.

It's necessary to delete both *NewField1* and *NewField2* each time you run some variation of this procedure, since otherwise Access will display a "Can't define field more than once" error message.

- Refreshing is required to keep objects created through multiple invocations of CurrentDb current, belying the purpose of CurrentDb to some extent.
- On the other hand, the Access interface does not require refreshing—it reflects the latest operations performed using any of the invocations of CurrentDb.

These issues notwithstanding, it makes sense to follow Microsoft's recommendation to use CurrentDb, since it does reflect the current state of the Access environment more accurately than DBEngine(0)(0). Just be advised that some circumspection (refreshing) is needed when creating more than one variable through CurrentDb.

Finally, if you do use CurrentDb, then you should use it according to Microsoft's rules, found in the Access 7.0 readme file *acreadme.txt* (but missing from the Access 8.0 readme file *acread80.wri*). Its text is reproduced here. Note the use of the word "once."

Using the CurrentDb Function to Return a Reference to the Current Database

When you write code that includes a reference to the current database, you should declare a variable of type Database and use the CurrentDb function once to assign to it a pointer to the current database. You should avoid using CurrentDb to return the current database in a statement that also returns a reference to another object, such as a Set statement. It was possible to do this in some beta versions of Microsoft Access, but in Microsoft Access for Windows 95, your code may not run properly. For example, to determine the number of Document objects in the Documents collection, you should write code such as that shown in the following two examples:

```
Dim dbs As Database, con As Container
Set dbs = CurrentDb
Set con = dbs.Containers!Forms
Debug.Print con.Documents.Count
```

-or-

```
Debug.Print _
    CurrentDb.Containers!Forms.Documents.Count
```

Code such as the following will not work:

```
Dim con As Container
Set con = CurrentDb.Containers!Forms
Debug.Print con.Documents.Count
```

CHAPTER 15

Programming DAO: Data Definition Language

In the overview of DAO, I noted that Data Access Objects consists of two conceptually distinct components: a data definition language (DDL), which allows us to create or access some basic database system objects, like databases, table definitions, and indexes; and a data manipulation language (DML), which allows us to perform the practical operations of adding data (records) to our tables, deleting unwanted data, and modifying existing data. In this chapter, I discuss the DDL aspects of DAO.

Let us begin by noting the following:

- To indicate variables of a certain type, I will write the type name followed by the suffix *Var*. For example, *DatabaseVar* denotes a variable of type *Database,* and *TableDefVar* denotes a variable of type *TableDef*.

- In describing the syntax of certain methods, I will use square brackets ([ ]) to indicate optional items.

- I will generally give the full syntax of methods, but will only give details on the more common options. Of course, full details are available through the Access help system.

Creating a Database

Databases are created using the CreateDatabase method of a *Workspace* object. The general syntax of this method is:

```
Set DatabaseVar = [WorkspaceVar.]CreateDatabase _
(DatabaseName, locale [, options])
```

where:

- *DatabaseName* is a string expression representing the full path and name of the database file for the database being created. If you don't supply a filename extension, then the extension *.mdb* is automatically appended.

- *locale* is a string expression used to specify collating order for creating the database. You must supply this argument, or an error will occur. For the English language, use the built-in constant dbLangGeneral.

- *options* relates to specifying encryption or use of a specific version of the Jet database engine. For more information, please see Access help.

Notes

- The CreateDatabase method creates a new *Database* object, appends the database to the *Databases* collection, saves the database on disk, and then returns an opened *Database* object, but the database has no structure or content at this point.

- To duplicate a database, you can use the CompactDatabase method of a *Workspace* object, specifying a different name for the compacted database.

- A database cannot be deleted programmatically through DAO. To delete a database programatically, use the KILL statement in VBA.

Example 15-1 creates a new database named *MoreBks.mdb* on the directory *c:/temp* and then lists the tables that are contained in the database.

Example 15-1. A CreateDatabase method example

```
Sub exaCreateDb( )

Dim dbNew As DATABASE
Dim tbl As TableDef

Set dbNew = CreateDatabase _
("c:\temp\MoreBks", dbLangGeneral)

For Each tbl In dbNew.TableDefs
    Debug.Print tbl.Name
Next

dbNew.Close

End Sub
```

The program in Example 15-1 displays the following list of tables:

> *MSysACEs*
> *MSysObjects*
> *MSysQueries*
> *MSysRelationships*

These tables are created by Microsoft Access for its own use.

Opening a Database

To open an existing database, use the OpenDatabase method of a *Workspace* object. The syntax is:

```
Set DatabaseVar = [WorkspaceVar.]OpenDatabase _
(DatabaseName[, exclusive[, read-only[, source]]])
```

where *DatabaseName* is the name of an existing database. (As indicated by the square brackets, the other parameters are optional.) For information about the optional parameters, see the Access help system.

It is important to remember to close a database opened through the OpenDatabase method. This removes the database from the *Databases* collection.

Creating a Table and Its Fields

Tables are created using the CreateTableDef method of a *Database* object. The full syntax of this method is:

```
Set TableDefVar = DatabaseVar.CreateTableDef _
([TableDefName[, attributes[, source[, connect]]]])
```

where:

- *TableDefName* is a string or string variable holding the name of the new *TableDef* object.
- For information about the optional parameters, see the Access help system.

Notes

- The new *TableDef* object must be appended to the *TableDefs* collection using the Append method. However, before appending, the table must have at least one field.
- CreateTableDef does not check for an already used *TableDefName*. If *TableDefName* does refer to an object already in the *TableDefs* collection, an error will occur when you use the *Append* method, but not before.
- To remove a *TableDef* object from a *TableDefs* collection, use the Delete method.

Fields are created for a table using the CreateField method of the *TableDef* object. The syntax is:

```
Set FieldVar =TableDefVar.CreateField _
([FieldName[, type [, size]]])
```

where:

- *FieldName* is a string or string variable that names the new *Field* object.
- *type* is an integer constant that determines the data type of the new *Field* object. (See Table 15-1.)
- *size* is an integer between 1 and 255 that indicates the maximum size, in bytes, for a text field. This argument is ignored for other types of fields.

Table 15-1. Constants for the Type property

Data type	Constant	Numerical value
Boolean	dbBoolean	1
Byte	dbByte	2
Integer	dbInteger	3
Long	dbLong	4
Currency	dbCurrency	5
Single	dbSingle	6
Double	dbDouble	7
Date/Time	dbDate	8
Text	dbText	10
Long Binary (OLE Object)	dbLongBinary	11
Memo	dbMemo	12
GUID	dbGUID	15

Note

To remove a field from a *TableDef* object, use the Delete method.

Field objects have a variety of properties, among which are:

AllowZeroLength
> True if a zero-length value is valid for a text or memo field. (Setting this property for a nontext field generates an error.)

DefaultValue
> Sets or returns the default value of a *Field* object.

Required
> True indicates that a null value is not allowed.

ValidationRule and ValidationText
> Used for validation of field values. (See the following example.)

The procedure in Example 15-2 creates a new table named *NewTable*, creates a new field named *NewField*, sets certain properties of the field and appends it to the *Fields* collection, and then appends the new table to the *TableDefs* collection.

Example 15-2. A CreateTableDef method example

```
Sub exaCreateTable( )

Dim db As DATABASE
Dim tblNew As TableDef
Dim fld As Field

Set db = CurrentDb

Set tblNew = db.CreateTableDef("NewTable")
Set fld = tblNew.CreateField("NewField", dbText, 100)

' Set properties of field BEFORE appending

' zero length value is OK
fld.AllowZeroLength = True
' default value is 'Unknown'
fld.DefaultValue = "Unknown"
' Null value not allowed
fld.Required = True
' Validation
fld.ValidationRule = "Like 'A*' or Like 'Unknown'"
fld.ValidationText = "Known value must begin with A"

' Append field to Fields collection
tblNew.Fields.Append fld

' Append table to TableDef collection
db.TableDefs.Append tblNew

End Sub
```

Setting the validation properties of a field requires setting two properties. The ValidationRule property is a text string that describes the rule for validation, and the ValidationText is a string that is displayed to the user when validation fails. After running the code from Example 15-2, a new table appears in the Access Database window. (You may need to move away from the *Tables* tab and then return to that tab to see the new table.) Opening this table in Design View shows the window in Figure 15-1. Note that the *Field Properties* setting reflects the properties set in our code.

Incidentally, *TableDef* objects also have ValidationRule and ValidationText properties, used to set validation rules that involve multiple fields in the table.

Changing the Properties of an Existing Table or Field

I have remarked that some properties that are read/write before the object is appended to its collection become read-only after appending. One such example is the Type property of a field. On the other hand, the Name property of a field can be changed. This is an example of a change that can be made using DAO but not by using SQL.

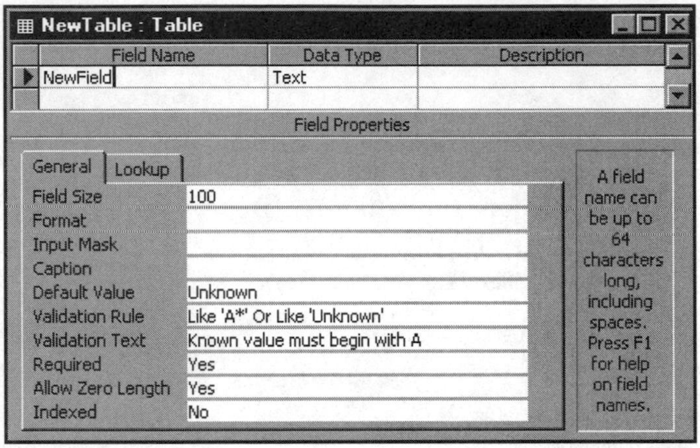

Figure 15-1. Design view of table generated from running exaCreateTable

Creating an Index

Indexes are created using the CreateIndex method for a *TableDef* object. Here is the syntax:

```
Set IndexVar = TableDefVar.CreateIndex([IndexName])
```

Creating an index by itself does nothing. We must append one or more fields to the *Fields* collection of the index in order to actually index the table. Moreover, the order in which the fields are appended (when there is more than one field) has an effect on the index order. This is demonstrated in Example 15-3, in which a new index called *PriceTitle* is added to the BOOKS table.

Example 15-3. A CreateIndex method example

```
Sub exaCreateIndex( )

Dim db As DATABASE
Dim tdf As TableDef
Dim idx As INDEX
Dim fld As Field

Set db = CurrentDb
Set tdf = db.TableDefs!BOOKS

' Create index by the name of PriceTitle
Set idx = tdf.CreateIndex("PriceTitle")

' Append the price and then the Title fields
' to the Fields collection of the index
Set fld = idx.CreateField("Price")
idx.Fields.Append fld
```

Example 15-3. A CreateIndex method example (continued)

```
Set fld = idx.CreateField("Title")
idx.Fields.Append fld

' Append the index to the indexes collection
' for BOOKS
tdf.Indexes.Append idx
```

End Sub

Figure 15-2 shows the result of running the program from Example 15-3. (To view this dialog box, open the BOOKS table in design view, and select the *Indexes* option from the *View* menu.) The figure shows clearly why we first create two fields—*Price* and *Title*—and append them, in that order, to the *Fields* collection of the index.

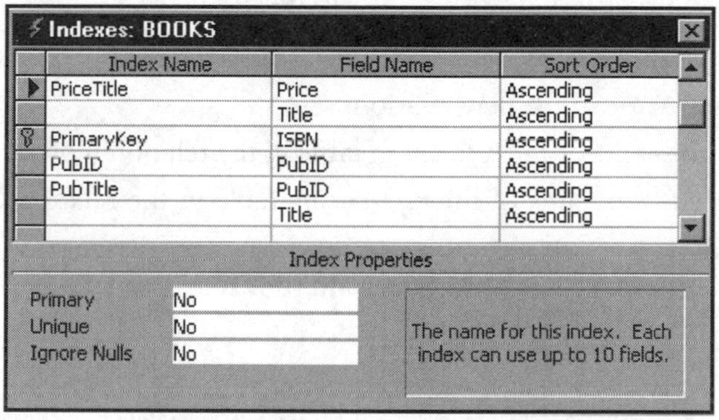

Figure 15-2. Indexes view of BOOKS table from running exaCreateIndex

As we discussed in an earlier chapter, an index for a table is actually a file that contains the values of the fields that make up the index, along with a pointer to the corresponding records in the table. Microsoft tends to blur the distinction between an index (as a file) and the fields that contribute to the index. Thus, to say that an index is *primary* is to say that the fields (actually, the *attributes*) that make up the index constitute a primary key.

With this in mind, some of the important index properties are:

DistinctCount
> Gives the number of *distinct* values in the index.

IgnoreNulls
> Determines whether a record with a null value in the index field (or fields) should be included in the index.

Primary
> Indicates that the index fields constitute the primary key for the table.

Required

Determines whether all of the fields in a multifield index must be filled in.

Unique

Determines whether the values in a index must be unique, thus making the index fields a key for the table.

Note that the difference between a *primary* key index and a *unique* values index is that a primary key is not allowed to have NULL values.

Creating a Relation

Relations are created in DAO using the CreateRelation method. The syntax is:

```
Set RelationVar = DatabaseVar.CreateRelation _
([RelName[, KeyTable[, ForeignTable[, Attributes]]]])
```

where:

- RelName is the name of the new relation.
- KeyTable is the name of the *referenced* table in the relation (containing the key).
- ForeignTable is the name of the *referencing* table in the relation (containing the foreign key).
- Attributes is a constant, whose values are shown in Table 15-2.

Table 15-2. Attributes for a Relation object

Constant	Description
dbRelationUnique	Relationship is one-to-one
dbRelationDontEnforce	No referential integrity
dbRelationInherited	Relationship exists in a noncurrent database that contains the two attached tables
dbRelationUpdateCascade	Cascading updates enabled
dbRelationDeleteCascade	Cascading deletions enabled

Notes

- All of the properties of a *Relation* object become read-only after the object is appended to a *Relations* collection.
- *Field* objects for the referenced and referencing tables must be appended to the *Fields* collection prior to appending the *Relation* object to the *Relations* collection.
- Duplicate or invalid names will cause an error when the Append method is invoked.
- To remove a *Relation* object from a collection, use the Delete method for that collection.

Example 15-4 illustrates the use of *Relation* objects. In this example, we will create a new relation in the LIBRARY database. The first step is to create a new table, using Microsoft Access. Call the table SALESREGIONS, and add two text fields: *PubID* and *SalesRegions*. Then add a few rows shown in Table 15-3 to the table.

Table 15-3. The SALESREGIONS table

PubID	SalesRegions
1	United States
1	Europe
1	Asia
2	United States
2	Latin America

The code in Example 15-4 creates a relation between the PubID field of the PUBLISHERS table (the primary key) and the PubID field of the SALESREGIONS table (the foreign key).

Example 15-4. A CreateRelation method example

```
Sub exaRelations( )

Dim db As DATABASE
Dim rel As Relation
Dim fld As Field

Set db = CurrentDb

' Create relation
Sct rcl = db.CreateRelation("PublisherRegions", _
"PUBLISHERS", "SALESREGIONS")

' Set referential integrity with cascading updates
rel.Attributes = dbRelationUpdateCascade

' Specify the key field in referenced table
Set fld = rel.CreateField("PubID")

' Specify foreign key field in referencing table.
fld.ForeignName = "PubID"

'Append Field object to Fields collection of
' Relation object.
rel.Fields.Append fld

' Append Relation object to Relations collection.
db.Relations.Append rel

End Sub
```

After running this code, make sure the *Database* window is active, and select *Tools* →
Relationships from the *Access* menu bar. Then select *Relationships* → *Show All*, and
you should see a window similar to that in Figure 15-3, showing the new relationship.

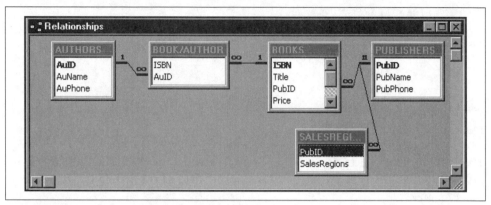

Figure 15-3. Relationships window after running exaRelations

Creating a QueryDef

Creating a *QueryDef* object is done using the CreateQueryDef method. The syntax is:

```
Set QueryDefVar = DatabaseVar.CreateQueryDef _
([QueryDefName][, SQLText])
```

where *QueryDefName* is the name of the new *QueryDef* object and *SQLText* is a string
expression that constitutes a valid Access SQL statement.

Notes

- If you include *QueryDefName*, the *QueryDef* is automatically saved (appended to
  the appropriate *QueryDefs* collection) when it is created. The Name property
  and the SQL property of a *QueryDef* can be changed at any time.

- You can create a temporary *QueryDef*, which is not appended to a collection, by
  setting the *QueryDefName* property to a zero-length string (""). You cannot change
  the name of a temporary *QueryDef*.

- If you omit the *SQLText* argument, you can define the *QueryDef* by setting its
  SQL property before or after you append it to a collection.

- To remove a *QueryDef* object from a *QueryDefs* collection, use the Delete
  method.

Running a Query

Recall from Chapter 6 that Microsoft Access supports several types of queries. In particular, a *select query* returns a recordset. An *action query* does not return a recordset, but rather takes action on existing data, such as making a new table, deleting rows from a table, appending rows to a table, or updating the values in a table.

If a *QueryDef* object represents an action query, then we can use its Execute statement to run the query. If the *QueryDef* object represents a select query, then we can open the corresponding result table (recordset) using the OpenRecordset method on the *QueryDef* object. Let us illustrate. The code in Example 15-5 creates a new select query and displays the record count for the resulting recordset.

Example 15-5. A CreateQueryDef method example

```
Sub exaCreateSelect( )

Dim db As DATABASE
Dim qdf As QueryDef
Dim strSQL As String
Dim rs As Recordset

Set db = CurrentDb

' Create an SQL SELECT statement
strSQL = "SELECT * FROM BOOKS WHERE Price > 20"

' Create a new QueryDef object
Set qdf = db.CreateQueryDef("NewQuery", strSQL)

' Open a recordset for this query
Set rs = qdf.OpenRecordset

' Move to end of recordset
rs.MoveLast

' Show record count
MsgBox "There  are " & rs.RecordCount & " books with price exceeding $20"

End Sub
```

The code in Example 15-6 creates a new action query and executes it. The effect is to raise the price of each book in the BOOKS table by 10%.

Example 15-6. A new action query example

```
Sub exaCreateAction( )

' Creates an action query and executes it
```

Example 15-6. A new action query example (continued)

```
Dim db As DATABASE
Dim qdf As QueryDef
Dim strSQL As String

Set db = CurrentDb

' Create an SQL UPDATE statement
' to raise prices by 10%
strSQL = "UPDATE BOOKS SET Price = Price*1.1"

' Create a new QueryDef object
Set qdf = db.CreateQueryDef("PriceInc", strSQL)

qdf.Execute

End Sub
```

Note that once a *QueryDef* object exists, we may still use the OpenRecordset or Execute methods to run the query. The Execute method can also be used on a *Database* object to run an SQL statement. Here is an example that reduces the price of each book in the BOOKS table by 10%:

```
Dim db As DATABASE
Set db = CurrentDb
db.Execute "UPDATE BOOKS SET Price = Price*0.9"
```

Properties of a QueryDef Object

When a *QueryDef* object is created or changed, Jet sets certain properties, such as DateCreated, LastUpdated, and Type. (Note that the *QueryDefs* collection may need refreshing before these properties can be read.) Some of the possible query types are listed in Table 15-4.

Table 15-4. Possible query-type constants

Constant	Query type	Value
dbQSelect	Select	0
dbQAction	Action	240
dbQCrosstab	Crosstab	16
dbQDelete	Delete	32
dbQUpdate	Update	48
dbQAppend	Append	64
dbQMakeTable	Make-table	80

The RecordsAffected property returns the number of records affected by the last application of the Execute method. Let us illustrate.

Example 15-7 modifies the earlier action-query example to perform the action (10% price increase) if and only if the increase will affect more than 15 books in the table. This is done using the BeginTrans, Committrans, and Rollback properties of the current *Workspace* object.

Example 15-7. A RecordsAffected property example

```
Sub exaCreateAction2( )

Dim ws As Workspace
Dim db As DATABASE
Dim qdf As QueryDef
Dim strSQL As String

Set ws = DBEngine(0)
Set db = CurrentDb

' Create an SQL UPDATE statement
' to raise prices by 10%
strSQL = "UPDATE BOOKS SET Price = Price*1.1"

' Create a new QueryDef object
Set qdf = db.CreateQueryDef("PriceInc", strSQL)

' Begin a transaction
ws.BeginTrans

' Execute the query
qdf.Execute

' Check the number of records affected and either roll back transaction or proceed
If qdf.RecordsAffected  <= 15 Then
    MsgBox qdf.RecordsAffected & " records affected " & _
            "by this query. Transaction cancelled."
    ws.Rollback
Else
    MsgBox qdf.RecordsAffected & " records affected " & _
            "by this query. Transaction completed."
    ws.CommitTrans
End If

End Sub
```

CHAPTER 16

Programming DAO: Data Manipulation Language

In Chapter 15 we examined how to use DAO to create and access the major components of a database, like its tables, its indexes, or its query definitions. For the most part, though, the focus of a database application is on accessing and manipulating discrete items of data stored in one or more records. In this chapter, we'll continue our overview of Data Access Objects by examining its data manipulation component, which allows you to perform such practical maintenance operations as adding, deleting, and updating records and accessing the records that your application is to display.

Recordset Objects

The main tool for manipulating data is the *Recordset* object. There are three types of *Recordset* objects:

Table-type Recordset object

> A representation of the records in a *single table* of the database. It is like a window into the table. Thus, operations on this type of recordset directly affect the table. I emphasize that a table-type recordset can be opened for a single table only. It cannot be opened for a join of more than one table or for a query. A table-type recordset can be indexed using a table index. This provides for quick manuvering within the table, using the Seek method, which we will discuss later in the chapter.

Dynaset-type Recordset object

> A *dynamic* (changeable) set of records that can contain fields from one or more tables or queries. Dynaset-type recordsets are generally updatable in both directions. Thus, changes in the recordset are reflected in the underlying tables or queries, and changes in the underlying tables or queries, are reflected in the dynaset-type recordset. With a dynaset-type recordset, no data is brought into memory. Rather, a unique key is brought into memory to reference each row of data. Searching through a dynaset-type recordset is done with the Find method, which is generally slower than the Seek method (which uses one of the table's indexes).

Snapshot-type Recordset object
> A *static* (nonchangeable) set of records that can contain fields from one or more tables or queries. These recordsets cannot be updated. For searching, a snapshot-type recordset can be faster than a dynaset-type recordset.

Opening a Recordset

To create or open a recordset, Jet provides the OpenRecordset method. This method can be used on *Database*, *TableDef*, *QueryDef*, or existing *Recordset* objects. The syntax is:

```
Set RecSetVar = DatabaseVar.OpenRecordset _
(source[, type[, options]])
```

or:

```
Set RecSetVar = ObjectVar.OpenRecordset _
([type[, options]])
```

where:

- *ObjectVar* points to an existing *TableDef*, *QueryDef*, or *Recordset* object.
- When opening a recordset based upon a database (the first syntax), *source* is a string specifying the source of the records for the new recordset. The source can be a table name, a query name, or an SQL statement that returns records. For table-type *Recordset* objects, the source can only be a table name.
- If you do not specify a type, then a table-type recordset is created if possible. Otherwise, the *type* value can be one of the following integer constants:
  - dbOpenTable to open a table-type Recordset object
  - dbOpenDynaset to open a dynaset-type Recordset object
  - dbOpenSnapshot to open a snapshot-type Recordset object
- *options* has several possible values related to multiuser situations. It also can take the value dbForwardOnly, which means that the recordset is a forward-only scrolling snapshot. This type of snapshot is useful for rapid searching.

Note

A new *Recordset* object is automatically added to the *Recordsets* collection when you open the object, and it is automatically removed when you close it using the Close method.

The code in Example 16-1 opens and then closes a recordset of each type, based on the BOOKS table. It also displays (in the debug window) the value of the RecordCount property for these recordsets. For a dynaset- and snapshot-type recordset, the Record-Count property is the number of records *accessed*. Accordingly, to determine the total number of records in such a recordset, we need to invoke the MoveLast method, thereby accessing all records. For a table-type recordset, the RecordCount property gives the total number of records. (We will discuss the MoveLast method later.)

Example 16-1. An OpenRecordset method example

```
Sub exaRecordsets()

Dim db As DATABASE
Dim rsTable As Recordset
Dim rsDyna As Recordset
Dim rsSnap As Recordset

Set db = CurrentDb

' Open table-type recordset
Set rsTable = db.OpenRecordset("Books")
Debug.Print "TableCount: " & rsTable.RecordCount

' Open dynaset-type recordset
Set rsDyna = db.OpenRecordset("Books", dbOpenDynaset)
Debug.Print "DynaCount: " & rsDyna.RecordCount
rsDyna.MoveLast
Debug.Print "DynaCount: " & rsDyna.RecordCount

' Open snapshot-type recordset
Set rsSnap = db.OpenRecordset("Books", dbOpenSnapshot)
Debug.Print "SnapCount: " & rsSnap.RecordCount
rsSnap.MoveLast
Debug.Print "SnapCount: " & rsSnap.RecordCount

' Close all
rsTable.Close
rsDyna.Close
rsSnap.Close

End Sub
```

Default Recordset Types

If you do not specify a type in the OpenRecordset method, Jet will choose one for you according to the following rules:

- The default *Type* when opening a recordset on a *Database* object (first syntax) or a *TableDef* object (second syntax) is a table-type *Recordset* object.
- The default *Type* when opening a recordset on a *QueryDef* object is a dynaset-type *Recordset* object. (Table-type recordsets are not available.)
- The default *Type* when opening a recordset on an existing table-type *Recordset* object is a dynaset-type recordset. If the recordset is not table-type, then the new recordset has the same type as the original.

Moving Through a Recordset

All recordsets have a *current position* (pointed to by the *current record pointer*) and a *current record*. Normally, the current record is the record at the current position. However, there are two exceptions. The current position can be:

- *Before* the first record
- *After* the last record

in which cases there is no current record.

To change the current position (and hence the current record), Jet provides several Move methods:

MoveFirst
> Moves to the first record.

MoveLast
> Moves to the last record.

MoveNext
> Moves to the next record.

MovePrevious
> Moves to the previous record.

Move[n]
> Moves forward or backward n positions.

In each case the syntax has the form:

    RecordSetVar.MoveCommand

BOF and EOF

The properties BOF (Beginning of File) and EOF (End of File) are set by Jet after each Move command. The concepts of BOF, EOF, current record, and current position can be confusing. Perhaps the following notes will help.

Notes on the BOF and EOF properties

- BOF is True when the current position is before the first record in the recordset, not *at* the first record.
- EOF is True when the current position is after the last record in the recordset, not at the last record.
- If either of BOF or EOF is True, then there is no current record.
- If you open a recordset containing no records, then BOF and EOF are set to True. If the recordset has some records, then Jet does a tacit MoveFirst so the first record becomes the current record and both BOF and EOF are set to False.
- If you delete the last remaining record in a recordset, then BOF and EOF remain False until you attempt to change the current position.

Notes on the Move methods

- If you use MovePrevious when the first record is current, the BOF property is set to True, and there is no current record. A further MovePrevious will produce an error, and BOF remains True.

- If you use MoveNext when the last record is current, the EOF property is set to True, and there is no current record. A further MoveNext will produce an error, and EOF remains True.

- If the recordset is a table-type recordset, then movement follows the current index, which is set using the Index property of the *Recordset* object. If no index is set (or if the recordset is not table-type), the order of returned records is not predictable.

The most common use of the Move methods is to cycle through each record in a recordset. Example 16-2 illustrates this. It creates both a table-type and a dynaset-type recordset on BOOKS and prints (in the debug window) a list of PubIDs and Titles. Note the use of the:

```
Do While Not rs.EOF
```

statement, which is typical of this type of procedure. Also, note the presence of this line:

```
rsTable.MoveNext
```

within the Do loop. It is a common error to forget to advance the current record pointer, in which case the PC will enter an endless loop, in this case printing the same line over and over again!

Example 16-2. Moving through a Recordset

```
Sub exaRecordsetMove( )

Dim db As DATABASE
Dim rsTable As Recordset
Dim rsDyna As Recordset

Set db = CurrentDb

Set rsTable = db.OpenRecordset("Books")
Debug.Print "Books indexed by PubID/Title:"

' Move through table-type recordset using PubTitle index
rsTable.INDEX = "PubTitle"
rsTable.MoveFirst
Do While Not rsTable.EOF
    Debug.Print rsTable!PubID & " / " & rsTable!Title
    rsTable.MoveNext
Loop

Debug.Print
```

Example 16-2. Moving through a Recordset (continued)

```
' Move through dynaset-type recordset
Debug.Print "Dynaset-type recordset order:"
Set rsDyna = db.OpenRecordset("Books", dbOpenDynaset)
rsDyna.MoveFirst
Do While Not rsDyna.EOF
    Debug.Print rsDyna!PubID & " / " & rsDyna!Title
    rsDyna.MoveNext
Loop

rsTable.Close
rsDyna.Close

End Sub
```

It is worth remarking that, for a dynaset-type or snapshot-type recordset, or for a table-type recordset for which the Index property has not been set, you cannot predict or rely on the order of records in the recordset.

In this connection, two Recordset properties of particular use are AbsolutePosition and PercentPosition, which give the ordinal position of the current record in a dynaset-type or snapshot-type recordset and the percent position, respectively. Let us illustrate by modifying Example 16-2, as shown in Example 16-3.

Example 16-3. The modified Recordset position example

```
Sub exaRecordsetPosition( )

Dim db As DATABASE
Dim rsDyna As Recordset
Dim strMsg As String

Set db = CurrentDb

Set rsDyna = db.OpenRecordset("Books", dbOpenDynaset)

' Move through recordset and display position
rsDyna.MoveFirst
Do While Not rsDyna.EOF

    strMsg = rsDyna!PubID & " / " & rsDyna!Title
    strMsg = strMsg & " / " & _
str$(rsDyna.AbsolutePosition)
    strMsg = strMsg & " / " & _
Format$(rsDyna.PercentPosition, "##")
    Debug.Print strMsg

    rsDyna.MoveNext
Loop

rsDyna.Close

End Sub
```

Finding Records in a Recordset

The method used to search for a record in a recordset is different for indexed table-type recordsets than for other recordsets.

Finding Records in a Table-Type Recordset

To locate a record in an indexed table-type recordset, you use the Seek method. Note that the recordset's Index property must be set before the Seek method can be used. The syntax of the Seek method is:

```
TableTypeRecSetVar.Seek comparison, key1, key2,...
```

where *comparison* is one of the following strings:

```
"<"
"<="
"="
">="
">"
```

and *key1, key2,...* are values corresponding to each field in the current index.

Notes

- The Seek method searches through the specified key fields and locates the first matching record. Once found, it makes that record current, and the NoMatch property of the recordset is set to False. If the Seek method fails to locate a match, the NoMatch property is set to True, and the current record is undefined.

- If *comparison* is equal to (=), greater than or equal to (>=), or greater than (>), Seek starts its search at the beginning of the index. If *comparison* is less than (<) or less than or equal to (<=), Seek starts its search at the end of the index and searches backward unless there are duplicate index entries at the end. In this case, Seek starts at an arbitrary entry among the duplicate index entries at the end of the index.

The code in Example 16-4 uses the Seek method on the *Title* index of BOOKS to find the first title that begins with the word "On."

Example 16-4. A Seek method example

```
Sub exaRecordsetSeek( )

Dim db As DATABASE
Dim rsTable As Recordset

Set db = CurrentDb

Set rsTable = db.OpenRecordset("Books")
```

Example 16-4. A Seek method example (continued)

```
' Find first book (if any) with title beginning
' with the word "On".
rsTable.INDEX = "Title"
rsTable.Seek "=", "On"
If Not rsTable.NoMatch Then
    MsgBox rsTable!Title
Else
    MsgBox "No title beginning with word 'On'."
End If

rsTable.Close

End Sub
```

Finding Records in a Dynaset-Type or Snapshot-Type Recordset

To search for a record in a dynaset-type or snapshot-type recordset, Jet provides various Find methods:

FindFirst
> Finds the first matching record in the recordset.

FindNext
> Finds the next matching record, starting at the current record.

FindPrevious
> Finds the previous matching record, starting at the current record.

FindLast
> Finds the last matching record in the recordset.

The syntax of these methods is:

```
RecordsetVar.FindMethod criteria
```

where:

- *RecordsetVar* represents an existing dynaset-type or snapshot-type *Recordset* object.
- *criteria* is a string expression, using the same syntax as a WHERE SQL clause (but without the word WHERE).

It is important to note that, if a record matching the criteria is not located, the NoMatch property is set to True, the current position is undetermined, and so there is no current record. It is thus important to position the current record pointer. This is usually done by setting a *bookmark* at the current record before starting the search. Then, if the search fails, the original position can be restored using the bookmark. In fact, a bookmark is a system-generated string that Jet can use to identify a record.

Thus, by setting a bookmark on the current record and then moving to another record, we can return to the bookmarked record. Let us illustrate.

The code in Example 16-5 displays all book titles starting with "M" and then returns to the current record before the search.

Example 16-5. A Find method example

```
Sub exaRecordsetFind( )

Dim db As DATABASE
Dim rs As Recordset
Dim bmkReturnHere As Variant

Set db = CurrentDb

Set rs = db.OpenRecordset("Books", dbOpenDynaset)

' Display current title
Debug.Print "Current title: " & rs!Title

' Set bookmark at current record
bmkReturnHere = rs.Bookmark

' Find books (if any) with first letter of title
' equal to 'M'.
rs.FindFirst "Left$(Title,1) = 'M'"
Do While Not rs.NoMatch
    Debug.Print rs!Title
    rs.FindNext "Left$(Title,1) = 'M'"
Loop

' Return to original location
rs.Bookmark = bmkReturnHere
Debug.Print "Returned to: " & rs!Title

rs.Close

End Sub
```

Editing Data Using a Recordset

Let us now discuss the methods used to edit, add, or delete data from a table-type or dynaset-type recordset. Snapshot-type recordsets are static, so data in such a recordset cannot be changed. Thus, in this section, the term *recordset* will refer to table-type or dynaset-type recordsets. Recall that any changes made to a recordset are reflected in the underlying tables or queries.

Editing an Existing Record

Editing an existing record is done in four steps:

1. Make the record the current record.
2. Invoke the Edit method for the recordset.
3. Make the desired changes to the record.
4. Invoke the Update method for the recordset.

It is important to note that if you move the current record pointer *before* invoking the Update method, any changes to the record will be lost.

The code in Example 16-6 changes all of the titles in a copy of the BOOKS table to uppercase. Before running this code, you should use the *Copy* and *Paste* menu options (under the *Edit* menu) to make a copy of BOOKS, called *Books Copy*. (Select BOOKS in the Database window, choose *Edit → Copy*, then choose *Edit → Paste*.)

Example 16-6. Editing data with Recordset

```
Sub exaRecordsetEdit( )

Dim db As DATABASE
Dim rs As Recordset

Set db = CurrentDb

Set rs = db.OpenRecordset("Books Copy")

rs.MoveFirst
Do While Not rs.EOF
    rs.Edit
    rs!Title = UCase$(rs!Title)
    rs.UPDATE
    rs.MoveNext
Loop

rs.Close

End Sub
```

To emphasize an earlier point, you might want to start over with a fresh *Books Copy* table and run the previous code without the line:

```
    rs.Update
```

to see that no changes are made to the table.

Deleting an Existing Record

Deleting the current record is done with the Delete method of the *Recordset* object. The syntax is simply:

```
RecordSetVar.Delete
```

Notes

- Deletions are made without any warning or confirmation. If you want confirmation, you must write appropriate code to do so.

- Note that immediately after a record is deleted, there is no valid current record. The current record pointer must be moved to an existing record (usually by invoking MoveNext).

The procedure in Example 16-7 deletes all books that have a price greater than $20.00 in a copy of the BOOKS table, after asking for confirmation. Before running this code, you should use the *Copy* and *Paste* commands to make a copy of BOOKS, called *Books Copy*.

Example 16-7. Using the Delete method with Recordset

```
Sub exaRecordsetDelete( )

' Demonstrates deleting records
' Deletes all books that have a price greater than
' $20.00 in a copy of the BOOKS table.
' Before running this, use Copy, Paste to make a
' copy of the BOOKS table

Dim db As DATABASE
Dim rs As Recordset
Dim DeleteCt As Integer

Set db = CurrentDb

Set rs = db.OpenRecordset("Books Copy")
DeleteCt = 0

rs.MoveFirst
Do While Not rs.EOF
    If rs!Price > 20 Then
        If MsgBox("Delete " & rs!Title & "(" & _
Format(rs!Price, "Currency") & ")?", vbYesNo) = _
vbYes Then
            rs.Delete
            DeleteCt = DeleteCt + 1
        End If
    End If
    rs.MoveNext
Loop

rs.Close

MsgBox Format$(DeleteCt) & " records deleted."

End Sub
```

Adding a New Record

Adding a new record to a recordset is done in three steps:

1. Invoke the AddNew method to create a blank record, which Jet makes the current record.
2. Fill in the fields of the record.
3. Invoke the Update method to save the record.

The syntax of the AddNew method is simply:

```
RecordsetVar.AddNew
```

Notes

- Once the Update method is invoked, the record that was the current record *prior* to invoking the AddNew method again becomes the current record. To make the new record current, use a bookmark together with the LastModified property, as shown in Example 16-8.
- In a table-type recordset, the new record is placed in its proper order with respect to the current index. In a dynaset-type recordset, the new record is placed at the end of the recordset. If the recordset has a sort order (such as might be inherited from an underlying query), the new record can be repositioned using the Requery method.

Example 16-8 adds a new book to the BOOKS table and makes it the current record. It also demonstrates the With...End With construct.

Example 16-8. Adding a record with Recordset

```
Sub exaRecordsetAddNew( )

Dim db As DATABASE
Dim rs As Recordset

Set db = CurrentDb

' Open recordset
Set rs = db.OpenRecordset("Books")

Debug.Print "Current title: " & rs!Title

' Use With...End With construct
With rs
    .AddNew              ' Add new record
    !ISBN = "0-000"      ' Set fields
    !Title = "New Book"
    !PubID = 1
    !Price = 100
    .UPDATE              ' Save changes.
```

Example 16-8. Adding a record with Recordset (continued)

```
        .Bookmark = rs.LastModified    ' Go to new record
    Debug.Print "Current title: " & rs!Title
End With

rs.Close

End Sub
```

ActiveX Data Objects

Part VI

ActiveX Data Objects

CHAPTER 17

ADO and OLE DB

What Is ADO?

In this chapter, we will discuss Microsoft's latest database programming object model, called *ActiveX Data Objects*, or ADO. This object model is a successor to DAO and is intended to replace DAO. Of course, the arrival of ADO raises the question of whether to redo existing DAO applications in ADO, as well as whether to write new applications in ADO.

As to the former, I can't see any immediate need to do so unless the application would benefit by some new feature of ADO. One possibility is that ADO may provide superior performance, but this is an ad hoc issue that will require experimentation in each situation. As to the latter, this decision is somewhat of a moving target. While DAO is more established and has proven to be reliable and stable, ADO is Microsoft's current wave of the future. For instance, the new VB6 DataBinding object model is just a frontend for an OLE DB data client and is designed to use ADO. In order to keep up with Microsoft's latest technologies—clearly a desirable goal—we will need to get on the ADO bandwagon. We can only hope that Microsoft will offer us other good reasons to join this bandwagon.

Actually, ADO is the immediate successor to *Remote Data Objects* (RDO), which is, in turn, the immediate successor to DAO. Since RDO did not get much first-string playing time, we will not discuss it in this book. My plan is to discuss the terminology related to ADO and its underlying technology, called OLE DB. Then we will look at the ADO object model and do a few examples, such as connecting to a Jet database, an Excel spreadsheet, and a text file. This will give you a solid foundation in ADO and OLE DB—certainly enough to understand the documentation (such as it is) and dig more deeply if the need arises.

It appears from the documentation that I have seen (from Microsoft and others) that most writers feel that the most important use of ADO is to connect to an SQL Server data provider. However, in my consulting practice, I seldom encounter SQL Server (or perhaps I just unconsciously avoid it). Much more often, I encounter the need to connect to an Excel spreadsheet, for instance. A great many business clients like to do database management in Excel, probably because they are familiar with that application, since they use it for financial analysis (which is its intended purpose). It seems that it is only the VBA consultant, and not those who hire her, who appreciates how limited Excel is when it comes to database management!

There seem to be three approaches to dealing with Excel "databases" (and I have used all three):

- We can twist and coerce Excel into doing more database management than it is intended to do. However, this creates bloated Excel workbooks with code that runs at a snail's pace.

- We can migrate the data from Excel into Access, where it really belongs.

- We can connect directly to an Excel spreadsheet using *Open Database Connectivity* (ODBC) for programming in ADO (or DAO).

We will discuss the latter approach in this chapter. This does seem to work, but for major data manipulation, I definitely prefer the second alternative.

Installing ADO

I should mention a word about installing ADO. ADO is installed along with Office 2000, but not with Office 97.

To see if you have ADO installed on your system, first open an Access code module, and then open the *References* dialog box, under the *Tools* menu. If you see an entry such as the one highlighted in Figure 17-1, you're all set.

If, on the other hand, you have no such listing, you might want to do a file search of your hard disk, looking for *MSADOxx.DLL*. If you don't have the file, then you can download the required software components from Microsoft's web site. At the time of this writing, the URL is *http://www.microsoft.com/data/mdac2.htm*. (If this URL is no longer valid, try searching for ADO or MDAC, which stands for Microsoft Data Access Components.) Note that the small version of the software kit is over 5 MB! Enjoy.

Note also that there is considerable confusion when it comes to versions of ADO, a situation that Microsoft does not seem to want to clarify. Version 2.0 refers to the following items, as reported by the type library itself (or the VBA IDE References dialog box). Note the different version numbers:

- Implementation: *msado15.dll*
- Object library name: *msado15.dll*
- Object Library Version: 2.0
- Documentation String: Microsoft ActiveX Data Objects 1.5 Library
- Help File: *msado10.hlp*

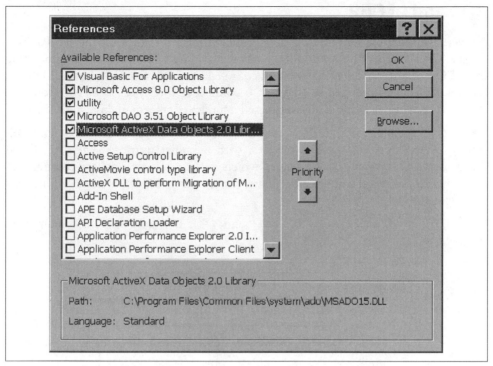

Figure 17-1. Reference to the ADO object library

On the other hand, Version 2.1 of ADO refers to the following items:

- Implementation: *msado15.dll*
- Object library name: *msado20.tlb*
- Object Library Version: 2.0
- Documentation String: Microsoft ActiveX Data Objects 2.0 Library
- Help File: (none)

Thus, Version 2.1 uses the same implementation as Version 2.0, which is presumably the same as Version 1.5! (Put another way, referring to Figure 17-1, if you highlight a reference to ADO 2.1, you will still see a reference to the *msado15.dll* library!)

The type library has changed for Version 2.1 of ADO, having been extracted from within the implementing DLL. However, this new type library does not report a help file, although the file *ado20.chm* appears to be such a file. (Accordingly, the type library contains no context-sensitive help references.)

Frankly, this situation does not seem to make much sense to me, but the bottom line is that ADO appears to be implemented by the same file (*msado15.dll*) through several "versions."

ADO and OLE DB

As we have seen, the DAO model is the programming interface for the Jet database engine. On the other hand, ADO has a more ambitious goal—it is the programming model for a *universal* data-access interface called OLE DB. Simply put, OLE DB is a technology that is intended to be used to connect to *any* type of data—traditional database data, spreadsheet data, web-based data, text data, email data, and so on.

Technically speaking, OLE DB is a set of COM interfaces. An *interface* is just a collection of functions, also called services, with a similar purpose. The term COM refers to the *Component Object Model*, which is Microsoft's model for communication between software components. Thus, simply put, OLE DB is a set of functions or services.

Figure 17-2 gives an overview of ADO and OLE DB from a VB programmer's perspective.

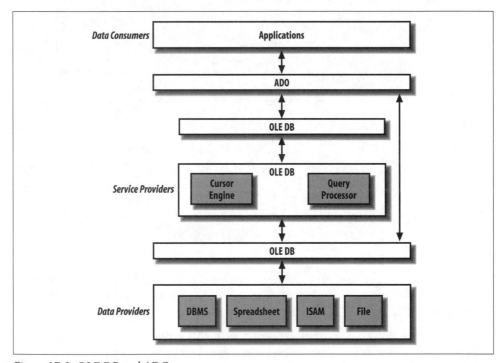

Figure 17-2. OLE DB and ADO

Data Stores

The purpose of OLE DB is to provide applications with universal data access—that is, with a common method for accessing data in essentially any format, including traditional database formats, text formats, spreadsheet formats, email formats, file system formats, web-based formats, and more. OLE DB uses the term *data store* to refer to any data that can be accessed through the OLE DB services. The term *data source* seems to be a synonym for data store, although this term is used in different ways in other related contexts (such as the VB6 DataBinding object model). Indeed, the term "data source" is one of the most abused in Microsoft's arsenal.

Data Providers

In order to create access to a particular type of data, a developer must write an OLE DB *data provider* for that type of data store. This is usually done in a C-type development environment such as Visual C++, but it can be done in VB as well.

The purpose of an OLE DB data provider is to expose the data in data stores of a particular type in *tabular* format, with rows (records) and columns (fields). In other words, the role of a data provider is to make data from a data store look like a table, even if the raw format does not resemble a table. For this reason, a data provider usually has direct access to the data in data stores of that type.

Note that some data providers may also implement more sophisticated data-retrieval and manipulation techniques, such as SQL. However, this is not a requirement. This is in distinction to ODBC, where an ODBC data provider *must* implement a form of SQL. (For more on this, see Appendix C.)

Here is a sampling of the OLE DB data providers available at the time of this writing:

- Microsoft OLE DB Simple Provider (a JavaBeans-related interface)
- Microsoft OLE DB Provider for ODBC Drivers (for Open Database Connectivity)
- Microsoft OLE DB Provider for Oracle (for Oracle databases)
- Microsoft Jet 3.51 OLE DB Provider (for Jet databases)
- Microsoft OLE DB Provider for SQL Server (for SQL Server databases)
- Microsoft OLE DB Provider for Directory Services (provides directory services— that is, logon, administration, and replication services—for Windows NT Server networks)

Two of these providers are especially interesting for us: the Microsoft Jet 3.51 OLE DB Provider and the Microsoft OLE DB Provider for ODBC Drivers. The ODBC provider is the default data provider and can be used to connect to a variety of data sources, such as an Excel spreadsheet or a text file, through ODBC. We will consider examples of how to use these providers later in the chapter.

It seems as though the distinction between data provider and data store (or data source) is often blurred. Thus, the term "data provider" may refer to a combination of both the data store (the raw data) and the data provider (the software component that implements OLE DB for that type of data store).

Data Consumers

An OLE DB *data consumer* is a software component that communicates with a data provider in order to gain access to and manipulate a data store. To a data consumer, all OLE DB data has a tabular format, with rows and columns.

Service Providers

In addition to the standard data providers, a developer may implement custom *service providers* (see Figure 17-2), which do not have direct access to the data (in the parlance of OLE DB, service providers do not *own* data). The purpose of a service provider is to provide additional services (features) for that particular type of data store through the use of OLE DB interfaces.

Here are some examples of OLE DB data services:

The Microsoft Data Shaping Service for OLE DB
  Provides support for the construction of hierarchical (shaped) *Recordset* objects from one or more data providers. A *hierarchical recordset* is one in which the value in a particular field can be another *Recordset* object, which would then be considered a child of the first (parent) recordset.

The Microsoft OLE DB Persistence Provider
  Provides support for saving a *Recordset* object to a file and restoring a *Recordset* object from a file.

The Microsoft OLE DB Remoting Provider
  Enables a user on a local machine to invoke data providers that reside on a remote machine.

Actually, an OLE DB service provider is both an OLE DB consumer and an OLE DB data provider. For example, consider a heterogeneous query processor. (The term *heterogeneous* refers to the fact that the query processor can process queries that reference data in more than one data source.) When a consumer asks the query processor to provide data from multiple OLE DB data sources, the query processor acts like a consumer when it submits the query to multiple data providers and retrieves the data from the data sources (through each source's data provider), and it acts like a provider when it returns the results of the query to the consumer that requested the data.

The ADO Object Model

OLE DB is designed for C programmers. In order to make it accessible to VB programmers, Microsoft created the ADO object model. This model gives VB programmers access to certain aspects of the OLE DB paradigm, by allowing the programmer to program an object model, rather than having to use the OLE DB API functions directly. For instance, a VB programmer can get access to a data provider by creating a *Connection* object and setting its Provider property. Thus, the *Connection* object represents a connection to a data store through a data provider.

The ADO object model is actually quite small, even smaller than the DAO object model. Table 17-1 shows the complete list of ADO objects (along with corresponding collection objects).

Table 17-1. The ADO objects

Command

Connection

Error (Errors)

Field (Fields)

Parameter (Parameters)

Property (Properties)

Recordset

The ADO object model is shown in Figure 17-3. Unlike the DAO model, which has a single object (*DBEngine*) at the top of the model, the ADO object model is headed by a triumvirate of three *externally creatable* objects: *Command*, *Connection*, and *Recordset*. (The *Parameter* object is also externally creatable.)

An externally creatable object is an object that can be created *directly* using the VBA New operator, as in:

```
Dim rs As New Recordset
```

or, alternatively:

```
Dim rs As Recordset
Set rs = New Recordset
```

Thus, as we will see, unlike DAO, a *Recordset* object can be created independently at the "beginning" of an ADO session.

Let us emphasize that while DAO is centered around the *DBEngine* object, through which almost all action begins, in ADO, as we will soon see, the "action" can begin with any of the three main ADO objects: *Connection*, *Command*, or *Recordset*. If you are accustomed to programming in DAO, this can take a bit of getting used to.

Incidentally, the tree-like view of the ADO object model shown in Figure 17-3 is from my Object Browser software program. For more on this, please see the card at the end of the book. You can also get more information on this object browser at my web site: *http://www.romanpress.com*.

Our plan is to take a look at the *Command, Connection, Field, Property*, and *Recordset* objects, along with their properties and methods. (We will also touch lightly upon the *Parameter* object.)

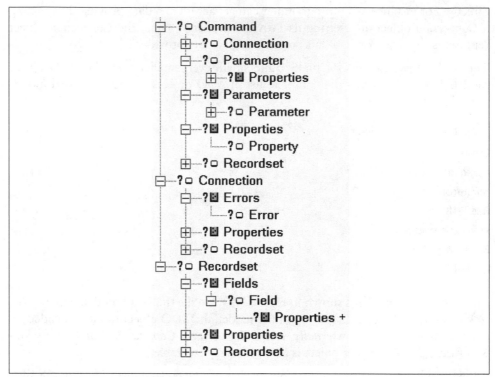

Figure 17-3. The ADO object model

It is important to emphasize that some features (objects, properties, or methods) of the ADO object model may not be implemented (or implemented fully) by a particular data provider. This is in contrast to the DAO object model, where the entire model is implemented. This is important enough to bear repeating:

> *To a large extent, it is up to a data provider to decide which features of the ADO object model to support.*

There are potentially four ways in which to determine whether a particular feature is supported by a particular data provider:

- Check the documentation for the data provider (if you can find it).
- Use the Supports method of the *Recordset* object to determine whether certain features are supported (but this only applies to the *Recordset* object).
- Use dynamic properties, discussed later.
- Experiment. If you get the error message shown in Figure 17-4, then you know that the operation that caused the message is not supported!

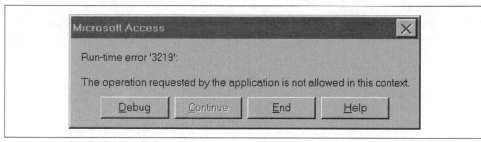

Figure 17-4. An "operation not supported" message

Note that we will discuss most of the properties and methods in the ADO object model, with the primary exception of those that relate to batch processing or transaction processing.

For the record, *batch* processing refers to sending multiple commands at one time. When communication between consumer and provider takes place over a network, this can save considerable time. *Transaction processing* refers to the grouping of multiple operations into a single transaction. At the end of the transaction, the programmer can commit the operations or rollback the data source to its state prior to any of the operations in the transaction. One use for this is in updating related tables (as in transferring money from one table to another). If the entire group of operations is not completed successfully, then a rollback is probably desirable.

The Three-Pronged Approach to Data Manipulation

As far as data manipulation is concerned (as opposed to data definition), the main purpose of ADO is to create a recordset that provides access to the data. As is indicated by the object model in Figure 17-3, there are three ways to obtain a *Recordset* object. The three methods are:

- Create a *Recordset* object directly, and use its Open method, as in:

  ```
  Dim rs As ADODB.Recordset
  Set rs = New ADODB.Recordset

  rs.Open ...
  ```

- Create a *Connection* object, and use its Execute method to return a recordset, as in:

  ```
  Dim cn As ADODB.Connection
  Dim rs As ADODB.Recordset

  cn.Provider = ...
  cn.ConnectionString = ...
  cn.Open

  Set rs = cn.Execute(...)
  ```

- Create a Command object:

```
Dim cmd As ADODB.Command
Dim rs As ADODB.Recordset

Set cmd = New ADODB.Command
Set cmd.ActiveConnection = ...
cmd.CommandText = ...

Set rs = cmd.Execute
```

Note that we will tend to qualify all ADO objects with the prefix ADODB. This will help distinguish between ADO objects and DAO objects of the same name. In fact, the line:

```
Dim rs As Recordset
```

will be interpreted by VBA as either an ADO or a DAO recordset depending on which of the references to the corresponding object library has higher priority in the *References* dialog box (under the *Tools* menu). Since it is a dangerous practice to rely on this priority (which can easily differ from system to system), it is best to always qualify:

```
Dim rs1 As ADODB.Recordset
Dim rs2 As DAO.Recordset
```

The RecordsetExample procedure shown in Example 17-1 illustrates each of the previous approaches to creating a recordset. Note, however, that only the first method (using the Open method of the *Recordset* object) allows us to set various recordset options. The other methods create read-only, forward-only recordsets. We will discuss this issue in detail at the appropriate time.

Example 17-1. Three methods of creating a Recordset object

```
Sub RecordsetExample( )

' Creating recordsets in different ways

Dim rs As ADODB.Recordset
Dim cn As ADODB.Connection

' Set up connection
Set cn = New ADODB.Connection
cn.Provider = "Microsoft Jet 3.51 OLE DB Provider"

cn.ConnectionString = "Data Source=D:\BkAccessII\AccessCode.mdb"
cn.Open


' --------------------------------
' Use rs.Open with table (or SQL)
' This is the most flexible method
' --------------------------------
Set rs = New ADODB.Recordset
rs.Open "Names", cn, adOpenDynamic, adLockReadOnly, adCmdTable
```

Example 17-1. Three methods of creating a Recordset object (continued)

```
rs.MoveFirst
Debug.Print "Use rs.Open: "
Debug.Print "ActiveConnection: " & rs.ActiveConnection
Debug.Print "Source: " & rs.Source
rs.Close


' ----------------------------------------
' Use cn.Execute
' Always a read-only, forward only cursor
' ----------------------------------------
Set rs = cn.Execute("SELECT * FROM Names")

rs.MoveFirst
Debug.Print
Debug.Print "Use cn.Execute: "
Debug.Print "ActiveConnection: " & rs.ActiveConnection
Debug.Print "Source: " & rs.Source
rs.Close


' ----------------------------------------
' Use Command object
' Always a read-only, forward only cursor
' ----------------------------------------
Dim cmd As ADODB.Command
Set cmd = New ADODB.Command
Set cmd.ActiveConnection = cn
cmd.CommandText = "SELECT * FROM Names"
Set rs = cmd.Execute

rs.MoveFirst
Debug.Print
Debug.Print "Use Command object: "
Debug.Print "ActiveConnection: " & rs.ActiveConnection
Debug.Print "Source: " & rs.Source
rs.Close

cn.Close

End Sub
```

For future reference, let us note the output from the Debug.Print statements in Example 17-1. In each case, the ActiveConnection property of the recordset is the same. I have broken the string into multiple lines to aid readability:

```
Provider=Microsoft.Jet.OLEDB.3.51;
Persist Security Info=False;
User ID=Admin;
Data Source=D:\BkAccessII\AccessCode.mdb;
Mode=Share Deny None;
Extended Properties=";
COUNTRY=0;
CP=1252;
```

```
LANGID=0x0409";
Locale Identifier=1033;
Jet OLEDB:System database="";
Jet OLEDB:Registry Path="";
Jet OLEDB:Database Password="";
Jet OLEDB:Global Partial Bulk Ops=2
```

As we will see when we discuss connection strings in more detail later in the chapter, this after-the-fact approach is one of the best (read: *only*) ways to actually see what a complete connection string looks like.

As for the Source property, here is the output:

```
Use rs.Open with table:
Source: select * from Names

Use cn.Execute:
Source: SELECT * FROM Names

Use Command object:
Source: SELECT * FROM Names
```

We will refer to this output when we discuss the Source property.

Let us now take a look at the various objects in the ADO object model. Our intention is not to be comprehensive, but to cover the main objects and their main properties and methods. After looking at the ADO model, we will look at several examples of connecting to a variety of data sources.

The Connection Object

The *Connection* object represents a connection to a data store through a data provider.

Properties of the Connection object

The main properties of the *Connection* object are:

CommandTimeout
> Sets the length of time to wait for a response to a command from the data source before issuing a timeout error message.

ConnectionString
> Holds the information needed to make the connection. This may include the name of the data provider, the name of the data source, a password, and a user ID. We will discuss connection strings at some length later in the chapter.

ConnectionTimeout
> Sets the length of time to wait for a connection to be made before issuing a timeout error message.

CursorLocation

Sets a recordset's *cursor* (which is a device used to traverse the recordset and which defines the current recordset) to reside on the client side of the connection or on the server side. Typically, client-side cursors offer more capabilities than server-side, but server-side cursors may be better at reflecting changes to the data source made by other users. Ultimately, the choice of which type of cursor to use depends on the capabilities of the data provider and on the particular needs at the time. We will see examples of using both types of cursors later on.

DefaultDatabase

Setting a default database for a particular connection avoids the need to qualify each table name in an SQL statement with the database name.

Errors

Returns the *Errors* collection of all *Error* objects (if any) for the previous command.

Mode

Specifies the access mode for the connection and can be set to any one of the following:

adModeUnknown

Signals that permission has not yet been set or cannot be determined. This is the default.

adModeRead

Is read-only permission.

adModeWrite

Is write-only permission.

adModeReadWrite

Is read/write permission.

adModeShareDenyRead

Prevents other users from opening the connection with read permission.

adModeShareDenyWrite

Prevents other users from opening the connection with write permission.

adModeShareExclusive

Prevents other users from opening the connection.

adModeShareDenyNone

Prevents other users from opening the connection with any permission.

Provider

Specifies the data provider. Note that the data provider can alternatively be specified in the ConnectionString property.

State

Returns the state of the connection (read-only). The possible values are given by the following enum:

```
Enum ObjectStateEnum
    adStateClosed = 0
    adStateOpen = 1
    adStateConnecting = 2
    adStateExecuting = 4
    adStateFetching = 8
End Enum
```

Version

Returns the ADO version number as a string.

Methods of the Connection object

The main methods of the *Connection* object are:

Close

Closes the connection. Its syntax is simply:

```
cn.Close
```

Execute

Executes a command. A command can be a database query, an SQL statement, a stored procedure, or a provider-specific command in text form. We emphasize that the form of command depends on the data provider. For instance, not all data providers support stored procedures or even SQL statements.

Note that some commands return a recordset and some do not. Accordingly, there are two syntaxes for the Execute method:

```
' Syntax for a non recordset-returning command
ConnectionObject.Execute CommandText, RecordsAffected, Options

' Syntax for a recordset-returning command
Dim rs As ADODB.Recordset
Set rs = ConnectionObject.Execute(CommandText, RecordsAffected, Options)
```

We will see several examples of the use of the Execute method. *RecordsAffected* is a Long parameter that we must supply. ADO will fill this variable with the number of records that are affected by the command. The optional *Options* parameter can assume a variety of values indicating how the data provider should interpret the *CommandText* argument. The possible values are:

adCmdText

CommandText is a textual definition of a command.

adCmdTable

CommandText is a table name. The rows of this table should be returned by an SQL query created internally by ADO.

adCmdTableDirect

> *CommandText* is a table name. The provider should return all rows from this table.

adCmdStoredProc

> *CommandText* is the name of a stored procedure.

adCmdUnknown

> The type of command in the *CommandText* argument is not known.

adAsyncExecute

> The command should execute asynchronously. (This means that the command will execute and then fire the *ExecuteComplete* event to signal that it has completed.)

adAsyncFetch

> The remaining rows after the initial quantity specified in the CacheSize property should be fetched asynchronously.

Open

> Opens a connection; that is, it creates an actual connection to the data provider. Its syntax is:
>
> ```
> connection.Open ConnectionString, UserID, Password, Options
> ```
>
> where all parameters are optional. The *ConnectionString* parameter is the tricky one here. We will discuss connection strings at length later in the chapter. Note that the *Connection* object has a ConnectionString property that can be used to set the connection string as well. However, the *ConnectionString* parameter will override any setting of the ConnectionString property.
>
> Microsoft warns that we should not pass UserID and password values in *both* the ConnectionString property and the *ConnectionString* parameter of the Open method, for this may lead to unpredictable results. (And here I thought that computers did not produce unpredictable results.)
>
> Note that it is important to close a connection using the Close method when the connection is no longer required. However, closing the connection does not remove the *Connection* object from memory, so its properties may still be accessed or altered. In order to remove the *Connection* object from memory, we must set the variable that references the *Connection* object to Nothing.
>
> The *Options* parameter can assume one of the following values:
>
> *adConnectUnspecified*
>
> > The default value. Opens the connection synchronously. Code execution pauses until the connection is made.
>
> *adAsyncConnect*
>
> > Opens the connection asynchronously. The ConnectComplete event is fired when the connection is complete.

OpenSchema

Gets database information from the data provider. The simplest syntax for this method is:

```
ConnectionObject.OpenSchema(QueryType)
```

where *QueryType* can be one of several constants specifying the type of information to retrieve. The method returns a *Recordset* object with the requested data.

For instance, the following code lists the tables in a Jet database:

```
' Get list of tables

Set rs = cn.OpenSchema(adSchemaTables)

Do While Not rs.EOF
    Debug.Print rs!TABLE_NAME & "  Type: " & rs!TABLE_TYPE
    rs.MoveNext
Loop
```

The Recordset Object

A *Recordset* object represents a recordset. To quote the documentation, "When you use ADO, you manipulate data almost entirely using Recordset objects."

Recordsets are created using the Open method with code such as:

```
Dim rs As ADODB.Recordset

Set rs = New ADODB.Recordset

rs.CursorType = adOpenDynamic
rs.CursorLocation = adUseServer
rs.Open "SELECT * FROM Names", cn
```

As we have seen, a *Recordset* object may also be created using the Execute method of the *Connection* object or the *Command* object.

Let us reiterate that even though the raw data in a particular data store (such as a text file or mail store) may not have the appearance of a traditional table with rows and columns, all ADO recordsets are structured with rows (records) and columns (fields). In fact, that is the primary purpose of ADO—to give all forms of raw data a table-like format.

Cursors

A recordset *cursor* is a device that is used to traverse the records (or rows) in a recordset. Recordsets (and their cursors) can reside on the *client side* of the connection or on the *server side*. Although we will not discuss remote connections—that is, connections over a network—in this introduction to ADO, the terminology is still valid. For instance, if we connect to a local Excel spreadsheet using the OLE DB provider for ODBC, then the dividing line between client and server is still the connection, even though both "sides" of this connection are on the same computer.

The cursor location is set using the CursorLocation property of the *Recordset* object; its value can be adUseClient or adUseServer.

ADO supports four types of cursors, determined by the CursorType property setting:

Dynamic cursor (CursorType = adOpenDynamic)
> This type of cursor is automatically updated to show additions, deletions, and edits to the recordset made by other users. It also permits all forms of movement through the recordset that do not use bookmarks, as well as those that do use bookmarks if the provider supports bookmarks. (Note, however, that the provider must support bookmarks or backward cursor movement in order to use the MovePrevious method.)

Keyset cursor (CursorType = adOpenKeyset)
> This type of cursor is similar to a dynamic cursor, except that it does not show records that have been added by other users, nor does it allow access to records that have been deleted by other users. However, edits by other users are visible. Keyset cursors must support bookmarks and therefore allow all forms of movement through the recordset.

Static cursor (CursorType = adOpenStatic)
> This type of cursor provides a *static copy* of a set of records. This is like a snapshot DAO recordset. Static cursors are used to find data or to generate reports. They must support bookmarks and therefore allow all forms of recordset movement. However, additions, deletions, and edits by other users are not visible. Note that all client-side cursors are static cursors. Even if we specify a different type of cursor for a client-side cursor, ADO will open a static cursor instead.

Forward-only cursor (CursorType = adOpenForwardOnly)
> This type of cursor behaves identically to a dynamic cursor except that it permits only forward scrolling. This is the analog of supplying the dbForwardOnly constant as an argument to the DAO OpenRecordset method. As with forward-only DAO recordsets, forward-only cursors perform more efficiently when we need to make only a single pass through the recordset.

LockType

The LockType property is a key property for recordsets. This property indicates the type of lock that is placed on the records during editing. It can be one of the following values:

adLockReadOnly
> Records are read-only. Note that this is the default value, which means that if we want to do any editing, we must set this property to another value.

adLockPessimistic
> In this case, the data provider ensures successful editing of records, usually by locking records at the data source as soon as the Edit method is called. This is termed pessimistic locking. It occurs on a record-by-record basis.

`adLockOptimistic`
> In this case, the provider locks records only when the `Update` method is called. This is termed optimistic locking. It occurs on a record-by-record basis.

`adLockBatchOptimistic`
> Optimistic batch updates are required for batch update mode.

I emphasize that `adLockReadOnly` is the default value, which means that if we want to do any editing, we must set this property to another value.

Properties of the Recordset object

The main properties of the *Recordset* object are described here:

AbsolutePage, PageCount, and PageSize
> To help the user page through the data in a recordset (especially when that data is intended to be displayed on the Web), ADO allows us to group the data into *logical pages*. (The page count starts at 1, by the way.) The PageSize property is used to specify the number of records per page (the default is 10 records per page).
>
> The PageCount property returns the number of pages in the recordset. If a data provider does not support pages, it will indicate this by always returning a Page-Count value of −1.
>
> The AbsolutePage property is used either to set the current record at the beginning of a page or to return the page number of the current record. The return value of AbsolutePage may be a page number or one of the following values:

`adPosUnknown`
> Indicates that the current position is unknown, the recordset is empty, or the data provider does not support pages.

`adPosBOF`
> Indicates that the current record pointer is pointed at BOF (BOF is `True`).

`adPosEOF`
> Indicates that the current record pointer is pointed at EOF (EOF is `True`).

AbsolutePosition
> This property works like the corresponding DAO property; namely, it provides the ordinal position of the current record in the recordset (the first position is position 1). As with DAO, however, the AbsolutePosition property can change when another record is deleted or if the recordset is refreshed. Thus, we cannot rely on the value of AbsolutePosition to return to a given record at a later time. To mark a record for later retrieval, we should use bookmarks.

ActiveConnection
> The ActiveConnection property of a recordset returns the connection string for the corresponding connection. If there is no active connection, it returns `Nothing`. For instance, in the code:

```
Dim rs As New ADODB.Recordset

Debug.Print rs.ActiveConnection
Debug.Print rs.ActiveConnection Is Nothing
```

the second line will produce a runtime error, whereas the third line will return True.

Thus, if the recordset rs is associated with the connection cn, then the following values are the same:

```
cn.ConnectionString
rs.ActiveConnection
```

For an open recordset, this property is read-only (as you would expect). However, for a closed recordset, we can set the ActiveConnection property to a valid connection string, and ADO will open the connection for us automatically. Setting the property to Nothing will disconnect the recordset from any provider.

Note that the ActiveConnection property can be set either to a string that specifies the connection or to a valid Connection object variable name.

We will have much more to say about connection strings later in the chapter. For now, we refer the reader to the *RecordsetExample* subroutine in Example 17-1 for an example of the ActiveConnection property. As mentioned earlier, querying the ActiveConnection property is one of the best ways to get the full syntax of a connection string for a data provider. Needing to resort to this technique is a reflection on the poor quality of the documentation for OLE DB data providers, especially when it comes to connect strings.

BOF and EOF

As with DAO, these Boolean properties indicate whether the current record pointer lies before the first record (BOF is True) or after the last record (EOF is True). In either case, there is no current record.

Bookmark

Each record in an ADO recordset has a bookmark associated with it. (A bookmark has Variant data type.) We can retrieve this bookmark and store it in a variable with code such as:

```
bk = rs.Bookmark
```

We can then return to this record at any time by writing:

```
rs.Bookmark = bk
```

CacheSize

This specifies the number of records that will be placed in the client-side memory buffer at one time. Put another way, it is the number of records that are fetched from the data store at one time.

CursorLocation

As discussed earlier, this property specifies the location of the cursor: client-side or server-side.

CursorType

As discussed earlier, this property specifies the type of cursor: dynamic, keyset, static, or forward-only.

EditMode

Like DAO, ADO uses a temporary editing buffer for the current record. The EditMode property indicates the current status of the data in this buffer. Its possible values are:

adEditNone

Indicates that no editing operation is in progress.

adEditInProgress

Indicates that the data in the current record buffer has been modified but has not yet been saved.

adEditAdd

Indicates that the AddNew method has been invoked and the new data in the current record buffer has not yet been saved.

adEditDelete

Indicates that the current record has been deleted.

Fields

This returns the *Fields* collection for the given recordset. We will discuss *Field* objects later in the chapter.

Filter

Filters the current recordset by restricting the records that are visible. Thus, for instance, after executing the code:

```
rs.Filter = "Lastname = 'Smith' OR FirstName Like 'A*'"
```

the recordset referenced by rs is filtered so that we have access only to those records that meet the filter condition. We can release the filter by writing:

```
rs.Filter = ""
```

Note that after setting a filter, the current record pointer is moved to the first record that fits the filter criteria. Note also that Microsoft warns that it is preferable to define and open a new recordset on the data source than to make extensive use of filters.

LockType

This property, discussed earlier, indicates the type of lock that is placed on the records during editing.

MaxRecords

This limits the number of records returned by a query. The default value of 0 indicates that all matching records should be returned. This property is read-only for an open recordset.

RecordCount

> This indicates the number of records in an open recordset. The property returns -1 when ADO cannot determine the number.

> Note that if the recordset supports either approximate positioning or book-marks (as indicated, for example, by the Supports method discussed later), then the RecordCount value is always correct regardless of whether the recordset has been fully populated by using the MoveLast method. Thus, if neither positioning nor bookmarks are supported, the only way to make sure that the RecordCount property is accurate is to populate the recordset fully, which may place a significant drain on resources because all records in the recordset will need to be retrieved from the data source.

Source

> This Variant property gives the source of the data for the recordset. It is read-only when the recordset is open. It can be set to a valid Command object variable name, an SQL statement, a table name, or a stored procedure call. (As always with ADO, this depends on the level of support from the data provider.) See the *RecordsetExample* subroutine in Example 17-1 for examples of the Source property.

State

> This read-only property returns the state of the recordset. The possible values are given by the following enum:

```
Enum ObjectStateEnum
    adStateClosed = 0
    adStateOpen = 1
    adStateConnecting = 2
    adStateExecuting = 4
    adStateFetching = 8
End Enum
```

Methods of the Recordset object

The main methods of the *Recordset* object are described in this section.

AddNew

> Adds new records to a recordset, provided that the data provider and the current cursor type support this feature, of course. The general syntax is:

```
recordset.AddNew Fields, Values
```

> where *Fields* is an optional single field name or an array of field names and the optional *Values* is the corresponding value (for a single field) or value array (for a field array) to assign to the fields in the new record. For instance, the code:

```
rs.AddNew Array(LastName, FirstName), Array("Einstein", "Albert")
```

> adds a new record with values LastName = "Einstein" and FirstName = "Albert".

Clone

> Creates a new *Recordset* object that is a duplicate of the *Recordset* object to which it is applied. It is important to note, however, that a cloned *Recordset* object is not entirely independent of its parent. Here is what the documentation says about cloned recordsets:

> Changes made to one *Recordset* object are visible in all of its clones regardless of cursor type. However, after you execute *Requery* on the original *Recordset*, the clones will no longer be synchronized to the original.

> Closing the original *Recordset* does not close its copies; closing a copy does not close the original or any of the other copies.

> You can only clone a *Recordset* object that supports bookmarks. Bookmark values are interchangeable; that is, a bookmark reference from one *Recordset* object refers to the same record in any of its clones.

Close

> Closes the recordset.

Delete

> Deletes one or more records. Its syntax is:

> > rs.Delete AffectRecords

> where AffectRecords is one of the following constants:

> adAffectCurrent

> > Deletes the current record.

> adAffectGroup

> > Causes all records that match the current filter only to be deleted.

> adAffectAll

> > Deletes all records.

> adAffectAllChapters

> > Deletes all chapter records.

GetRows

> Retrieves multiple records into an array. The syntax is:

> > array = recordset.GetRows(*Rows, Start, Fields*)

> *Rows* is an optional Long parameter that specifies the number of rows to retrieve. Its default is adGetRowsRest, indicating that the method should retrieve all of the remaining records in the recordset. The optional *Start* parameter specifies the starting row to retrieve. It should be either a bookmark or one of the values: adBookmarkCurrent (start at the current record; this is the default), adBookmarkFirst (start at the first record), or adBookmarkLast (start at the last record). Finally, *Fields* can be a single field name (or ordinal position) or an array of field names (or ordinal positions). If the *Fields* parameter is not missing, only those fields will be returned; otherwise, all fields will be returned.

> Note that the DAO version of the GetRows method has a different syntax.

Here are some things to keep in mind concerning the GetRows method:

- The first subscript in the array identifies the field, and the second identifies the record. This is counterintuitive.

- The lower bound on the returned array is 0, whereas the upper bound is one less than the number of records actually returned. Thus, if we specify more rows than are returned, the upper bound provides a way to get the number of rows actually returned. (Use the VBA UBound function to get the upper bound, and add 1 to get the number of records returned.)

- After a call to GetRows, the current record is the next unread record, or EOF if there are no more records. Thus, subsequent calls to GetRows can be made without specifying the *Start* parameter.

Move, MoveFirst, MoveLast, MoveNext, MovePrevious

Are used to move the current record pointer.

The Move method has the syntax:

```
recordset.Move NumRecords, Start
```

where *NumRecords* is a Long specifying the number of records to move the current record pointer relative to *Start*, which is either a bookmark or one of the values adBookmarkCurrent, adBookmarkFirst, or adBookmarkLast.

According to the documentation, "the Move method is supported on all Recordset objects." Of course, exactly what this means is unclear. Does it refer to all types of recordsets for a provider that supports the Move method, or does it mean that all providers must support this method?

If you are experiencing performance problems with Move, you might want to consider whether the CacheSize setting is causing too many retrievals. It may be possible to improve performance by setting the CacheSize value to a larger number. This is a tradeoff between performance and memory usage (as always).

Note that if the *Recordset* object to which we apply the Move method is forward-only, we can still pass a *NumRecords* value that is less than zero, provided that the destination is within the current set of cached records. If not, an error will occur. On the other hand, a call to MovePrevious will generate an error even if the resulting move lies within the currently cached group of records.

The MoveFirst, MoveLast, MoveNext, and MovePrevious methods work similarly to those methods in DAO. Note, however, that the *Recordset* object must support bookmarks or backward cursor movement in order to use the MovePrevious method. Otherwise, the method will generate an error. On the other hand, the MoveFirst method will work on a forward-only recordset, but it may cause the provider to re-execute the command that retrieved the *Recordset* object in the first place.

NextRecordset

Makes it possible to set up a *compound command* that contains several individual commands. For instance, the statement:

```
SELECT * FROM table1;SELECT * FROM table2
```

consists of two separate SQL statements. If we execute this command using the `Execute` method, ADO will execute and retrieve only the first SQL statement. To execute the second command and get the corresponding recordset, we use the `NextRecordset` method. For more on this, we refer the reader to the ADO documentation.

Open

Opens a recordset. The full syntax is:

```
recordset.Open Source, ActiveConnection, CursorType, LockType, Options
```

As with the *Connection* object, the parameters are optional and can be specified separately using properties of the *Recordset* object.

The *Source* parameter specifies the data source. Setting this parameter will override the setting of the *Source* property (if any). The parameter can be set to a Variant that identifies a valid *Command* object variable name, or to an SQL statement, a table name, or a stored procedure call (if supported by the data provider, as usual).

Setting the `ActiveConnection` parameter will override the current value of the ActiveConnection property (if any). The setting can be the name of a valid *Connection* object variable or a string that describes the connection. This will cause ADO to establish (open) the connection.

For a discussion of the `CursorType` and `LockType` parameters, see the "Cursors" and "LockType" sections in the discussion of the "The Recordset Object" earlier in this chapter. Note that if we set either of these parameters, the setting will also be made automatically in the corresponding property value.

The `Options` parameter is used when *Source* is a string (not a *Command* object) to identify the type of the *Source* argument. It can be one of the following values:

adCmdText

Treats the *Source* argument as a text string that describes a command.

adCmdTable

Treats the *Source* argument as a table name. ADO should generate an SQL query to return the table rows.

adCmdTableDirect

Treats the *Source* argument as a table name and returns all rows.

adCmdFile

Returns a recordset from the file named by *Source*.

adCmdStoredProc

Treats the *Source* argument as the name of a stored procedure.

adCmdUnknown

> The *Source* argument type is unknown.

These values can be combined with values that relate to asynchronous fetching of records:

adAsyncExecute

> The *Source* should be executed asynchronously. A FetchComplete event will fire when the operation is complete.

adAsyncFetch

> After the initial quantity specified in the Initial Fetch Size property is fetched, any remaining rows are fetched asynchronously. If a required row has not yet been fetched, further code execution is blocked (halted) until the requested row becomes available.

adAsyncFetchNonBlocking

> This is similar to adAsynchFetch, except that further code execution is never blocked. If the requested row has not been fetched, the current row automatically moves to the end of the file.

It is important to close a recordset using the Close method when the recordset is no longer required. However, closing the recordset does not remove the *Recordset* object from memory, so its properties may still be accessed or altered. In order to remove the *Recordset* object from memory, we must set the recordset variable that references the object to Nothing.

Requery

> Updates the recordset by requerying the data source.

Resync

> Resynchronizes the recordset with the underlying data. It differs from the Requery method in that it does not re-execute the original query that produced the recordset. Hence, it will cause any changes to existing records to be visible, but it will not show any new records.

Supports

> Gets information on what features are supported for recordsets of the specified type by the data provider. The syntax is:
>
>   boolean = recordset.Supports(CursorOptions)

The return value is True if the feature described by *CursorOptions* is supported and False otherwise.

Here is a list of the possible values for *CursorOptions*:

adAddNew

> The AddNew method is supported.

adApproxPosition

> The AbsolutePosition and AbsolutePage methods are supported.

adBookmark

> The Bookmark property is supported.

adDelete

> The Delete method is supported.

adHoldRecords

> With respect to transaction processing, we can retrieve more records or change the next retrieve position without committing all pending changes.

adMovePrevious

> The MovePrevious method is supported. Also, Move and GetRows can be used to move the current record pointer backwards without requiring the use of bookmarks.

adResync

> The Resync method is supported.

adUpdate

> The Update method is supported.

adUpdateBatch

> Batch updating is supported.

adSeek

> The Seek method is available.

adIndex

> The Index property with which to name an index is available (ADO 2.1 only).

To illustrate, the *SupportsExample* procedure in Example 17-2 compares static and dynamic cursors for a Jet connection.

Example 17-2. The SupportsExample procedure

```
Sub SupportsExample( )

' Compares support options for static and dynamic cursors

Dim rs As ADODB.Recordset
Dim cn As ADODB.Connection
Dim lRecordsAffected As Long

' Set up connection
Set cn = New ADODB.Connection
cn.Provider = "Microsoft Jet 3.51 OLE DB Provider"
cn.ConnectionString = "Data Source=D:\BkAccessII\AccessCode.mdb"
cn.Open

Set rs = New ADODB.Recordset
```

Example 17-2. The SupportsExample procedure (continued)

```
'   --------------------------------------------------
' Check support options for server-side static cursor
rs.CursorLocation = adUseServer
rs.Open "SELECT * FROM Names", cn, adOpenStatic, adLockOptimistic
' Get recordset support
Debug.Print
Debug.Print "Server-Side Static Recordset:"
Debug.Print "adAddNew: " & rs.Supports(adAddNew)
Debug.Print "adBookmark: " & rs.Supports(adBookmark)
Debug.Print "adDelete: " & rs.Supports(adDelete)
Debug.Print "adFind: " & rs.Supports(adFind)
Debug.Print "adUpdate: " & rs.Supports(adUpdate)
Debug.Print "adMovePrevious: " & rs.Supports(adMovePrevious)

rs.Close

'   ----------------------------------------------------
' Check support options for server-side dynamic cursor
rs.CursorLocation = adUseServer
rs.Open "SELECT * FROM Names", cn, adOpenDynamic, adLockOptimistic
' Get recordset support
Debug.Print
Debug.Print "Server-Side Dynamic Recordset:"
Debug.Print "adAddNew: " & rs.Supports(adAddNew)
Debug.Print "adBookmark: " & rs.Supports(adBookmark)
Debug.Print "adDelete: " & rs.Supports(adDelete)
Debug.Print "adFind: " & rs.Supports(adFind)
Debug.Print "adUpdate: " & rs.Supports(adUpdate)
Debug.Print "adMovePrevious: " & rs.Supports(adMovePrevious)

rs.Close

cn.Close

End Sub
```

The output is:

```
Server-Side Static Recordset:
adAddNew: True
adBookmark: True
adDelete: True
adFind: True
adUpdate: True
adMovePrevious: True

Server-Side Dynamic Recordset:
adAddNew: True
adBookmark: False
adDelete: True
adFind: True
adUpdate: True
adMovePrevious: True
```

Thus, we can see that static cursors support bookmarks, whereas dynamic cursors do not.

Update

Updates the current record after editing. This method can be used to set values as well, since its general syntax is:

```
recordset.Update Fields, Values
```

where *Fields* is a single field name or an array of field names, and *Values* are the corresponding values to assign to the fields in the record. For instance, the code:

```
rs.Update Array(LastName, FirstName), Array("Einstein", "Albert")
```

updates the record by setting `LastName = "Einstein"` and `FirstName = "Albert"`.

The Command Object

A *Command* object represents a definition of a command that may be executed by a data provider. We have seen an example (the `RecordsetExample` subroutine in Example 17-1) of how a *Command* object can be used to create a recordset. The `RecordsetExample` procedure also demonstrates that a *Command* object is not always required in order to execute a command. However, a *Command* object is required when we want to execute the same command more than once. Also, a *Command* object is needed to pass parameters to a query.

Command objects and connections

The ActiveConnection property is used to specify the connection over which the command will pass. The ActiveConnection property can be set either to a text string that describes the connection or to a *Connection* object variable that refers to a valid connection.

It is important to note that if we want to assign a single connection to multiple commands (at different times), a *Connection* object variable should be used. For if we use a text string, ADO will create a new *Connection* object for each command, even if the connection string is the same.

Setting the ActiveConnection property to `Nothing` disassociates the *Command* object from the current connection and causes the data provider to release any associated resources on the data source. This may or may not be required, depending on the data provider, before associating a new *Connection* object to the command.

Properties of the Command object

Let us discuss the main properties of the *Command* object.

ActiveConnection

Sets the connection over which the command will be sent. As discussed earlier, it can be a text string (a connection string) or a *Connection* object variable.

CommandText

Sets (or retrieves) the actual command. This is usually an SQL statement, but it can be any string that is recognized as a command by the data provider (such as a stored procedure call). According to the documentation, some data providers may alter the text of a command string. We can view any changes by examining the value of the CommandText property.

CommandTimeout

Sets or returns the length of time to wait for the command to execute before displaying a timeout error. The default is 30 seconds.

CommandType

Sets the type of command; it has the same values as the *Options* parameter in the Open method of the *Recordset* object:

adCmdText

A text string that describes a command.

adCmdTable

A table name whose records are returned by generating an internal SQL query.

adCmdTableDirect

A table name whose records are returned.

adCmdFile

The name of a file containing a recordset.

adCmdStoredProc

The name of a stored procedure.

adExecuteNoRecords

CommandText is a command or stored procedure that does not return rows. This value is always combined with either adCmdText or adCmd-StoredProc.

adCmdUnknown

Unknown type.

Name

Can be used to assign a name to a command.

Parameters

Returns a *Parameters* collection, which contains the parameters that are required by the command (if any). We will not discuss parameterized queries for ADO in this book.

Prepared

If set to True, the data provider will compile the command specified in the CommandText property, assuming that it supports this feature. This may slow execution the first time that the command is executed. However, subsequent executions of the same command should proceed more quickly. Note that if the data provider does not support command compilation, it may return an error as soon as this property is set to True, or it may simply ignore the request to prepare the command and set the Prepared property to False.

Methods of the Command object

Let us discuss the main methods of the *Command* object.

CreateParameter

Creates a *Parameter* object. A *Parameter* object represents a parameter that is associated with a parameterized query. We will not discuss parameterized queries for ADO in this book.

Execute

Executes the command represented by the *Command* object. As with the Execute method of the *Connection* object, there are two possible syntaxes based on whether or not the command returns a recordset:

```
' Syntax for a non recordset-returning command
CommandObject.Execute RecordsAffected, Parameters, Options

' Syntax for a recordset-returning command
Dim rs As ADODB.Recordset
Set rs = CommandObject.Execute(RecordsAffected, Parameters, Options )
```

Note that all parameters are optional.

The *RecordsAffected* parameter is a Long that returns the number of records affected by the command. The *Parameters* parameter is a Variant array of parameters that may be required by the SQL statement (if any). The values in this array will override any parameter values set through the Parameters property. (The order of parameters in the array is the order in which the parameters are passed.)

Finally, the *Options* parameter is equivalent to the CommandType property (and has the same possible values).

The Property Object and Dynamic Properties

The ADO objects:

Recordset
Parameter
Field
Connection
Command

each have a Properties property that returns a *Properties* collection. This collection contains a *Property* object for each dynamic property of the object.

ADO objects can have two types of properties: built-in and dynamic. *Built-in proper-ties* are the familiar properties implemented by ADO itself. These are the properties that we have been discussing up to now. Note that the *Properties* collection does not contain *Property* objects for built-in properties.

On the other hand, *dynamic properties* are defined by the data provider and are thus specific to a particular data provider. There is one *Property* object in the *Properties* collection for each dynamic property, and this *Properties* collection provides the only method for referencing a dynamic property, as in:

```
Object.Properties(PropertyName)
```

or:

```
Object.Properties(PropertyIndex)
```

Dynamic properties have four built-in properties of their own:

Name
> Identifies the property, as in the previous code.

Type
> An integer that specifies the data type of the property. It can be one of the values in Table 17-2.

Table 17-2. The values of the Type property

adEmpty = 0	adIUnknown = 13	adNumeric = 131
adSmallInt = 2	adDecimal = 14	adUserDefined = 132
adInteger = 3	adTinyInt = 16	adDBDate = 133
adSingle = 4	adUnsignedTinyInt = 17	adDBTime = 134
adDouble = 5	adUnsignedSmallInt = 18	adDBTimeStamp = 135
adCurrency = 6	adUnsignedInt = 19	adVarChar = 200
adDate = 7	adBigInt = 20	adLongVarChar = 201
adBSTR = 8	adUnsignedBigInt = 21	adVarWChar = 202
adIDispatch = 9	adGUID = 72	adLongVarWChar = 203
adError = 10	adBinary = 128	adVarBinary = 204
adBoolean = 11	adChar = 129	adLongVarBinary = 205
adVariant = 12	adWChar = 130	

Note also that the Type property can be set to a disjunction (ORing) of one of the constants in Table 17-2 and one of the following values:

adArray
> Indicates that the Type value is an array of values.

adByRef
> Indicates that the Type value is a pointer to a value.

adVector

> Indicates that the Type value is a `DBVECTOR` structure, as defined by OLE DB. This structure contains a count of elements and a pointer to data of type `DBTYPE_VECTOR`. For more on this, see the ADO documentation.

For example, the value:

```
adInteger OR adArray
```

represents an array of integers.

Value

> A Variant containing the value of the dynamic property.

Attributes

> A Long that describes attributes of the property. It can be a sum of one or more of the following values:

> *adPropNotSupported*
>
> > The property is not supported by the data provider.

> *adPropRequired*
>
> > The user must specify a value for this property before the data source is initialized.

> *adPropOptional*
>
> > The property is optional.

> *adPropRead*
>
> > The property can be read.

> *adPropWrite*
>
> > The property can be set.

To illustrate, consider the PropertiesExample procedure shown in Example 17-3.

Example 17-3. The PropertiesExample procedure

```
Sub PropertiesExample()

Dim rs As ADODB.Recordset
Dim cn As ADODB.Connection
Dim prop As ADODB.Property

' Set up connection
Set cn = New ADODB.Connection
cn.Provider = "Microsoft Jet 3.51 OLE DB Provider"

cn.ConnectionString = "Data Source=d:\BkAccessII\AccessCode.mdb"
cn.Open

' Open recordset
Set rs = New ADODB.Recordset
rs.Open "Names", cn, adOpenDynamic, adLockReadOnly, adCmdTable
```

Example 17-3. The PropertiesExample procedure (continued)

```
For Each prop In rs.Properties
    Debug.Print prop.Name
Next

rs.Close
cn.Close
End Sub
```

This procedure prints a list of dynamic property names for a Jet recordset. The rather impressive output is:

```
Preserve on Abort
Blocking Storage Objects
Use Bookmarks
Skip Deleted Bookmarks
Bookmark Type
Cache Deferred Columns
Fetch Backwards
Hold Rows
Scroll Backwards
Column Privileges
Preserve on Commit
Defer Column
Delay Storage Object Updates
Immobile Rows
Literal Bookmarks
Literal Row Identity
Maximum Open Rows
Maximum Pending Rows
Maximum Rows
Column Writable
Memory Usage
Notification Phases
Bookmarks Ordered
Others' Inserts Visible
Others' Changes Visible
Own Inserts Visible
Own Changes Visible
Quick Restart
Reentrant Events
Remove Deleted Rows
Report Multiple Changes
Row Privileges
Row Threading Model
Objects Transacted
Updatability
Strong Row Identity
IAccessor
IColumnsInfo
IColumnsRowset
IConnectionPointContainer
IRowset
```

```
IRowsetChange
IRowsetIdentity
IRowsetInfo
IRowsetLocate
IRowsetResynch
IRowsetScroll
IRowsetUpdate
ISupportErrorInfo
ILockBytes
ISequentialStream
IStorage
IStream
IRowsetIndex
Column Set Notification
Row Delete Notification
Row First Change Notification
Row Insert Notification
Row Resynchronization Notification
Rowset Release Notification
Rowset Fetch Position Change Notification
Row Undo Change Notification
Row Undo Delete Notification
Row Undo Insert Notification
Row Update Notification
Append-Only Rowset
Change Inserted Rows
Return Pending Inserts
IConvertType
Notification Granularity
Access Order
Lock Mode
Jet OLEDB:Partial Bulk Ops
Jet OLEDB:Pass Through Query Connect String
Jet OLEDB:ODBC Pass-Through Statement
Jet OLEDB:Grbit Value
Jet OLEDB:Use Grbit
Jet OLEDB:3.5 Enable IRowsetIndex
Bookmarkable
```

Of course, getting documentation on these properties is another matter. Let me know if you find any.

The Field Object

The *Field* object represents a field (or column) in a recordset. The Fields property of the *Recordset* object returns the *Fields* collection of all *Field* objects for that recordset.

The *Field* object has but two methods, AppendChunk and GetChunk, which are used with large text or binary fields. The reader should refer to the documentation for more on these methods.

Properties of the Field object

Here are the properties of the *Field* object:

ActualSize and DefinedSize

The DefinedSize property is used to set the size of a field as it is defined. The ActualSize property returns the size of the actual data stored in that field for the current record. Thus, for example, a *String* field named FirstName may have DefinedSize 25, but if the actual data in a given record at a particular time is "Albert", then the ActualSize property will return 6.

Attributes

The Attributes property of a *Field* object can be a sum of the following values. Note that for a *Field* object, the Attributes property is read-only.

adFldMayDefer

The field is deferred; that is, the field values are not retrieved from the data source when the record is retrieved. Instead, we must explicitly request the values.

adFldUpdatable

The field value is writable.

adFldUnknownUpdatable

The provider cannot determine if we can write to the field.

adFldFixed

The field contains fixed-length data.

adFldIsNullable

The field accepts Null values.

adFldMayBeNull

Null values can be read from the field.

adFldLong

The field is a long binary field. Hence, the AppendChunk and GetChunk methods are available for this field.

adFldRowID

The field contains some type of record ID, such as a record number or unique identifier.

adFldRowVersion

The field contains a time or date stamp used to track updates.

adFldCacheDeferred

The provider caches field values and subsequent reads are done from the cache.

Name

This is the name of the field. Note that the Name property is read-only for *Field* objects.

NumericScale and Precision

The read-only NumericScale property is used to return the number of digits to the right of the decimal place that is used to represent numeric values. The read-only Precision property returns the total number of digits used to represent a numeric value. Both are Byte properties.

Value, UnderlyingValue, and OriginalValue

The Value property sets or returns the value of the field for the current record.

The UnderlyingValue property returns the current field value from the database. This value may be the result of a recent update to the recordset by another transaction, whereas the OriginalValue property returns the original value that was retrieved from the recordset and thus does not reflect any updates by another transaction.

The UnderlyingValue and OriginalValue properties are read-only. To set a value, we must use the Value property.

Type

This specifies the data type for the field. The possible values are listed earlier in Table 17-1.

Finding OLE DB Providers

It is clearly important to be able to determine which OLE DB providers are installed on a particular system. The Windows registry contains entries for each installed OLE DB provider. An example is shown in Figure 17-5.

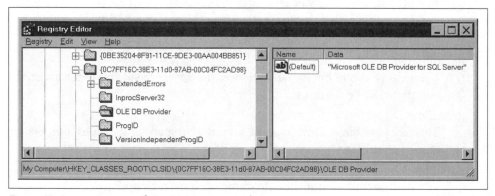

Figure 17-5. Registry entry for an OLE DB provider

Unfortunately, Windows does not make it a simple matter to extract this registry information using code. The ListDPs procedure shown in Example 17-4 will do the trick. You don't need to worry about all of the coding details related to the registry, but you may want to change some of the code, since it currently just prints the list of data providers to the Immediate window. Also, don't forget to include the code in the declarations section, also shown in Example 17-4.

Example 17-4. The ListDPs procedure

```
' Declarations for ListDPs

Type FILETIME
    dwLowDateTime As Long
    dwHighDateTime As Long
End Type

Public Const HKEY_CLASSES_ROOT = &H80000000

Public Const ERROR_SUCCESS = 0&
Public Const KEY_QUERY_VALUE = &H1
Public Const KEY_ENUMERATE_SUB_KEYS = &H8
Public Const KEY_NOTIFY = &H10
Public Const SYNCHRONIZE = &H100000
Public Const STANDARD_RIGHTS_READ = &H20000
Public Const KEY_READ = ((STANDARD_RIGHTS_READ Or KEY_QUERY_VALUE Or _
        KEY_ENUMERATE_SUB_KEYS Or KEY_NOTIFY) And (Not SYNCHRONIZE))

Public Const REG_SZ = 1

Declare Function RegOpenKeyEx Lib "advapi32.dll" Alias _
    "RegOpenKeyExA" (ByVal hKey As Long, ByVal lpSubKey As String, _
    ByVal ulOptions As Long, ByVal samDesired As Long, _
    phkResult As Long) As Long
Declare Function RegCloseKey Lib "advapi32.dll" _
    (ByVal hKey As Long) As Long
Declare Function RegEnumKeyEx Lib "advapi32.dll" Alias _
    "RegEnumKeyExA" (ByVal hKey As Long, ByVal dwIndex As Long, _
    ByVal lpName As String, lpcbName As Long, _
    ByVal lpReserved As Long, ByVal lpClass As String, _
    lpcbClass As Long, lpftLastWriteTime As FILETIME) As Long
Declare Function RegQueryValueEx Lib "advapi32.dll" Alias _
    "RegQueryValueExA" (ByVal hKey As Long, ByVal lpValueName As String, _
    ByVal lpReserved As Long, lpType As Long, lpData As Any, _
    lpcbData As Long) As Long
Declare Function RegQueryValueExStr Lib "advapi32.dll" Alias _
    "RegQueryValueExA" (ByVal hKey As Long, ByVal lpValueName As String, _
    ByVal lpReserved As Long, lpType As Long, ByVal lpData As String, _
    lpcbData As Long) As Long


Private Sub ListDPs()

' Search the registry for Data Providers

Const BUF_LEN As Long = 2048

Dim lret As Long, lret2 As Long, lret3 As Long
Dim hCLSIDKey As Long, hClassKey As Long, hClassSubKey As Long
```

Example 17-4. The ListDPs procedure (continued)

```vb
Dim lbufKeyName As Long
Dim bufKeyName As String * BUF_LEN
Dim lbufClassName As Long
Dim bufClassName As String * BUF_LEN

Dim lbufKeyName2 As Long
Dim bufKeyName2 As String * BUF_LEN
Dim lbufClassName2 As Long
Dim bufClassName2 As String * BUF_LEN

Dim lbufValue As Long
Dim bufValue As String * BUF_LEN

Dim ft As FILETIME, ft2 As FILETIME
Dim lxKey As Long, lxKey2 As Long
Dim lValueType As Long

Dim bProvider As Boolean
Dim sDPs As String
Dim sName As String

' --------------
' Open CLSID key
' --------------
lret = RegOpenKeyEx(HKEY_CLASSES_ROOT, "CLSID", 0, KEY_READ, hCLSIDKey)

If lret <> ERROR_SUCCESS Then
    MsgBox "Cannot open CLSID key", vbCritical
    Exit Sub
End If

lxKey = 0
Do
    lbufKeyName = BUF_LEN
    bufKeyName = String(BUF_LEN, Chr$(0))
    lbufClassName = BUF_LEN
    bufClassName = String(BUF_LEN, Chr$(0))
    lret = RegEnumKeyEx(hCLSIDKey, lxKey, bufKeyName, lbufKeyName, _
        0, bufClassName, lbufClassName, ft)
    lxKey = lxKey + 1
    DoEvents
    If lret = ERROR_SUCCESS Then
        ' We have a subkey of CLSID (a class key) -
        '   check its subkeys for OLE DB Provider key
        lret2 = RegOpenKeyEx(HKEY_CLASSES_ROOT, "CLSID\" & _
                Left$(bufKeyName, lbufKeyName), 0, KEY_READ, hClassKey)
        If lret2 <> ERROR_SUCCESS Then
            MsgBox "Cannot open key " & Left$(bufKeyName, lbufKeyName)
            RegCloseKey hCLSIDKey
            Exit Sub
        End If
```

Example 17-4. The ListDPs procedure (continued)

```
' Got a class key, check its subkeys
' We compile the subkeys and their default values in sDPs
' to be discarded if the class is not a provider
sDPs = ""
bProvider = False
lxKey2 = 0
Do
    lbufKeyName2 = BUF_LEN
    bufKeyName2 = String(BUF_LEN, Chr$(0))
    lbufClassName2 = BUF_LEN
    bufClassName2 = String(BUF_LEN, Chr$(0))
    lret2 = RegEnumKeyEx(hClassKey, lxKey2, bufKeyName2, _
        lbufKeyName2, 0, bufClassName2, lbufClassName2, ft2)
    If lret2 = ERROR_SUCCESS Then
        ' Test for OLE DB Provider
        If LCase$(Left$(bufKeyName2, lbufKeyName2)) = _
                "ole db provider" Then
            bProvider = True
            Exit Do
        End If
    End If
    lxKey2 = lxKey2 + 1
Loop While lret2 = ERROR_SUCCESS
' Finished looping through subkeys of the class key
' If a provider, display all key values
If bProvider Then
    Debug.Print ""
    Debug.Print "***NEW PROVIDER***"
    Debug.Print "CLSID = " & Left$(bufKeyName, lbufKeyName)
    lxKey2 = 0
    Do
        lbufValue = 0   '''this causes a GPF --> BUF_LEN
        bufValue = String(BUF_LEN, Chr$(0))
        lbufKeyName2 = BUF_LEN
        bufKeyName2 = String(BUF_LEN, Chr$(0))
        lbufClassName2 = BUF_LEN
        bufClassName2 = String(BUF_LEN, Chr$(0))
        lret2 = RegEnumKeyEx(hClassKey, lxKey2, bufKeyName2, _
            lbufKeyName2, 0, bufClassName2, lbufClassName2, ft2)
        If lret2 = ERROR_SUCCESS Then
            ' Open the key and get the default value
            lret3 = RegOpenKeyEx(HKEY_CLASSES_ROOT, _
                "CLSID\" & Left$(bufKeyName, lbufKeyName) & "\" & _
                Left$(bufKeyName2, lbufKeyName2), _
                0, KEY_QUERY_VALUE, hClassSubKey)
            If lret3 = ERROR_SUCCESS Then
                sName = ""
                ' Get the length and check for string
                lret3 = RegQueryValueEx(hClassSubKey, sName, 0&, _
                    lValueType, 0&, lbufValue)
```

Example 17-4. The ListDPs procedure (continued)

```
                ' Check for string
                If lValueType = REG_SZ Then

                    If lbufValue <> O Then
                        lret3 = RegQueryValueExStr(hClassSubKey, sName, _
                            0&, lValueType, bufValue, lbufValue)
                    End If

                    If Left$(bufKeyName2, lbufKeyName2) <> _
                            "ExtendedErrors" Then
                        Debug.Print Left$(bufKeyName2, lbufKeyName2) & _
                            " = " & Left$(bufValue, lbufValue)
                    End If
                End If   ' string
                RegCloseKey hClassSubKey
            End If
        End If
        lxKey2 = lxKey2 + 1
    Loop While lret2 = ERROR_SUCCESS

    End If

    RegCloseKey hClassKey
  End If
Loop While lret = ERROR_SUCCESS

RegCloseKey hCLSIDKey

End Sub
```

Here is the output of ListDPs on my system:

```
***NEW PROVIDER***
CLSID = {0C7FF16C-38E3-11d0-97AB-00C04FC2AD98}
InprocServer32 = C:\Program Files\Common Files\system\ole db\SQLOLEDB.DLL
OLE DB Provider = Microsoft OLE DB Provider for SQL Server
ProgID = SQLOLEDB.1
VersionIndependentProgID = SQLOLEDB

***NEW PROVIDER***
CLSID = {3449A1C8-C56C-11D0-AD72-00C04FC29863}
InprocServer32 = C:\Program Files\Common Files\system\msadc\MSADDS.DLL
OLE DB Provider = MSDataShape
ProgID = MSDataShape.1
VersionIndependentProgID = MSDataShape

***NEW PROVIDER***
CLSID = {c8b522cb-5cf3-11ce-ade5-00aa0044773d}
InprocServer32 = C:\Program Files\Common Files\System\OLE DB\MSDASQL.DLL
OLE DB Provider = Microsoft OLE DB Provider for ODBC Drivers
ProgID = MSDASQL.1
VersionIndependentProgID = MSDASQL
```

```
***NEW PROVIDER***
CLSID = {dee35060-506b-11cf-b1aa-00aa00b8de95}
InprocServer32 = C:\Program Files\Common Files\system\ole db\MSJTOR35.DLL
OLE DB Provider = Microsoft Jet 3.51 OLE DB Provider
ProgID = Microsoft.Jet.OLEDB.3.51
VersionIndependentProgID = Microsoft.Jet.OLEDB

***NEW PROVIDER***
CLSID = {dfc8bdc0-e378-11d0-9b30-0080c7e9fe95}
InprocServer32 = C:\Program Files\Common Files\system\ole db\MSDAOSP.DLL
OLE DB Provider = Microsoft OLE DB Simple Provider
ProgID = MSDAOSP.1
VersionIndependentProgID = MSDAOSP

***NEW PROVIDER***
CLSID = {e8cc4cbe-fdff-11d0-b865-00a0c9081c1d}
InprocServer32 = C:\Program Files\Common Files\system\ole db\MSDAORA.DLL
OLE DB Provider = Microsoft OLE DB Provider for Oracle
ProgID = MSDAORA.1
VersionIndependentProgID = MSDAORA

***NEW PROVIDER***
CLSID = {E8CCCB79-7C36-101B-AC3A-00AA0044773D}
InprocServer32 = C:\oledbsdk\bin\SAMPPROV.DLL
OLE DB Provider = Microsoft OLE DB Sample Provider
ProgID = SampProv
VersionIndependentProgID = SampProv
```

With reference to this output, a CLSID is a number that is intended to identify the data provider (in this case) or any software component (in more general settings) throughout the universe. This is why it is also referred to as a *globally unique identifier* (GUID). We have no use for this value, however.

The InprocServer32 entry shows the fully qualified name of the DLL that actually implements the data provider. For instance, the Jet provider has the filename *C:\Program Files\Common Files\system\ole db\MSJTOR35.DLL*.

The OLE DB Provider entry is the name of the provider. This can be used with the Provider property of the *Connection* object. The ProgID entry is the provider's *programmatic ID*, an identifying string that is friendlier than the CLSID and is supposed to be unique as well. The ProgID can also be used as the value of the Provider property.

A Closer Look at Connection Strings

It seems fair to say that the most confusing aspect of using ADO is determining the correct connection string required to establish a connection to an OLE DB provider. Certainly, this is one of the first confusing aspects of ADO, if not the only one.

In the beginning, there was only one OLE DB provider—Microsoft OLE DB Provider for ODBC Drivers. This was a good way for Microsoft to introduce OLE DB, because it meant that any ODBC provider automatically became an OLE DB provider.

Today, the list of OLE DB providers has grown to include the following (and presumably there are more of which I am not aware):

- Microsoft OLE DB Simple Provider (a JavaBeans-related interface)
- Microsoft OLE DB Provider for ODBC Drivers (for Open Database Connectivity)
- Microsoft OLE DB Provider for Oracle (for Oracle databases)
- Microsoft Jet 3.51 OLE DB Provider (for Jet databases)
- Microsoft OLE DB Provider for SQL Server (for SQL Server databases)
- Microsoft OLE DB Provider for Directory Services (provides directory services—that is, logon, administration and replication services—for Windows NT Server networks)

Aside from the ODBC provider, the SQL Server provider is used most often in examples, so we will not do so here. On the PC side, I think that the most interesting OLE DB providers are the Jet provider and the ODBC provider, especially since the latter can be used to connect to such things as Excel spreadsheets and text documents. Accordingly, we will take a look at how to set up connection strings using these two providers.

The Microsoft Jet 3.51 OLE DB Provider

Oddly enough, the MSDN Library (which is now the main source of documentation for Microsoft's development platforms) does not seem to document the Jet 3.51 OLE DB provider—at least I couldn't find any documentation on it. However, some experimentation will yield sufficient details to use the provider.

You may be wondering why you would want to use this OLE DB provider to connect to a Jet database when DAO was specifically designed for this purpose and works quite well. This is a fair question. I suppose one answer is that we had better stay current with Microsoft's technology, or we may find ourselves in trouble later on. Frankly, I wish I had a better answer at this time.

The place to start is with the results of the ListDPs procedure shown earlier for the Jet provider:

```
CLSID = {dee35060-506b-11cf-b1aa-00aa00b8de95}
InprocServer32 = C:\Program Files\Common Files\system\ole db\MSJTOR35.DLL
OLE DB Provider = Microsoft Jet 3.51 OLE DB Provider
ProgID = Microsoft.Jet.OLEDB.3.51
VersionIndependentProgID = Microsoft.Jet.OLEDB
```

Recall that we can use either the ProgID entry or the OLE DB Provider entry as the value of the Provider property of the *Connection* object.

The AccessExample procedure in Example 17-5 illustrates a connection to a Jet database.

Example 17-5. The AccessExample procedure

```
Sub AccessExample( )

Dim rs As ADODB.Recordset
Dim cn As ADODB.Connection

' Set up connection
Set cn = New ADODB.Connection
cn.Provider = "Microsoft Jet 3.51 OLE DB Provider"
cn.ConnectionString = "Data Source=D:\BkAccessII\AccessCode.mdb"
cn.Open

' Get full connection string after opening
Debug.Print "Full connection string: " & cn.ConnectionString

' Get list of 2s
Set rs = cn.OpenSchema(adSchemaTables)
Do While Not rs.EOF
    Debug.Print rs!TABLE_NAME & "  Type: " & rs!TABLE_TYPE
    rs.MoveNext
Loop

rs.Close
cn.Close

End Sub
```

After declaring and creating a *Connection* object:

```
Dim cn As ADODB.Connection
Set cn = New ADODB.Connection
```

we set the Provider property:

```
cn.Provider = "Microsoft Jet 3.51 OLE DB Provider"
```

As for the ConnectionString property, without knowing much about the connection string format, we try specifying just a data source:

```
cn.ConnectionString = "Data Source=D:\BkAccessII\AccessCode.mdb"
```

Then we open the connection and print the ConnectionString property:

```
cn.Open
Debug.Print "Full connection string: " & cn.ConnectionString
```

The resulting output gives us a full connection string, which in this case is:

```
Provider=Microsoft.Jet.OLEDB.3.51; _
Persist Security Info=False; _
User ID=Admin; _
Data Source=D:\BkAccessII\AccessCode.mdb; _
Mode=Share Deny None; _
Extended Properties=";COUNTRY=0;CP=1252;LANGID=0x0409"; _
Locale Identifier=1033; _
```

```
Jet OLEDB:System database=""; _
Jet OLEDB:Registry Path=""; _
Jet OLEDB:Database Password=""; _
Jet OLEDB:Global Partial Bulk Ops=2
```

Much of this connection string, such as the Persist Security Info, is obscure. Fortunately, we don't seem to need it. Note that the *Provider* parameter is the ProgID rather than the text description that we used to set this value.

Finally, to test the connection, we also print out a list of all of the tables in the database using the OpenSchema method of the *Connection* object. The result is:

```
MSysACEs  Type: SYSTEM TABLE
MSysIMEXColumns  Type: TABLE
MSysIMEXSpecs  Type: TABLE
MSysModules  Type: TABLE
MSysModules2  Type: TABLE
MSysObjects  Type: SYSTEM TABLE
MSysQueries  Type: SYSTEM TABLE
MSysRelationships  Type: SYSTEM TABLE
Names  Type: TABLE
Table1  Type: TABLE
```

The Microsoft OLE DB Provider for ODBC Drivers

Open Database Connectivity (ODBC) for short, is an Application Programming Interface (API) designed for connecting to databases of various types. The term database is used here in a very general sense to refer not only to traditional relational databases, such as Access, FoxPro, Oracle, or SQL Server databases, but also to less traditional "databases," such as delimited text files or Excel worksheets.

Since ODBC is still very commonly used and will be for some time, I have included Appendix C, which describes this technology in some detail. For now, we want to discuss how to connect to an ODBC data source through the OLE DB provider for ODBC. To understand the process completely and create your own connection strings, you must be familiar with ODBC Data Source Names. These are discussed in Appendix C. However, to modify the connection strings for the Excel files and text files that we will discuss later, you don't really need to know anything about DSNs beyond the following.

The term *Data Source Name* (DSN) refers not simply to the name of the data source, but to a description of the data source and its accompanying driver, as well as the attributes of a connection between the two. For instance, a DSN includes the name of the data source, the complete path of the data source, the name of the driver, and details about the connection to the data source, such as whether the connection is read-only. As we will see in the Appendix C, there are various types of DSNs. A DSN is created using the ODBC Administrator, which can be activated by clicking on the ODBC icon in the Windows Control Panel. Appendix C discusses how to use this applet.

Again referring to the output of the ListDPs procedure described earlier, we first note that the Provider property of the *Connection* object can be set to either MSDASQL (or its version-dependent counterpart, MSDASQL.1) or the string "Microsoft Jet 3.51 OLE DB Provider". Also, since this provider is the default, we can simply omit the Provider property altogether.

Fortunately, there is some documentation for the Microsoft OLE DB provider for ODBC, and, equally fortunately, it is quite clearly written, as far as it goes. Here is what the documentation says about the connect string (this is from the Microsoft MSDN Library CD):

> Because you can omit the Provider parameter, you can therefore compose an ADO connection string that is identical to an ODBC connection string for the same data source, using the same parameter names (DRIVER=, DATABASE=, DSN=, and so on), values, and syntax as you would when composing an ODBC connection string. You can connect with or without a predefined data source name (DSN) or FileDSN.
>
> Syntax with a DSN or FileDSN:
>
> "[Provider=MSDASQL;] { DSN=name | FileDSN=filename } ; [DATABASE=database;] UID=user; PWD=password"
>
> Syntax without a DSN (DSN-less connection):
>
> "[Provider=MSDASQL;] DRIVER=driver; SERVER=server; DATABASE=database; UID=user; PWD=password"
>
> If you use a DSN or FileDSN, it must be defined through the ODBC Administrator in the Windows Control Panel. As an alternative to setting a DSN, you can specify the ODBC driver (DRIVER=), such as "SQLServer," the server name (SERVER=), and the database name (DATABASE=).
>
> You can also specify a user account name (UID=), and the password for the user account (PWD=) in the ODBC-specific parameters or in the standard ADO-defined User ID and Password parameters. If you include both the ADO and the ODBC-specific parameters for these values, the ADO parameters take precedence.
>
> Although a DSN definition already specifies a database, you can specify a DATABASE parameter in addition to a DSN to connect to a different database. This also changes the DSN definition to include the specified database. It is a good idea to always include the DATABASE parameter when you use a DSN. This will ensure that you connect to the proper database because another user may have changed the default database parameter since you last checked the DSN definition.

This seems to be saying that when we omit the provider portion of the connection string (which can always be supplied using the Provider property), an OLE DB connection string is identical with an ODBC connection string. Of course, this begs the question: "How do we compose an ODBC connection string?"

The simplest answer is to let Windows do this for us. However, the starting point for this is a DSN that we must create, probably using the ODBC Administrator. The GetODBCConnectString procedure in Example 17-6 will extract a connection string from a DSN. The procedure first uses DAO (yes, DAO) to create an ODBC workspace. Then the OpenConnection method:

```
Set c = ws.OpenConnection("", dbDriverPrompt, , "ODBC;")
```

causes Windows to display the ODBC Administrator so we can create a DSN. Once this is done, the procedure prints the complete connection string.

Example 17-6. The GetODBCConnectString procedure

```
Private Sub GetODBCConnectString( )

' Create an ODBC workspace and get the connect string for a DSN

Dim db As Database, ws As Workspace, rs As Recordset
Dim cn As Connection

Set ws = CreateWorkspace("NewODBC", "admin", "", dbUseODBC)

' The following causes a prompt for the DSN
Set cn = ws.OpenConnection("", dbDriverPrompt, , "ODBC;")
Debug.Print cn.Connect
cn.Close

End Sub
```

Actually, there are two types of ODBC connection strings—DSN and DSN-less. Here are examples of the two types of connection strings for a connection to an Excel worksheet and to a text file. These strings were obtained using the GetODBCConnectString procedure:

```
' Excel DSN-less connection string
ODBC; _
DBQ=D:\BkAccessII\Connect.xls; _
DefaultDir=D:\bkado; _
Driver={Microsoft Excel Driver (*.xls)}; _
DriverId=790; _
FIL=excel 5.0; _
ImplicitCommitSync=Yes; _
MaxBufferSize=512; _
MaxScanRows=8; _
PageTimeout=5; _
ReadOnly=0; _
SafeTransactions=0; _
Threads=3; _
UID=admin; _
UserCommitSync=Yes;

' Excel DSN connection string
ODBC; _
DSN=ConnectExcel; _
DBQ=D:\BkAccessII\Connect.xls; _
DefaultDir=D:\bkado; _
DriverId=790; _
FIL=excel 5.0; _
MaxBufferSize=512; _
PageTimeout=5; _
UID=admin;
```

```
' Text file DSN-less connection string
ODBC; _
DefaultDir=D:\bkado; _
Driver={Microsoft Text Driver (*.txt;*.csv)}; _
DriverId=27; _
Extensions=txt,csv,tab,asc; _
FIL=text; _
ImplicitCommitSync=Yes; _
MaxBufferSize=512; _
MaxScanRows=25; _
PageTimeout=5; _
SafeTransactions=0; _
Threads=3; _
UID=admin; _
UserCommitSync=Yes;

' Text file DSN connection string
ODBC; _
DSN=ConnectText; _
DBQ=D:\bkado; _
DefaultDir=D:\bkado; _
DriverId=27; _
FIL=text; _
MaxBufferSize=512; _
PageTimeout=5; _
UID=admin; _
```

The main difference between the two types of connection strings is that in a DSN connection string, the DSN file is referenced so that ODBC can get information from that file. In a DSN-less string, all required information must be supplied directly. Thus, in many ways DSN-less connection strings are superior since they do not require an external DSN file.

Let me reiterate (lest you become annoyed with me) that we will discuss creating DSNs using the ODBC Administrator in Appendix C. At this point, however, you should just keep the following in mind:

- If you just want to connect to an Excel spreadsheet or text file, you can modify and use the connection strings in the upcoming examples.

- If you want to create a connection string for a different ODBC provider, you can use the GetODBCConnectString procedure to get the proper connection string, but for this you will need to use the ODBC Administrator to create a DSN. A discussion of how to do this is given in Appendix C, along with more details on DSNs and ODBC in general. As we will see in the appendix, by creating a File DSN, the GetODBCConnectString procedure will produce a DSN-less connection string!

So let us turn to some actual examples.

Connecting to an Excel workbook

The ExcelExample procedure shown in Example 17-7 illustrates how to connect to an Excel worksheet named MasterTable (shown in Figure 17-6) in the workbook *D:\BkAccessII\Connect.xls*.

	A	B	C	D	E
1	a	b	c	d	e
2	u	2	2	2	2
3	v	3	3	3	3
4	w	4	4	4	4
5	x	5	5	5	5
6	y	6	6	6	6
7					

Figure 17-6. A test Excel worksheet

The procedure uses the SQL statement:

```
"SELECT * FROM [MasterTable$]"
```

to open a recordset based on this table. (I can't tell you how long it took me to determine that a dollar sign must be appended to the end of an Excel worksheet name.)

We set the connect string to:

```
' Connection string
cn.ConnectionString = _
    "DRIVER={Microsoft Excel Driver (*.xls)};DBQ=D:\BkAccessII\Connect.xls;"
```

Note the *DBQ* parameter. Based on the documentation from Microsoft that I quoted earlier, I first tried to use the parameter name *DATABASE*, but was rudely rewarded with the message "Operation cancelled" at the line:

```
cn.Open
```

(In case you are wondering how I discovered that DBQ was the correct name, I used the ODBC Administrator to create a DSN and inspected the DSN file with a text editor.)

The *ExcelExample* procedure in Example 17-7 prints the full connection string, which in this case is:

```
Provider=MSDASQL.1; _
Connect Timeout=15; _
Extended Properties="DBQ=D:\BkAccessII\Connect.xls; _
    Driver={Microsoft Excel Driver (*.xls)}; _
    DriverId=790; _
    MaxBufferSize=512; _
    PageTimeout=5;"; _
Locale Identifier=1033
```

Next, the procedure prints the field names for the Excel worksheet, which are the entries in the first row. (I didn't know this until I ran this code.) It then prints the remaining rows of the table. Note the use of the GetRows function to grab all of the records in the recordset at once.

Finally, the procedure gathers some support information for future reference.

Example 17-7. The ExcelExample procedure

```
Sub ExcelExample( )

Dim r As Integer, f As Integer
Dim vrecs As Variant

Dim rs As ADODB.Recordset
Dim cn As ADODB.Connection
Dim fld As ADODB.Field

' Set up connection
Set cn = New ADODB.Connection

' Set provider
' Note we can also use the ProgID: "MSDASQL.1", or nothing!
cn.Provider = "Microsoft OLE DB Provider for ODBC Drivers"

' Connection string
cn.ConnectionString = _
    "DRIVER={Microsoft Excel Driver (*.xls)};DBQ=D:\BkAccessII\Connect.xls;"

' Open the connection
cn.Open

' Get full connection string after opening
Debug.Print "Full connection string: " & cn.ConnectionString

' Get recordset using rs.open SQL statement
Set rs = New ADODB.Recordset
rs.CursorLocation = adUseClient
rs.Open "SELECT * FROM [MasterTable$]", cn, adOpenDynamic, adLockOptimistic

' Print the field names (from first row)
For Each fld In rs.Fields
    Debug.Print fld.Name,
Next
Debug.Print

' Get the rows all at once
vrecs = rs.GetRows(6)

For r = 0 To UBound(vrecs, 2)
    For f = 0 To UBound(vrecs, 1)
        Debug.Print vrecs(f, r),
    Next
    Debug.Print
Next
```

Example 17-7. The ExcelExample procedure (continued)

```
' Check support options while we are here
Debug.Print
Debug.Print "Client-Side Dynamic Recordset:"
Debug.Print "adAddNew: " & rs.Supports(adAddNew)
Debug.Print "adBookmark: " & rs.Supports(adBookmark)
Debug.Print "adDelete: " & rs.Supports(adDelete)
Debug.Print "adFind: " & rs.Supports(adFind)
Debug.Print "adUpdate: " & rs.Supports(adUpdate)
Debug.Print "adMovePrevious: " & rs.Supports(adMovePrevious)

rs.Close
cn.Close

End Sub
```

The output from the support information code is:

```
Client-Side Dynamic Recordset:
adAddNew: True
adBookmark: True
adDelete: True
adFind: True
adUpdate: True
adMovePrevious: True
```

This shows that ADO provides pretty good access to an Excel worksheet.

Connecting to a text file

The TextExample procedure, shown in Example 17-8, illustrates how to create a text file and add text to it using the ODBC provider for OLE DB. (Before running this procedure, you will probably want to change the DefaultDir value.)

Example 17-8. The TestExample procedure

```
Sub TextExample( )

Dim rs As ADODB.Recordset
Dim cn As ADODB.Connection
Dim sCS As String
Dim sSQL As String

' Declare new connection
Set cn = New ADODB.Connection

' Form connection string
sCS = "DefaultDir=d:\bkado;"
sCS = sCS & "Driver={Microsoft Text Driver (*.txt; *.csv)};"
sCS = sCS & "DriverId=27;"
cn.ConnectionString = sCS
```

Example 17-8. The TestExample procedure (continued)

```
cn.Open

' Get full connection string after opening
Debug.Print "Full connection string: " & cn.ConnectionString

' Create a new text file and add a line
On Error Resume Next
cn.Execute "CREATE TABLE [newfile.txt] (FirstName TEXT, LastName TEXT);"

If Err.Number <> 0 And Err.Number <> vbObjectError + 3604 Then
    MsgBox "Error: " & Err.Number & ": " & Err.Description
    Err.Clear
End If

sSQL = "INSERT INTO [newfile.txt] (FirstName, LastName) Values ('steve', 'roman');"
cn.Execute sSQL

' Open a recordset
Set rs = New ADODB.Recordset
rs.Open "SELECT * FROM NewFile.txt", cn, adOpenDynamic, adLockOptimistic

' Check support options while we are here
Debug.Print
Debug.Print "Client-Side Dynamic Recordset:"
Debug.Print "adAddNew: " & rs.Supports(adAddNew)
Debug.Print "adBookmark: " & rs.Supports(adBookmark)
Debug.Print "adDelete: " & rs.Supports(adDelete)
Debug.Print "adFind: " & rs.Supports(adFind)
Debug.Print "adUpdate: " & rs.Supports(adUpdate)
Debug.Print "adMovePrevious: " & rs.Supports(adMovePrevious)

rs.Close
cn.Close

End Sub
```

In this case, there is a wrinkle in the connection-string requirements. We seem to need the clause:

```
DriverId = 27;
```

in the connection string, even though the driver name is also given. Without the DriverId, we get the confusing error message "Data source name not found and no default driver specified." As with the Excel example, to figure this out, I created a DSN with the ODBC Administrator and inspected the resulting file. Starting with the entire connection string based on that file, I slowly eliminated entries until I got a minimal working connection string.

Note also that when creating a new text file, we need to deal with the possibility that the file already exists. The line:

```
On Error Resume Next
```

tells VBA that if an error occurs, it should simply skip the line that produced the error and execute the next line. Now consider the code that will handle an error:

```
If Err.Number <> 0 And Err.Number <> vbObjectError + 3604 Then
    MsgBox "Error: " & Err.Number & ": " & Err.Description
    Err.Clear
End If
```

If we remove the On Error Resume Next line, the second time we run the procedure, we will get the error message in Figure 17-7.

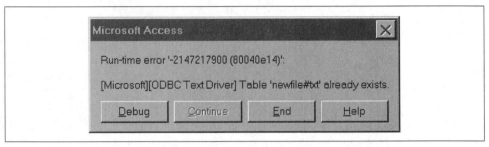

Figure 17-7. An error message

Now, VBA uses error numbers starting with the constant vbObjectError (which equals &H8004000) to indicate object errors. The error number in Figure 17-7 is thus:

```
&H8004000 + &H0e14 = vbObjectError + 3604
```

So, the error-handling code:

```
If Err.Number <> 0 And Err.Number <> vbObjectError + 3604 Then
    MsgBox "Error: " & Err.Number & ": " & Err.Description
    Exit Sub
End If
```

looks for errors message other than error number vbObjectError+3604. If it finds such an error, it displays a message and exits. However, if the error is the one shown in Figure 17-7, then the procedure just ignores it. This is what we want, because the next line of code just inserts a line in the existing file.

The full connection string for this text connection is:

```
Provider=MSDASQL.1; _
Connect Timeout=15; _
Extended Properties="DefaultDir=d:\bkado; _
...Driver={Microsoft Text Driver (*.txt; *.csv)}; _
...DriverId=27;MaxBufferSize=512;PageTimeout=5;"; _
Locale Identifier=1033
```

and the support-related output is:

```
Client-Side Dynamic Recordset:
adAddNew: True
adBookmark: False
adDelete: True
```

```
adFind: True
adUpdate: True
adMovePrevious: True
```

Thus, we even have pretty good access to a text file, but we cannot use bookmarks.

ODBC support

The documentation for the ODBC data provider does include some useful tables that describe which features are available for various recordset types. These tables are reproduced here as Tables 17-3 and 17-4.

Table 17-3. Availability of properties by Recordset

Property	ForwardOnly	Dynamic	Keyset	Static
AbsolutePage	Not available	Not available	Read/write	Read/write
AbsolutePosition	Not available	Not available	Read/write	Read/write
ActiveConnection	Read/write	Read/write	Read/write	Read/write
BOF	Read-only	Read-only	Read-only	Read-only
Bookmark	Not available	Not available	Read/write	Read/write
CacheSize	Read/write	Read/write	Read/write	Read/write
CursorLocation	Read/write	Read/write	Read/write	Read/write
CursorType	Read/write	Read/write	Read/write	Read/write
EditMode	Read-only	Read-only	Read-only	Read-only
EOF	Read-only	Read-only	Read-only	Read-only
Filter	Read/write	Read/write	Read/write	Read/write
LockType	Read/write	Read/write	Read/write	Read/write
MarshalOptions	Read/write	Read/write	Read/write	Read/write
MaxRecords	Read/write	Read/write	Read/write	Read/write
PageCount	Not available	Not available	Read-only	Read-only
PageSize	Read/write	Read/write	Read/write	Read/write
RecordCount	Not available	Not available	Read-only	Read-only
Source	Read/write	Read/write	Read/write	Read/write
State	Read-only	Read-only	Read-only	Read-only
Status	Read-only	Read-only	Read-only	Read-only

Table 17-4. Availability of methods by Recordset

Method	ForwardOnly	Dynamic	Keyset	Static
AddNew	Yes	Yes	Yes	Yes
CancelBatch	Yes	Yes	Yes	Yes
CancelUpdate	Yes	Yes	Yes	Yes
Clone	No	No	Yes	Yes

Table 17-4. *Availability of methods by Recordset (continued)*

Method	ForwardOnly	Dynamic	Keyset	Static
Close	Yes	Yes	Yes	Yes
Delete	Yes	Yes	Yes	Yes
GetRows	Yes	Yes	Yes	Yes
Move	Yes	Yes	Yes	Yes
MoveFirst	Yes	Yes	Yes	Yes
MoveLast	No	Yes	Yes	Yes
MoveNext	Yes	Yes	Yes	Yes
MovePrevious	No	Yes	Yes	Yes
NextRecordset (except Jet)	Yes	Yes	Yes	Yes
Open	Yes	Yes	Yes	Yes
Requery	Yes	Yes	Yes	Yes
Resync	No	No	Yes	Yes
Supports	Yes	Yes	Yes	Yes
Update	Yes	Yes	Yes	Yes
UpdateBatch	Yes	Yes	Yes	Yes

An Example: Using ADO over the Web

Let us conclude this chapter with a simple real-world illustration of the use of ADO. Many web sites expose data from an underlying database. Now, it is quite easy to save an Access table in the form of an HTML page, using Access' Export feature. However, the resulting data is static. To generate dynamic data in response to a user's input, we need to do some programming.

One of my duties is to maintain a web site called The Mathematics Online Bookshelf (*http://www.mathbookshelf.com*). This site is essentially a frontend for a searchable Jet database of several thousand high-level mathematics books. The user can fill in a search form and click a Search button. All matching records will be returned to the user over the Web. Let's look at a simplified version of the ADO code used to search the database. (Incidentally, the context of this code is an *Active Server Pages* (ASP) file, and the scripting language is VBScript. However, you don't need to know anything about these technologies.)

Figure 17-8 shows a greatly simplified version of the search form. This version allows user input of author, title, and publisher, and the principle is the same for more complicated forms.

We begin by noting that in VBScript, the Like operator uses a percent sign (%) to represent any string and an underscore (_) to denote any single character. (This is the syntax of regular expressions.)

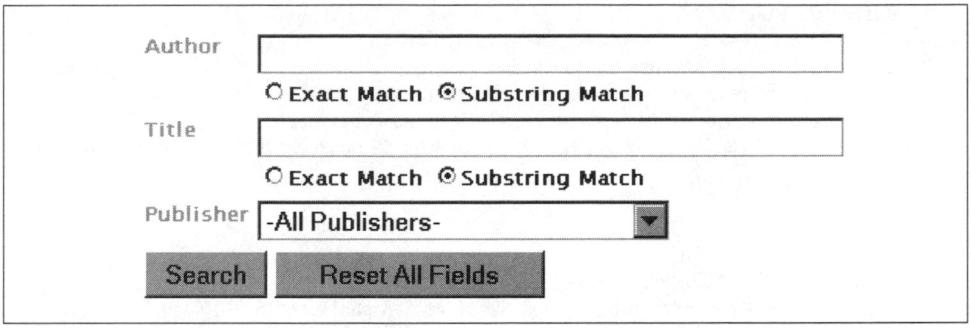

Figure 17-8. A search page

First, we declare some variables. Since this code is written as VBScript, variables are declared without a type. Note that we include variables that correspond to the values of each search-form control.

```
' Declare variables
Dim cn, rs, sSQL
Dim author, authorexact, title, titleexact, publisher
Dim connective
Dim cMatches
```

Then we assign the variables to the control's values, as returned by the ASP *Request* object.

```
' Gather input from search form
author = Request("txtAuthor")
authorexact = Request("optAuthor")
title = Request("txtTitle")
titleexact = Request("optTitle")
publisher = Request("lstPublishers")
```

Now we open an ADO connection to the database, which is called MobBooks, and declare a recordset variable for later use.

```
' Open a connection to MobBooks database
Set cn = Server.CreateObject("ADODB.Connection")
Set rs = Server.CreateObject("ADODB.Recordset")

cn.Provider = "Microsoft Jet 3.51 OLE DB Provider"
cn.ConnectionString = "Data Source=" & Server.MapPath("/MobBooks.mdb") & ";Jet OLEDB:
Database Password=""xxxxx"""
cn.Open
```

Now we can build an SQL statement based on the contents of the search form, as contained in the variables.

We begin by creating a JOIN between the MobBooks and the MobPubs tables. The reason is that the PUB field in the MobBooks table contains abbreviations for the publisher names, but we want to display the full publisher names, which are in the MobPubs table.

```
' Build SQL statement

' Start with a join between MobBooks and
' Publishers to pick up Long name of publisher
sSQL = "SELECT MobBooks.*, MobPubs.[LONG NAME] AS Publisher"
sSQL = sSQL & " FROM MobBooks INNER JOIN MobPubs ON MobBooks.PUB = MobPubs.PUBLISHER"

connective = " WHERE "

' Publisher
If publisher <> "-All Publishers-" Then
    sSQL = sSQL & connective & "([Long Name] = '" & publisher & "')"
    connective = " AND "
End If

' Author
if author <> "" then
    if authorexact = "exact" then
        sSQL = sSQL & connective & "(AU='" & author & "')"
    else
        sSQL = sSQL & connective & "(AU Like '%" & author & "%')"
    End If
    connective = " AND "
End If

' Title
if title <> "" then
    if titleexact = "exact" then
        sSQL = sSQL & connective & "(Title='" & title & "')"
    else
        sSQL = sSQL & connective & "(Title Like '%" & title & "%')"
    End If
    connective = " AND "
End If
```

Next we open the recordset:

```
' Open recordset
rs.Open sSQL, cn
```

Now we can write the search results to HTML output, using the Write method of the ASP *Response* object (the HTML header has already been written):

```
' Write search results to html output

' First write search form's control values for reference
connective = ""
Response.Write "<font color='Green'>Search Criteria</font><br>"
If title <> "" Then
    Response.Write connective & "<font color='Blue'>Title</font>:" & title
    connective = ";  "
end if
If author <> "" Then
    Response.Write connective & "<font color='Blue'>Author</font>:" & author
    connective = ";  "
```

```
End If
If publisher <> "" Then
    Response.Write connective & "<font color='Blue'>Pub</font>:" & publisher
End If
Response.Write "<br>"
connective = ""

' Loop through recordset
cMatches = 0
Do While Not rs.eof

    cMatches = cMatches + 1

    Response.Write "<HR><font color='Green'>" & cMatches & " - " &
    rs("Title") & "</font>"
    Response.Write "<br>" & rs("Au")

    ' Collect bibliographic data from recordset
    bib = ""
    if rs("Date") <> "" then bib = bib & ", " & rs("Date")
    if rs("ISBN") <> "" then bib = bib & ", " & rs("ISBN")
    if rs("Pages") <> "" then bib = bib & ", " & rs("Pages") & " pp."
    if rs("Price") <> "" then bib = bib & ", $" & rs("Price")

    ' Remove leading comma and space and print it
    bib = "<br>" & mid(bib, 2)
    Response.write bib

    ' Write TOC
    if rs("TOC") <> "" then Response.write
        "<br><font color='Green' ><i>Contents</i></font>: " & rs("TOC")

    rs.MoveNext
Loop

Response.Write "<HR>"

rs.close
cn.close
```

That's it. As you can see, a little ADO programming is all it takes to "publish" an Access database over the Web.

CHAPTER 18

ADOX: Jet Data Definition in ADO

ADOX is an acronym for *ADO Extensions for Data Definition and Security*. When making comparisons between ActiveX Data Objects (ADO) and Data Access Objects (DAO), proponents of DAO will point out that ADO does not include features for data definition—that is, features that can be used to create and alter databases and their components (tables, columns, indexes, etc.). This is precisely the purpose of ADOX, but not just in the context of Jet databases. ADOX is intended to be a universal data-definition object model. Of course, as with ADO, it requires support from OLE DB data providers. Our concern is with ADOX in relation to Jet.

I plan to discuss the role of ADOX in various data definition operations, such as creating a Jet database and creating and altering Jet database tables.

It is worth mentioning that ADOX is not a complete substitute for DAO's data-definition features. For example, query creation in ADOX has a serious wrinkle (at least for Access 2000). Namely, a query created using ADOX will not appear in the Access 2000 user interface! We will revisit this issue later in this chapter.

The ADOX Object Model

The ADOX object model is shown in Figure 18-1. The model has 9 object pairs (object/collection), about 75 properties, and about 50 methods—not a very large object model as Microsoft object models go (and smaller than the ADO object model). Unfortunately, the ADOX help documentation is among Microsoft's worst, which is saying a lot.

Let's now look at some of the more common data-definition operations from the perspective of ADOX.

Creating a Database

To create a Jet database, use the `Create` method of the *Catalog* object. Its syntax is:

```
CatObject.Create(ConnectString)
```

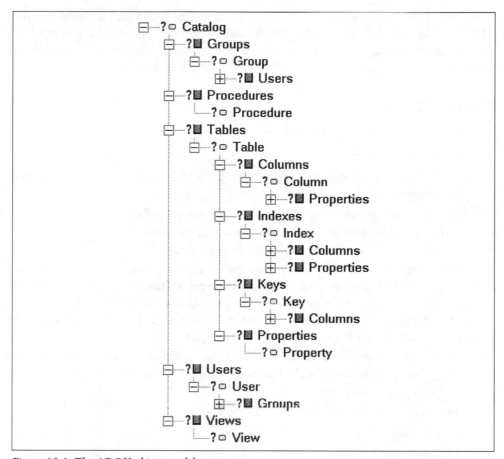

Figure 18-1. The ADOX object model

where *ConnectString* is a connection string that must also define the database to be created.

The following code creates a new Jet database:

```
Sub CreateDatabase( )

Dim cat As New Catalog

' Must use version 3.51 of data provider in order
' to create a database compatible with Access 97.
' If this is not required, can use version 4.0.
cat.Create "Provider=Microsoft.Jet.OLEDB.4.0;" & _
    "Data Source=d:\temp\ADOXExample.mdb"

End Sub
```

Note that if the database already exists, an error will be generated. Incidentally, the ADOX documentation says: "The Create method creates and opens a new ADO Connection to the data source specified in ConnectString." This seems to imply that the data source must already exist, which is, of course, not the case.

Creating Tables

A Jet table in ADOX is created as follows:

1. Create a *Table* object.

2. Give it a name by assigning a string containing the name to the *Table* object's Name property.

3. Append some columns to the *Table* object's *Columns* collection. Do this by calling the Append method of the *Column* collection. Its syntax is:

    ```
    TableObject.Columns.Append Item[, Type[, DefinedSize]]
    ```

    where *Item* is either a *Column* object or the string containing the name of the column. The remaining two parameters are optional if *Item* is a *Column* object that contains all column information. *Type* is an optional Long or a member of the DataTypeEnum enumeration (the default is adVarWChar), and *DefinedSize* is an optional Long that determines the column size.

4. Append the *Table* object to the *Catalog* object's *Tables* collection. Do this by calling the Append method of the *Tables* collection. Its syntax is:

    ```
    TablesObject.Append Item
    ```

    where *Item* is the *Table* object added to the collection.

Here is a sample:

```
Sub CreateTable( )

Dim cat As New ADOX.Catalog
Dim tbl As New ADOX.Table

' Open catalog
cat.ActiveConnection = "Provider=Microsoft.Jet.OLEDB.4.0;" & _
   "Data Source=d:\temp\ADOXExample.mdb"

' Assign table name and some columns
With tbl
   .Name = "NewTable"
   .Columns.Append "Column1", adVarWChar, 250
   .Columns.Append "Column2", adInteger
   .Columns.Append "Column3", adInteger
End With

cat.Tables.Append tbl

End Sub
```

To rename a column, we use the Name property of the *Column* object. To delete a column, we use the `Delete` method of the *Columns* collection. Its syntax is:

```
ColumnsObject.Delete Item
```

where *Item* is a string containing the name of the column to delete. Here is an example:

```
Sub ChangeColumn()

Dim cat As New ADOX.Catalog
Dim tbl As New ADOX.Table

cat.ActiveConnection = "Provider=Microsoft.Jet.OLEDB.4.0;" & _
    "Data Source=d:\temp\ADOXExample.mdb"

' Assign table name and some columns
Set tbl = cat.Tables("Newtable")

' Rename a column
tbl.Columns("Column2").Name = "Column2X"

' Delete a column
tbl.Columns.Delete "Column3"

End Sub
```

You may have noticed the use of the data type constant `adVarWChar` to create a string column. Table 18-1 compares the field data type constants of DAO and ADOX.

Table 18-1. DAO/ADOX field data type constants

DAO data type	ADOX data type
dbBinary	adBinary
dbBoolean	adBoolean
dbByte	adUnsignedTinyInt
dbCurrency	adCurrency
dbDate	adDate
dbDecimal	adNumeric
dbDouble	adDouble
dbGUID	adGUID
dbInteger	adSmallInt
dbLong	adInteger
dbLongBinary	adLongVarBinary
dbMemo	adLongVarWChar
dbSingle	adSingle
dbText	adVarWChar

The Tables Collection

Unlike DAO, the ADO *Tables* collection may contain objects other than Jet tables. For example, the *Tables* collection contains row-returning, nonparameterized queries (which are considered Views by ADO).

To determine the actual type of a *Table* object, we can use the Type property. Table 18-2 lists the possible values for the Type property (in the context of the Jet Data Provider). Note that the Type property is read-only and returns a string.

Table 18-2. Return values of the Table object's Type property

Type property returns	Description
ACCESS TABLE	A Microsoft Access system table
LINK	A linked table from a non-ODBC data source
PASS-THROUGH	A linked table from an ODBC data source
SYSTEM TABLE	A Microsoft Jet system table
TABLE	A Jet table
VIEW	A row-returning, nonparameterized query

For instance, the following code:

```
Sub ListTables()

Dim cat As New ADOX.Catalog
Dim tbl As ADOX.Table

cat.ActiveConnection = "Provider=Microsoft.Jet.OLEDB.4.0;" & _
    "Data Source=d:\temp\ADOXExample.mdb;"

For Each tbl In cat.Tables
    Debug.Print tbl.Name, tbl.Type
Next
End Sub
```

may produce the following output:

```
MSysAccessObjects       ACCESS TABLE
MSysACEs                SYSTEM TABLE
MSysObjects             SYSTEM TABLE
MSysQueries             SYSTEM TABLE
MSysRelationships       SYSTEM TABLE
NewQuery                VIEW
NewTable                TABLE
```

Creating Indexes

The process for creating a table index is the same in ADOX as it is in DAO:

1. Create the index by creating an *Index* object and assigning a name to it.

2. Append columns one by one to the *Index* object's *Columns* collection. Call the *Columns* collection's Append method; its syntax was discussed in "The Tables Collection" section earlier in this chapter.

3. Append the index to the *Table* object's *Indexes* collection. The syntax of the Append method is:

```
TableObject.Indexes.Append Index[, Columns]
```

where *Index* is the *Index* object to be appended or a string containing the name of the index to create, and *Columns* is an optional variant specifying the columns to be indexed.

Here is an example:

```
Sub ADOCreateIndex()

Dim cat As New ADOX.Catalog
Dim tbl As ADOX.Table
Dim idx As New ADOX.Index

' Open the catalog
cat.ActiveConnection = "Provider=Microsoft.Jet.OLEDB.4.0;" & _
    "Data Source=d:\temp\ADOXExample.mdb;"

Set tbl = cat.Tables("Newtable")

' Create Index object and append table column to it
idx.Name = "Newindex"
idx.Columns.Append "Column1"

' Allow Null values
idx.IndexNulls = adIndexNullsAllow

' Append the Index object to the table's Indexes collection
tbl.Indexes.Append idx

End Sub
```

The DAO *Index* object has two properties that determine the behavior of Nulls within an index: Required and IgnoreNulls. Both of these properties are False by default, implying that Null values are allowed in the index and that an index entry is added for each row with a Null value in the index field.

On the other hand, ADO has a single property, called IndexNulls, that governs the behavior of Null values in indexes. By default, the IndexNulls property is set to adIndexNullsDisallow, implying that Null values are not allowed in the index and that no index entry will be added if a field contains Null. Table 18-3 compares the relevant settings in DAO and ADOX.

Table 18-3. Comparison of constants for treating nulls

DAORequired	DAO IgnoreNulls	ADOX IndexNulls	Description
True	False	adIndexNullsDisallow	Null value not allowed in index field; no index entry added
False	True	adIndexNullsIgnore	Null value allowed in index field; no index entry added
False	False	adIndexNullsAllow	Null value allowed in index field; index entry added

Creating a Primary Key

In DAO, primary keys are created by setting the Primary property of the *Index* object to True. In ADOX, we proceed as follows:

1. Create a *Key* object.
2. Set its Type property to Primary using the adKeyPrimary constant.
3. Append some columns to the *Key* object's *Columns* collection.
4. Append the *Key* object to the *Index* object's *Keys* collection.

Here is an example:

```
Sub ADOCreatePrimaryKey()

Dim cat As New ADOX.Catalog
Dim tbl As ADOX.Table
Dim pk As New ADOX.Key

cat.ActiveConnection = "Provider=Microsoft.Jet.OLEDB.4.0;" & _
    "Data Source=d:\temp\ADOXExample.mdb;"

Set tbl = cat.Tables("Newtable")

' Create the Primary Key
pk.Name = "PrimaryKey"
pk.Type = adKeyPrimary
pk.Columns.Append "Column1"

' Append the Key object to the Keys collection of Table
tbl.Keys.Append pk

End Sub
```

Creating a Query

To create a query, we use the ADO *Command* object to create a new ADO command. This can be appended to the *Views* (or *Procedures*) collection of the catalog to create a new query. Its syntax is:

```
ViewsObj.Append Name, Command
```

where *Name* is a string containing the name of the object, and *Command* is a *Command* object.

Here is an example:

```
Sub CreateQuery()

Dim cat As New ADOX.Catalog
Dim cd As New ADODB.Command
Dim sSQL As String

cat.ActiveConnection = "Provider=Microsoft.Jet.OLEDB.4.0;" & _
    "Data Source=d:\temp\ADOXExample.mdb;"

sSQL = "SELECT * FROM Newtable"

cd.CommandText = sSQL

cat.Views.Append "Newquery", cd

End Sub
```

Now, the bad news. Here is a quotation from MSDN:

> Although it is possible to create and modify a stored query in an Access database by using Microsoft ActiveX® Data Objects Extensions for Data Definition Language and Security (ADOX), if you do so your query won't be visible in the Access Database window or in any other part of the Access user interface...

The reason behind this invisibility is explained further in MSDN:

> This is so because the Microsoft Jet 4.0 database engine can run in two modes: one mode that supports the same Jet SQL commands used in previous versions of Access, a new mode that supports new Jet SQL commands and syntax that are more compliant with the ANSI SQL-92 standard.

> Queries created with ADOX can support the new Jet SQL mode, and so are flagged internally to identify them as using that mode, whether the query contains the new commands or not. Access 2000 can open an Access database only while using the mode that supports the older Jet SQL commands and syntax. To prevent error messages and conflicts between the new Jet SQL commands and syntax and the Access query editing tools, Access hides queries that are flagged as containing the new Jet SQL commands and syntax.

An interesting thing happens with Access 2003. Access 2003 does see the query, probably because it can handle the newer Jet SQL syntax; however, the Design view of the query does not show the output fields of the query!

Conclusion

I wish Microsoft would continue to support DAO. It is well understood, easy to use, does what is necessary, seems quite stable, and is optimized for Jet.

Sony supports a variety of TVs; General Motors supports a variety of cars; General Electric supports a variety of refrigerators; so why can't Microsoft support two types of data access? Imagine General Motors saying: "We make only one model of car, but it is designed to be universal. Whether you want a convertible sports car, or a car to haul around ten sheets of plywood, or a car to race on weekends, or a car to do off-roading, this is the car for you." Ridiculous.

PART VII

Programming Problems

CHAPTER 19

Some Common Data Manipulation Problems

In this chapter, I discuss a number of problems that you may encounter when dealing with data, along with possible solutions. I suggest that you try to find a solution before reading the solution in the text. Also, I should mention that there are usually many different ways of solving a given problem. In fact, you may very well be able to find a more efficient solution than the one given. The main purpose of these problems and solutions is to give you some food for thought.

Before beginning, let us note that many of the upcoming solutions involve the use of subqueries. We discussed subqueries in Chapter 6, but let us review quickly here.

Access SQL permits the use of SELECT statements within other SELECT statements (as well as in other statements, such as INSERT INTO statements). The internal, or nested, SELECT statement is referred to as a *subquery*.

Note that you may include a nested SELECT statement within a main SELECT statement only if the internal SELECT statement returns *at most one record*. To illustrate, consider the main SQL statement:

```
SELECT Hour,
  (SELECT Count(Interval) FROM StartTimes WHERE (StartTime <= Hour))
  FROM Hours
```

Here, the internal SQL statement:

```
SELECT Count(Interval) FROM StartTimes WHERE (StartTime <= Hour)
```

returns at most a single record, because it returns a Count. Note also that the WHERE clause in the internal SQL statement refers to the *Hour* field that is part of the main SQL, thus linking the return value of the internal statement to the current record in the HOURS table.

Running Sums

The computation of *running sums* is a common operation. To illustrate, consider Table 19-1, which contains the duration (in hours, say) for various events.

Table 19-1. A running sum

Event	Duration
1	1
2	5
3	6
4	3
5	4
6	1
7	8
8	2

For each event, we want to compute the sum of all the durations of the events that precede that event. This sum is a running sum.

Solution

One approach is to use the Cartesian product of the table with itself. In this way, we can access all records whose Event number precedes that of a given record. For instance, for the record with Event number 5, we need access to the records with Event numbers 1 through 4. The Cartesian product provides us with these records.

Here is the SQL statement that does the job:

```
SELECT Running.Event, Sum(RunningCopy.Duration) AS StartTime
FROM Running, Running AS RunningCopy
WHERE (RunningCopy.Event < Running.Event)
GROUP BY Running.Event
```

The FROM clause creates the Cartesian product of the table with itself. The WHERE clause restricts the records to those for which:

```
RunningCopy.Event < Running.Event
```

that is, to the records that provide information about the records *preceding* each record in Table 19-1. Finally, we GROUP BY Event and compute the sum of the durations.

The problem is that Cartesian products are very inefficient and use a lot of resources. (If Table 19-1 has 100,000 rows, then the Cartesian product has $100{,}000 \times 100{,}000 = 10{,}000{,}000{,}000$ rows!)

A more efficient solution is to use a nested SELECT statement, that is, to use a SELECT statement within the main SELECT statement. Recall that this is permitted in Access SQL, provided that the internal SELECT statement returns *at most one record*.

In the following SQL statement, note the use of table aliases, which are needed because we must refer to Table 19-1 in two contexts:

```
SELECT R1.Event,
(SELECT SUM(R2.Duration) FROM Running As R2 WHERE R2.Event < R1.Event)
    AS StartTime
FROM Running As R1
```

The internal SQL statement:

```
SELECT SUM(R2.Duration) FROM Running As R2 WHERE R2.Event < R1.Event
```

returns the sum of the duration for all events *preceding* the current event, which is denoted by R1.Event.

Example 19-1 shows a VBA procedure to execute this SQL statement. The *DoCmd* object is used in VBA to run an Access action. Thus, the line DoCmd.OpenQuery opens a query in Access.

Example 19-1. Calculating running sums using nested SQL statements

```
Private Sub RunningSumSQL( )

Dim db As Database
Set db = CurrentDb

Dim qry As QueryDef
Dim sSQL As String

On Error Resume Next
db.QueryDefs.Delete "temp"
On Error GoTo 0

sSQL = "SELECT R1.Event," & _
" (SELECT SUM(R2.Duration)" & _
" FROM Running As R2" & _
" WHERE R2.Event < R1.Event)" & _
" AS StartTime" & _
" FROM Running As R1"

Set qry = db.CreateQueryDef("temp", sSQL)

DoCmd.OpenQuery qry.Name

End Sub
```

Another approach is to use DAO, which provides a very simple solution in this case. It creates a permanent result table, whereas the previous solution creates a select query. Example 19-2 shows the DAO code performing the same operation. The results are placed in Table 19-1.

Example 19-2. Calculating a running sum using DAO

```
Private Sub RunningSumDAO( )

Dim db As Database
Dim rs As Recordset
Dim lRunningSum As Long

Set db = CurrentDb

lRunningSum = 0
```

Example 19-2. Calculating a running sum using DAO (continued)

```
Set rs = db.OpenRecordset("SELECT * FROM Running ORDER BY Event")
Do While Not rs.EOF
    rs.Edit
    rs!RunningSum = lRunningSum
    rs.Update
    lRunningSum = lRunningSum + rs!Duration
    rs.MoveNext
Loop

rs.Close

End Sub
```

Overlapping Intervals I

In Table 19-2, the rows denote intervals of time. The problem is determining, for each hour of the day, the number of intervals that contain this hour.

Table 19-2. Overlap table: Rows denote time intervals

Interval	StartTime	EndTime
1	4:00:00 PM	7:00:00 PM
2	5:00:00 PM	9:00:00 PM
3	2:00:00 PM	6:00:00 PM
4	8:00:00 PM	11:59:00 PM
5	12:00:00 PM	4:00:00 PM

For this, we also use an HOURS table (see Table 19-3).

Table 19-3. Hours table

Hours
12:00:00 PM
1:00:00 PM
2:00:00 PM
3:00:00 PM
4:00:00 PM
5:00:00 PM
6:00:00 PM
7:00:00 PM
8:00:00 PM
9:00:00 PM
10:00:00 PM
11:00:00 PM
11:59:00 PM

Solution

This problem can be solved using a nested SELECT statement (that is, a subquery). Here is the code:

```
Private Sub OverlappingIntervals()

Dim db As Database
Set db = CurrentDb

Dim qry As QueryDef
Dim sSQL As String

On Error Resume Next
db.QueryDefs.Delete "temp"
On Error GoTo 0

sSQL = "SELECT Hours.Hour," & _
" (SELECT Count(Interval) AS CountOfIntervals" & _
" FROM Overlap" & _
" WHERE (StartTime <= Hours.Hour) And" & _
" (Hours.Hour < EndTime))" & _
" FROM Hours"

Set qry = db.CreateQueryDef("temp", sSQL)

DoCmd.OpenQuery qry.Name

End Sub
```

We invite you to create a DAO solution. The problem in the next section illustrates the overlapping intervals technique.

Overlapping Intervals II

A company employs workers and supervisors. During a typical day, each worker and supervisor works one or more shifts, which consist of consecutive hours. Table 19-4 shows a typical day (from 12 noon to 12 midnight).

Table 19-4. Superload table: Hours worked by supervisors and workers

EmpID	EmpType	StartHour	EndHour
1	Super	12:00:00 PM	5:59:00 PM
2	Super	6:00:00 PM	11:59:00 PM
3	Super	4:00:00 PM	8:59:00 PM
4	Worker	4:00:00 PM	6:59:00 PM
5	Worker	5:00:00 PM	8:59:00 PM
6	Worker	2:00:00 PM	5:59:00 PM
7	Worker	8:00:00 PM	11:59:00 PM
8	Worker	12:00:00 PM	3:59:00 PM

We want to compute the *maximum* number of workers that each supervisor must supervise at one time.

Solution

This problem can be handled in a two-step process. First, we count the number of workers in each hour. Consider the following SQL statement:

```
SELECT Hours.Hour,
(SELECT Count(EmpType) FROM SuperLoad
 WHERE (Starthour <= Hours.Hour) And (Hours.Hour < EndHour)
   And (EmpType='Worker')) AS CountOfWorkers
FROM Hours
```

This, again, uses a subquery that returns a single record giving the number of workers that are working during a given hour.

Using this SQL statement, we make a query named qry1, so it can be used in the next step. See Table 19-5 for the result of this query.

Table 19-5. Number of workers working at a particular hour

Hours	CountOfWorkers
12:00:00 PM	1
1:00:00 PM	1
2:00:00 PM	2
3:00:00 PM	2
4:00:00 PM	2
5:00:00 PM	3
6:00:00 PM	2
7:00:00 PM	1
8:00:00 PM	2
9:00:00 PM	1
10:00:00 PM	1
11:00:00 PM	1

The next step is computing the supervisor load as the maximum number of workers in each supervisor's shift. Do this by using the name of the query from the previous step in the following SQL statement:

```
sSQL2 = "SELECT SuperLoad.EmpID, SuperLoad.EmpType," & _
" (SELECT Max(CountOfWorkers) AS WorkerLoad" & _
" FROM [" & qry1.Name & "]" & _
" WHERE ((Hours.Hour >= StartHour) And (Hours.Hour < Endhour)))" & _
" FROM SuperLoad" & _
" WHERE SuperLoad.EmpType = 'Super'"
```

The results are shown in Table 19-6.

Table 19-6. Maximum number of workers per supervisor

EmpID	EmpType	WorkerLoad
1	Super	3
2	Super	2
3	Super	3

The complete code for this solution is in Example 19-3.

Example 19-3. Calculating the maximum number of workers per supervisor

```
Private Sub SupervisorLoad( )

Dim db As Database
Set db = CurrentDb

Dim qry1 As QueryDef
Dim qry2 As QueryDef
Dim sSQL1 As String
Dim sSQL2 As String

On Error Resume Next
db.QueryDefs.Delete "temp1"
db.QueryDefs.Delete "temp2"
On Error GoTo 0

sSQL1 = "SELECT Hours.Hour," & _
" (SELECT Count(EmpType) FROM SuperLoad" & _
" WHERE (Starthour <= Hours.Hour) And (Hours.Hour < EndHour)" & _
" And (EmpType='Worker'))" & _
" AS CountOfWorkers" & _
" FROM Hours"

Set qry1 = db.CreateQueryDef("temp1", sSQL1)

' Uncomment to see how this step looks
'DoCmd.OpenQuery qry1.Name

sSQL2 = "SELECT SuperLoad.EmpID, SuperLoad.EmpType," & _
" (SELECT Max(CountOfWorkers) AS WorkerLoad" & _
" FROM [" & qry1.Name & "]" & _
" WHERE ((Hours.Hour >= StartHour) And (Hours.Hour < Endhour)))" & _
" FROM SuperLoad" & _
" WHERE SuperLoad.EmpType = 'Super'"

Set qry2 = db.CreateQueryDef("temp2", sSQL2)

DoCmd.OpenQuery qry2.Name

End Sub
```

Making Assignments with Default

Imagine a conference where your task is assigning conference rooms to attendees. Table 19-7 shows the preregistered attendees along with corresponding room numbers.

Table 19-7. Assignment table

Name	Room
_default	15
_default	14
_default	13
_default	12
Bach	123
Beethoven	231
Mozart	455
Chopin	455
Elgar	231
Gluck	123
Liszt	455

Note that the table contains several default choices. If an individual is not in the table, then you want to assign one of the default rooms to that individual. Moreover, to avoid overcrowding, you want to assign the default room numbers randomly. How do you do this?

Solution

This problem can be solved in a variety of ways, one of which provides a nice use of both subqueries and the UNION statement. First, consider the SQL statement:

```
sSQL1 = "SELECT Room FROM Assignment WHERE (Name = [Enter Name])"
```

Recall that [Enter name] is a parameter. When the query is run, the user will be prompted for a name, which will be substituted for [Enter name]. This statement will return the record associated with a given name if it is in the table; otherwise, it will return the empty recordset.

Now consider the statement:

```
sSQL2 = "SELECT Room FROM Assignment
        WHERE (Name = '_default') AND
        ([Enter Name] NOT IN (SELECT Name FROM Assignment))"
```

The clause:

```
[Enter Name] NOT IN (SELECT Name FROM Assignment)
```

returns TRUE if and only if the name entered by the user is *not* in the table. Hence, the clause sSQL2 can be rewritten based on two cases, name in table:

```
sSQL2 = "SELECT Room FROM Assignment WHERE (Name = '_default') AND FALSE"
```

and name not in table:

```
sSQL1 = "SELECT Room FROM Assignment WHERE (Name = '_default') AND TRUE"
```

This simplifies further to name in table:

```
sSQL2 = "SELECT Room FROM Assignment WHERE FALSE"
```

and name not in table:

```
sSQL1 = "SELECT Room FROM Assignment WHERE (Name = '_default')"
```

Thus, this statement returns the empty recordset if the name *is* in the table and the default records if the name is *not* in the table.

Now we take the union:

```
sSQL3 = sSQL1 & " UNION " & sSQL2
```

This SQL statement will return the room number for a name if the name is in the table; otherwise, it returns the default records.

Now, all we need to do is return a random record! Note that this will work in either case, because if the name is in the table, there is only one record, so a randomly chosen record must be that record.

The complete code is shown in Example 19-4.

Example 19-4. Handling preregistered and default room assignments

```
Private Sub AssignmentWithDefault()

Dim db As Database
Set db = CurrentDb

Dim sName As String
Dim qry1 As QueryDef
Dim rs As Recordset
Dim sSQL1 As String
Dim sSQL2 As String
Dim sSQL3 As String

Dim lRandom As Long
Dim lcRecords As Long

On Error Resume Next
db.QueryDefs.Delete "temp1"
On Error GoTo 0

sSQL1 = "SELECT Room FROM Assignment" & _
" WHERE (Name = [Enter Name])"
```

```
sSQL2 = "SELECT Room FROM Assignment" & _
" WHERE (Name = '_default') AND ([Enter Name] NOT IN (SELECT Name FROM Assignment))"

sSQL3 = sSQL1 & " UNION " & sSQL2

Set qry1 = db.CreateQueryDef("temp1", sSQL3)

sName = InputBox("Enter name")
qry1.Parameters(0) = sName

' To see the results
''DoCmd.OpenQuery qry1.Name

Set rs = qry1.OpenRecordset

' Populate and get recordcount
rs.MoveLast
lcRecords = rs.RecordCount

' Random record
Randomize Timer
' lRandom is between 0 and lcRecords-1
lRandom = Int(lcRecords * Rnd)

rs.MoveFirst
rs.Move lRandom

MsgBox "Room for " & sName & " is " & rs!Room

End Sub
```

Time to Completion I

Here is a simple time-to-completion problem. Table 19-8 shows the status of widget production for your company. At various stages in the production process, the workers enter a record into the table indicating the remaining time to completion for the widget.

We want to identify those widgets that are not yet completed.

Solution

The next SQL statement does the job. Note the use of the NOT IN form of subquery, which is discussed in the "Subqueries" section in Chapter 6.

```
SELECT DISTINCT WidgetID FROM Widgets As W1
WHERE 0 NOT IN
(SELECT TimeToCompletion FROM Widgets As W2
WHERE W2.WidgetID = W1.WidgetID)
```

Table 19-8. Widgets table: Time to completion for widgets

WidgetID	TimeToCompletion
1	5
1	3
1	2
1	1
2	6
2	3
2	0
3	8
3	7
3	6
3	4
4	9
4	4
4	2
4	0

Time to Completion II

Let's make the time-to-completion problem more complicated. Imagine again that you are keeping track of the status of widget production for your company. Each widget is composed of four modules, each of which is assembled separately. Table 19-9 shows some sample data.

We are trying to determine the widgets in which Module 1 is the *only* completed module—that is, where TimeToCompletion is equal to zero for Module 1, but not for any of the other modules in the widget. Thus, for our table, Widgets 1 and 4 qualify.

Solution

Consider the following SQL statement:

```
SELECT WidgetID
FROM Widgets AS W1
WHERE (TimeToCompletion = 0) AND
0 NOT IN
(SELECT TimeToCompletion FROM Widgets AS W2
WHERE (W2.WidgetID=W1.WidgetID) AND (W2.ModuleID <> 1))
```

The subquery selects, for a particular widget, all TimeToCompletions for all modules except the first module. We can then test to see if that set of TimeToCompletions contains a zero.

Table 19-9. Widgets table: Time to completion of multimodule widgets

WidgetID	ModuleID	TimeToCompletion
1	1	0
1	2	1
1	3	2
1	4	1
2	1	1
2	2	2
2	3	3
2	4	4
3	1	0
3	2	5
3	3	4
3	4	0
4	1	0
4	2	1
4	3	1
4	4	2

Example 19-5 shows the complete code.

Example 19-5. TimeToCompletion example

```
Private Sub TimeToCompletion( )

Dim db As Database
Set db = CurrentDb

Dim qry1 As QueryDef
Dim sSQL1 As String

On Error Resume Next
db.QueryDefs.Delete "temp1"
On Error GoTo 0

sSQL1 = "SELECT WidgetID FROM Widgets AS W1" & _
" WHERE (TimeToCompletion = 0) AND" & _
" 0 NOT IN" & _
" (SELECT TimeToCompletion FROM Widgets AS W2" & _
" WHERE (W2.WidgetID=W1.WidgetID) AND (W2.ModuleID <> 1))"

Set qry1 = db.CreateQueryDef("temp1", sSQL1)

DoCmd.OpenQuery qry1.Name

End Sub
```

Time to Completion III—A MaxMin Problem

Let's make the time-to-completion problem even more involved. Suppose each module is composed of several parts. Periodically, the workers involved with a particular part will make an entry into a database table, as shown in Table 19-10.

Table 19-10. Widgets table: Time to completion of a widget whose modules consist of multiple parts

WidgetID	ModuleID	PartID	TimeToCompletion
1	1	1	3
1	1	1	4
1	1	1	5
1	1	2	2
1	1	2	4
1	1	2	1
1	2	1	6
1	2	1	5
1	2	1	3
1	2	2	7
1	2	2	4
1	2	2	3
1	2	3	4
1	2	3	5
1	2	3	6
1	3	1	8
1	3	1	5
1	3	2	2
1	3	2	4

We want to compute the time to completion for each part, module, and widget. Note that there may be several entries for a given part. The time to complete a given part is the minimum of the times in these rows.

Solution 1

Let's take a step-by-step approach to the solution. Later, we can present a more elegant, but less readable, solution.

First, we create an SQL statement that returns only those rows of the table that, for each widget/module, have the smallest part TimeToCompletion. We can do this in two steps. The first SQL statement selects the TimeToCompletion field for all records in Widgets2 that have a given WidgetID, ModuleID, and PartID.

```
' Times to completion for given WidgetID/ModuleID/PartID
```

```
sSQL1 = "SELECT TimeToCompletion FROM Widgets2 AS W2" & _
" WHERE (W2.WidgetID = W1.WidgetID)" & _
" And (W2.ModuleID = W1.ModuleID)" & _
" And (W2.PartID = W1.PartID)"
```

The second SQL statement returns all records whose TimeToCompletion is less than or equal to *all* records returned in the first SQL statement—that is, all records for the given WidgetID, ModuleID, and PartID:

```
' Those records that have minimum time to completion for each part
sSQL2 = "SELECT WidgetID, ModuleID, PartID," & _
" TimeToCompletion AS TimeToFinishPart FROM Widgets2 AS W1" & _
" WHERE TimeToCompletion <= ALL (" & sSQL1 & ")"
```

An alternative approach is to use a single nested SELECT statement:

```
sSQL2 = "SELECT DISTINCT WidgetID, ModuleID, PartID," & _
" (SELECT MIN(TimeToCompletion)" & _
" FROM Widgets2 as W2 WHERE" & _
" (W2.WidgetID = W1.WidgetID) And" & _
" (W2.ModuleID = W1.ModuleID) And" & _
" (W2.PartID = W1.PartID))" & _
" AS TimeToFinishPart" & _
" FROM Widgets2 AS W1"
```

Running this query

```
Set qry1 = db.CreateQueryDef("temp1", sSQL2)
DoCmd.OpenQuery qry1.Name
```

will result in Table 19-11.

Table 19-11. Results table for qry1

WidgetID	ModuleID	PartID	TimeToFinishPart
1	1	1	3
1	1	2	1
1	2	1	3
1	2	2	3
1	2	3	4
1	3	1	5
1	3	2	2

Using this query, it is simple to get the time to completion for each module:

```
' Time to finish each module
sSQL3 = "SELECT WidgetID, ModuleID," & _
" Max(TimeToFinishPart) AS TimeToFinishModule FROM " & qry1.Name & _
" GROUP BY WidgetID, ModuleID"

Set qry2 = db.CreateQueryDef("temp2", sSQL3)
```

```
' Show it
DoCmd.OpenQuery qry2.Name
```

This query results in Table 19-12.

Table 19-12. Results table for qry2

WidgetID	ModuleID	TimeToFinishModule
1	1	3
1	2	4
1	3	5

Finally, we can compute the time to completion for each widget:

```
' Time to finish each Widget
sSQL4 = "SELECT WidgetID," & _
" Max(TimeToFinishModule) AS TimeToFinishWidget FROM " & qry2.Name & _
" GROUP BY WidgetID"

Set qry3 = db.CreateQueryDef("temp3", sSQL4)
```

This results in Table 19-13.

Table 19-13. Results table for qry3

WidgetID	TimeToFinishWidget
1	5

Solution 2

It is possible to get the time to completion in a single SQL statement, although I definitely do not recommend doing so. The result may be more elegant, but it is also harder to read. For instance, for modules, we have:

```
sSQL1 = "SELECT DISTINCT WidgetID, ModuleID," & _
" TimeToCompletion FROM Widgets2 AS W1" & _
" WHERE TimeToCompletion =" & _
"    (SELECT MAX(TimeToCompletion) FROM Widgets2 As W2" & _
"    WHERE TimeToCompletion =" & _
"      (SELECT MIN(TimeToCompletion) FROM Widgets2 AS W3" & _
"      WHERE (W3.WidgetID = W2.WidgetID)" & _
"            And (W3.ModuleID = W2.ModuleID)" & _
"            And (W3.PartID = W2.PartID)" & _
"      Group BY W3.WidgetID, W3.ModuleID, W3.PartID)" & _
"    AND (W2.WidgetID = W1.WidgetID) And (W2.ModuleID = W1.ModuleID)" & _
"    GROUP BY W2.WidgetID, W2.ModuleID)"
```

Digesting this SQL statement will probably take time, and I hope it will make you reconsider using such a statement in your own applications.

Vertical to Horizontal

Imagine a database of personal statistics with two tables (Tables 19-14 and 19-15).

Table 19-14. Composers table

EmpID	Name
1	Beethoven
2	Chopin
3	Mozart
4	Schubert
5	Brahms
6	Liszt

Notice that Table 19-15 has one row per statistic. Thus, the data for an individual person is arranged vertically. Notice also that some data is missing. For instance, there is no data at all for Liszt.

Table 19-15. ComposersData table

EmpID	StatType	Value
1	Age	45
1	Height	63
1	Weight	150
2	Age	46
2	Height	67
3	Age	35
3	Weight	135
4	Age	44
5	Height	76

Now, we want to view the data horizontally, as in Table 19-16.

Table 19-16. Combination of Tables 19-14 and 19-15

EmpID	Name	Age	Height	Weight
1	Beethoven	45	63	150
2	Chopin	46	67	
3	Mozart	35		135
4	Schubert	44		
5	Brahms		76	
6	Liszt			

Solution

One solution is given by the following SQL statement:

```
SELECT DISTINCT Composers.EmpID, Name,
  (SELECT Value FROM ComposerData As T2 WHERE
    (T2.StatType='Age') And (T2.EmpID=Composers.EmpID)) As Age,
  (SELECT Value FROM ComposerData As T2 WHERE
    (T2.StatType='Height') And (T2.EmpID=Composers.EmpID)) As Height,
  (SELECT Value FROM ComposerData As T2 WHERE
    (T2.StatType='Weight') And (T2.EmpID=Composers.EmpID)) As Weight
FROM (Composers INNER JOIN ComposerData
ON Composers.EmpID=ComposerData.EmpID)
```

Here, we have multiple SELECT subquery statements within the main SELECT clause. For instance, the clause:

```
(SELECT Value FROM ComposerData As T2 WHERE
    (T2.StatType='Age') And (T2.EmpID=Composers.EmpID)) As Age,
```

selects the age for the person selected by the main SELECT clause.

As the number of statistics grows, this SQL statement becomes more complex. Example 19-6 shows an alternative solution using DAO that does not require adjusting when additional statistics are added.

Example 19-6. VerticalToHorizontal example

```
Private Sub VerticalToHorizontal2( )

Dim db As Database
Set db = CurrentDb

Dim rsEmp As Recordset
Dim rsData As Recordset
Dim rsHor As Recordset

Set rsEmp = db.OpenRecordset("Composers")
Set rsHor = db.OpenRecordset("ComposersOutput")

Do While Not rsEmp.EOF

    Set rsData = db.OpenRecordset( _
        "SELECT * FROM ComposerData WHERE EmpID = " & rsEmp!EmpID)
    rsHor.AddNew
    rsHor!EmpID = rsEmp!EmpID
    rsHor!Name = rsEmp!Name
    Do While Not rsData.EOF
        rsHor.Fields(rsData!StatType).Value = rsData!Value
        rsData.MoveNext
    Loop
    rsHor.Update

    rsEmp.MoveNext
Loop
```

Example 19-6. VerticalToHorizontal example (continued)

```
rsEmp.Close
rsData.Close
rsHor.Close

End Sub
```

A Matching Problem

Table 19-17 presents programmers and their language skills. Table 19-18 specifies the language requirements for a number of different jobs. We want to display a list of the jobs and their respective qualified programmers.

Table 19-17. Programmers table: Programmers and their language skills

Name	Language
Blaise Pascal	VB
Blaise Pascal	C++
Blaise Pascal	Access
Blaise Pascal	Excel
Gauss	VB
Gauss	Access
Gauss	Delphi
Gauss	SQL Server
Smith	C++
Von Neuman	VB
Von Neuman	C++
Wordsworth	Delphi
Wordsworth	C++
Wordsworth	Word

Table 19-18. ProgrammingJobs table

JobID	Language
1	VB
1	Access
2	C++
3	C++
3	SQL Server
4	Delphi
5	VB
5	Pascal

Solution

One solution is given by the following SQL statement:

```
SELECT ProgrammingJobs.JobID, Programmers.Name
FROM Programmers INNER JOIN ProgrammingJobs
ON Programmers.Language = ProgrammingJobs.Language
GROUP BY ProgrammingJobs.JobID, Programmers.Name
HAVING Count(Programmers.Language)=
(SELECT Count([Language]) FROM ProgrammingJobs AS PJ
WHERE PJ.JobID=ProgrammingJobs.JobID)
```

We begin with an INNER JOIN of the two tables on the *Language* field. For each job/programmer pair, this INNER JOIN creates a set of records of the form:

```
JobID X - Language 1 - ProgrammerName Y
JobID X - Language 2 - ProgrammerName Y
JobID X - Language 3 - ProgrammerName Y
  . . .
```

where the job requires the language, and the programmer is skilled in that language.

Now, for each job/programmer pair, we need to ensure that the number of such records is the same as the number of languages required by that job. This is accomplished by grouping the records by job/programmer pair and then using a HAVING clause that compares a count of those records with the count of languages for that job. The resulting table is Table 19-19.

Table 19-19. Jobs and programmers qualified for these jobs

JobID	Name
1	Blaise Pascal
1	Gauss
2	Blaise Pascal
2	Smith
2	Von Neuman
2	Wordsworth
4	Gauss
4	Wordsworth

Equality of Sets

A common problem is determining when two sets are equal, that is, when they have the same elements. Consider Table 19-20, which shows five sets and their members. To simplify this as much as possible, we simply number the sets and assume they contain numbers themselves. We want to get a list of which sets are equal.

Table 19-20. Equality

Set	Member
1	1
1	2
1	3
2	1
2	2
2	3
3	1
3	2
3	3
3	4
4	1
4	2
4	3
4	4
5	1
5	2
5	8

Solution

This problem has an elegant solution using a single SQL statement. While, in general, SQL does not permit us to compare two sets directly, as in:

```
(SELECT Members FROM Equality WHERE Set=1) = (SELECT Members FROM Equality WHERE _
    Set=2)
```

it will accept such clauses if the two SELECT statements return a single value.

Consider now the SQL statement:

```
SELECT Equality.Set, E2.Set
FROM Equality INNER JOIN Equality AS E2 ON
  (Equality.Member = E2.Member) And (Equality.Set < E2.Set)
GROUP BY Equality.Set, E2.Set
HAVING
((SELECT Count(Member) FROM Equality As E3 WHERE E3.Set=Equality.Set) =
  (SELECT Count(Member) FROM Equality As E3 WHERE E3.Set=E2.Set))
AND
(Count(Equality.Set) =
  (SELECT Count(Member) FROM Equality As E3 WHERE E3.Set=E2.Set))
```

The INNER JOIN is on the clause:

```
(Equality.Member = E2.Member) And (Equality.Set < E2.Set)
```

The important part of this clause is the first part. It states that we want all set pairs that have a common member. The second part prevents returning duplicate set pairs. For instance, if sets 1 and 2 both contain the number 3, we don't want to return both pairs [(1,2) and (2,1)].

To illustrate further, since the number 3 is in sets 1, 2, 3, and 4, the records returned for the member 3 are as follows:

```
(1,2) (from member 3)
(1,3) (from member 3)
(1,4) (from member 3)
(2,3) (from member 3)
(2,4) (from member 3)
(3,4) (from member 3)
```

If it were not for the clause Equality.Set < E2.Set, we would also be getting (1,1), (2,2), ... (4,4), as well as (2,1), (3,1), and so on.

Now we ask the question, "How many times will a given set pair appear?" A given set pair, say (1,2), will appear as many times as there are common elements between the two sets. That is, it will appear as many times as the size of the intersection of the two sets.

So if we GROUP BY set pair, we can examine these intersections and restrict the returns using a HAVING clause. The HAVING clause we want says that the two sets are equal. But two sets A and B are equal if the sizes of A, B, and the intersection of A and B are all the same! The clause:

```
(SELECT Count(Member) FROM Equality As E3 WHERE E3.Set=Equality.Set) =
  (SELECT Count(Member) FROM Equality As E3 WHERE E3.Set=E2.Set)
```

says that, for a given set pair (Equality.Set, E2.Set) from the main SELECT clause, the size of Equality.Set is equal to the size of E2.Set. The clause:

```
Count(Equality.Set) =
  (SELECT Count(Member) FROM Equality As E3 WHERE E3.Set=E2.Set)
```

says that the size of the intersection of Equality.Set and E2.Set is the same as the size of E2.Set. That's it.

PART VIII

Appendixes

DAO 3.0/3.5 Collections, Properties, and Methods

Microsoft Access 97 comes with a utility known as the *Object Browser*, which can be used to explore the DAO object hierarchy. Figure A-1 shows the Object Browser, which can be invoked from an Access code module by striking the F2 function key (or from the *View* menu).

Figure A-1. The Object Browser

The Object Browser can be a very useful tool, but there are times when a hardcopy reference is also useful. Accordingly, this appendix contains information on the collections, properties, and methods of each of the objects in the DAO 3.0 object hierarchy (which underlies Access 95) and the DAO 3.5 (which underlies Access 97). If nothing else, this information should help point you to the right spot in the Access Online Help System.

In this DAO reference, a table listing the classes and collections available in DAO is followed by tables listing the properties and methods exposed by each class, as well as the collections that are accessible from each object. The tables also indicate whether each item applies to DAO 3.0, DAO 3.5, or both. Finally, there is a summary description of each item.

DAO Classes

Class name	Version	Description
Connection	3.5	An open ODBCDirect connection
Connections	3.5	A collection of Connection objects
Container	3.0/3.5	Storage for information about a predefined object type
Containers	3.0/3.5	A collection of Container objects
Database	3.0/3.5	An open database
Databases	3.0/3.5	A collection of Database objects
DBEngine	3.0/3.5	The Jet database engine
Document	3.0/3.5	Information about a saved, predefined object
Documents	3.0/3.5	A collection of Document objects
Error	3.0/3.5	Information about any error that occurred with a DAO object
Errors	3.0/3.5	A collection of Error objects
Field	3.0/3.5	A column that is part of a table, query, index, relation, or recordset
Fields	3.0/3.5	A collection of Field objects
Group	3.0/3.5	A group of user accounts
Groups	3.0/3.5	A collection of Group objects
Index	3.0/3.5	Object used to order values and provide efficient access to a recordset
Indexes	3.0/3.5	A collection of Index objects
Parameter	3.0/3.5	Parameter for a parameter query
Parameters	3.0/3.5	A collection of Parameter objects
Properties	3.0/3.5	A collection of Property objects
Property	3.0/3.5	A built-in or user-defined property

Class name	Version	Description
QueryDef	3.0/3.5	A saved query definition
QueryDefs	3.0/3.5	A collection of Querydef objects
Recordset	3.0/3.5	The representation of the records in a table or that result from a query
Recordsets	3.0/3.5	A collection of Recordset objects
Relation	3.0/3.5	A relationship between fields in tables and queries
Relations	3.0/3.5	A collection of Relation objects
TableDef	3.0/3.5	A saved table definition
TableDefs	3.0/3.5	A collection of Tabledef objects
User	3.0/3.5	A user account
Users	3.0/3.5	A collection of User objects
Workspace	3.0/3.5	A session of the Jet database engine
Workspaces	3.0/3.5	A collection of Workspace objects

A Collection Object

Each of the *Collection* objects listed earlier in "DAO Classes" supports a single method and a single property.

Methods

Method	Type	Version	Description
Refresh	Sub	3.0/3.5	Updates the collection to reflect recent changes

Properties

Property	Type	Version	Description
Count	Integer	3.0/3.5	Number of objects in the collection (read-only)

In addition, *DynaCollection* objects—that is, *Collection* objects whose members can be dynamically added and removed—have the two additional methods.

Methods

Method	Parameters	Returns	Version	Description
Append	Object As Object	Sub	3.0/3.5	Appends an object to the collection
Delete	Name As String	Sub	3.0/3.5	Deletes an object from the collection

Connection Object (DAO 3.5 Only)

Collections

Property	Type	Version	Description
Database	Database	3.5	Returns a Database reference to this Connection object
QueryDefs	QueryDefs	3.5	A collection of QueryDef objects
Recordsets	RecordSets	3.5	A collection of Recordset objects open in this connection

Methods

Method	Parameters	Returns	Version	Description
Cancel		Sub	3.5	Cancels execution of an asynchronous Execute or OpenRecordset method
Close		Sub	3.5	Closes the Connection object and everything it contains
CreateQueryDef	[Name], [SQLText]	QueryDef	3.5	Creates a new QueryDef object
Execute	Query As String, [Options]	Sub	3.5	Executes an SQL statement
OpenRecordSet	Name As String, [Type], [Options], [LockEdit]	Recordset	3.5	Creates a new Recordset object

Properties

Property	Type	Version	Description
Connect	String	3.5	Information saved from the Connect argument of the OpenDatabase method
Name	String	3.5	Name of the Connection object
QueryTimeout	Integer	3.5	Number of seconds before timeout occurs when executing an ODBC query
RecordsAffected	Long	3.5	Number of records affected by the last Execute method
StillExecuting	Boolean	3.5	Indicates whether an asynchronous method call is still executing
Transactions	Boolean	3.5	Indicates whether the DAO object supports transactions
Updatable	Boolean	3.5	Indicates whether the connection allows data to be updated

Container Object

Collections

Property	Type	Version	Description
Documents	Documents	3.0/3.5	Collection of Document objects in the container

Properties

Property	Type	Version	Description
AllPermissions	Long	3.0/3.5	All permissions that apply to the current username
Inherit	Boolean	3.0/3.5	Indicates whether new Document objects inherit default permissions properties
Name	String	3.0/3.5	The name of this object
Owner	String	3.0/3.5	Sets or returns the owner of the object
Permissions	Long	3.0/3.5	Sets or returns permissions for the user or group indicated by the UserName property when accessing the object
UserName	String	3.0/3.5	User or group to which the Permissions property applies

Database Object

Collections

Property	Type	Version	Description
Connection	Connection	3.5	An open ODBCDirect connection
Containers	Containers	3.0/3.5	Collection of Container objects in the Database object
QueryDefs	QueryDefs	3.0/3.5	Collection of QueryDef objects in the Database object
Recordsets	Recordsets	3.0/3.5	Collection of Recordset objects open in Database object
Relations	Relations	3.0/3.5	Collection of Relation objects in the Database object
TableDefs	TableDefs	3.0/3.5	Collection of TableDef objects in the Database object

Methods

Method	Parameters	Returns	Version	Description
Close		Sub	3.0/3.5	Closes the Database object and everything it contains
CreateProperty	[Name], [Type], [Value], [DDL]	Property	3.0/3.5	Creates a new user-defined Property object
CreateQueryDef	[Name], [SQLText]	QueryDef	3.0/3.5	Creates a new QueryDef object
CreateRelation	[Name], [Table], [ForeignTable], [Attributes]	Relation	3.0/3.5	Creates a new Relation object
CreateTableDef	[Name], [Attributes], [SourceTableName], [Connect]	TableDef	3.0/3.5	Creates a new TableDef object
Execute	Query As String, [Options]	Sub	3.0/3.5	Executes a query
MakeReplica	PathName As String, Description As String, [Options]	Sub	3.0/3.5	Makes a new replica based on the current replicable database
NewPassword	bstrOld As String, bstrNew As String	Sub	3.0/3.5	Changes the password of an existing database

Method	Parameters	Returns	Version	Description
OpenRecordset	Name As String, [Type], [Options]	Recordset	3.0/3.5	Creates a new Recordset object
PopulatePartial	DbPathName As String	Sub	3.5	Synchronizes a partial replica
Synchronize	DbPathName As String, [ExchangeType]	Sub	3.0/3.5	Synchronizes the database object

Properties

Property	Type	Version	Description
CollatingOrder	Long	3.0/3.5	Defines the order used for sorting and comparisons
Connect	String		Information saved from the Connect argument of the OpenDatabase method
DesignMasterID	String	3.0/3.5	Unique identifier for a replica design master
Name	String	3.0/3.5	The name of this Database object
QueryTimeout	Integer	3.0/3.5	Number of seconds before timeout occurs when executing an ODBC query
RecordsAffected	Long	3.0/3.5	Number of records affected by the last Execute method
ReplicaID	String	3.0/3.5	Unique identifier for a replica
Transactions	Boolean	3.0/3.5	Indicates whether the Database object supports transactions
Updatable	Boolean	3.0/3.5	Indicates whether the Database object can be modified
Version	String	3.0/3.5	Version number of the Database object format

DBEngine Object

Collections

Property	Type	Version	Description
Errors	Errors	3.0./3.5	Collection of errors from the most recently failed DAO operation
Properties	Properties	3.0/3.5	Collection of Property objects
Workspaces	Workspaces	3.0/3.5	Collection of open Workspace objects

Methods

Method	Parameters	Returns	Version	Description
BeginTrans		Sub	3.0/3.5	Begins a new transaction
CommitTrans		Sub	3.0	Ends the transaction and saves any changes
CommitTrans	[Option as Long]	Sub	3.5	Ends the transaction and saves any changes

Method	Parameters	Returns	Version	Description
CompactDatabase	SrcName As String, DstName As String, [DstConnect], [Options], [SrcConnect]	Sub	3.0	Compacts a closed database
CompactDatabase	SrcName As String, DstName As String, [DstLocale], [Options], [SrcLocale]	Sub	3.5	Compacts a closed database
CreateDatabase	Name As String, Connect As String, [Option]	Database	3.0	Creates a new database
CreateDatabase	Name As String, Locale As String, [Option]	Database	3.5	Creates a new .mdb database
CreateWorkspace	Name As String, UserName As String, Password As String	Workspace	3.0	Creates a new Workspace object
CreateWorkspace	Name As String, UserName As String, Password As String, [UseType]	Workspace	3.5	Creates a new Workspace object
Idle	[Action]	Sub	3.0/3.5	Completes pending engine tasks such as lock removal
OpenConnection	Name As String, [Options], [ReadOnly], [Connect]	Connection	3.5	Opens a connection to a database
OpenDatabase	Name As String, [Exclusive], [ReadOnly], [Connect]	Database	3.0	Opens a specified database
OpenDatabase	Name As String, [Options], [ReadOnly], [Connect]	Database	3.5	Opens a specified database
RegisterDatabase	Dsn As String, Driver As String, Silent As Boolean, Attributes As String	Sub	3.0/3.5	Enters connection information for an ODBC data source
RepairDatabase	Name As String	Sub	3.0/3.5	Repairs a corrupted database
Rollback		Sub	3.0/3.5	Rolls back any changes since the last BeginTrans
SetOption	Option As Long, Value	Sub	3.5	Overrides Jet registry settings

Properties

Property	Type	Version	Description
DefaultPassword	String	3.0/3.5	Password if a Workspace object is created without a password
DefaultType	Long	3.5	Sets the default Workspace type
DefaultUser	String	3.0/3.5	Username if a Workspace object is created without a username
IniPath	String	3.0/3.5	Path and filename of the initialization file (in Jet 3.0) or the complete Registry path (Jet 3.5) containing Jet engine settings
LoginTimeout	Integer	3.0/3.5	Number of seconds allowed for logging in to an ODBC database
SystemDB	String	3.0/3.5	Path to the system database
Version	String	3.0/3.5	Version number of the Jet database engine

Document Object

Methods

Method	Parameters	Returns	Version	Description
CreateProperty	[Name], [Type], [Value], [DDL]	Property	3.0/3.5	Creates a new user-defined Property object

Properties

Property	Type	Version	Description
AllPermissions	Long	3.0/3.5	All permissions that apply to the current username
Container	String	3.0/3.5	Name of the Container object to which this Document object belongs
DateCreated	Variant	3.0/3.5	Date and time the Document object was created
LastUpdated	Variant	3.0/3.5	Date and time of the most recent change to the Document object
Name	String	3.0/3.5	Name of this Document object
Owner	String	3.0/3.5	The owner of the object
Permissions	Long	3.0/3.5	Permissions for user or group accessing the Document object
UserName	String	3.0/3.5	User or group for which the Permissions property applies

Error Object

Properties

Property	Type	Version	Description
Description	String	3.0/3.5	Description of the error
HelpContext	Long	3.0/3.5	Help context ID for a topic describing the error
HelpFile	String	3.0/3.5	Path to Help file describing the error
Number	Long	3.0/3.5	Error code of the most recent error
Source	String	3.0/3.5	Name of the object class that generated the error

Field Object

Collections

Property	Type	Version	Description
Properties	Properties	3.0/3.5	Collection of Property objects

Methods

Method	Parameters	Returns	Version	Description
AppendChunk	Val	Sub	3.0/3.5	Writes long binary data to a field
CreateProperty	[Name], [Type], [Value], [DDL]	Property	3.0/3.5	Creates a new user-defined Property object
FieldSize		Long	3.0	Returns the FieldSize field
GetChunk	Offset As Long, Bytes As Long	Byte	3.0/3.5	Reads binary data from a field

Properties

Property	Type	Version	Description
AllowZeroLength	Boolean	3.0/3.5	Indicates whether a zero-length string is valid for this field
Attributes	Long	3.0/3.5	Value indicating characteristics of this Field object
CollatingOrder	Long	3.0/3.5	Language used for sorting and comparisons
DataUpdatable	Boolean	3.0/3.5	Indicates whether the data in the field are updatable
DefaultValue	String	3.0/3.5	Default value of the field for a new record
FieldSize	Long	3.5	The size of a memo field or a long binary field
ForeignName	String	3.0/3.5	The name of the foreign field
Name	String	3.0/3.5	The name of this Field object
OrdinalPosition	Integer	3.0/3.5	The relative position of this field object
OriginalValue	Variant	3.5	Value stored in the database server at the start of a batch update
Required	Boolean	3.0/3.5	Indicates whether the Field requires a non-Null value
Size	Long	3.0/3.5	Maximum size of the field
SourceField	String	3.0/3.5	Name of the original source of data for a Field object
SourceTable	String	3.0/3.5	Name of the original source table
Type	Integer	3.0/3.5	Data type of the field
ValidateOnSet	Boolean	3.0/3.5	Determines whether validation occurs immediately (a True value) or is delayed until an update (a False value)
ValidationRule	String	3.0/3.5	Expression that must evaluate to True for a successful update
ValidationText	String	3.0/3.5	Message to display if validation with ValidationRule fails
Value	Variant	3.0/3.5	The Field object's data
VisibleValue	Variant	3.5	Data currently stored in the database server

Group Object

Collections

Property	Type	Version	Description
Properties	Properties	3.0/3.5	A collection of Property objects
Users	Users	3.0/3.5	A collection of User objects

Methods

Method	Parameters	Returns	Version	Description
CreateUser	[Name], [PID], [Password]	User	3.0/3.5	Creates a new User object

Properties

Property	Type	Version	Description
Name	String	3.0/3.5	Name of the Group object
PID	String	3.0/3.5	Personal identifier (PID) for the group or user account

Index Object

Collections

Property	Type	Version	Description
Fields	Fields	3.0/3.5	Collection of fields in the Index object
Properties	Properties	3.0/3.5	Collection of Property objects

Methods

Method	Parameters	Returns	Version	Description
CreateField	[Name], [Type], [Size]	Field	3.0/3.5	Creates a new Field object
CreateProperty	[Name], [Type], [Value], [DDL]	Property	3.0/3.5	Creates a new user-defined Property object

Properties

Property	Type	Version	Description
Clustered	Boolean	3.0/3.5	Indicates whether the index is clustered
DistinctCount	Long	3.0/3.5	Number of unique values in this Index object
Foreign	Boolean	3.0/3.5	Indicates whether an Index object represents a foreign key
IgnoreNulls	Boolean	3.0/3.5	Indicates whether Null values are stored in the index
Name	String	3.0/3.5	Name of this Index object
Primary	Boolean	3.0/3.5	Indicates whether this is a primary index
Required	Boolean	3.0/3.5	Indicates whether the index requires a non-Null value
Unique	Boolean	3.0/3.5	Indicates whether this is a unique index for a table

Parameter Object

Properties

Property	Type	Version	Description
Direction	Integer	3.5	Indicates whether a Parameter is for input, output, or returned values
Name	String	3.0/3.5	Name of this Parameter object
Type	Integer	3.0/3.5	Data type of the object
Value	Variant	3.0/3.5	The object's value

Property Object

Properties

Property	Type	Version	Description
Inherited	Boolean	3.0/3.5	Indicates whether a property is inherited from an underlying object
Name	String	3.0/3.5	Name of the Property object
Type	Integer	3.0/3.5	The Property object's data type
Value	Variant	3.0/3.5	The property value

QueryDef Object

Collections

Property	Type	Version	Description
Fields	Fields	3.0/3.5	Collection of fields in the QueryDef object
Parameters	Parameters	3.0/3.5	Collection of Parameter objects in the QueryDef object
Properties	Properties	3.0/3.5	Collection of Property objects in the QueryDef object

Methods

Method	Parameters	Returns	Version	Description
Cancel		Sub	3.5	Cancels execution of an asynchronous OpenRecordset method
Close		Sub	3.0/3.5	Closes the open QueryDef object
CreateProperty	[Name], [Type], [Value], [DDL]	Property	3.0/3.5	Creates a new user-defined Property object
Execute	[Options]	Sub	3.0/3.5	Execute the Querydef

Method	Parameters	Returns	Version	Description
OpenRecordset	[Type], [Options]	Recordset	3.0	Creates a new Recordset object
OpenRecordset	[Type], [Options], [LockEdit]	Recordset	3.5	Creates a new Recordset object

Properties

Property	Type	Version	Description
CacheSize	Long	3.5	Number of records to be locally cached from an ODBC data source
Connect	String	3.0/3.5	Value providing information about a data source for a QueryDef
DateCreated	Variant	3.0/3.5	Date and time the QueryDef was created
LastUpdated	Variant	3.0/3.5	Date and time of the most recent change to the QueryDef
MaxRecords	Long	3.5	Maximum number of records to return from the query
Name	String	3.0/3.5	Name of this QueryDef object
ODBCTimeout	Integer	3.0/3.5	Number of seconds to wait before a timeout occurs when querying an ODBC database
Prepare	Variant	3.5	Indicates whether to prepare a temporary stored procedure from the query
RecordsAffected	Long	3.0/3.5	Number of records affected by the last Execute method
ReturnsRecords	Boolean	3.0/3.5	Indicates whether an SQL pass-through query returns records
SQL	String	3.0/3.5	SQL statement that defines the query
StillExecuting	Boolean	3.5	Indicates whether an asynchronous method call is still executing
Type	Integer	3.0/3.5	The data type of the object
Updatable	Boolean	3.0/3.5	Indicates whether the query definition can be changed

Recordset Object

Collections

Property	Type	Version	Description
Connection	Connection	3.5	Indicates which Connection owns the Recordset
Fields	Fields	3.0/3.5	Collection of fields in the Recordset object

Methods

Method	Parameters	Returns	Version	Description
AddNew		Sub	3.0/3.5	Adds a new record to the Recordset
Cancel		Sub	3.5	Cancels execution of an asynchronous Execute, OpenRecordset, or OpenConnection method
CancelUpdate		Sub	3.0/3.5	Cancels any pending AddNew or Update statements

Method	Parameters	Returns	Version	Description
Clone		Recordset	3.0/3.5	Creates a duplicate Recordset
Close		Sub	3.0/3.5	Closes an open Recordset object
CopyQueryDef		QueryDef	3.0/3.5	Returns a copy of the QueryDef that created the Recordset
Delete		Sub	3.0/3.5	Deletes a record from the Recordset
Edit		Sub	3.0/3.5	Prepares a row of the Recordset for editing
FillCache	[Rows], [StartBookmark]	Sub	3.0/3.5	Fills the cache for an ODBC-derived Recordset
FindFirst	Criteria As String	Sub	3.0/3.5	Locates the first record that satisfies the criteria
FindLast	Criteria As String	Sub	3.0/3.5	Locates the last record that satisfies the criteria
FindNext	Criteria As String	Sub	3.0/3.5	Locates the next record that satisfies the criteria
FindPrevious	Criteria As String	Sub	3.0/3.5	Locates the previous record that satisfies the criteria
GetRows	[cRows]	Variant	3.0/3.5	Writes multiple records into an array
Move	Rows As Long, [StartBookmark]	Sub	3.0/3.5	Repositions the record pointer relative to the current position or to a bookmark
MoveFirst		Sub	3.0/3.5	Moves to the first record in the Recordset
MoveLast		Sub	3.0	Moves to the last record in the Recordset
MoveLast	[Options As Long]	Sub	3.5	Moves to the last record in the Recordset
MoveNext		Sub	3.0/3.5	Moves to the next record in the Recordset
MovePrevious		Sub	3.0/3.5	Moves to the previous record in the Recordset
NextRecordset		Boolean	3.5	Retrieves the next recordset in a multiquery Recordset
OpenRecordset	[Type], [Options]	Recordset	3.0/3.5	Creates a new Recordset object
Requery	[NewQueryDef]	Sub	3.0/3.5	Re-executes the query on which the Recordset is based
Seek	Comparison As String, Key1...	Sub	3.0/3.5	Locates a record in a table-type Recordset
Update		Sub	3.0/3.5	Saves changes initiated by the Edit or AddNew methods

Properties

Property	Type	Version	Description
AbsolutePosition	Long	3.0/3.5	Returns or sets the relative record number of the current record
BatchCollision-Count	Long	3.5	Indicates the number of rows having collisions in the last batch update
BatchCollisions	Variant	3.5	Indicates which rows had collisions in the last batch update
BatchSize	Long	3.5	Determines how many updates to include in a batch
BOF	Boolean	3.0/3.5	Indicates whether the current record position is before the first record
Bookmark As	Byte	3.0/3.5	Uniquely identifies a particular record in a Recordset
Bookmarkable	Boolean	3.0/3.5	Indicates whether a Recordset supports bookmarks
CacheSize	Long	3.0/3.5	Indicates the number of records from an ODBC data source to be cached locally

Property	Type	Version	Description
CacheStart As	Byte	3.0/3.5	Bookmarks the first record to be cached from an ODBC data source
DateCreated	Variant	3.0/3.5	Indicates the date and time when the underlying base table was created
EditMode	Integer	3.0/3.5	Indicates the state of editing for the current record
EOF	Boolean	3.0/3.5	Indicates whether the current record position is after the last record
Filter	String	3.0/3.5	Defines a filter to apply to a Recordset
Index	String	3.0/3.5	Indicates the name of the current Index object (table-type Recordset only)
LastModified As	Byte	3.0/3.5	Bookmarks indicating the most recently added or changed record
LastUpdated	Variant	3.0/3.5	Indicates the date and time of the most recent change to the underlying base table
LockEdits	Boolean	3.0/3.5	Indicates the type of locking (optimistic or pessimistic) in effect during editing
Name	String	3.0/3.5	Indicates the name of the Recordset object
NoMatch	Boolean	3.0/3.5	Indicates whether the Seek or Find methods succeeded in finding a record
PercentPosition	Single	3.0/3.5	Indicates or changes the approximate location of the current record
RecordCount	Long	3.0/3.5	Indicates the number of records in the Recordset object
RecordStatus	Integer	3.5	Indicates the batch-update status of the current record
Restartable	Boolean	3.0/3.5	Indicates whether the Recordset supports the Requery method
Sort	String	3.0/3.5	Defines the sort order for records in a Recordset
StillExecuting	Boolean	3.5	Indicates whether an asynchronous method call is still executing
Transactions	Boolean	3.0/3.5	Indicates whether the Recordset supports transactions
Type	Integer	3.0/3.5	Indicates the object's data type
Updatable	Boolean	3.0/3.5	Indicates whether records in the Recordset can be updated
UpdateOptions	Long	3.5	Determines how a batch update query will be constructed
ValidationRule	String	3.0/3.5	Contains an expression that must evaluate True for a successful update
ValidationText	String	3.0/3.5	Indicates the message to appear if ValidationRule fails

Relation Object

Collections

Property	Type	Version	Description
Fields	Fields	3.0/3.5	Collection of fields in this Relation object
Properties	Properties	3.0/3.5	Collection of Property objects

Methods

Method	Parameters	Returns	Version	Description
CreateField	[Name], [Type], [Size]	Field	3.0/3.5	Creates a new Field object

Properties

Property	Type	Version	Description
Attributes	Long	3.0/3.5	Miscellaneous characteristics of the Relation object
ForeignTable	String	3.0/3.5	Specifies the name of the foreign (referencing) table in a relationship
Name	String	3.0/3.5	Name of this Relation object
PartialReplica	Boolean	3.5	Indicates whether the relation provides a partial replica's synchronizing rules
Table	String	3.0/3.5	Specifies the primary (referenced) TableDef or Querydef

TableDef Object

Collections

Property	Type	Version	Description
Fields	Fields	3.0/3.5	Collection of fields in this TableDef object
Indexes	Indexes	3.0/3.5	Collection of indexes associated with this TableDef object
Properties	Properties	3.0/3.5	Collection of Property objects

Methods

Method	Parameters	Returns	Version	Description
CreateField	[Name], [Type], [Size]	Field	3.0/3.5	Creates a new Field object
CreateIndex	[Name]	Index	3.0/3.5	Creates a new Index object
CreateProperty	[Name], [Type], [Value], [DDL]	Property	3.0/3.5	Creates a new user-defined Property object
OpenRecordset	[Type], [Options]	Recordset	3.0/3.5	Creates a new Recordset object
RefreshLink		Sub	3.0/3.5	Updates connection information for an attached table

Properties

Property	Type	Version	Description
Attributes	Long	3.0/3.5	Miscellaneous characteristics of the TableDef object
ConflictTable	String	3.0/3.5	Name of table containing records that conflicted during replica synchronization
Connect	String	3.0/3.5	Data source for the TableDef
DateCreated	Variant	3.0/3.5	Date and time when the table was created
LastUpdated	Variant	3.0/3.5	Date and time when the TableDef was last changed
Name	String	3.0/3.5	Name of the TableDef
RecordCount	Long	3.0/3.5	Number of records

Property	Type	Version	Description
ReplicaFilter	Variant	3.5	Indicates which records to include in a partial replica
SourceTableName	String	3.0/3.5	Name of a linked table's original source table
Updatable	Boolean	3.0/3.5	Indicates whether the TableDef definition can be changed
ValidationRule	String	3.0/3.5	Expression that must evaluate to True for a successful update
ValidationText	String	3.0/3.5	Message to display if ValidationRule fails

User Object

Collections

Property	Type	Version	Description
Groups	Groups	3.0/3.5	Collection of Group objects in a User object
Properties	Properties	3.0/3.5	Collection of Property objects

Methods

Method	Parameters	Returns	Version	Description
CreateGroup	[Name], [PID]	Group	3.0/3.5	Creates a new Group object
NewPassword	bstrOld As String, bstrNew As String	Sub	3.0/3.5	Changes the password of an existing user account

Properties

Property	Type	Version	Description
Name	String	3.0/3.5	The name of the User object
Password	String	3.0/3.5	Password for the user account
PID	String	3.0/3.5	Personal identifier (PID) for a group or user account

Workspace Object

Collections

Property	Type	Version	Description
Connections	Connections	3.5	Collection of Connection objects
Databases	Databases	3.0/3.5	Collection of open Database objects
Groups	Groups		Collection of Group objects in a Workspace object
Users	Users	3.0/3.5	Collection of User objects for a Workspace object

Methods

Method	Parameters	Returns	Version	Description
BeginTrans		Sub	3.0/3.5	Begins a new transaction
Close		Sub	3.0/3.5	Close the Workspace object
CommitTrans		Sub	3.0/3.5	Ends the transaction and saves any changes
CreateDatabase	Name As String, Connect As String, [Option]	Database	3.0/3.5	Creates a new Microsoft Jet database (.mdb)
CreateGroup	[Name], [PID]	Group	3.0/3.5	Creates a new Group object
CreateUser	[Name], [PID], [Password]	User	3.0/3.5	Creates a new User object
OpenConnection	Name As String, [Options], [ReadOnly], [Connect]	Connection	3.5	Opens a connection to a database
OpenDatabase	Name As String, [Exclusive], [ReadOnly], [Connect]	Database	3.0/3.5	Opens a database
Rollback		Sub	3.0/3.5	Undoes any changes since the last BeginTrans

Properties

Property	Type	Version	Description
DefaultCursorDriver	Long	3.5	Selects the ODBC cursor library
IsolateODBCTrans	Integer	3.0/3.5	Indicates whether multiple transactions are isolated (ODBC only)
LoginTimeout	Long	3.5	Number of seconds allowed for logging in to an ODBC database
Name	String	3.0/3.5	Name of this Workspace object
UserName	String	3.0/3.5	User that created the Workspace object

The Quotient: An Additional Operation of the Relational Algebra

The quotient of two tables is not used often, but has a very specific use. It arises when we wish to select those rows of a table that are sufficient to provide all possible values in certain columns. As an example, imagine a business that makes furniture. The database for this business has a table on the types of wood that they use, as well as on suppliers of wood and which types they supply. Examples are shown in Tables B-1 and B-2 (of course, these tables would include more columns, but this is just to illustrate the point).

Table B-1. WOOD

Type
Mahogany
Red oak
Poplar
Walnut

Note that there are four types of wood. Suppose we want to know which suppliers supply *all* four types—a reasonable question. The answer, which is shown in Table B-3 is called the *quotient* of the table SUPPLIERS/TYPE by WOOD, written SUPPLIER/TYPE ÷ WOOD.

As you can see, the quotient can certainly come up in real-life situations. The reason for defining a specific operation for this purpose is that expressing the quotient in terms of the other relations is a bit complex. Let's do it to illustrate the virtue of the quotient.

The idea is actually relatively simple. We first get a table, called T, containing all rows that are not in the SUPPLIER/TYPE table. This new table will involve only those suppliers who have not supplied all types of wood. (If a supplier supplies all four types of wood, then there will be four rows in the SUPPLIER/TYPE table and therefore no rows in T.) Then we subtract this from a table containing all (participating) suppliers. Here is the step-by-step procedure.

Table B-2. SUPPLIER/TYPE

Sname	Type
Jones Wood Supply	mahogany
Austin Hardwoods	red oak
Orange Coast	mahogany
Jones Wood Supply	poplar
West Lumber	poplar
Jones Wood Supply	walnut
Austin Hardwoods	walnut
Jones Wood Supply	red oak
Orange Coast	walnut
West Lumber	red oak
Orange Coast	poplar
Orange Coast	red oak
Fred's Woods	walnut

Table B-3. SUPPLIER/TYPE WOOD

Sname
Jones Wood Supply
Orange Coast

Step 1. Form the table:

```
R = [projSName(SUPPLIER/TYPE) ↔ WOOD] - SUPPLIER/TYPE
```

Table B-4, the table R, contains all rows of the form (*SName, Type*) that are not in the SUPPLIER/TYPE table. Put another way, it is the set of "missing possibilities" in the Cartesian product (which is the set of all possibilities).

Table B-4. R

Sname	Type
Austin Hardwoods	poplar
West Lumber	walnut
Austin Hardwoods	mahogany
West Lumber	mahogany
Fred's Woods	walnut

Step 2. Form the table:

```
projSName(R)
```

That is, project the table R onto the *SName* column, giving the SUPPLIERS that do not supply all types of wood, as shown in Table B-5.

Table B-5. projSName(R)

SName
Austin Hardwoods
West Lumber
Fred's Woods

Step 3. Finally, form the table:

```
projSName(SUPPLIERS/TYPE) - projSName (R)
```

That is, subtract the table in Step 2 from the first column of the SUPPLIERS/TYPE table. This gives the suppliers that supply all four types of wood, as Table B-6 illustrates.

Table B-6. SUPPLIER/TYPE ÷ WOOD

SName
Jones Wood Supply
Orange Coast

Open Database Connectivity (ODBC)

In this appendix, we take a close look at ODBC, which is a part of both DAO and ADO and probably will be for some time to come, despite Microsoft's desire to replace all previous database technologies with OLE DB and ADO.

ODBC is part of DAO in the sense that DAO supports ODBC workspaces for connecting to ODBC providers. Also, ODBC is part of OLE DB in the sense that the first OLE DB data provider was for ODBC data sources and this is still the most flexible OLE DB provider.

Our discussion of ODBC will be fairly detailed, but it will not be reference-like. However, you should feel free to skim through this appendix for whatever information suits your particular needs. If you get more deeply involved in database connectivity, you may find that some of this information will prove useful later on.

Incidentally, all of the code examples in this chapter are available on my web site: *http://www.romanpress.com*.

Introduction

Open Database Connectivity, or ODBC for short, is an Application Programming Interface (API) for connecting to databases of various types. (An API is essentially just a set of functions, also called *services*, for performing various tasks. These functions are usually contained in one or more dynamic link libraries (DLLs).) The term database is used here in a very general sense to refer not only to traditional relational databases, such as Access or FoxPro databases, but also to less traditional "databases" such as delimited text files or Excel worksheets.

Typically, the functions in the ODBC API are implemented in database-specific *ODBC drivers*. In this way, an application is shielded from having to know the specifics of the various types of databases.

Figure C-1 shows the components involved in the use of ODBC.

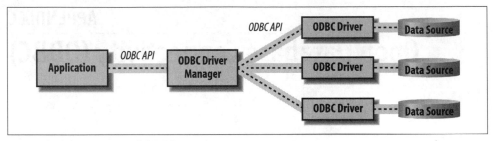

Figure C-1. An overview of ODBC

Since most data access is done using the SQL language, the primary ODBC-related task for an application is to submit SQL statements to the Driver Manager, which sends the commands to the appropriate driver and also processes any data that is returned as a result of the SQL statements.

The ODBC Driver Manager

The purpose of the *ODBC Driver Manager* is to manage communication between the application and the driver. The application communicates directly with the Driver Manager, which in turn either processes the command or sends it on (with or without some modification) to the driver. (It is possible for an application to communicate directly with a driver, but this is not usual.)

Generally, the Driver Manager just passes API function calls from the application to the correct driver. However, it does implement some API functions and also performs some basic error checking. In particular, it is responsible for implementing the following driver/data source information functions:

SQLDataSources
    Returns information about a data source

SQLDrivers
    Lists driver descriptions and attributes

SQLGetFunctions
    Determines whether a given driver supports a given ODBC function

The Driver Manager is also responsible for managing the connection to and disconnection from an ODBC driver. In particular, when an application wants to use a particular driver, the application calls one of the following connection functions:

SQLConnect
    Establishes a connection to a driver and a data source

SQLDriverConnect
    Establishes a connection using a connection string

SQLDriverBrowse
    Establishes a connection iteratively

Each of these functions must include information about the driver in its parameters (in different forms, however). Using this driver information, the Driver Manager loads the driver (if it is not already loaded) and calls the appropriate connection function (SQLConnect, SQLDriverConnect, or SQLDriverBrowse) in the driver.

When the application is done using the driver, it calls SQLDisconnect. The Driver Manager passes this call to the driver, which disconnects from the data source.

The ODBC Driver

An ODBC driver is a code component that implements the functions in the ODBC API. Each driver is specific to a particular database type. Drivers expose the capabilities of the underlying database management system (DBMS) but do not, in general, enhance its capabilities. The main exception is that drivers for DBMSs that do not have standalone database engines, as is the case with dBASE, Xbase, and ASCII text, for example, must implement a database engine that supports a minimal amount of SQL.

In particular, an ODBC driver must implement the following tasks (among others):

- Connecting to and disconnecting from the data source.
- Sending data to and retrieving data from the data source.
- Checking for API function errors that are not checked by the Driver Manager.
- Submitting SQL statements to the data source for execution. For this, the driver may need to modify the ODBC-style SQL statements to a form of SQL that the DBMS understands.

Driver Types

In general, there are two types of ODBC drivers. A *file-based driver* accesses the physical data in the database directly. Thus, it must process not only ODBC function calls, but also SQL statements. Put another way, a file-based driver must also be a database engine that can process ODBC SQL (at a minimum). For example, dBASE drivers are file-based drivers because dBASE does not provide a standalone database engine the driver can use.

By contrast, a *DBMS-based driver* accesses the physical data only through a separate database engine. In this case the driver processes ODBC calls but passes SQL statements to the database engine for processing. For example, Microsoft Access provides a standalone database engine called Jet, so an Access driver can be DBMS-based. (There are also file-based Access database drivers that communicate directly with MDB files.)

The advantage of DBMS-based drivers is that they can accept and pass along the DBMS's specific brand of SQL. For instance, a DBMS-based driver for Microsoft Access can pass Access SQL statements to the Access database (Jet) engine for processing. On the other hand, a file-based Access driver, which contains its own proprietary database engine that accesses MDB files directly, may support only ODBC SQL, in which case attempts to pass Access-specific SQL statements to the driver are likely to result in errors.

Data Sources

A *data source* is, in general, a source of data. However, this term is one of the most abused and inconsistently misused terms in database-related programming (at least in Microsoft's arsenal). For instance, when the data is contained in a text file, then the term "data source" refers simply to the physical data in the file. Similarly, when the data is contained in an Access database file (extension *.mbd*) that is being accessed by a file-based driver, the term data source refers to the MDB file. On the other hand, when the data are contained in an Access database file that is being accessed by a DBMS-based driver, then the data source is considered to be the combination of the Access DBMS and the MDB file. On the other hand, in the context of the new VB6 DataBinding object model, the term data source refers to a source for the data binding, which is often a VB6 class module that has its DataSourceBehavior property set to vbDataSource. In this case, the data source itself contains no data whatsoever!

Thus, just what constitutes a data source depends upon the circumstances. In fact, since a data source is always associated with a particular driver under ODBC, we will usually think of the pair together. This view is supported by the fact that when configuring a data source using the ODBC Administrator, we are first required to select a driver.

The term data source is also sometimes used (unfortunately) to stand for the *description* of a data source—that is, the name and path of the database, password, user name, connection attributes, and so on. What a mess.

DSNs and Data Source Types

The ODBC literature uses the term *Data Source Name* (DSN) quite frequently. Unfortunately, it does not refer simply to the name of the data source! Rather, it refers to a description of the data source, the accompanying driver, and the attributes of a connection between the two. For instance, a DSN includes the name of the data source, the complete path of the data source, the name of the driver, and details about the connection to the data source, such as whether or not the connection is read-only. We will see examples of DSNs a little later. The important thing to keep in mind is that the name DSN is quite misleading. Perhaps a better term would have been *Data Connection Description* (DCD).

Machine data sources

Data sources are said to fall into two categories: *machine data sources* and *file data sources*. Note, however, that it is really the DSNs that fall into these categories. The difference is in where and how the DSN (and *not* the data source itself) is stored.

For a machine data source, the DSN is stored in the system registry of a machine under a specific name, called the *Data Source Name name* (DSN name). A machine data source can be registered under one of two registry keys:

- HKEY_LOCAL_MACHINE/SOFTWARE/ODBC/ODBC.INI
- HKEY_CURRENT_USER/SOFTWARE/ODBC/ODBC.INI

In the former case, the DSN is available to all users of the machine. In the latter case, the DSN is available only to the user under whose name it is registered. When a DSN is stored in the HKEY_LOCAL_MACHINE key, the data source is referred to as a *system data source*, although again this term should really be applied to the DSN. When the DSN is stored in the HKEY_CURRENT_USER key, the data source (actually DSN) is referred to as a *user data source*.

Incidentally, the registry key HKEY_LOCAL_MACHINE/SOFTWARE/ODBC/ODBCINST.INI contains information about each installed ODBC component, including drivers. This is a good place to find the filename of a driver, should you be interested.

File data sources

For a file data source, the DSN is kept in an ordinary text file, with extension *.dsn*, and is accessible to anyone with access to the file. This is so that a file data source (that is, a file DSN) is not registered to any one user or machine. Thus, a file DSN docs not have a DSN name *per se* (under which it is registered). It does have a filename, of course.

The main advantage of a file data source is that it can be copied to any machine, so that identical data sources can be used by several machines. A file data source can also be shared by more than one application.

Creating DSNs: The ODBC Administrator

DSNs are generally created by the user with a program called the *ODBC Administrator*. This program is accessed by clicking on the ODBC icon in the Windows Control Panel. The opening dialog box is shown in Figure C-2.

Once the type of DSN (User, System, or File) is chosen and the user clicks the Add button, the dialog box in Figure C-3 is displayed, prompting the user for the name of the driver.

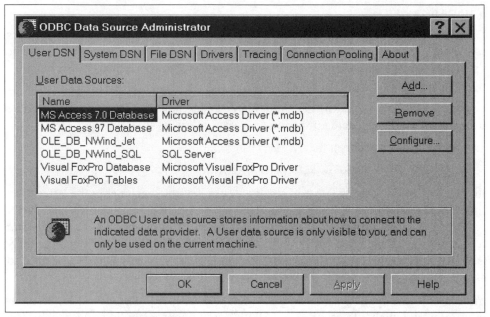

Figure C-2. The ODBC Administrator

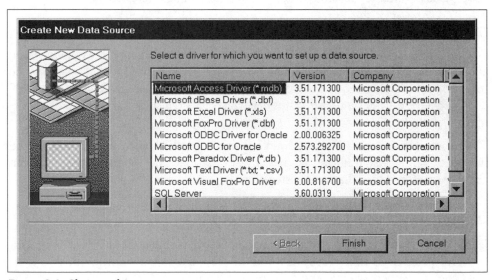

Figure C-3. Choose a driver

The ODBC Administrator then calls the driver so it can display any of its dialog boxes that request specific information required by the driver to connect to the data source. (Thus, these dialog boxes vary from driver to driver.) After the user enters the information, the DSN data is stored in the appropriate place (the registry or a DSN file).

Example DSNs

It is helpful to take a look at a few examples of DSNs created using the ODBC Administrator.

Excel system data source

Here is an example of the registry entries for a system DSN consisting of an Excel workbook. The DSN name is *ConnectExcel*:

```
[HKEY_LOCAL_MACHINE\SOFTWARE\ODBC\ODBC.INI\ConnectExcel]
"Driver"="C:\\WINNT\\System32\\odbcjt32.dll"
"DBQ"="d:\\bkado\\connect.xls"
"DefaultDir"="d:\\bkado"
"Description"="An example Excel data source"
"DriverId"=dword:00000316
"FIL"="excel 5.0;"
"ReadOnly"=hex:00
"SafeTransactions"=dword:00000000
"UID"=""

[HKEY_LOCAL_MACHINE\SOFTWARE\ODBC\ODBC.INI\ConnectExcel\Engines]

[HKEY_LOCAL_MACHINE\SOFTWARE\ODBC\ODBC.INI\ConnectExcel\Engines\Excel]
"ImplicitCommitSync"="Yes"
"MaxScanRows"=dword:00000008
"Threads"=dword:00000003
"UserCommitSync"="Yes"
"FirstRowHasNames"=hex:01
```

As you can see, the Driver value entry holds the name of the ODBC driver for Excel. The DBQ value entry gives the name of the Excel workbook, which is the database in this case. Each worksheet in the workbook is a database table. (For some reason, the value of FIL is "excel 5.0", even though the version of Excel that I used here is Excel 97.) The Engines\Excel subkey reports, among other things, whether the Excel tables (worksheets) use the first row for field names.

The ODBC Administrator dialog boxes that created this data source are shown in Figures C-4 and C-5.

Excel file data source

The contents of an Excel file DSN are shown here:

```
[ODBC]
DRIVER=Microsoft Excel Driver (*.xls)
UID=admin
UserCommitSync=Yes
Threads=3
SafeTransactions=0
ReadOnly=0
PageTimeout=5
MaxScanRows=8
```

```
MaxBufferSize=512
ImplicitCommitSync=Yes
FIL=excel 5.0
DriverId=790
DefaultDir=D:\bkado
DBQ=D:\BkAccessII\Connect.xls
```

Note that this is not as extensive as the system DSN. For instance, it does not include the FirstRowHasNames value.

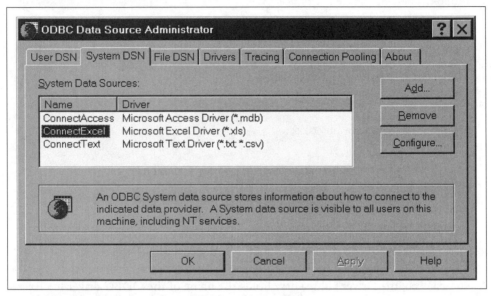

Figure C-4. Creating an Excel data source, Part 1

Text-system data source

Here is an example for a text data source. In this case, a "table" is a text file with extension *.txt*, *.csv*, *.tab*, or *.asc*.

```
[HKEY_LOCAL_MACHINE\SOFTWARE\ODBC\ODBC.INI\ConnectText]
"Driver"="C:\\WINNT\\System32\\odbcjt32.dll"
"DefaultDir"="D:\\bkado"
"Description"="A text data source"
"DriverId"=dword:0000001b
"FIL"="text;"
"SafeTransactions"=dword:00000000
"UID"=""

[HKEY_LOCAL_MACHINE\SOFTWARE\ODBC\ODBC.INI\ConnectText\Engines]

[HKEY_LOCAL_MACHINE\SOFTWARE\ODBC\ODBC.INI\ConnectText\Engines\Text]
"Extensions"="txt,csv,tab,asc"
"ImplicitCommitSync"="Yes"
"Threads"=dword:00000003
"UserCommitSync"="Yes"
```

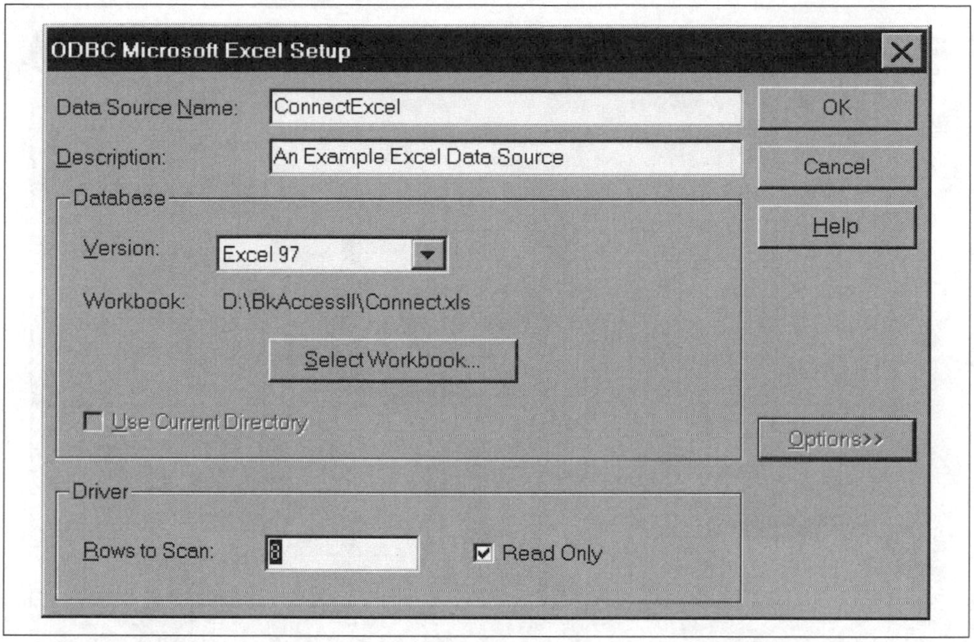

Figure C-5. Creating an Excel data source, Part 2

Note that nowhere in the registry is there a reference to the actual table (text file) or tables for this data source. This information is placed in a special text file called *schema.ini* that is created by the ODBC Administrator. The file is placed in the directory *DefaultDir*. Here are the contents of the *schema.ini* file, which in this case actually describes two separate text connections:

```
[donna.txt]
ColNameHeader=True
Format=TabDelimited
MaxScanRows=25
CharacterSet=OEM
Col1=FIRSTNAME Char Width 255
Col2=LASTNAME Char Width 255

[textfile.csv]
ColNameHeader=False
Format=CSVDelimited
MaxScanRows=25
CharacterSet=OEM
Col1=F1 Char Width 255
Col2=F2 Char Width 255
```

Note that if new text "tables" are added to the connection, additional sections are created in the *schema.ini* file. The ODBC dialog boxes that created the first connection are shown in Figures C-6 and C-7.

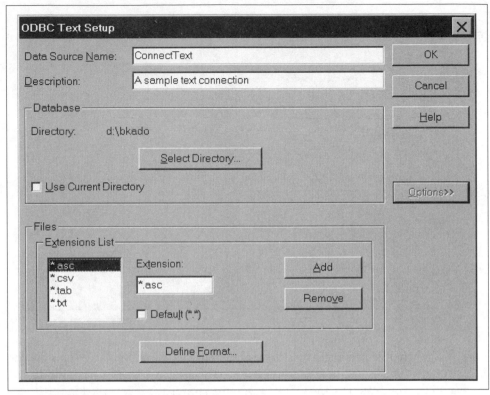

Figure C-6. Text data-source setup

Connecting to a Data Source

It is not my intention to go into the details of the ODBC API functions. However, I do want to discuss the functions briefly that are used to establish a data-source connection, since this will shed some light on the issues of DSNs and the infamous *connection string*.

The ODBC API has three functions for establishing data-source connections: SQLConnect, SQLDriverConnect, and SQLBrowseConnect. I will briefly discuss the first two.

The SQLConnect Function

SQLConnect is the simplest connection function. The parameters to this function consist of a DSN and optionally a user ID and password. This function is the best choice when the DSN contains all of the information required for the connection. Note that this is not always the case. For instance, suppose that the connection requires one password to log on to a server and a second password to log onto a specific database on the server. The first password can be included as an argument to SQLConnect, but

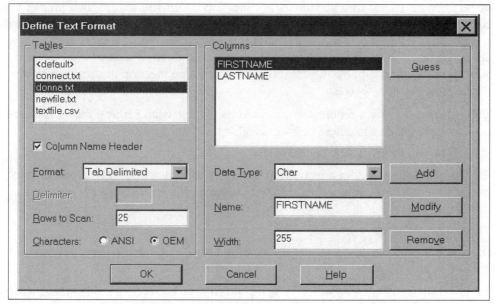

Figure C-7. Setup for the donna.txt source file

the second password must be stored in the DSN. If you don't want to store a password in a DSN, the DSN will not be sufficient to make the connection, and so the SQLConnect function will not be appropriate.

Since SQLConnect does not interact with the user (unlike the other connection functions), it is the correct choice when the programmer wants to write his own interaction code (such as prompting the user for a user ID or passwords).

Connection Strings

A *connection string* is a text string that contains information used for establishing a data-source connection. Note, however, that a connection string may or may not contain all of the required information (just as a DSN may not be complete). A connection string consists of a series of keyword/value pairs separated by semicolons. As you will see, a connection string is used by SQLDriverConnect. Note that SQLConnect does not use a connection string. Since DSNs serve essentially the same purpose, connection strings and DSNs are basically just two sides of the same coin. (In fact, connection strings are built from DSNs by ODBC.)

SQLDriverConnect

When the parameters to SQLConnect—a DSN, a password, and a user ID—are not sufficient to make the desired connection, the SQLDriverConnect function may do the job. There are two reasons to use SQLDriverConnect rather than SQLConnect. First, if a system DSN does not contain suffcient connection information, it is much simpler to construct a custom connection string in code than it is to alter the registry entries in a DSN. (For a file DSN, this issue is mitigated somewhat, but it is still easier to create a connection string in code than to open and alter a text file.) Second, SQLDriverConnect is capable of prompting the user for connection information by displaying ODBC dialog boxes.

To illustrate, if a driver requires two passwords (as discussed earlier), then a connection string could contain these passwords (along with other data):

```
UID=SRoman;ServerPWD=SubRosa;DBPWD=Secret;
```

As we mentioned, if a connection string is not complete, SQLDriverConnect may prompt the user for additional connection information. For example, if the connection string is:

```
DSN=ConnectToWhatever;
```

this might cause the driver to display a dialog box asking for the necessary user ID and password.

In addition, if SQLDriverConnect receives an empty connection string, the Driver Manager displays a dialog box prompting the user for the correct DSN.

Getting ODBC Driver Help

You may be able to get some limited help for an ODBC driver by starting the DSN creation process through the ODBC Administrator and then clicking the Help button once a driver-specific dialog box appears. This brings up the ODBC Microsoft Desktop Database Drivers Help file. However, this information is at best sketchy and often misleading. For instance, under the topic "Connection Strings," the help file says that a connection string includes the following keywords:

DSN
    Name of the data source

DBQ
    Name of the directory

DRIVERID
    An integer ID for the driver

FIL
    File type

However, as you will see in the upcoming examples, the DBQ value is the name of the directory for the Microsoft Text Driver, but not the name of the actual *workbook* for the Microsoft Excel Driver! The help file also does not give any indication as to when or whether these keywords are always required. Nevertheless, the information contained in the help file can be very useful.

Getting ODBC Information Using Visual Basic

It is clear that in order to use ODBC effectively, the programmer may need to know what drivers and data sources exist on a particular computer. This information is accessible through a few ODBC API calls.

The following code includes a procedure called ListODBCSources, which prints (to the Immediate window) a list of all data sources on a system, and ListODBCDrivers, which prints a list of ODBC drivers on the system. This code can be placed in an Access code module:

```
Const SQL_NULL_HANDLE = 0
Const SQL_HANDLE_ENV = 1
Const SQL_FETCH_NEXT = 1
Const SQL_FETCH_FIRST = 2
Const SQL_SUCCESS = 0
Const SQL_ATTR_ODBC_VERSION = 200
Const SQL_OV_ODBC2 = 2
Const SQL_IS_INTEGER = -6

Dim nRetCode  As Long

Declare Function SQLDrivers Lib "odbc32.dll" (ByVal _
    EnvironmentHandle As Long, ByVal Direction As Integer, _
    ByVal DriverDescription As String, ByVal BufferLength1 As Integer, _
    DescriptionLengthPtr As Integer, ByVal DriverAttributes As String, _
    ByVal BufferLength2 As Integer, AttributesLengthPtr As Integer) _
    As  Integer

' Note that pointers to numbers are passed as numbers by reference!
Declare Function SQLDataSources Lib "odbc32.dll" (ByVal _
    EnvironmentHandle As Long, ByVal Direction As Integer, _
    ByVal ServerName As String, ByVal BufferLength1 As Integer, _
    NameLength1Ptr As Integer, ByVal Description As String, _
    ByVal BufferLength2 As Integer, NameLength2Ptr As Integer) As Integer

Declare Function SQLFreeHandle Lib "odbc32.dll" (ByVal _
    HandleType As Integer, ByVal Handle As Long) As Integer

Declare Function SQLAllocHandle Lib "odbc32.dll" (ByVal _
    HandleType As Integer, ByVal InputHandle As Long, _
    OutputHandlePtr As Long) As Integer

Declare Function SQLSetEnvAttr Lib "odbc32.dll" (ByVal _
    EnvironmentHandle As Long, ByVal EnvAttribute As Long, _
    ByVal ValuePtr As Long, ByVal StringLength As Long) As Integer

Declare Function SQLDisconnect Lib "odbc32.dll" (ByVal _
    ConnectionHandle As Long) As Integer

Public Function Trim0(sName As String) As String
```

```
' Keep left portion of string sName up to first 0.

Dim x As Integer
x = InStr(sName, Chr$(0))
If x > 0 Then Trim0 = Left$(sName, x - 1) Else Trim0 = sName

End Function


Private Sub ListODBCSources()

' Prints a list of ODBC data soruces/drivers on system

Dim lHEnv               As Long
Dim sServerName         As String * 32
Dim sDescription        As String * 128
Dim nServerNameLength   As Integer
Dim nDescriptionLength As Integer

' Allocate an environment handle.
nRetCode = SQLAllocHandle(SQL_HANDLE_ENV, SQL_NULL_HANDLE, lHEnv)

' Set ODBC behavior
nRetCode = SQLSetEnvAttr(lHEnv, SQL_ATTR_ODBC_VERSION, _
    SQL_OV_ODBC2, SQL_IS_INTEGER)

' Put first data source name in sServerName
nRetCode = SQLDataSources(lHEnv, SQL_FETCH_FIRST, sServerName, _
    Len(sServerName), nServerNameLength, sDescription, _
    Len(sDescription), nDescriptionLength)

Debug.Print "DATA SOURCE / DRIVER"
Do While nRetCode = SQL_SUCCESS

    Debug.Print Left$(sServerName, _
        nServerNameLength) & " / " & Trim0(sDescription)

    ' Next data source
    nRetCode = SQLDataSources(lHEnv, SQL_FETCH_NEXT, _
        sServerName, Len(sServerName), nServerNameLength, _
        sDescription, Len(sDescription), nDescriptionLength)

Loop

nRetCode = SQLFreeHandle(SQL_HANDLE_ENV, lHEnv)

End Sub

' ----------------------------------------

Private Sub ListODBCDrivers()

' Prints a list of ODBC drivers on system
```

```
Dim lHEnv              As Long
Dim sDriverDesc        As String * 1024
Dim sDriverAttr        As String * 1024
Dim sDriverAttributes As String
Dim nDriverDescLength  As Integer
Dim nAttrLength As Integer
Dim x As Integer
Dim sAll As String

' Allocate an environment handle.
nRetCode = SQLAllocHandle(SQL_HANDLE_ENV, SQL_NULL_HANDLE, lHEnv)

' Set ODBC behavior
nRetCode = SQLSetEnvAttr(lHEnv, SQL_ATTR_ODBC_VERSION, _
    SQL_OV_ODBC2, SQL_IS_INTEGER)

' Get first driver
nRetCode = SQLDrivers(lHEnv, SQL_FETCH_FIRST, sDriverDesc, _
    Len(sDriverDesc), nDriverDescLength, sDriverAttr, _
    Len(sDriverAttr), nAttrLength)

sAll = ""
Do While nRetCode = SQL_SUCCESS

    ' Replace NULL separators with colons
    sDriverAttributes = Left$(sDriverAttr, nAttrLength - 1)
    Do
        x = InStr(sDriverAttributes, Chr$(0))
        If x = 0 Then Exit Do
        sDriverAttributes = Left$(sDriverAttributes, x - 1) & _
          " : " & Mid$(sDriverAttributes, x + 1)
    Loop

    sAll = sAll & Left$(sDriverDesc, nDriverDescLength) & _
      " / " & sDriverAttributes & vbCrLf

    ' Next data source
    nRetCode = SQLDrivers(lHEnv, SQL_FETCH_NEXT, sDriverDesc, _
        Len(sDriverDesc), nDriverDescLength, sDriverAttr, _
        Len(sDriverAttr), nAttrLength)

Loop

Debug.Print "ODBC Drivers"
Debug.Print sAll

nRetCode = SQLFreeHandle(SQL_HANDLE_ENV, lHEnv)

End Sub
```

The output produced by running ListODBCSources on my system is:

```
DATA SOURCE / DRIVER
MS Access 7.0 Database / Microsoft Access Driver (*.mdb)
```

```
Visual FoxPro Tables / Microsoft Visual FoxPro Driver
Visual FoxPro Database / Microsoft Visual FoxPro Driver
MS Access 97 Database / Microsoft Access Driver (*.mdb)
OLE_DB_NWind_Jet / Microsoft Access Driver (*.mdb)
OLE_DB_NWind_SQL / SQL Server
ConnectExcel / Microsoft Excel Driver (*.xls)
ConnectAccess / Microsoft Access Driver (*.mdb)
ConnectText / Microsoft Text Driver (*.txt; *.csv)
```

The output of `ListODBCDrivers` is:

```
ODBC Drivers

SQL Server / UsageCount=10 : SQLLevel=1 : FileUsage=0 :
DriverODBCVer=02.50 : ConnectFunctions=YYY : APILevel=2 :
\Setup=sqlsrv32.dll : .01= : : s=YYN : DSNConverted=F : CPTimeout=60 :
FileExtns=Null

Microsoft ODBC Driver for Oracle / UsageCount=3 : SQLLevel=1 :
FileUsage=0 : DriverODBCVer=02.50 : ConnectFunctions=YYY : APILevel=1

Microsoft Access Driver (*.mdb) / UsageCount=10 : APILevel=1 :
ConnectFunctions=YYN : DriverODBCVer=02.50 : FileUsage=2 :
FileExtns=*.mdb : SQLLevel=0 : s=YYN

Microsoft dBase Driver (*.dbf) / UsageCount=6 : APILevel=1 :
ConnectFunctions=YYN : DriverODBCVer=02.50 : FileUsage=1 :
FileExtns=*.dbf,*.ndx,*.mdx : SQLLevel=0 : [g= :  = : ;g= :  g=

Microsoft FoxPro Driver (*.dbf) / UsageCount=6 : APILevel=1 :
ConnectFunctions=YYN : DriverODBCVer=02.50 : FileUsage=1 :
FileExtns=*.dbf,*.cdx,*.idx,*.ftp : SQLLevel=0

Microsoft Excel Driver (*.xls) / UsageCount=4 : APILevel=1 :
ConnectFunctions=YYN : DriverODBCVer=02.50 : FileUsage=1 :
FileExtns=*.xls : SQLLevel=0

Microsoft Paradox Driver (*.db ) / UsageCount=3 : APILevel=1 :
ConnectFunctions=YYN : DriverODBCVer=02.50 : FileUsage=1 :
FileExtns=*.db : SQLLevel=0

Microsoft Text Driver (*.txt; *.csv) / UsageCount=4 : APILevel=1 :
ConnectFunctions=YYN : DriverODBCVer=02.50 : FileUsage=1 :
FileExtns=*.,*.asc,*.csv,*.tab,*.txt,*.csv : SQLLevel=0

Microsoft ODBC for Oracle / UsageCount=2 : SQLLevel=1 : FileUsage=0 :
DriverODBCVer=02.50 : ConnectFunctions=YYY : APILevel=1 : CPTimeout=120

Microsoft Visual FoxPro Driver / UsageCount=2 : APILevel=0 :
ConnectFunctions=YYN : DriverODBCVer=02.50 : FileUsage=1 :
FileExtns=*.dbc,*.dbf : SQLLevel=0
```

Let us briefly describe the ODBC functions used in these procedures. You can skip this material if it does not interest you.

Preliminaries

Before using the ODBC functions we are interested in, we must first get a handle to the ODBC environment. Obtaining an environment handle is done by calling SQLAllocHandle, whose Visual Basic declaration is:

```
Declare Function SQLAllocHandle Lib "odbc32.dll" (
    ByVal HandleType As Integer, _
    ByVal InputHandle As Long, _
    OutputHandlePtr As Long) As Integer
```

The actual call to use is:

```
nRetCode = SQLAllocHandle(SQL_HANDLE_ENV, SQL_NULL_HANDLE, lHEnv)
```

The return value is an error code or 0 if no error has occured, in which case lHEnv will receive the handle as a Long.

Once we have obtained an environment handle, we must set the environment attribute known as ODBC behavior, using the SQLSetEnvAttr function, as follows:

```
' Set ODBC behavior
nRetCode = SQLSetEnvAttr(lHEnv, SQL_ATTR_ODBC_VERSION, _
    SQL_OV_ODBC2, SQL_IS_INTEGER)
```

Note the use of the lHEnv argument to identify the environment handle. This function call sets the ODBC behavior to ODBC Version 2.x (SQL_OV_ODBC2). Actually, it does not seem to matter whether we set the behavior to ODBC Version 2 or Version 3 (SQL_OV_ODBC3) as long as we set it to one of these values!

Getting Driver Information

To get information about the installed ODBC drivers on a system, we use the SQLDrivers function. The declaration for this function is:

```
Declare Function SQLDriverConnect Lib "odbc32.dll" ( _
    ByVal ConnectionHandle As Long, ByVal WindowHandle As Long, _
    ByVal InConnectionString As String, ByVal StringLength1 As Integer, _
    ByVal OutConnectionString As String, ByVal BufferLength As Integer, _
    StringLength2Ptr As Integer, ByVal DriverCompletion As Integer) As Integer
```

The following is the complete procedure to list all drivers and their attributes in a text box. (This procedure and the following ones are bare-bones, with no error checking. Feel free to augment them for your own use.)

```
    Private Sub ListODBCDrivers()

Dim lHEnv              As Long
Dim sDriverDesc        As String * 1024
Dim sDriverAttr        As String * 1024
Dim sDriverAttributes As String
Dim nDriverDescLength  As Integer
Dim nAttrLength As Integer
Dim x As Integer
Dim sAll As String
```

```
txtDrivers = ""

' Allocate an environment handle.
nRetCode = SQLAllocHandle(SQL_HANDLE_ENV, SQL_NULL_HANDLE, lHEnv)

' Set ODBC behavior
nRetCode = SQLSetEnvAttr(lHEnv, SQL_ATTR_ODBC_VERSION, _
    SQL_OV_ODBC2, SQL_IS_INTEGER)

' Get first driver
nRetCode = SQLDrivers(lHEnv, SQL_FETCH_FIRST, sDriverDesc, _
    Len(sDriverDesc), nDriverDescLength, sDriverAttr, _
    Len(sDriverAttr), nAttrLength)

sAll = ""
Do While nRetCode = SQL_SUCCESS

    ' Replace NULL separators between atributes with colons
    sDriverAttributes = Left$(sDriverAttr, nAttrLength - 1)
    Do
        x = InStr(sDriverAttributes, Chr$(0))
        If x = 0 Then Exit Do
        sDriverAttributes = Left$(sDriverAttributes, x - 1) _
            & " : " & Mid$(sDriverAttributes, x + 1)
    Loop

      ' Save it
    sAll = sAll & Left$(sDriverDesc, nDriverDescLength) _
        & " / " & sDriverAttributes & vbCrLf

      ' Next data source
    nRetCode = SQLDrivers(lHEnv, SQL_FETCH_NEXT, sDriverDesc, _
        Len(sDriverDesc), nDriverDescLength, sDriverAttr, _
        Len(sDriverAttr), nAttrLength)

Loop

txtDrivers = sAll

nRetCode = SQLFreeHandle(SQL_HANDLE_ENV, lHEnv)

End Sub
```

Some of the driver attributes are worth discussing briefly:

DriverODBCVersion

Gives the version of ODBC that the driver supports. Note that even though the drivers on my system are Version 3.5 or later, their ODBC Versions are only 2.5. Thus, they support only ODBC 2.5.

SQLLevel

Describes, in general terms, the level of compliance of the driver to SQL. Level 0 is basic SQL-92 compliance. Level 1 is FIPS127-2 Transitional (whatever that is); Level 2 is SQL-92 Intermediate; Level 3 is SQL-92 Full.

ConnectionFunctions

Indicates which of the three connection-related functions (SQLConnect, SQLDriverConnect, or SQLBrowseConnect) are supported by this driver. The value has the form XXX, where X is Y or N. Thus, a value of YYN means that the driver supports SQLConnect and SQLDriverConnect but not SQLBrowseConnect.

FileExtns

For file-based drivers (that access the physical data directly), indicates which file-name extensions the driver recognizes.

FileUsage

Indicates how a file-based driver views the data in the physical database. A value of 0 indicates that the driver is not file-based. A value of 1 indicates that a file-based driver treats data-source files as tables. A value of 2 indicates that the driver treats the data files as databases.

Getting Data Sources

The process of getting a list of all data sources is quite similar. It uses the function SQLDataSources, whose syntax is similar to SQLDrivers. The Visual Basic declaration is:

```
Declare Function SQLDataSources Lib "odbc32.dll" (ByVal _
    EnvironmentHandle As Long, ByVal Direction As Integer, _
    ByVal ServerName As String, ByVal BufferLength1 As Integer, _
    NameLength1Ptr As Integer, ByVal Description As String, _
    ByVal BufferLength2 As Integer, NameLength2Ptr As Integer) As Integer
```

The complete code is:

```
Private Sub ListODBCSources()

Dim lHEnv              As Long
Dim sServerName        As String * 32
Dim sDescription       As String * 128
Dim nServerNameLength  As Integer
Dim nDescriptionLength As Integer

lstDataSources.Clear

' Allocate an environment handle.
nRetCode = SQLAllocHandle(SQL_HANDLE_ENV, SQL_NULL_HANDLE, lHEnv)

' Set ODBC behavior
nRetCode = SQLSetEnvAttr(lHEnv, SQL_ATTR_ODBC_VERSION, _
    SQL_OV_ODBC2, SQL_IS_INTEGER)

' Put first data source name in sServerName
nRetCode = SQLDataSources(lHEnv, SQL_FETCH_FIRST, sServerName, _
    Len(sServerName), nServerNameLength, sDescription, _
    Len(sDescription), nDescriptionLength)
```

```
        lstDataSources.AddItem "DATA SOURCE / DRIVER"
        Do While nRetCode = SQL_SUCCESS

            lstDataSources.AddItem Left$(sServerName, _
                nServerNameLength) & " / " & TrimO(sDescription)

            ' Next data source
            nRetCode = SQLDataSources(lHEnv, SQL_FETCH_NEXT, _
                sServerName, Len(sServerName), nServerNameLength, _
                sDescription, Len(sDescription), nDescriptionLength)

        Loop

        nRetCode = SQLFreeHandle(SQL_HANDLE_ENV, lHEnv)

        End Sub
```

Obtaining or Creating
the Sample Database

The sample flat file "database," as well as the Access database and the sample programs, are all available for free download from the O'Reilly Internet site. You can choose from any of the following methods to download the data that accompanies the book:

Via the World Wide Web

The sample files are available from *ftp://ftp.ora.com/published/oreilly/windows/access.design2/CodeAccess3.zip.*

Via an ftp client program

You can use an ftp client such as WS_FTP32 to ftp to *ftp.ora.com*, change to the directory *published/oreilly/windows/access.design3/*, and get the file *example.zip.*

In each case, the sample files are stored in a single file compressed using the PKZip file format. If you don't own a utility program capable of decompressing the software (or if you're still doing these things from the command line), I highly recommend that you download an evaluation copy of the shareware utility WinZip, from Nico Mak Computing, Inc.; it is available at *http://www.winzip.com.*

EXAMPLE.ZIP contains *LIBRARY_FLAT.DOC* (the flat database created with Microsoft Word), as well as *LIBRARY95.MDB* (the sample Access database for Access for Office 95), and *LIBRARY97.MBD* (the sample Access database for Access for Office 97). (The two versions perform optimally when using different file formats.) The *.mbd* file itself contains the following:

- The four tables (BOOKS, AUTHORS, PUBLISHERS, and BOOK/AUTHOR) and their primary indexes

- A code module, *Examples*, that contains all of the example programs from the book

It does not, however, contain definitions of relationships, nor does it include any query definitions. The book assumes that you'll be creating these from scratch.

If you don't have access to the Internet or to an email account from a service provider with a gateway to the Internet, it is quite easy to create the sample files yourself. In the remainder of this section, we'll guide you through the steps required to create each of the tables in the Library database, *LIBRARY.MDB*.

Creating the Database

The first step is to create the database itself by doing the following:

1. Start Microsoft Access.
2. When the Microsoft Access dialog box appears over the main Microsoft Access window, as shown in Figure D-1, select the *Blank Database* button, and Click *OK*. Access opens the *File New Database* dialog box.

Figure D-1. The Microsoft Access dialog box

3. Navigate to the directory in which you'd like to save the database file. If the directory doesn't exist, you can create it by clicking on the *Create New Folder* button (the third button from the left on the toolbar); you should then navigate to the newly created directory. In the *File name* text box, type in `library.mdb`. Then click the *Create* button.

Access creates the new database and opens the Library Database window, which should resemble Figure D-2. This is a completely empty database; it doesn't even contain any tables that are capable of holding data. Our next step is to define each of those tables and enter some data into them.

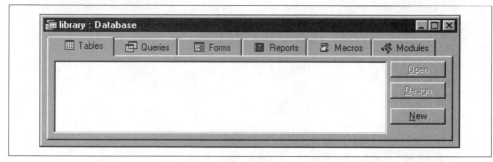

Figure D-2. The Library Database window

Creating the BOOKS Table

To define the design of the BOOKS table, perform the following steps:

1. Click the *New* button in the Library Database window. Access opens the *New Table* dialog box, which contains a listbox with a variety of options. Select *Design View*, and click *OK*. Access opens the Table1 Table window, as shown in Figure D-3, which allows you to define the fields in a new database table.

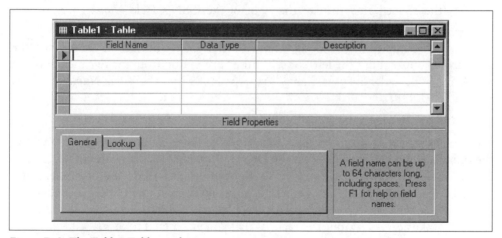

Figure D-3. The Table1 Table window

2. Enter the information shown in Table D-1 into the *Field Name* and *Data Type* columns of the Table1 Table window. Note that you can select the data type from a drop-down listbox.

3. When you select a field, its properties are displayed in the lower portion of the dialog box. Next, enter the individual field properties shown in Table D-2 in the *Field Properties* portion of the dialog box. Note that you don't have to add or modify any properties of the *Price* field.

Table D-1. Fields of the BOOKS table

Field Name	Data Type
ISBN	Text
Title	Text
PubID	Text
Price	Currency

Table D-2. Nondefault properties of the BOOKS table

Field Name	Property	Value
ISBN	Indexed	Yes (No Duplicates)
Title	Field Size	200
	Indexed	Yes (Duplicates OK)
PubID	Indexed	Yes (Duplicates OK)
Price	Format	Currency

4. Designate ISBN as the table's primary key. To do this, either click on the *Primary Key* button on the toolbar (the 11th button from the left of the toolbar, and immediately to the left of the *Undo* button), or right-click on the row selector (the shaded gray field to the right of the ISBN's *Field Name* column) and select *Primary Key* from the pop-up menu.

5. Save the completed table design. Either click the *Save* button on the toolbar (the second button from the left), or select the *Save* option from the *File* menu. When Access opens the *Save As* dialog box, type BOOKS into the *Table Name* text box, and click *OK*.

6. Close the BOOKS table in Design View.

You're now ready to begin entering data into the table. Select the *BOOKS* table in the database window, and click on the *Open* button. Access opens the BOOKS table in Datasheet View, which allows you to input information into the database. Enter the data shown in Table D-3. When you've finished, close the table. Note that you don't have to save the data explicitly that you've entered into the table; Access automatically takes care of writing the records that you've entered to disk.

Creating the AUTHORS Table

To create the AUTHORS table, follow the same basic steps listed in the previous section, "Creating the BOOKS Table." The field definitions for the AUTHORS table are shown in Table D-4.

There is only a single property that you need to set, as shown in Table D-5.

When you've finished creating the fields and assigning their attributes, define AuID as the table's primary key. Then save the table, assigning it the name AUTHORS.

Table D-3. Data for the BOOKS table

ISBN	Title	PubID	Price
0-555-55555-9	Macbeth	2	12.00
0-91-335678-7	Faerie Queene	1	15.00
0-99-999999-9	Emma	1	20.00
0-91-045678-5	Hamlet	2	20.00
0-55-123456-9	Main Street	3	22.95
1-22-233700-0	Visual Basic	1	25.00
0-12-333433-3	On Liberty	1	25.00
0-103-45678-9	Iliad	1	25.00
1-1111-1111-1	C++	1	29.95
0-321-32132-1	Balloon	3	34.00
0-123-45678-0	Ulysses	2	34.00
0-99-777777-7	King Lear	2	49.00
0-12-345678-9	Jane Eyre	3	49.00
0-11-345678-9	Moby-Dick	3	49.00

Table D-4. Fields of the AUTHORS table

Field Name	Data Type
AuID	Text
AuName	Text
AuPhone	Text

Table D 5. Single property to be set in the AUTIIORS table

Field Name:	AuID
Property:	Indexed
Value:	Yes (No Duplicates)

Next, enter the author data into the table; it is shown in Table D-6.

Creating the PUBLISHERS Table

Once again, follow the same basic steps listed in the earlier section "Creating the BOOKS Table" to create the PUBLISHERS table. Field definitions for the PUBLISHERS table are shown in Table D-7.

Once again, there is only a single property that you need to set, as shown in Table D-8.

Designate PubID as the primary key, and save the table as PUBLISHERS.

Table D-6. Data for the AUTHORS table

AuID	AuName	AuPhone
1	Austen	111-111-1111
12	Grumpy	321-321-0000
3	Homer	333-333-3333
10	Jones	123-333-3333
6	Joyce	666-666-6666
2	Meville	222-222-2222
8	Mill	888-888-8888
4	Roman	444-444-4444
5	Shakespeare	555-555-5555
13	Sleepy	321-321-1111
9	Smith	123-222-2222
11	Snoopy	321-321-2222
7	Spenser	777-777-7777

Table D-7. Fields of the PUBLISHERS table

Field Name	Data Type
PubID	Text
PubName	Text
PubPhone	Text

Table D-8. Single property to set for the PUBLISHERS table

Field Name:	PubID
Property:	Indexed
Value:	Yes (No Duplicates)

Once you've finished creating the PUBLISHERS table, you can enter data into it. The PUBLISHERS table contains records for only three publishers; these are shown in Table D-9.

Table D-9. Data for the PUBLISHERS table

PubID	PubName	PubPhone
1	Big House	123-456-7890
2	Alpha Press	999-999-9999
3	Small House	714-000-0000

Creating the BOOK/AUTHOR Table

The BOOK/AUTHOR table is the final table needed for our examples. Once again, create it following the same basic steps described earlier in "Creating the BOOKS Table." It consists of only two fields, as shown in Table D-10. Once you've entered the field names and data types into the table definition, change the two properties listed in Table D-11, and save the table as BOOK/AUTHOR. When you save the table, Access will open the dialog box shown in Figure D-4. The table does not have a primary key, so click on the *No* button; Access will save the table without designating a primary key.

Table D-10. Fields of the BOOK/AUTHOR table

Field Name	Data Type
ISBN	text
AuID	text

Table D-11. Nondefault properties of the BOOK/AUTHOR table

Field Name	Property	Value
ISBN	Indexed	Yes (Duplicates OK)
AuID	Indexed	Yes (Duplicates OK)

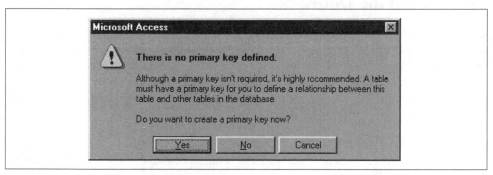

Figure D-4. The "no primary key" warning dialog box

Once you've created the BOOK/AUTHOR table, you can enter the data shown in Table D-12 into it.

Once you've finished this data entry, you'll still have to define the relationships among the tables. This is discussed in detail in "Setting Up the Relationships in Access," in Chapter 3. Once this detail is taken care of, you can use the tables to create the queries and to run the programs discussed in the text of the book.

Table D-12. Data for the BOOK/AUTHOR table

ISBN	AuID
0-103-45678-9	3
0-11-345678-9	2
0-12-333433-3	8
0-12-345678-9	1
0-123-45678-0	6
0-321-32132-1	11
0-321-32132-1	12
0-321-32132-1	13
0-55-123456-9	9
0-55-123456-9	10
0-555-55555-9	5
0-91-045678-5	5
0-91-335678-7	7
0-99-777777-7	5
0-99-999999-9	1
1-1111-1111-1	4
1-22-233700-0	4

Backing Up the Database

Once you've created the BOOKS database, it's a good idea to make a backup copy of each of the tables. That way, you can feel free to make modifications to individual tables, to try out the book's sample programs, and generally to experiment with the data, the tables, and the database, without having to be concerned that you'll corrupt the data. You can make a backup copy by following this procedure for each of the four tables of the BOOKS database:

1. Highlight the table you'd like to back up.

2. Select the *Save As* option from the *File* menu. Access opens the *Save As...* dialog box shown in Figure D-5.

3. Select the *Within the current database* button. Access will suggest a filename for your backup copy, such as *Copy of BOOKS*, as shown in Figure D-5.

4. Click the *OK* button to create the backup copy. It will appear in the *Tables* property sheet of the *Database* dialog box.

If the data in any of your tables does become lost or corrupted, you can restore the table as follows:

1. Highlight the backup copy of the table in the database window.

2. Select the *Save As* option from the *File* menu. Access again opens the *Save As...* dialog box shown in Figure D-5.

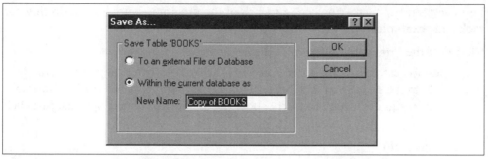

Figure D-5. The Save As... dialog box

3. Select the *Within the current database* button.

4. Replace Access' suggested filename (*Copy of Copy of...*) with the name of the original table, and click *OK*.

5. Access displays a message warning that the name you entered has already been assigned to another table and asking whether you want to replace it. Click *OK*.

 Before replacing any of the tables that participate in relationships with other tables, you'll have to delete that table's relationships. To do this, select the *Relationships* option from the *Tools* menu. When Access opens the *Relationships* window, right click on the line depicting each relationship in which a table participates, then select the *Delete* option from the pop-up menu.

Entering and Running the Sample Programs

If you've downloaded the sample file from O'Reilly & Associates, your database already includes a code module, *Examples*, that contains all of the book's sample VBA programs. If not, you can create a code module yourself and enter programs into it. To create the code module:

1. Select the *Modules* tab when the Library database is open in the *Database* window.

2. Click on the *New* button to create a new code module.

3. When Access opens a new code module (which it will usually name Module1, unless your database already contains code modules saved with their default names), click on the *Save* button on the toolbar.

4. When Access displays the *Save As* dialog box, enter the name of your new code module, *Examples*, in the *Module Name* text box, and click *OK*.

You can then begin entering code for each of the program examples. To do this, for each code example:

1. Select the *Procedure* option from the *Insert* menu.
2. When Access opens the *Insert Procedure* dialog box, enter the name of the procedure in the *Name* text box. Since all of the programs listed in the book are subroutines, you don't have to worry about the dialog box's other options. Just click *OK*.

To run a program:

1. Select the *Modules* tab in the *Database* window, and open the *Examples* module.
2. Select the *Debug Window* option from the *View* menu.
3. When Access opens the *Debug* window, simply type in the name of the program you'd like to run.

Suggestions for Further Reading

Here is a brief list of some books on database theory:

Atzeni, P., and V. De Antonellis. *Relational Database Theory*. Benjamin Cummings: 1993. (A highly theoretical and mathematical treatment of the subject.)

Codd, E. F. *The Relational Model for Database Management: Version 2*. Addison-Wesley: 1990. (The classic exposition of the relational model by one of its creators and chief proponents.)

Date, C. J. *An Introduction to Database Systems*, 6th Edition. Addison-Wesley: 1995. (A less formal and highly readable book.)

Simovici, D., and R. Tenney. *Relational Database Systems*. Academic Press: 1995. (This is a very mathematical treatment of the subject. Much better written than the Atzeni and De Antonellis book.)

Ullman, J. *Principles of Database and Knowledge-Base Systems, Volume 1: Classical Database Systems*. Computer Science Press: 1988. (A book with a somewhat different point of view. Not as mathematical as Atzeni or Simovici, but more mathematical than Date.)

Index

Symbols

' (apostrophe), 146
! (bang) operator, 211, 212
. (dot) operator, 212
" " (double quotation marks), 147
∞ ("many") symbol, 17
(number sign), 147
[ ] (square brackets), 174
θ-joins (theta-joins), 71, 74, 91

Numbers

1NF (first normal form), 38
2NF (second normal form), 40
3NF (third normal form), 41

A

AbsolutePage property, 286
AbsolutePosition property (ADO), 286
AbsolutePosition property (DAO), 259
ac symbolic constants, 147
Access
    CurrentDb function for, 234–240
    housekeeping in, 216
    Object data types for, 154
    object model for, 209
Access collections, 215
Access forms, 131
Access IDE, 129–136
    starting, 129
access modes, 281
access permissions, 229

Access SQL, 56, 81–85
    data types for, 87
    DDL component of, 86–90
    DML component of, 90–111
    query types for, 83
    reasons for using, 84
    syntax conventions for, 85
action queries, 83, 251
ActiveConnection property, 286, 296
ActiveX Data Objects (see ADO)
ActualSize property, 303
Add method, 216
adding
    columns to tables, 89
    foreign keys to tables, 24
    records to recordsets, 265
AddNew method, 265, 289
address, memory and, 203
adjacent quotation marks, 152
ADO (ActiveX Data Objects), 269–325
    vs. DAO and ADOX, 326
    installing, 270
    object model for, 274–304
        treelike view of, 275
    OLE DB and, 272–274
    using over the Web, 322–325
ADO Extensions for Data Definition and
        Security (ADOX), 326–334
ADO objects, 280–304
ADODB prefix, 278
ADOX (ADO Extensions for Data Definition
        and Security), 326–334
    object model for, 326

We'd like to hear your suggestions for improving our indexes. Send email to *index@oreilly.com*.

algebraic query languages, 53–55
ALL option
    SELECT statement and, 93
    UNION statement and, 103
AllowZeroLength property, 244
ALTER TABLE command, 89
anomalies, 8
apostrophe (') indicating comments, 146
Append method, 216
append queries, 83
AppendChunk method, 302
application-defined properties, 221
application modal dialog box, 174
architecture of databases, 115–125
arguments, 167–170
    vs. parameters, 167
arrays, 155–157
As Object declaration, 155
assignments, 344–346
atomic attributes, 38
attribute dependency, 37
attribute names (see table schemes)
attributes, 12–15, 21
    atomic, 38
    environment, 397
    fully qualified attribute names and, 62
    indivisible, 38
    of ODBC drivers, 397–399
    for Relation objects, 248
    renaming, 56
    scalar, 38
    strictly informational, 36
    structured, 38
Attributes property, 300, 303
automatic syntax checking, 141

B

backing up databases, 408
bang (!) operator, 211, 212
base tables, 53
BCNF (Boyce-Codd normal form), 42
Beep statement, 183
BOF property (ADO), 287
BOF property (DAO), 257
Bookmark property, 287
bookmarks, 138, 285
Boolean data types, 152
Boyce-Codd normal form (BCNF), 42
break mode, 139
breakpoint, 140
bugs (see errors)
built-in functions, 173–183

built-in properties (ADO), 299
built-in properties (DAO), 221
Button types, 175
buttons, 174–176
ByRef parameters, 169
ByVal parameters, 169

C

CacheSize property, 287
call stack, 186
calling (see declaring)
calling procedure, error-handling in, 185
candidate keys, 16
Cartesian product of tables, 62
cascading updates/deletions, 26
Case Else part, 196
case-insensitive comparison, 179
Catalog object, 326
characters, repeated, 178
class modules, 131
classes, 12
    DAO, list of, 362–377
    entity (see entity classes)
client side, 284
client/server architecture, 124
Clone method, 290
Close method (ADO)
    of Connection object, 282, 283
    of Recordset object, 290, 293
Close method (DAO), 225
closing objects, 225
code
    bookmarking, 138
    debugging, 143–145
    error handling and, 183–190
    executing, 134, 143
        in break mode, 145
    long lines of, handling, 146
    sample, for ODBC, 381
Code window, 132–134
collections, 207–209, 215–220
    Collection objects and, 363
    DAO collections and, 226–234
    default, 213
    for objects, 362–377
    Properties collection and, 220–225
    refreshing, 219, 237
    types of, 215
    user-defined, 216
columns
    adding/deleting, 89
    constraint clauses for, 88

definition for, 87
headings for, 20
order of, 20
projection and, 63
COM (Component Object Model), 272
Command objects, 296–298
commands
in ADO, 282, 332
compound, 292
executing, 134
CommandText property, 297
CommandTimeout property, 280, 297
CommandType property, 297
comments, 146
compile errors, 141
compiling programs, 142
Component Object Model (COM), 272
compound commands, 292
conceptual databases, 117
Connection objects, 280–284
connection strings, 309–322, 391
ConnectionFunction attribute, 399
ConnectionString property, 280
ConnectionTimeout property, 280
constants, 147
enums and, 148
scope of, 159
for Type property, 223, 244
VBA string functions and, 177–180
constraints, 88
referential, 26
Container objects, 209, 230–232, 364
continuation, 146
control statements, 191–197
Controls collection, 215
Count property, 215
user-defined collections and, 216
counter, For loop and, 192–195
CreateDatabase method, 241
CreateField method, 243
CREATE INDEX command, 90
CreateIndex method, 246
CreateParameter method, 298
CreateQueryDef method, 250
CreateRelation method, 248
CREATE TABLE command, 87–89
CreateTableDef method, 243
creating
databases, 241
fields, 243–245
indexes
in ADOX, 330–332
in DAO, 246–248

Jet databases, 326–328
Jet tables, 328
primary keys in ADOX, 332
queries
in ADOX, 332
in DAO, 250–253
QueryDefs objects, 250–253
relations, 248–250
sample database, 401–410
tables, 243–245
text files, 197
crosstab queries, 83, 106–109
current position/record in recordsets, 257
CurrentDb function, 234–240
cursors, 284
CursorLocation property, 281, 285, 287
CursorType property, 288

D

dangling references, 9, 26
DAO (Data Access Objects), 115, 119,
        201–266
ADO and, 269, 326
ADOX and, 326
DDL programming and, 241–253
DML programming and, 254–266
Microsoft support for, 333
Object data types for, 154
object model for, 207–209
Properties collection and, 220–225
referencing objects and, 211–215
DAO classes, list of, 362–377
DAO collections, 215–220
DAO objects, 226–234
list of, 363–377
data, 9
editing using recordsets, 262–266
manipulating in database, 122
NULL values and, 33
persistent, 11
solving manipulation problems
        with, 337–357
viewing vertically/horizontally, 352–354
Data Access Objects (see DAO)
data consumers, 274
data definition, ADOX for, 326–334
data definition language (see DDL)
data dictionary/catalog, 119
data manipulation language (see DML)
data providers, 273, 276, 281
Data Source Name (see DSN)
data source types, 384

data sources, 272, 384–392
    examples of, 387–389
    existing on system, 393–396, 399
    functions for connecting to, 390
    list of, 393–396, 399
    (see also DSN)
data stores, 272, 273
data types, 87, 149–155
    object, 154, 202
    of properties, 221
database management system (see DBMS)
Database objects, 207, 225, 229, 365
Databases container, 230
database programming, 9
    ADO and, 269–271
    DAO DDL, 241–253
    DAO DML, 254–266
    VBA and, 115
database systems, 117
databases, 11
    architecture of, 115–125
    backing up, 408
    conceptual, 117
    creating
        in DAO, 241
        host languages for, 120
        sample database, 401–410
    CurrentDb function for, 234–240
    deleting, 242
    design and, 3–9
    duplicates of, 119, 242
    flat, 5
    new, defining, 121
    normalizing, 43–48
    opening, 243
    programming (see database programming)
    relational (see relational databases)
    resources for further reading, 411
data-definition queries, 83
date constants, 147
Date data type, 153
date-related functions, 197
dates, formatting, 198
DBEngine object, 226, 366
DBMS (database management system), 3,
        81, 118
    client/server architecture for, 124
    (see also Jet DBMS)
DBMS-based drivers, 383
DBQ parameter, 316

DDL (data definition language)
    as component of Access SQL, 86–90
    DAO and, 241–253
    for Jet DBMS, 121
debugging, 135, 143–145
    commenting out code and, 146
    debug mode, exiting from, 145
    (see also problem-solving; runtime errors)
declaration statements
    location of in procedures, 151
    Require Variable Declaration option
        and, 152
declaring
    functions, 165
    subroutines, 166
    variables, 150
decomposition of table schemes, 45–48
DefaultDatabase property, 281
defaults
    button, 175
    collections, 213
    recordset types, 256
DefaultValue property, 244
DefinedSize property, 303
degree of table, 20, 57
deleting
    cascading deletions and, 26
    columns from tables, 89
    databases, 242
    Delete method and (ADO), 290
    Delete method and (DAO), 216, 263
    delete queries and, 83, 104
    DELETE statement and, 104
    deletion anomalies and, 8
    records, 263
    tables, 90
deletion anomalies, 8
dependency
    attribute, 37
    functional, 39
    loss of, 46
    trivial/nontrivial, 40
dependency-preserving decomposition, 47
derived tables, 53
design mode, 139
    Step Into feature and, 144
design-time errors, 141
dialog boxes, 174
difference of tables, 60–62
dimensions of an array, 156

directories, housekeeping in, 197
DISTINCT option, 93–95, 99
DISTINCTROW option, 93–100
DistinctCount property, 247
DLL (dynamic link library), 119, 381
DML (data manipulation language)
    as component of Access SQL, 90–111
    DAO and, 254–266
    for Jet DBMS, 122
Do... loop statement, 194
docked windows, 135
Document objects, 209, 232, 368
domains, 20
dot (.) operator, 212
double quotation marks (" "), 147
downloads, for LIBRARY sample
            database, 401
driver types, 383
DriverODBCVersion attribute, 398
drivers
    ODBC, 383, 392, 397–399
    ODBC Driver Manager and, 382
DROP statement, 90
DSN (Data Source Name), 312, 319,
            384–389
    connection strings and, 391
    creating, 385
    examples of, 387–389
    types of, 385
duplicate data (see redundancy)
duplicate Recordset objects, 290
duplicate rows, 64
dynamic arrays, 156
dynamic cursors, 285
dynamic data, 322
dynamic link library (see DLL)
dynamic properties, 298–302
dynaset-type Recordset objects, 254, 261

E

E/R (entity-relationship) diagram, 16
editing buffer, 288
editing with recordsets, 262–266
EditMode property, 288
ElseIf parts, 191
empty strings, 33
End statement, 171
Enforce Referential Integrity box, 30
entities, 11–15, 21
    E/R diagrams for, 16
    implementing, 18–20
    relationships between, 16

entity classes, 12–15, 21, 25
    implementing, 18
    superkeys and, 15, 21
entity sets, 12, 21
    implementing, 19
    superkeys and, 15
entity-relationship (E/R) diagram, 16
entity-relationship model, 11
enums, 148
environment handle, 397
EOF property (ADO), 287
EOF property (DAO), 257
equality of sets, 355–357
equi-joins, 67, 73
error messages
    "Data source name not found...", 319
    "Invalid use of Null", 183
    "Item not found...", 220
    "Project Unviewable", 130
error object (Err), 187
Error objects, 227, 368
errors, 140–143
    error dialog boxes and, 139
    handling in code, 183–190
    resources for further reading, 183
    runtime (see runtime errors)
    trapping, 185
Errors property, 281
event procedures, 186
example of DSNs, 387–389
EXAMPLE.ZIP file, 401
Excel (see Microsoft Excel)
Execute method, 282, 298
Exit Do statement, 195
Exit For statement, 193
exiting
    debug mode, 145
    procedures, 171
expressions, query (see views)
external level of database, 118
externally creatable objects, 275

F

Field objects, 233, 302–304, 368
    properties of, 244
fields, 31
    creating for tables, 243–245
    properties of, 244
Fields property, 288
file-based drivers, 383
file data sources, 385
FileExtns attribute, 399

files, 197
  (see also tables)
FileUsage attribute, 399
Filter property, 288
Find methods, 261
first normal form (1NF), 38
fixed-length string variables, 152
flat databases, 5
floating windows, 135
For Each loop, 194
For...Next statement (For loop), 192
foreign keys, 23
  referential integrity and, 26
Format function, 198
forms, 37–43
Forms collection, 210, 215
Forms container, 230
forward-only cursors, 285
FROM clause, 101
frontends, 124
full-module view, 132
fully qualified attribute names, 62
fully qualified object names, 212, 213
fully qualified procedure names, 172
functional dependency, 39
  decomposition and, 46
functions, 180
  built-in, 173–183
  connection, 382
  for data source connections, 390
  date- and time-related, 197
  declaring, 165
  file-related, 197
  ODBC, 396
  VBA, 177–183

G

GetChunk method, 302
GetRows method, 290
global variables, 159
glossary of database terms, 21
GROUP BY option, 102
Group objects, 229, 369

H

HAVING option, 102
help files, 138
  for ODBC drivers, 392
host applications, 124
host languages, 120, 123

housekeeping
  in Access, 216
  for files and directories, 197

I

Icon types, 175
IDE (Integrated Development
    Environment), 129
  keyboard shortcuts for, 137
If...Then statement, 191
IgnoreNulls property, 247
Immediate If function (IIf function), 181
Immediate window, 134
implementing
  entities, 18–20
  LIBRARY database, 27–31
  relationships, 22–27
index files, 31–33
Index objects, 234, 331, 370
Index property, 258
Indexed Sequential Access Method
    (ISAM), 119
indexes
  ALTER TABLE statement for, 89
  creating
    in ADOX, 330–332
    in DAO, 246–248
Indexes dialog box, 33
indivisible attributes, 38
information, loss of, 45
Inherited property, 222
initialized variables, 163
in-line error checking, 188
INNER JOIN clause, 91
inner joins, 67–72, 91
  outer joins and, 72
  semi-joins and, 77–79
InputBox function, 176
INSERT INTO statement, 105
insertion anomalies, 8
Instr function, 177
Integrated Development Environment (see
    IDE)
integrity (see referential integrity)
Internal ISAM Component, 119
internal level of database, 117
intersection of tables, 59
Is function, 180
ISAM (Indexed Sequential Access
    Method), 119

IsDate function, 180
IsEmpty function, 180
IsMissing function, 168
IsNull function, 180, 182
IsNumeric function, 181
Item method, 216

J

Jet Database Engine (see Jet DBMS)
Jet databases
    ADOX data definition and, 326–334
    creating, 326–328
Jet DBMS, 119–124
    integration with Access and Visual
        Basic, 124
Jet Query Engine, 119
Jet tables, 328
JOIN statement, 91
joins, 67–73, 91–93
    implementing in Access, 73–76
    semi-joins and, 77–79

K

keyboard shortcuts, 137
keys, 15, 21
    candidate, 16
    constraint clauses for, 88
    foreign, 23
    functional dependency and, 39
    NULLs appearing in, 34
    primary, 16, 32
    referenced, 24
    unique indexes and, 32
keyset cursors, 285
keywords, 167–172

L

labels, 184
languages
    algebraic query, 53–55
    data definition (see DDL)
    data manipulation (see DML)
    nonprocedural, 53
    host (see host languages)
    structured query (see SQL)
late binding, 155
LCase function, 177
Left function, 177
left outer joins, 61, 72, 76
left semi-joins, 77
Len function, 177

LIBRARY sample database, 3–8, 11–14
    downloading files for, 401
    entity-relationship diagram for, 22
    implementing, 27–31
    primary keys in, 16
    Properties collection and, 223
    Relation objects and, 249
    TableDef objects and, 218
lifetime, 160–163
Like operator function, 179
line-continuation character, 146
ListDPs procedure, 304–309, 310
literal constants, 147
local constants/variables, 159
LockType property, 285, 288
logical errors, 142
logical pages, 286
logical structure of database, 117
long integers, 152
looping, 192–195
loss of data, 9
lossless decomposition, 47
LTrim function, 178

M

machine data sources, 385
Macros container, 230
make-table queries, 53, 83, 106
"many" (∞) symbol, 17
many-to-many relationships, 17, 25
matching elements, 354
MaxRecords property, 288
MDAC (Microsoft Data Access
        Components), 270
.mdb file, 226, 241
memory, data types and, 149
metadata, 119
methods
    of Command objects, 298
    of DAO collections, 216
    for objects, 206, 207, 362–377
    for Recordset objects, 289–296
    for recordsets, 321
    of user-defined collections, 216
Microsoft, support for DAO and, 333
Microsoft Access (see entries at Access)
Microsoft Data Access Components
        (MDAC), 270
Microsoft Excel, 270
    connecting to Microsoft OLE DB provider
        for ODBC, 316–318
    sample DSNs and, 387–389

Microsoft Jet OLE DB provider, 310–312
    connection test for, 312
Microsoft OLE DB provider for
        ODBC, 312–322
    connecting to Microsoft Excel, 316–318
    connecting to text files, 318–321
Mid function, 177
Mode property, 281
module-level constants/variables, 159
modules, 131
Modules container, 230
Move methods, 257, 291
moving through recordsets, 257–259
MsgBox function, 174–176
multicolumn constraints, 88
multiple-value problems, 7

N

Name property (ADO), 299, 303
Name property (DAO), 222, 297
named arguments, 168
names
    fully qualified object, 212, 213
    fully qualified procedure, 172
    for projects, 131
    for variables, 205
naming conventions for variables, 157, 205
natural joins (nat-joins), 69–71, 73
navigating recordsets, 257–259
nested joins, 91
NextRecordset method, 292
nodes, 129, 131
NoMatch property, 260
nonprocedural languages, 53
nontrivial dependency, 40
normal forms, 37–43
    functional dependency and, 39
normalization, 38, 43–48
NULL values, 8, 33
number sign (#), 147
numbers
    converting to strings, 178
    formatting, 198
    in InputBox, 176
Numeric data types, 152
NumericScale property, 304

O

Object box, 133
Object Browser utility, 361
object-collection relationships, 209

object data types, 154, 202
object models
    Access, 209
    ADO, 274–304
    ADOX, 326
    COM, 272
    DAO, 207–209
object properties, 209
object variables, 202–206, 213
    naming, 205
    vs. standard, 202
objects, 201–207
    ADO, 280–304
    As Object declaration for, 155
    closing, 225
    collections and, 215–220
        default collections for, 213
    Command, 296–298
    Connection, 280–284
    DAO, 226–234
    error (Err), 187
    externally creatable, 275
    fully qualified names for, 212
    referencing, 206, 211–215
    Set statement and, 155
    viewing, 133
ODBC Administrator, 312, 385
ODBC Driver Manager, 382
ODBC drivers, 383
    help files for, 392
    lists of, obtaining, 393–399
ODBC functions, 396
ODBC (Open Database Connectivity), 312,
        381–400
    (see also Microsoft OLE DB provider for
        ODBC)
OLE DB providers, 309–322
    finding in Windows registry, 304–309
OLE DB (technology), 269, 272–274
On Error statements, 183, 187
one-to-many relationships, 17, 23
one-to-one relationships, 17, 24
Open Database Connectivity (see ODBC)
Open method, 283, 292
Open statement, 197
OpenDatabase method, 243
opening
    databases, 243
    recordsets, 255
OpenRecordset method, 255
OpenSchema method, 284, 312
operators, VBA and, 164
optimization, 79

Option Explicit, 152
optional arguments, 167
optional parameters, 174
Options parameter, 282, 283
ORDER BY option, 93, 103
order of columns/table rows, 20
OriginalValue property (ADO), 304
outer joins, 72, 76, 91
overlapping intervals, 340–343

P

PageCount/PageSize property, 286
Parameter objects, 233, 371
parameter queries, 83, 111
parameters, 167
    to a function, 165
    optional, 174
Parameters property, 297
PARAMETERS statement, 111
pass-through queries, 83
pattern matching, 179
PercentPosition property, 259
persistent data, 11
physical database, 117
    Internal ISAM component and, 119
pointer variables, 203
positional arguments, 169
Precision property (ADO), 304
predicate (the), 93
Prepared property, 297
primary index, 32
primary keys, 16, 32
    creating in ADOX, 332
Primary property, 247
private constants/variables, 159
Private/Public procedures, 171
problem-solving, 337–357
procedural languages, 53
Procedure list box, 133
procedure-level constants/variables, 159
procedures, 131, 138–140, 171
    creating, 138
    executing, 139
    exiting, 171
    Private/Public, 171
    stepping and, 144
    viewing, 132
programmatic ID, 309
programming (see database programming)
Project Explorer, 129–132
projection, 63
    (see also SELECT statement)

projects, 129
    names of, 131
properties, 207
    application-defined, 221
    built-in (ADO), 299
    built-in (DAO), 221
    of Command objects, 296
    of DAO collections, 216
    editing, 245
    of fields, 244
    of indexes, 247
    of Microsoft Access collections, 215
    for objects, 362–377
    of QueryDef objects, 252
    recordset available, 321
    of Recordset objects, 286–289
    referencing, 206
    types of, 221
    user-defined, 224
    of user-defined collections, 216
Properties collection (ADO), 298
Properties collection (DAO), 220–225
Properties property, 298
Properties window, 132
Property objects (ADO), 298–302
Property objects (DAO), 220, 222, 371
Provider property, 281
public constants/variables, 159

Q

qualified attribute names, 62
queries, 52, 83
    Access design of, 81
    creating
        in ADOX, 332
        in DAO, 250–253
    Jet Query Engine for, 119
    make-table, 53
    parameter, 83, 111
    running, 251
    subqueries and, 84, 109–111
    updatable, 83, 91, 104
Query Design window, 55, 82
query expressions (see views)
query types, 83
QueryDef objects, 229, 371
    creating, 250–253
    properties of, 252
quotation marks
    adjacent, 152
    double, 147
quotients, 79, 378–380

R

read-only properties, 222
read/write properties, 222
readability
  improved
    by named arguments, 169
    by object variables, 213
  of VBA programs, 157
RecordCount property, 289
records (see rows)
RecordsAffected parameter, 282
RecordsAffected property, 252
Recordsets collection, 255
recordset cursors, 284
Recordset objects, 225, 230, 254–266,
      284–296, 372
  creating, 284
  duplicating, 290
  methods of, 289–296
  obtaining in ADO, 277
  opening, 255
  properties of, 286–289
  searching, 260–262
  snapshot-type, 255
recordset types, 256, 321
recordsets
  adding records to, 265
  Do... loops and, 195
  navigating, 257–259
redimensioning arrays, 156
redundancy, 5–7, 35–37
referenced keys, 24
referenced table schemes, 24
referencing methods and properties, 206
referencing objects, 203, 211–215
referential constraints, 26
referential integrity, 9, 26
  NULL in primary keys and, 34
Refresh method, 216
refreshing collections, 219, 237
Relations collection, 230
Relations container, 230
Relation objects, 248–250, 374
relational algebra, 53–80
relational calculus, 53–55
relational databases, 5–9, 22
  entity-relationship model of, 11
relations
  creating, 248–250
  VBA, 164

relationships
  between entities, 16
  between tables, 92
  implementing, 22–27
  integrity of (see referential integrity)
  object-collection, 209
  types of, 17
Relationships view, 29
remote database model, 124
Remove method, 216
renaming table attributes, 56
repeated characters, 178
Replication Engine, 119
Reports collection, 215
Reports container, 230
Requery method, 293
Require Variable Declaration option, 152
Required property, 244, 248
resources for further reading
  databases, 411
  errors, 183
  Visual Basic, 132
  Visual Basic for Applications, 196
restriction of tables (selection), 65–67
result tables, 52
Resume statements, 188
Resync method, 293
Right function, 177
right outer joins, 72, 76
right semi-joins, 77
rows, 31
  deleting, 263
  duplicate, 64, 93
  inserting into tables, 105
  order of, 20
  selection and, 65–67
RTrim function, 178
run mode, 139
Run to Cursor feature, 145
running queries, 251
running sums, 337–340
runtime errors, 142, 183–190

S

sample database, obtaining, 401–410
sample DSNs, 387–389
scalar attributes, 38
schema.ini, 389
scope, 159
  vs. lifetime, 160

SDI (single document interface), 130
searching recordsets, 260–262
second normal form (2NF), 40
secondary index, 32
Seek method, 260
Select Case statement, 195
SELECT... INTO statement, 106
select queries, 83, 251
SELECT statement, 93–103, 337
    DISTINCT option and, 93–95, 99
    DISTINCTROW option and, 93, 99
    for subqueries, 109–111
selection, 65–67
self-joins, 92
semantic models, 16
semi-joins, 77–79
semiqualified names, 212
SEQUEL, 81
server side, 284
service providers, 274
Set Next Statement feature, 145
Set statement, 155
sets, equality of, 355–357
single-column constraints, 88
single document interface (SDI), 130
snapshot-type Recordset objects, 255, 261
Source property, 289
Space function, 178
spaces, 178
split-screens, 135
SQL (Structured Query Language), 56, 84
    DAO and, 116
    (see also Access SQL)
SQLBrowseConnect function, 399
SQLConnect function, 390, 399
SQLDataSources function, 399
SQLDriverConnect function, 391, 399
SQLDrivers function, 397
SQLLevel attribute, 398
SQL queries, 83
SQL Server, 269
SQLSetEnvAttr function, 397
SQL View, 82
square brackets [ ] indicating optional
            parameters, 174
standard modules, 131
State property, 282, 289
statements, 180–190
    changing order of execution for, 145
    control, 191–197
    error-handling, 183–190

stepping and, 144
VBA and, 173–183
static cursors, 285
static variables, 161–163
Step Into feature, 144
Step Out feature, 145
Step Over feature, 144
stepping, 143–145
Stop statement, 140
StrCmp function, 179
Str function, 178
strictly informational attributes, 36, 40
String data types, 152
String function, 178
strings
    comparing, 179
    converting to number, 178
    formatting, 198
    string constants and, 147
structured attributes, 38
Structured Query Language (see SQL)
subqueries, 84, 109–111, 337
subroutines, declaring, 166
subschemes (see views)
subsets of tables
    projection and, 63
    selection (restriction) of, 65–67
suffixes, 151
superkeys, 15, 21
    functional dependency and, 39
Supports method, 293
Switch function, 182
symbolic constants, 147
syntax conventions, 85
syntax errors, checking for, 141
system data sources, 385
system modal dialog box, 174

T

table schemes, 18, 116
    attributes of, 35
    decomposing, 45–48
    normal forms for, 37–43
TableDef objects, 218, 229, 375
tables, 19, 21
    ALTER TABLE command and, 89
    base, 53
    Cartesian product of, 62
    CREATE TABLE command and, 87–89
    creating in DAO, 243–245

tables (*continued*)
degree of, 20, 57
deleting or deleting from, 90, 104
derived, 53
difference of, 60–62
inserting data into other, 106
intersection of, 59
joins and, 67–76, 91–93
optimization and, 79
printing list of, 312
projection of, 63
quotients of, 378–380
relationships between, 92
result, 52
rows, inserting into, 105
selection (restriction) and, 65–67
semi-joins and, 77–79
union of, 57–59, 83, 103
updating, 104
virtual (see views)
Tables collection, 330
Tables container, 230
table-type Recordset objects, 254, 260
tabular format, 273, 284
text files
connecting to ODBC provider, 318–321
creating, 197
sample DSNs and, 388
theta-joins, 71, 74, 91
third normal form (3NF), 41
three-tier structure, 117
time, 154, 197
time to completion, 346–351
TOP option (SELECT statement), 93
tracing, 143–145
TRANSFORM statement, 106–109
Trim function, 178
trivial/nontrivial dependency, 40
type conversion functions, 178
Type property (ADO), 299, 304
Type property (DAO), 222
type-declaration suffixes, 151
types
recordset, 321
Type property and, 244
types (see data types)

U

UBound function, 156
UCase function, 177
UnderlyingValue property (ADO), 304

underscore, for line continuation, 146
union of tables, 57–59, 103
union queries and, 83
UNION statement, 103
unique indexes, 32
Unique property, 248
update anomalies, 8
Update method, 263, 265, 296
UPDATE statement, 104
updates
cascading, 26
for records, 263
updatable queries and, 83, 91, 104
URLs
MDAC, 270
for this book, xviii
user data sources, 385
user-defined collections, 216
user-defined properties, 224
User objects, 229, 376
users
beeping, 183
displaying messages to, 174–176
event procedures and, 186
getting input from, 176, 391, 392

V

Val function, 178
ValidationRule and ValidationText
properties, 245
Value property (ADO), 300, 304
Value property (DAO), 223
values, NULL values and, 8, 33
variable counter, 192–195
variable-length string variables, 153
variables, 149
changing value of, 170
declaring, 150
initialized, 163, 180
IsNull function and, 180
lifetime of, 160–163
naming conventions for, 157, 205
object, 202–206, 213
naming, 205
vs. standard, 202
pointer, 203
scope of, 159
VBA string functions for, 177–180
Variant data types, 150, 154
variants, 150, 154
vb symbolic constants, 147

VBA (Visual Basic for Applications), 115, 119, 129–145
  built-in functions and statements for, 173–180
  control statements for, 191–197
  debugging, 143–145
  help files for, 138
    using for further study, 197
  miscellaneous functions and statements for, 180–183
  procedures for, 131
  programs and, 409
    readability of, 157
  resources for further reading, 196
  rules for initializing variables and, 163
  string functions for, 177–180
VBA data types, list of, 149
VBA operators/relations, 164
Version property, 282
viewing
  data vertically/horizontally, 352–354
  objects, 133
  output, 134
  procedures, 132
  split-screen, 135

views, 9, 53, 118
virtual tables, 53
Visual Basic
  resources for further reading, 132
  using to obtain ODBC information, 393–400
Visual Basic Editor, 129
  keyboard shortcuts for, 137
Visual Basic for Applications (see VBA)

W

watch statement, 140
Web, using ADO over, 322–325
WHERE clause
  SELECT statement and, 93, 101
  UPDATE statement and, 104
windows, docked/floating, 135
Workspace objects, 207, 226, 228, 376
write-only properties, 222

About the Author

Steven Roman is a Professor Emeritus of mathematics at the California State University, Fullerton. He has taught at a number of other universities, including the Massachusetts Institute of Technology, the University of California at Santa Barbara, and the University of South Florida. Dr. Roman received his B.A. degree from the University of California at Los Angeles and his Ph.D. from the University of Washington. He has authored over 35 books in mathematics and personal computing.

Dr. Roman's other computing books include: *VB .NET Language in a Nutshell*, *Writing Word Macros*, *Writing Excel Macros*, *Developing Visual Basic Add-Ins*, and *Win32 API Programming with Visual Basic*, all published by O'Reilly & Associates, as well as *Concepts of Object-Oriented Programming with Visual Basic* and *Understanding Personal Computer Hardware*, published by Springer-Verlag. He has also written a number of software applications, including Object Model Browser, a browser that displays a structured view of virtually any type library. For more information on Dr. Roman's books, articles, and software, visit his web site at *http://www.romanpress.com*.

Colophon

Our look is the result of reader comments, our own experimentation, and feedback from distribution channels. Distinctive covers complement our distinctive approach to technical topics, breathing personality and life into potentially dry subjects.

The animal on the cover of *Access Database Design and Programming* is a Southern tamandua (*Tamandua tetradactyla*), one of three species comprising the anteater family. The Southern tamandua is also known as the collared anteater (although vested anteater might be a better name). Tamanduas live in the tropical rainforest. They spend much of their time in the forest canopy, feasting on ants and termites; they often move awkwardly when they descend to the ground. Tamanduas use their powerful forearms for self-defense. When attacked, they will back up against a rock or cling to a tree branch with their hind legs, while fighting and clawing with their forearms. Amazonian Indians sometimes use tamanduas to clear their homes of ants and termites. Despite this useful trait, the tamandua is an endangered species. They are often killed for their tails, the tendons of which are used to make ropes.

Jeffrey Holcomb was the production editor and proofreader for *Access Database Design and Programming*. Clairemarie Fisher O'Leary and Tatiana Apandi Diaz were the copyeditors. Rachel Wheeler, Matt Hutchinson, and Claire Cloutier provided quality control. Brenda Miller wrote the index.

Edie Freedman designed the cover of this book. The cover image is a 19th-century engraving from the Dover Pictorial Archive. Emma Colby produced the cover layout with QuarkXPress 4.1 using Adobe's ITC Garamond font.

David Futato designed the interior layout. Mihaela Maier converted the files from Microsoft Word to FrameMaker 5.5.6 using tools created by Mike Sierra. The text font is Linotype Birka; the heading font is Adobe Myriad Condensed; and the code font is LucasFont's TheSans Mono Condensed. The illustrations that appear in the book were produced by Robert Romano and Jessamyn Read using Macromedia Free-Hand 9 and Adobe Photoshop 6. The tip and warning icons were drawn by Christopher Bing. This colophon was written by Clairemarie Fisher O'Leary.

Whenever possible, our books use a durable and flexible lay-flat binding.